Child-friendly Justice

Stockholm Studies in Child Law and Children's Rights

VOLUME 1

The titles published in this series are listed at *brill.com/sscl*

Child-friendly Justice

A Quarter of a Century of the UN *Convention on the Rights of the Child*

Edited by

Said Mahmoudi
Pernilla Leviner
Anna Kaldal
Katrin Lainpelto

BRILL

NIJHOFF

LEIDEN | BOSTON

Library of Congress Cataloging-in-Publication Data

Child-friendly justice : a quarter of a century of the UN Convention on the Rights of the Child / Edited by Said Mahmoudi, Pernilla Leviner, Anna Kaldal, Katrin Lainpelto.
    pages cm. -- (Stockholm studies in child law and children's rights ; volume 1)
    Includes index.
    ISBN 978-90-04-29742-5 (hardback : alk. paper) -- ISBN 978-90-04-29743-2 (e-book) 1. Convention on the Rights of the Child (1989 November 20) 2. Children (International law) 3. Children--Legal status, laws, etc. I. Mahmoudi, Said, 1948- editor.

K639.A41989C44 2015
341.4'8572--dc23

2015014569

This publication has been typeset in the multilingual "Brill" typeface. With over 5,100 characters covering Latin, IPA, Greek, and Cyrillic, this typeface is especially suitable for use in the humanities. For more information, please see www.brill.com/brill-typeface.

ISSN 2405-8343
ISBN 978-90-04-29742-5 (hardback)
ISBN 978-90-04-29743-2 (e-book)

Contents

Preface and Acknowledgments

The concept of child-friendly justice has been current in the child-related meetings of many governmental, intergovernmental, non-governmental and academic organizations in the past ten years. The development of child law, like many other fields of law, has moved from an initial focus on a linear and sectorial approach to separate issues to a more comprehensive and integrated treatment of all matters where children are involved. "Justice" has thus become the common denominator of the latter approach.

There have been many efforts to define the exact content of child-friendly justice, primarily in the context of the Council of Europe, but also in several international conferences in Africa and Europe. One important example was the child-friendly justice conference organized by the Swedish Government in 2008. Notwithstanding these efforts, the concept seems still to need elaboration. The UN Convention on the Rights of the Child (CRC) as a global instrument with almost total memberships of the countries of the world, can be a suitable instrument for harmonizing national interpretations of child-friendly justice.

The 25th anniversary of the adoption of the CRC in 2014 was an important occasion for the Stockholm Centre for the Rights of the Child (BRC) to organize an international conference in Stockholm 16–18 May 2014. The Conference was entitled Child-friendly Justice: What It Means and How It is Realized. The purpose was to reassess the effect of the CRC in the elucidation of the concept of justice in child-related matters and the Convention's contribution to the promotion of child-friendly justice systems at national level.

World-leading experts representing various academic disciplines and professions spoke at the Conference. They presented their views in eight panels on a diversity of issues from the perspective of the relation between the CRC and the concept of child-friendly justice. The present volume contains the proceedings of this Conference. The book is the first in a new series of academic works on child law/children's rights launched by the BRC in cooperation with Martinus Nijhoff Publishers.

I would like to thank the Swedish Ministry for Social Affairs, the Bank of Sweden Tercentenary Foundation and the Justice Edvard Cassel Foundation for the generous financial contributions that made this event possible. I am also grateful to the staff of the BRC for their untiring efforts and invaluable assistance in connection with the Conference.

Stockholm, January 2015

Said Mahmoudi
Professor of International Law at Stockholm University
Chairman of the Conference Organizing Committee

Abbreviations

ACPF	African Child Policy Forum
ADHD	Attention Deficit/Hyperactivity Disorder
AIR	All Indian Report
ALR	Australian Law Reports
ASD	Autism Spectrum Disorders
CAC	Children's Advocacy Center
CAPTA	Child Abuse Prevention and Treatment Act
CBCA	Criterion-based Content Analysis
CCTV	Closed Circuit Television
Cf.	Compare
CJ-S-CH	Council of Europe Group of Specialists on Child-Friendly Justice
CLR	Common Law Reports
CMW	International Convention on the Protection of the Rights of All Migrant Workers and Members of their Families
CNDS	French National Security Ethics Commission
COPE	Children of Prisoners Europe
COPING	Children of Prisoners, Interventions and Mitigations to Strengthen Mental Health
CPCR	Commission for the Protection of Child Rights (India)
CPT	European Committee for the Prevention of Torture and Inhuman or Degrading Treatment or Punishment
CrPC	Criminal Procedure Code (India)
CRC	Convention on the Rights of the Child
CrLJ	Criminal Law Journal (India)
CRIA	Child-Rights Impact Assessment
CRIN	Child Rights International Network
CRPD	Convention on the Rights of Persons with Disabilities
CWC	Child Welfare Committee
DCI	Defence for Children International
DHS	Department of Human Services
ENOC	European Network of Ombudspersons for Children
ECHR	European Convention for the Protection of Human Rights and Fundamental Freedoms
ETS	European Treaty Series
FIDH	International Federation of Human Rights Leagues
FLR	Federal Law Reports (Australia)
GAL	Guardian *ad litem*

GC	General Comment
GIP	Guidelines on International Protection
HCR	High Commissioner for Refugees
IACHR	Inter-American Commission on Human Rights
ICCPR	International Covenant on Civil and Political Rights
ICSECR	International Covenant on Social, Economic and Cultural Rights
ILO	International Labour Organization
INGO	Intergovernmental Organization
IPC	Indian Penal Code
J4C	Justice for Children
MACR	Minimum age of criminal responsibility
MDG	United Nations Millennium Development Goals
NSPCC	National Society for the Prevention of Cruelty to Children (UK)
NNA	Niños, Niñas y Adolescentes (child boys, child girls and adolescents)
OHCHR	Office of the High Commissioner for Human Rights
Para.	Paragraph
POCSO	The Protection of Children from Sexual Offences (India)
PTSD	Posttraumatic Stress Disorder
SCPCR	State Commission for Protection of Child Rights (India)
SIJS	Special Immigrant Juvenile Status (USA)
SLL	Special and Local Laws
SRA	Statement Reality Analysis
UDHR	Universal declaration of Human Rights
UKSC	The Supreme Court of the United Kingdom
UNHCR	United Nations High Commissioner for Refugees
UNICEF	United Nations Children's Fund
UNODC	United Nations Office on Drug and Crime
UNTS	United Nations Treaty Series
WHO	World Health Organization

List of Contributors

Asha Bajpai

is the Dean and Professor of Law of the School of Law, Rights and Constitutional Governance at the Tata Institute of Social Sciences (TISS), Mumbai, India. Her teaching and research interests include laws and rights relating to children, women, youth, and other vulnerable sections of the society. She has been extensively involved in law reform assignments both for governments and international organizations. She was a Fulbright Visiting Lecturer at the Washington College of Law, American University, where she designed and taught a course on Child Rights and Laws- International and Comparative Perspectives. She has published extensively on various issues relating to child law and rights of the child, particularly from the perspective of India and South Asia.

Ann-Christin Cederborg

is Professor of Child and Youth Studies at Stockholm University, Sweden. She is also the head of the Department of Child and Youth Studies. Her research concerns vulnerable children, for example, children in migration, children exposed to sexual and physical abuse, children as offenders, and children in sex trade. She has published numerous articles, books and book chapters and since 2007 she has trained police officers in half-year courses in investigative interviewing of child witnesses at the police academy in Stockholm. She is also frequently requested by social workers, prosecutors or police officers to give lectures on her research findings and she serves as an expert in court assessments of child witnesses.

Mary E. Crock

is Professor of Public Law and Associate Dean (Research) at the Faculty of Law, University of Sydney. She has worked in the area of immigration and refugee law since 1985. An Accredited Specialist in Immigration Law, she has been Chief examiner/ Head Assessor in various Specialist Accreditation programs in Immigration Law across Australia since 1994. She helped to establish and run the Victorian Immigration Advice and Rights Centre Inc. in Melbourne, now the Refugee and Immigration Law Centre (Vic). She is author of eight books and reports and many articles on immigration and refugee law. Her special interest is in vulnerable migrants, particularly children and migrants with disabilities.

Joan E. Durrant

is Professor of Family Social Sciences at the University of Manitoba in Canada, where she teaches courses on violence against children with a focus on children's rights. For 25 years, her research has focused on punitive violence, from psychological, cultural, human rights, and legal perspectives. She co-edited, "Global Pathways to Abolishing Physical Punishment of Children: Realizing Children's Rights" and "Eliminating Corporal Punishment: The Way Forward to Constructive Discipline." She is co-author of the Canadian Joint Statement on Physical Punishment of Children and Youth, and was a member of the Research Advisory Committee of the United Nations Secretary-General's Study on Violence against Children. With Save the Children Sweden, she has co-created child-rights-based programs for parents and teachers on non-violent discipline, now implemented in more than 30 countries.

Hrefna Friðriksdóttir

is Cand. Jur. from the University of Iceland (1989), LLM from Harvard Law School (1996), and is Associate Professor of Family Law at the University of Iceland. She is currently Vice Dean of the Law Faculty of the University of Iceland and chairperson of the Ármann Snævarr Research Institute on Family Affairs. Her main research areas are family law and the law on inheritance. She has researched and published on issues relating to marriage, non-marital cohabitation and sexual orientation law, children's rights, parental responsibility, child protection, adoption and reproductive technologies.

Elisabet Fura

is doctor *h.c.* from the Faculty of Law, Stockholm University, Chief Parliamentary Ombudsman in Sweden, and former judge of the European Court of Human Rights. She served as a lawyer in private practice for more than 20 years in Stockholm and Paris and was elected chair of the Swedish Bar Association in 1999. She took part in the establishment of ILAC (International Legal Assistance Consortium), an umbrella organization for associations of legal and human rights experts, in 2002. As ombudsman, her area of responsibility includes, among others, the armed forces, the prisons and probation services and national insurance.

Deborah A. Goldfarb

is a developmental psychology graduate student at the University of California, Davis. Prior to attending graduate school, she worked as an attorney in civil litigation, including two years as a law clerk to a federal district court judge. She graduated *cum laude* with a Juris Doctor from the University of Michigan Law School and a Bachelor of Science in Psychology from the University of Illinois.

Her research focuses on attitudes towards and effects of interacting with the legal system. Her recent research includes a longitudinal study of children indicated for maltreatment, an international study on family court laws, and an experimental study on the influence of generic language on children's and adults' conviction rates.

Gail S. Goodman

is Distinguished Professor of Psychology at the University of California, Davis. She obtained her PhD from UCLA and conducted postdoctoral studies at the University of Denver and the Université René Descartes in Paris. Her research concerns trauma and memory, memory development, child maltreatment, and children in the legal system. She has received many awards for her research and writings, including the James McKeen Cattell Award for Lifetime Contributions to Applied Psychological Research from the Association for Psychological Science and two Distinguished Contributions awards from the *American Psychological Association* (APA). She has published widely and her research has been cited in U.S. Supreme Court decisions. She has consulted with numerous governments and agencies throughout the world on policies and research concerning child victims in the legal system.

Elisabeth Gording Stang

is Associate Professor at the Oslo and Akershus University College of Applied Sciences since 2008. She is teaching human rights law, family law, immigration law and administrative law at the child welfare bachelor education. She also gives external lectures and courses in child law at other universities, as well as for employees in several social services and public departments. She has published extensively on children's rights, with a specific focus on children under the child protection legislation, asylum seeking children and children exposed to violence and abuse. She is the chairperson of the first board on administrative law established under the Norwegian Association of Lawyers in 2014, and member of the editorial board of the Nordic law journal Retfærd since 2007.

Alex Hirschfield

is Professor of Criminology and Director of the Applied Criminology Centre at the University of Huddersfield UK. He is an inter-disciplinary criminologist with an earlier background in human geography and public health. He has published widely in the field of environmental criminology and has led major evaluations of crime reduction programmes both in the UK and internationally. He is a former Senior Advisor to the UK Home Office, served as a member of the Advisory Panel of Lord John Stevens Commission on the Future of Policing and is a Fellow of the Faculty of Public Health.

Adele D. Jones

is Professor of Social Work at the Centre for Applied Childhood Studies at the University of Huddersfield, UK. Previously at the University of the West Indies, Republic of Trinidad and Tobago, She specializes in international children's rights. She has conducted research throughout the Caribbean, in Uganda, Nepal, South Africa, Romania, Germany, Sweden and the UK and is the author of over 100 publications and conference papers on various issues affecting children worldwide: child abuse, residential care, migration, child refugees, gender, HIV-AIDS and the impact on children of parental imprisonment.

Anna Kaldal

is Associate Professor in Procedural Law at the Faculty of Law, Stockholm University and a member of the board of the Stockholm Centre for the Rights of the Child. She teaches procedural law, evidential law, law and psychology and child law. Her research interests include the right of the child, in particular in legal proceedings, such as criminal-, family- and child protection proceedings, gathering and evaluation of statements given by a child and decision-making in family and child protection cases. She is Sweden's representative in the Nordic research network about children house models. She has published reports, articles and books on various aspects of child law and served as expert and carried out assignments for government agencies.

Françoise Kempf

has been working in the Office of the Council of Europe Commissioner for Human Rights since March 2012. She is, *inter alia*, the Commissioner's adviser on children's rights and on the human rights of minorities. Within the Council of Europe, she has previously worked on minority rights (2005–2012), social rights (2003–2005) and human rights of the Roma (1994–2002). She has also established, and worked for, a human rights NGO based in Spain (Centre for Legal and Social Investigations, Madrid; 2002). She holds a Master in international relations from Geneva Graduate Institute of International Studies.

Katrin Lainpelto

is Senior Lecturer in Procedural Law at the Faculty of Law, Stockholm University, where she teaches criminal procedure, criminal investigation, child law, forensic psychology, and evidential law. Her research interests include procedural and evidential matters concerning crimes against women, children, youth, and other vulnerable groups in the society. Her doctoral dissertation "Corroborating Evidence" (2012) concerns the legal evaluation of corroborating evidence in child sexual abuse cases. The current research project concerns children with neuropsychiatric disorder, with the overall aim to study how children with these types of disorders are treated in the Swedish legal system.

Michael J. Lawler

is Dean and Professor at the School of Health Sciences, University of South Dakota, United States. His areas of published research include child welfare services, juvenile justice, foster care, parent-child relationships, forensic psychology, child well-being, public health, and professional education. He is associate editor of Training & Development in Human Services, co-author of the Application Potential of Professional Learning Inventory, and United States Principal Investigator of Children's Worlds: International Survey of Children's Well-Being. He received a PhD in human development from the University of California, Davis and MSW from the University of California, Berkeley.

Pernilla Leviner

is the Deputy Head of the Stockholm Centre for the Rights of the Child and Associate Professor at the Faculty of Law, Stockholm University. She teaches constitutional law, administrative law, family law and child law. Her research interests lie within and on the border of the fields of public and family law, and more specifically the societal responsibility of protecting children from harm and neglect. Her doctoral thesis addresses the legal dilemmas within the Swedish child protection system and the difficult balancing act between children's rights to protection and the fundamental rights to private and family life. Her recent research has focused on the role and function of courts in child protection cases, the right to a fair trial from a child's perspective as well as children's right to participation and issues relating to the legal representation of children.

Fredrik Malmberg

has been Ombudsman for Children in Sweden since 2008. He has previously worked for Save the Children in Asia, Africa and Sweden. He has a Master of Science in Business Administration and Economics. Since 2012 he is a member of the Management Board of the European Union Fundamental Rights Agency.

Mats Melin

is President of the Swedish Supreme Administrative Court. He has served as a judge at all levels of Swedish courts of law and has also worked, for a number of years, at the Court of Justice of the European Union. Immediately before taking up his present position, he served as Chief Parliamentary Ombudsman in Sweden. He is a member of the Permanent Court of Arbitration.

Rusudan Mikhelidze

holds a master's degree in law from Tbilisi State University and is LL.M in Public International Law from the University of Helsinki. She has attended the Executive Education Programs at Harvard Kennedy School and Massachusetts Institute of Technology. She has served eight years in the Ministry of Justice of Georgia, including at the positions of the director of Analytical Department, the Secretary of the Criminal Justice Reform Council and the Chair of the Juvenile Justice Interagency working group co-chaired by UNICEF Georgia. She is the co-author of the Juvenile Diversion and Mediation Program in Georgia. Currently, she works for the Organization for Economic Co-operation and Development.

Nils Muižnieks

has been Council of Europe Commissioner for Human Rights since 1 April 2012. He is a Latvian national educated in the United States of America, where he obtained a PhD in political science at the University of California at Berkeley. Prior to his appointment as Commissioner for Human Rights, he had served as Director of the Advanced Social and Political Research Institute at the Faculty of Social Sciences of the University of Latvia in Riga (2005–2012); Chairman of the European Commission against Racism and Intolerance (2010–2012), Latvian minister responsible for social integration, anti-discrimination, minority rights, and civil society development (2002–2004), and Director of the Latvian Centre for Human Rights and Ethnic Studies – now Latvian Human Rights Centre (1994–2002). He has published extensively on human rights issues, in particular on racism, discrimination and minority rights.

Peter Newell

is a long-term advocate for and commentator on the rights of children, in the UK and internationally. He is the Coordinator of the Global Initiative to End All Corporal Punishment of Children (www.endcorporalpunishment.org), that he launched together with the Former Council of Europe Commissioner for Human Rights Thomas Hammarberg in 2001. He was a member of the editorial board for the UN Secretary General's Study on Violence against Children. He has been Adviser to the European Network of Ombudspersons for Children (ENOC) since its inception in 1997 and chaired the Council of the Child Rights

International Network (CRIN) from 2008 to 2014. He is co-author of UNICEF's *Implementation Handbook for the CRC*, now in its third edition.

Rosa Maria Ortiz

is member of the Inter-American Commission on Human Rights and its Rapporteur on the Rights of Children. She has a degree in social communications media and is an expert in children's human rights. She has served as Vice-Chairperson of the Committee on the Rights of the Child, and as a human rights and cultural diversity adviser to the Paraguayan Presidency's National Secretariat of Culture. She is founder and member of several human rights organizations in Paraguay, including Decidamos, Global, Tekoha, Callescuela and Communication and Popular Education. In 2003, she was recognized with the award "Paraguayan Women of the Paraguayan Presidency's Women's Secretariat," and in 2010 she received the Peter Benenson for the Defense of Human Rights Award from the Paraguay Section of Amnesty International. She has numerous publications on the rights of the child.

Marta Santos Pais

is the Special Representative of the United Nations Secretary-General on Violence against Children. She served as the Director of the UNICEF Innocenti Research Centre, the UNICEF Director of Evaluation, Policy and Planning, and as the Rapporteur of the United Nations Committee on the Rights of the Child. She was a member of the drafting group of the Convention on the Rights of the Child and of its Optional Protocols and participated in the development of other key international human rights instruments. She has researched and published widely on children's rights, human rights and legal issues and holds a law degree from the University of Lisbon.

Paulo Sérgio Pinheiro

is Adjunct Professor of International Studies at the Watson Institute of International Studies, Brown University and a research associate at the Center for the Study of Violence, University of São Paulo, NEV/USP. He has also taught at Columbia, Notre Dame, USA and Oxford universities and at the École des Hautes Études en Sciences Sociales, Paris. He chairs the UN independent international commission of inquiry on the Syrian Arab Rpublic since 2011 . He was a commissioner of the Brazilian National Truth Commission, 2012 to 2014, and served as Minister of the Secretariat of State for Human Rights, under President Cardoso, Brazil.

Julia Sloth-Nielsen

is a senior professor at the University of the Western Cape. She also holds a chair in Children's Rights in the Developing World at Leiden University. She has published extensively on children's rights, with a specific focus on children's rights in African context. She serves as the second vice chair of the African Committee of Experts on the Rights and Welfare of the Child, and has consulted to governments on child law reform in South Africa, Mozambique, Botswana, Kenya, Ethiopia, Lesotho, Namibia, Zambia, and Tanzania, amongst others. She was a member of the South African Law Reform Commission project committee that drafted the Child Justice Act 75 of 2008 as well as the Children's Act 38 of 2005.

Ashley Stewart-Tufescu

is a PhD Candidate in Applied Health Sciences at the University of Manitoba and faculty member in the Department of Early Childhood Education, School of Health Sciences and Community Services at Red River College in Winnipeg, Canada. Her areas of research expertise include child rights, child developmental health, and violence against children. She is the Canadian Principal Investigator for the *Children's Worlds: International Survey of Subjective Well-being* (ISCWeB), a multi-national, rights-based study of children's well-being. In addition to her academic work, she is a practicing social worker and a Master Trainer for *Positive Discipline in Everyday Parenting,* working with caregivers and teachers to reduce physical and humiliating punishment in Bangladesh, Canada, Indonesia, Japan, Jordan, the Occupied Palestinian Territories, Peru, and the Philippines.

Carl Göran Svedin

is Professor in Child and Adolescent Psychiatry at the Faculty of Health Sciences, Linköping University. He earned an MD (1973), a PhD (1984), and docent (associate professorship, 1994). He was professor in Lund 2002–2006, and after that he moved back to Linköping to be a professor in child and adolescent psychiatry. He has long clinical experience and his major research interests are trauma and abuse in children and adolescents. Has been the initiator of the child and youth psychiatry specialist unit BUP-Elefanten and the two Child Advocacy Centres (CAC) in Lund and Linköping. Co-author of more than 100 original scientific papers published in international peer-reviewed journals, of which 76 have been published in Pub Med. Board member and treasurer in Nordic Association for Prevention of Child Abuse and Neglect (NASPCAN) since the start 1998.

Rebecca Thorburn Stern

is Associate Professor of International Law at the Faculty of Law, Uppsala University where she teaches international law, human rights and migration law. She is the Coordinator of L/UMIN (the Lund/Uppsala Migration Law Network), a research network aimed at promoting, facilitating and developing national and international migration law research in Sweden. Her research interests include the rights of the child, in particular the child's right to participation, different aspects of asylum law and the relationship between national and international law in an increasingly globalized world. She defended her doctoral thesis "The Child's Right to Participation – Reality or Rhetoric?" in 2006 and has since published articles and books in Swedish and English on various aspects of human rights and asylum law.

Trond Waage

is head of the pedagogical department at Telemark University College. He has served as advisor on the rights of the child to many governments and international bodies. For eight years he was the Ombudsman for Children in Norway with focus on policy review and monitoring from an independent position. In the role as ombudsman he initiated the European Network of Ombudspersons for Children (ENOC) and supported governments and parliaments in setting up Ombudsman for Children offices worldwide. His research concerns independent human rights institutions for children and their effectiveness of champion children's rights. He has served as Senior fellow at UNICEF International Research Centre and has been Director of Research at Childwatch International Research Network, University of Oslo.

Jean Zermatten

is doctor *h.c.* from the University of Fribourg (2007) and from the University of Geneva (2014), He served as member of the UN Committee for the Rights of the Child since 2005, its Vice-Chair 2007–11, and Chairperson 2011–2013. He was President of the juvenile Court of the Canton of Valais (Switzerland) between 1980 to 2005. He is also the Founder and Director of the International Institute for the Rights of the Child (IDE) in Sion/Switzerland (www.childsrights.org) (1995–2014) and has been lecturer at the University of Fribourg (Law Faculty). He has initiated and launched the Master in Children's Rights, in collaboration with the University of Fribourg and the Institut Universitaire Kurt Bösch.

Introduction

Pernilla Leviner, Anna Kaldal and Katrin Lainpelto

As Nelson Mandela proclaimed at the inauguration of a children's fund in Pretoria in 1995 "there can be no keener revelation of a society's soul than the way in which it treats its children." This is especially true for how a society treats children in vulnerable situations, and particularly when they meet government agencies and courts as victims, offenders or otherwise in civil, criminal or administrative proceedings.

Today, 25 years after the UN Convention on the Rights of the Child (CRC) was adopted, the existence of children's rights is taken for granted. Nevertheless, how to achieve these rights still poses challenges. Now that children are recognized as legal subjects with their own individual rights, the time has come to ensure them access to justice and child-friendly judicial processes. This can be seen as the second phase in realizing children's rights. Adopting a child-rights' perspective, and taking the next step in ensuring the fulfilment of these rights as enshrined in the CRC, is a delicate and complicated task. This is partly because children cannot always themselves assert their rights; but also because their needs and rights can conflict with parental rights as custodians. Moreover, taking children's rights seriously challenges the way we have organized judicial proceedings and how we have understood fundamental principles such as the right to a fair trial.

Efforts have been made internationally to provide States with recommendations on how to realize child-friendly justice systems. The United Nations Committee on the Rights of the Child, for example, has issued guidelines on how to ensure children the right to be heard in all judicial proceedings affecting them. The Committee also gives specific recommendations for the treatment of children in the criminal justice system. Two examples of important regional efforts here are the 2010 Council of Europe Guidelines of the Committee of Ministers of the Council of Europe on child-friendly justice and the 2011 African Guidelines on child-friendly justice. The overall aim of these guidelines is to enhance children's access to and treatment in justice. They apply to all the circumstances in which children are likely, on any ground and in any capacity, to be in contact with the criminal, civil or administrative justice system. They recall and promote the principles of the best interests of the child, care and respect, participation, equal treatment and the rule of law.

In line with these international recommendations, States clearly need to integrate child-specific considerations in the organization and development of their justice systems. However, the guidelines and recommendations are fairly

© KONINKLIJKE BRILL NV, LEIDEN, 2015 | DOI 10.1163/9789004297432_002

non-specific. Hence, States can quite easily argue that they are fulfilling the requirements set out. This is heatedly and repeatedly contested in country reports by the United Nations Committee on the Rights of the Child and by other organizations focusing on children's rights, and also in scholarly writing. Much indicates that many of the world's justice systems are not at all child-friendly, or are at best deficient in this aspect.

The realization of children's fundamental rights rests squarely on ensuring them access to justice, and on creating child-friendly justice systems. This in turn clearly encompasses many challenges including the obvious need for further analysis and discussion, and this was one of the aims of the conference, *Child-friendly Justice – What it means and how it is realized*, organized by the Stockholm Centre for the Rights of the Child in May 2014. Central questions addressed were what child-friendly justice actually means and how it can and should be realized, now 25 years after the CRC was adopted. The aspiration was to identify and elaborate on these challenges. This includes where we stand in ensuring children access to child-friendly justice when they are in contact with public authorities and courts, what possibilities we have to create and promote child-friendly justice systems and what the next step should be.

The following papers, the proceedings of the Conference, address topics analysed by researchers in child law and the behavioural sciences focusing on children meeting the justice system. They also include contributions by representatives of organizations such as the United Nations, the European Council, the Inter-American Commission on Human Rights and the Ombudsman for Children in Sweden. The book's four parts have the following themes – (1) *Basic Components of Child-friendly Justice Systems,* (2) *Children and Criminal Justice Systems* (offender and victim perspectives), (3) *Children and Civil and Administrative Justice* and (4) *Child-friendly Justice – Continental Perspectives.*

In the first part – *Basic Components of Child-friendly Justice Systems* – Mats Melin, in his opening address to the Conference, underlines the CRC's fundamental impact on the position of children in our society and our social and legal culture. Concerning children affected by the administration of justice, Melin emphasizes the need for schemes to secure that children's views are heard and respected. He also underscores the importance of avoiding legal proceedings that unnecessarily add to the traumas underlying such proceedings.

The next two papers, by Marta Santos Pais and Paulo Sérgio Pinheiro respectively, address the core issues of children's fundamental right to protection against violence and the urgent need to stop the criminalization of children. Ashley Stewart-Tufescu & Joan E. Durrant then take up the need to ban corporal punishment, partly by synthesizing the research on its negative effects and partly by presenting a theoretical pathway from abused children to children themselves committing crimes.

In this first part of the book, two papers relate specifically to the basic principles of children's rights – the best interest of the child and children's right to participation. Jean Zermatten discusses different aspects of the first principle: the basis for a substantive right, a rule of procedure and a fundamental interpretative legal principle. Zermatten also addresses the potential conflict between the best interest of a child and other interests affecting legislation and/or decision-making. Hrefna Friðriksdóttir takes up children's right to participation and representation, suggesting the use of the concept of relational representation of children in order to acquire optimal representation and participation for children.

This first part also includes articles dealing with children's right to be heard from a behavioural-science perspective. The overall message is that a prerequisite for children's participation is that their voices are heard and interpreted in accordance with current knowledge and experience. Ann-Christin Cederborg stresses the importance of high-quality interviews and collaboration between professionals as ways of ensuring children's right to be heard from their own perspectives. The need for better ways of obtaining evidence from children is then highlighted by Deborah A. Goldfard, Gail S. Goodman & Michael J. Lawler. They emphasize that when investigative units, social service systems and courts appreciate the importance of proper experimental research design and open their doors to researchers, the legal system can both ensure that the goals of the CRC are met and help fix a non-optimal system to prevent re-traumatization.

The paper by Adele Jones & Alex Hirschfield takes up the question of the psychological impact on children of parental incarceration and the relation between this and children's later behavioural, educational and health outcomes. The dissonance between policy on criminal justice and that concerned with the welfare of children is highlighted: widespread adoption of a child-sensitive approach to justice would be a major step forward. In the last paper of the book's first part, Trond Waage pinpoints the shortcomings of the CRC and its implementation and suggests measures for improvement. He particularly elaborates the need for change in approaches, and underlines, among other things, the significance of closer contact between the "producers" of knowledge, *i.e.*, researchers, on the one hand and the "consumers," *i.e.* the child-law policymakers.

The various aspects of children's contact with criminal justice systems form the subject of the second part of the book – *Children and Criminal Justice Systems*. The two initial papers discuss child-friendly justice for *children in conflict with the law* – the child-offender perspective on criminal justice systems. The overall themes for Peter Newell are the harm done by criminalization of children and society's responsibility to promote the establishment of laws, procedures, authorities and institutions specifically applicable to children in conflict with the law. Fredrik Malmberg discusses the situation for children deprived of their liberty during police investigations. He points out that Sweden does not live up to the requirements of the CRC and that there is a clear need for a separate juvenile justice system for children in conflict with the law in Sweden. The paper by Rusudan Mikhelidze deals with diversion and mediation programmes as experienced in Georgia since 2010. The result of studies conducted on these measures shows that a culture of mediation and restorative justice has yet to grow in countries with limited resources, and the profession of mediator needs support, capacity-building and development.

The second part of the book also includes three papers addressing *child victims and witnesses in criminal justice* proceedings. Anna Kaldal & Carl Göran Svedin analyse the activities and the results, as well as challenges and possibilities, of the Swedish Children's Houses (*Barnahus*). Being a rather new institution in Sweden, based on the American Children's Advocacy Center model, the function of Barnahus is assessed in Kaldal's and Svedin's article and its possible future development is discussed. Asha Bajpai explores the nature and extent of child abuse in India. She describes how legislative, administrative and institutional changes have brought about a paradigm shift in the way child victims are handled; but that there is still a long way to go to further improve the status of child victims and child witnesses. Bajpai suggests that the adversarial system needs to be reviewed and that there is a need for legislative, procedural and even constitutional reform to create a child-friendly justice system. Katrin Lainpelto deals with the challenges of evidentiary difficulties in criminal proceedings when children with neuropsychiatric disorders are alleged victims of sexual abuse. Preliminary findings are presented from a case study dealing with how Swedish courts reason in such cases and the extent to which judgments are based on the involvement of experts. The overall conclusion is that courts should involve experts in the decision-making, a view that can favour both victims and defendants.

Turning to the third part of the book, which has the general theme of *Children and Civil and Administrative Justice*, two papers deal with migrant children and unaccompanied asylum-seeking minors. Mary Crock explores the extent to which the CRC can assist in addressing the vulnerability and precarious status of children in migration processes. She examines the relevance of two basic principles of the CRC to the situation of migrant children. These are the "best interests" principle and the notion that children should have the right to participate in all decisions affecting their future. Rebecca Thorburn Stern focuses on the assessment of asylum claims, raising the importance of applying a rights-based and child-sensitive perspective to the plight of unaccompanied and separated asylum-seeking children, and how the general principles of the CRC can best be employed here.

The question of children's right to protection of private and family life is addressed in the paper by Elisabeth Gording Stang, who provides a rather thorough analysis of the case law of the European Court of Human Rights in the light of the CRC. She highlights the tension between the broad definition of family and family life both in the CRC and in the case law of the court, and the fact that the very existence of biological bonds amounts automatically to a protection of family life at the cost of the child. This causes a paradoxical and unresolved legal situation. In the final paper in this part, Pernilla Leviner discusses the principle of the right to a fair trial in child-protection cases from a child's perspective. The need for a clearer definition of what a fair trial means from a child's perspective is demonstrated in order to enable reforms with a substantive-rights-based approach regarding specific needs of children in child-protection processes.

In the fourth part of the book—*Child-friendly Justice: Continental Perspectives*—four papers adopt a continent-specific approach and analyse children's rights and child-friendly justice. Two papers deal with the situation in Europe. Nils Muižnieks & Françoise Kempf point out that justice systems in Europe are not yet as child-friendly as they should be and often do not adequately reflect the principles contained in the Council of Europe Guidelines. These authors' general conclusion is that there is a lack of awareness of children's rights and of the relevant standards. Additionally, the two main goals of juvenile justice—prevention and reintegration—remain all too often ignored or neglected by policy-makers, who tend to favour punitive approaches, or still miss the key point that children have a right to be treated differently from adults. Elisabet Fura focuses on a rather recent European Court decision concerning the rights of an asylum-seeking family. Complaints were made against the French authorities regarding the administrative detention of the family and its adverse impact on their children. Fura describes how the Court in this landmark decision for the first time took children's rights seriously even though the children were neither applicants nor the objects of the detention order.

In a detailed and comprehensive study, Julia Sloth-Nielsen describes the complexity of the subject of children and justice and analyses the situation in Africa. The recent legal reforms in Africa are carefully presented and their gaps and strengths are elaborated. One important hypothesis is that the clear thrust of juvenile justice reform that was evident around 2000 in Africa has somehow been diluted by the introduction of the concept of Justice for Children (J4C) in 2006. This has shifted the focus to "protection of children" in general. Sloth-Nielsen concludes that the legal framework for driving reforms which under-pin a more child-friendly system is in place, both at continental and, by and large, at country level. However she notes that the need for the reform of insti-tutions linked to children's contact with justice systems is a serious concern.

The last paper, by Rosa Maria Ortiz, discusses access to justice in the Inter-American System. She describes the structure of the Inter-American Commission on Human Rights with particular focus on petitions relating to children. Almost 10 percent of the total workload of the Commission consists of petitions relating to children. Of these, a high percentage represent a lack of access to justice. Since 1989 the Commission has had a special children's rap-porteur who has published a number of specific reports.

The Conference sought to make a new effort to assess the content of child-friendly justice. Certain concepts, perhaps child-friendly justice among them, are easy to understand but difficult to define precisely in legal terms. The papers included in this volume have nonetheless undoubtedly contributed to the clarification of many aspects of the concept as understood today in state practice, in the doctrine of law and in several other scientific disciplines. As already seen from the brief presentation above, the concept of child-friendly justice is multi-facetted—both in terms of what it actually means, and regard-ing the challenges, potentials and possibilities it poses.

However, despite the plethora of expertise and subjects, many of these papers have common features and raise similar questions. One very strong message from the Conference proceedings is that before discussing how to make justice systems child-friendly, we have to ensure there are effective mechanisms to guarantee children the most fundamental right to protection from violence, abuse and neglect, whether at home or elsewhere. No justice system can ever be fair if children are not treated with dignity. Another core message is that children should not be criminalized. This stance was raised in many of the Conference presentations (*e.g.* Pinheiro, Santos Pais, Newell, Malmberg, Muižnieks & Kempf, Mikhelidze and Stewart-Tufescu & Durrant). This can be contrasted to the widespread trend in many parts of the world towards decreasing the minimum age of criminal responsibility and sentenc-ing children to longer imprisonment. In Pinheiro's words, "It is madness, and very inhumane, rights-violating madness, to criminalize and lock up children. We must stop criminalizing children altogether." Many of the contributors also emphasize that we should instead focus on rehabilitation and re-integration. This is especially true when taking into account, as Marta Santos Pais points out, that in many countries incarceration is being used as a substitute for child protection, cloaking the fact that many young offenders have been, and are, exposed to abuse and neglect.

Another aspect raised in these papers is that requirements for a child-friendly justice often imply a need for legislative reform and specific considerations in the organization and development of justice systems. An overall question is how far our traditional systems and procedures can be adapted and reformed so as to meet children's specific needs and rights, especially in situations where these may be in conflict with the rights of parents as custodians. Further, several papers raise the need for specific considerations regarding how public agencies and courts handle specifically vulnerable children such as those with disabilities and unaccompanied and separated asylum-seeking children. It is underlined in these papers that children in abusive situations, as well as children with special needs, require additional consideration with respect to justice systems in order to safeguard, and also exercise effectively, the rights that they enjoy, a point underlined by several authors here.

A central question for child-rights advocates and organizations has been how to make current justice systems more child-friendly. It cannot be underscored enough how important it is for justice systems to function with the primary goal of avoiding unnecessary additional traumas to children encountering legal proceedings. However, much suggests that the next step should be to consider how to change, or even rebuild, justice systems so that they have the true potential of fairness to children, as well as to other vulnerable groups. It might be that in many cases we cannot solve "new problems" within the framework of our old systems, or with old problem-solving models.

While many of the papers discuss the needs for reform and better implementation of children's rights in order to create child-friendly justice systems, positive examples and developments are also presented and discussed (see, e.g., Mikhelidze's paper). Advance is also identified by Julia Sloth-Nielsen in the legislative changes in Africa and by Elisabet Fura with respect to judicial practice in Europe. Since the adoption of the CRC in 1989, we have seen significant changes, many of which must be considered ground-breaking, both in furthering children's rights and in creating more child-friendly justice systems. There has certainly been significant progress, but we are facing challenges.

Remembering that the CRC was adopted a quarter of a century ago, it should be considered as a very creative and forward-looking instrument. Now, however, there is a need to re-think children's rights as enshrined in the Convention. For instance, much has been done to provide better modalities for actually *listening* to children and materializing their right to be heard and to express their views in accordance with the CRC's Article 12. But the time is now ripe to figure out *what to do* with what children are saying and expressing as their wishes. We need this knowledge for their right to participation to be truly realized, thereby ensuring that justice systems are fair and child-friendly. We need also to stress again and again that children have not only the same rights as adults, but also additional ones, including the right to be treated differently from adults, given their specific needs. One overall challenge is arguably how to work proactively so that children do not need to be in contact with the justice system at all, be it because of a direct conflict with the law, as victims or witnesses of crime, in child protection cases and custody disputes or as asylum seekers. Ideally, children should not have to meet the courts and public authorities, but instead have their needs supplied by supportive environments.

We all agree that the realization of children's rights is crucial for children themselves. Progress in this area is also of absolutely central importance in a democratic society. Nelson Mandela could not have said a truer word when he stated that the treatment of children reveals a society's soul. If we want children to participate and contribute to our societies in positive ways, both now and later as adults, we have to treat them with respect and dignity while considering their own specific rights and needs. Change and further progress here is a collective responsibility for international organizations, States, governmental bodies, academics and child-rights advocates everywhere.

PART 1

Basic Components of Child-friendly Justice Systems

∵

A Quarter of a Century with the UN Convention on the Rights of the Child*

Mats Melin

Your Majesty, Madam Vice-Chancellor, distinguished conference participants, ladies and gentlemen.

It is a great honor to have been asked to briefly address this assembly of experts and dedicated persons from all over the world, gathered here today for a Conference on the occasion of the 25th Anniversary of the adoption of the Convention on the Rights of the Child.

I suppose you could say that celebrating the 25th anniversary of any international instrument which has not quietly slipped into oblivion is an important occasion in itself. But this is not just *any* international instrument. It champions an especially noble and important cause.

It recognizes, as stated in the preamble, that children "need special safeguards and care, including appropriate legal protection."

And it aims to ensure, still in the words of the preamble, that children should be fully prepared to live an individual life in society, and be brought up in the spirit of the ideals proclaimed in the Charter of the United Nations, and in particular in the spirit of peace, dignity, tolerance, freedom, equality and solidarity.

With those words, I understand the Convention to proclaim firmly the rights of all children and of every individual child—but also that the Convention is based on the understanding that how children are treated today largely determines how our societies will be shaped and function tomorrow.

An upbringing marked by neglect, disrespect and authoritarian leadership may make it more difficult for tomorrow's fully capable citizens and decision-makers to honor the ideals of inclusiveness and openness and the spirit of democracy.

Not only has the Convention escaped from oblivion, it has in fact had a fundamental impact on our way of thinking, on our social and legal culture. I understand that one of the purposes of this conference is to evaluate the effects of the Convention. With all due respect for the work to be done during the next few days, I would argue that today, a quarter of century after the Convention's adoption, the position of children is fundamentally different, not only within the legal sphere.

This is certainly true in my country, as well as in many any legal orders of which I have some knowledge. I assume—or at least hope—that it is also true also for countries and legal orders which I am not familiar with.

---

* Keynote speech

I am of course aware that the situation may be different where the fight for survival is a daily challenge.

I wish to share with you just one, fairly simple and concrete, example from my own legal system.

Let us go back 25 years in time, to cases where one parent had to be given sole custody of a child—in itself of course a failure vis-à-vis the child.

In judgments delivered then, the excluded parent would be given the right to spend time with the child for certain defined periods, what is sometimes referred to as visitation rights.

Today, in that same situation, the *child* is given the right to spend time with the other parent. It is the child who has the right not to be deprived of his or her relation with the other parent. The legal effect might be essentially the same, but nevertheless, there has been a fundamental change of perspective.

Sweden belongs to the dualist tradition with regard to international law. International treaties are not automatically part of the national legal order.

There has been, and still is, a sometimes-heated debate in this country as to whether the Convention on the Rights of the Child should be incorporated into national law and thus be transformed into directly applicable provisions rather than an obligation under international law.

The importance of this issue has, to some extent, been reduced. In our part of the world, the European Union Charter of Fundamental rights is now part of EU primary law.

Article 24 of the Charter stipulates that:

1. Children shall have the right to such protection as is necessary for their well-being. They may express their views freely. Such views shall be taken into consideration on matters which concern them in accordance with their age and maturity.
2. In all actions relating to children, whether taken by public authorities or private institutions, the child's best interest must be a primary consideration.

The fact that this provision is part of the EU Charter is, I think, in itself a testimony to the tremendous impact of the Convention on the Rights of the Child. The courts and public authorities of 28 Member States are now, when implementing EU law, bound by these directly applicable provisions which, I think it is fair to say, contain the essence of the Convention of the Rights of the Child.

Let me just make one more specific remark about the position of children in the legal process. Children may be affected by the administration of justice but are rarely parties to the proceedings. It is of course essential that schemes are put in place to ensure that their interests are protected and that their views are heard and respected. This may be done, for example, by appointing a special legal counsel to protect the child's specific interest.

However, almost as important, to my mind, is that children also have the right to *abstain* from taking a stand, not least in cases of conflict between the parents, as in, for example, battles for custody.

Where the child does wish to take a stand, or when it is necessary for the child to be heard, as for example when he or she is the victim of a crime, we need to avoid obliging the child to appear before the full court in adversarial proceedings. Arrangements have to be made—while respecting the requisites of fair trial—for the child to testify in a calm and secure environment.

We need to avoid the legal proceedings unnecessarily adding to the trauma underlying the proceedings.

With those brief words of introduction, I wish to thank the Stockholm Centre for the Rights of the Child for taking the initiative to summon this conference. And I congratulate the Centre, and especially Professor Said Mahmoudi, for assembling such a distinguished set of panellists to represent the interdisciplinary character of this field of study.

I wish our guests from abroad a pleasant stay in a at least for the moment sunny Stockholm and all of you a successful conference with a fruitful exchange of views which, no doubt, will further enhance the rights of children in our respective legal orders and thus bring us closer to child-friendly justice.

Children's Rights, Freedom from Violence and Criminal Justice

Marta Santos Pais

Being held on a very special year, the year of the 25th anniversary of the adoption of the Convention on the Rights of the Child, the Stockholm Conference provides an excellent platform to commemorate positive developments, to reflect on prevailing challenges that compromise the protection of the rights of the child and to join efforts to accelerate progress in the realization of children's rights.

The Convention on the Rights of the Child (CRC) and its Optional Protocols provide a sound normative foundation to build upon!

In April 2014, the Third Protocol to the Convention on the Rights of the Child on a Communications Procedure entered into force. I cannot imagine a better way of starting the celebrations of the 25th Anniversary of the CRC than by increasing children's access to justice and effective remedies to safeguard their rights.

The Convention calls on all governments to take children seriously and to promote children's rights as a distinct priority: in laws and policies, in budget decisions and in daily actions across all levels of administration. One key dimension of this agenda is the imperative to safeguard the right of the child to freedom from violence.

I Violence against Children is a Human-rights Violation

Violence against children is indeed a violation of human rights that compromises all the rights of the child. Although it may manifest itself in different forms, in every single case it compromises the enjoyment of children's rights and undermines children's dignity and development. Violence inhibits positive relationships, provokes low self-esteem, emotional distress and depression; at times, it leads to risk-taking and aggressive behaviour. Violence has both a human and a social cost. In addition to the dramatic impact on individual children, it entails very high costs for society, reducing human capacity and compromising social development. As the UN Secretary-General's Study on Violence against Children puts it so well: No violence against children is justifiable and all violence is preventable.

© KONINKLIJKE BRILL NV, LEIDEN, 2015 | DOI 10.1163/9789004297432_004

To assess progress in children's protection from violence, in 2013 my office conducted a Global Survey on Violence against Children. The Global Survey confirms that protecting children from violence is an area where over the past years significant progress has been achieved. Our understanding of how and why children are exposed to violence has deepened, and strategic actions are under way in many countries to translate this endeavour into effective protection.

At the international level, there has been an ever-growing ratification and incremental implementation of treaties on children's protection from violence—including in the context of trafficking, gender violence and the sexual exploitation of children.

Translating international treaties into tangible action is an ethical and legal imperative. Unfortunately, it remains a distant reality for countless girls and boys exposed to violence in schools, in care and justice institutions, and within the home; for those lured into prostitution, portrayed in pornographic materials, groomed through the internet; trafficked for sexual or labour exploitation or illegal adoption; and for children placed in detention because of their migration status or for the lack of official documentation; as well as for the many girl victims of genital mutilation, forced into marriage or killed in the name of honour.

Despite the seriousness of these phenomena, child victims remain largely invisible and are often neglected in statistics and policy action.

Bridging the governance gap between rhetoric and effective enforcement remains a pressing challenge. But this is a challenge we can steadily overcome. One important dimension of this process is to ensure that children become fundamental actors in implementation! But for this to happen, young people must have access to, and understand and make use of, the provisions of child-rights treaties.

This is why it remains important to disseminate child-rights-friendly materials, such as those issued by my office on the Optional Protocols to the CRC. These publications benefited from the special advice of children in different regions of the world, who helped to shape the text and design of these publications. They are being translated into different national languages. We remain committed to joining hands with partners to help disseminate these important advocacy tools and to promote their inclusion in public awareness-raising initiatives and in child-rights education initiatives within the school system.

At the national level there is also good news to share. There is a clear increase in the number of countries with a comprehensive and multidisciplinary policy agenda to prevent and address violence against children. The legal protection of children from all forms of violence, including corporal punishment, is also gaining ground – globally, the number of countries with a legal prohibition has more than doubled since 2006, counting 38 today; in some cases such provisions have been included in the Constitution itself.

Significant information and awareness-raising campaigns have also been launched to keep violence concerns high on the agenda, to prevent abuse, to help child victims gain confidence to speak up and seek support, and to promote a change in attitudes and behaviour.

Although it is important to welcome these achievements, it is imperative to recognize that progress has been too slow, too uneven and too fragmented to make a genuine breakthrough. The urgency of this cause has clearly not diminished and some irrefutable figures illustrate this well. According to a recent WHO Report,[1] every year, across the European region, child maltreatment leads to the premature death of more than 850 children under 15 years; at least 18 million children suffer from sexual abuse, 44 million from physical abuse and 55 million from mental abuse. Shocking as they are, these figures are understood to be underestimations; in fact, it is believed that 90% of child maltreatment may go unreported.

Other United Nations reports,[2] including those addressed below, reveal dramatic figures on children's exposure to some serious forms of violence. According to ILO, child labour continues to compromise the rights of millions of children: 168 million child labourers, almost half (73 million) of primary school age (5–11); 85 million involved in hazardous work, and more than 11 million girls involved in domestic work often enduring physical, emotional and sexual abuse. Trafficking affects countless people everywhere and most victims find themselves in violent situations. As highlighted by UNODC, although it is hard to capture the real dimension of this phenomenon, the numbers of child victims have been on the increase; from 2007 to 2010, numbers rose by 27%. In some regions children constitute more than 60% of detected victims and although children may be trafficked for different purposes, girls are hardest hit.

Homicide rates are another serious reflection of this worrying pattern. As noted by UNODC, adolescent boys are highly represented amongst victims of homicide, as a result of their manipulation by drug dealers, association with gangs, possession of small arms or involvement in violence-prone activities. And when armed violence is prevalent, girls are at high risk of domestic

---

1   WHO Regional Office for Europe, "European Report on Preventing Child Maltreatment," 2013.
2   See for example: ILO, "Marking Progress against Child Labour: Global Estimate and Trends 2000-2012," 2013; UNODC, "Global Study on Homicide," 2013; UNODC, "Global Report on Trafficking in Persons," 2014.

violence and of being killed by their partners, while young children are at high risk of being witness of violence at home.

Some children are at particularly high risk. More often than not they come from disadvantaged populations. Children from deprived neighbourhoods are more likely to be admitted to hospital as a result of assault, and adolescents are highly represented amongst homicide rates.

This pattern has been aggravated by the recent economic crisis. High levels of unemployment and cutbacks in public health and welfare services have led to increasing levels of stress, depression, anxiety and suicidal thinking amongst affected families, undermining parent–child bonding and constituting serious risk factors for child neglect and abuse.

Cuts in child benefits and services, the loss of social safety nets and reductions in staff providing counselling and support to child victims have added a serious strain on millions of families, constituting aggravating factors for violence, abuse, and exploitation. These are concerns which we need to continue to seriously monitor, now and in the future.

Despite the magnitude and severity of this phenomenon, children continue to lack information about where to go and whom to call to get advice and assistance, especially when the perpetrator is someone they trust and feel close to.

In still too many countries, child-sensitive counselling, reporting and complaint mechanisms are unavailable or difficult to access. When in place, services frequently lack the resources and skills to address children's concerns and promote the healing and reintegration of child victims. With the economic crisis, the accessibility and quality of these mechanisms has also suffered. Even national, independent children's rights institutions, which play a particularly crucial role during such periods of economic recession and uncertainty, are facing increased demands with fewer resources.

When violence occurs, children often lack trust in existing services. They fear they will not be believed or taken seriously; and they are afraid of public exposure, stigmatization and possible reprisals if they tell their story. For particularly disadvantaged children, including those belonging to minorities, living and working on the streets, or children with disabilities, these challenges may become truly unsurmountable.

At the same time, professionals often lack the necessary skills to identify early signs of abuse and address incidents of violence in an ethical, and gender- and child-sensitive manner. They frequently have no guidance as to whether and how they are expected to report, or to whom to refer the case. And when incidents are indeed considered, there is a persistent risk of multiple and fragmented interventions by different professionals, working in disconnected disciplines. This in turn, generates renewed risks of re-victimization of the child and jeopardizes children's safety and effective protection.

For children deprived of liberty, surrounded by stigma and hidden from the public eye, these challenges tend to grow exponentially. They are exposed to serious risks of physical, psychological and sexual violence; they endure humiliating treatment by staff, as a form of control, discipline or punishment; and they risk torture, rape and abuse, especially when placed in facilities with adults.

II   Children, Freedom from Violence and Criminal Justice

The functioning of the juvenile justice system is an important indicator of how children are perceived and protected by society. It also constitutes a pivotal area where States' commitment to children's rights can be best expressed. A juvenile justice system framed by the rights of the child is indeed critical to safeguard children's effective access to justice and to prevent and respond to situations of violence.

Children's access to justice requires a system that fully respects and protects the rights of the child; and also a system that children understand, trust and feel empowered to use, including when they are exposed to violence as victims, witnesses or alleged offenders.

Access to justice is particularly important when children are at risk of criminalization and deprivation of liberty. Thousands of children around the world are confronted with such risks, awaiting trial for long periods of time; being held for minor offences and detained in inhuman conditions; victims of social stigma and still too often lacking alternatives to custodial measures and community-based programmes to support their effective rehabilitation and social reintegration.

Unfortunately, the justice system is an area where children's rights, including the right to protection from violence, continue to be put at risk.

Criminal justice, violence and children are closely interlinked.
· Firstly, the criminal justice system exists to prevent and respond to violent acts (a criminal offence) which often involve children as victims and witnesses, and also as offenders.
· Secondly, child victims of violence, abuse, and neglect are more likely to commit criminal offences later in life. The earlier protective measures can be provided to these children, the greater the chances of preventing offending in adult life.

- Thirdly, children are indeed exposed to serious risks of violence within the criminal justice system; violence remains in fact a persistent challenge, largely invisible, concealed and unreported, and rarely investigated and punished.
- Fourthly, the trauma and the stigma of detention increase children's vulnerability to social exclusion and violence once they are released.

The connections between criminal justice and violence are complex but can and need to be effectively addressed. The response goes beyond the criminal justice system itself, mirroring the complexity and multidimensionality of the phenomenon of violence and the need to assert everywhere and at all times the human rights and best interests of children.

(a)   *Young Offenders Have Often been Previously Exposed to Violence, Abuse and Neglect*

The criminal justice system is still used in many countries as a substitute for weak or incipient child protection institutions, generating approaches that further stigmatize socially excluded children, including those who have fled home as a result of violence and neglect, those who have been abandoned, and are homeless and poor, at times living and working on the street; and also those who suffer from mental health or substance abuse problems. Incarceration and criminalization of children in these situations may put them at risk of serious levels of depression, hopelessness and acute situational stress that can result in self-injurious or aggressive behaviour, or suicide.

According to some studies, child victims of sexual abuse are three to five times more likely to suffer post-traumatic stress disorder, to be dependent on drugs and alcohol, and to commit criminal offences later in life.[3] Child neglect increases the likelihood of arrest as a juvenile by 59 %. Emotional maltreatment, including as a result of witnessing domestic violence, leads to an increased risk of involvement in violent crime. In the case of child victims of abuse placed in non-relative foster care, the risk of arrest increases exponentially.

Moreover, some children are treated as offenders while they were in fact the main victims of incidents of violence. For instance, in a number of countries girls who are victims of violence, exploitation and abuse are still being made responsible for "moral offences" and crimes committed against them by adults.

---

3   For a review of studies on the impact of childhood sexual abuse see "Hidden in Plain Sight: A statistical analysis of violence against children," UNICEF, New York, 2014.

(b)   *Children are Exposed to Serious Risks of Violence within*
        the Criminal Justice System

Still today, there are countries where persons below 18 years of age risk being
convicted and sentenced to the death penalty or life imprisonment, and to
other forms of inhuman sentencing, including caning, flogging, stoning and
amputation. Such punishments are enshrined in legislation, prescribed by formal or informal justice systems.

Violence is frequently associated with situations of deprivation of liberty.
It can occur at the moment of arrest, during transfers in police vehicles, while
in police custody, during pre-trial detention and after conviction.

Around the world, it is estimated that at least one million children are
deprived of liberty. In the majority of cases, they should simply not be placed
in detention.

Frequently, these children are awaiting trial, often for months and even
years, lacking access to legal aid and in many cases without ever being convicted. Others are held for minor offences, placed in overcrowded facilities and
deprived of access to health services, education and vocational training, or
other options for genuine and long lasting reintegration. In many cases, there
are no children's courts, specialized prosecutors or judges, and children end up
being treated as adults and detained in adult prisons.

Children belonging to certain ethnic and minority groups are overrepre-
sented in the criminal justice system. At the same time, asylum-seeking and
migration are also becoming risk factors for children's deprivation of liberty.
These children face a constant risk of physical, psychological and sexual violence. Countless numbers endure violence and humiliating treatment by staff
in detention centres, as a form of control, discipline or punishment; and they
risk torture, rape and abuse, including when placed in facilities with adults. For
girls these risks tend to grow exponentially.

III   Unveiling the Truth about Children within the Criminal Justice
        System

Overall, the situation of children within the criminal justice system remains
hidden, surrounded by stigma and considered of low priority on the national
policy agenda. This explains why it remains difficult to access accurate data on
the numbers of children deprived of liberty and on the reasons leading to their
placement in justice institutions.

Professionals and personnel working with children in the juvenile justice
system often lack the necessary knowledge and skills to respect and protect

children's rights; in addition, oversight and ethical standards are frequently not in place. As a consequence, alternatives to detention are rarely used, even when clear options are foreseen by the legislation.

In still too many countries, national independent mechanisms are also not in place to monitor the safeguarding of children's rights in the justice system and to address any complaints presented by child victims.

Altogether this is a pattern that helps to create a culture of impunity and of tolerance of violence against children and adolescents. A situation that is at times aggravated by sensationalist media that promotes a misleading connection between juvenile delinquency, increases in crime rates and fear of social unrest. As a result, children and adolescents risk being portrayed as perpetrators of serious crimes, and security in society is largely perceived as dependent on the lowering of the minimum age of criminal responsibility and a rise in the length of measures of deprivation of liberty.

And yet, when statistical data is available and publicly known, what it reveals is that persons below 18 years of age are primarily and largely the victims, rather than actors of violence. Indeed, only an extremely low proportion of adolescents are associated with serious criminal offences.

As Special Representative of the Secretary-General on Violence against Children, I undertake many missions across regions and am committed to meet with young people deprived of liberty. Children involved with the criminal justice system convey a strong and persistent message: they feel perceived as human beings of no value and without values. Due to the real or perceived mistake of having infringed the law, they feel stigmatized as citizens and excluded from the opportunity of experiencing life with dignity.

In this overall scenario, more frequently than not, the principles and provisions of the Convention on the Rights of the Child become relegated to a second plane, while legal and policy solutions are shaped by emotions and assumptions, dictated by the pressure of the moment, rather than considered in the light of the child's best interests.

IV   Strengthening the Role of the Criminal Justice System in the Prevention and Elimination of Violence against Children

Clearly, it is urgent to narrow the governance gap between international human-rights standards and practices for the protection of children in the juvenile justice system. Also, it is imperative to promote a change from punitive responses to an increased investment in prevention, including through early-childhood initiatives, and children's quality education and reintegration, with a steady concern for the promotion of the child's sense of dignity and worth. Hence the development of a child-friendly justice system cannot be prepared in a vacuum but has to go hand-in-hand with the realization of a broader vision, that of a child-friendly society.

Recognizing the urgency of addressing these critical child-rights concerns, and, together with the Office of the High Commissioner on Human Rights and the United Nations Office on Drugs and Crime, I have issued a report on preventing and responding to violence against children within the juvenile justice system.[4] The report presents important recommendations designed to support national implementation efforts, particularly to raise public awareness and enhance the capacity of professionals working with and for children; to inform legislative and policy developments; and to build strong oversight and monitoring systems for violence prevention and for support to child victims, as well as to fight impunity.

To achieve these goals, action is urgently needed in four main areas: the building of a strong national child protection system, the prevention of the criminalization and penalization of vulnerable children, the promotion of restorative justice initiatives, and the urgency of establishing sound accountability mechanisms.

(a) *Building a Strong National Child Protection System*
Firstly, to prevent the involvement of children in the criminal justice system and lower the risk of related incidents of violence, it is critical to develop a strong and cohesive national child protection system. It is essential to address the root causes of child poverty and social exclusion, and provide access to basic social services of quality to all children, including early childhood initiatives and quality education. In addition, young people at risk need to benefit from targeted support to prevent situations where they may be exposed to violence or involved in criminal activities.

Resources are naturally needed to advance this process. Resource allocation for the realization of children's rights is both a human rights imperative and a question of good economics. Investment in prevention is indeed less costly and achieves better results than promoting punitive approaches. Underinvestment in children leads to a high price for society and to poor health, weak education achievement, early pregnancies and criminal behaviour, which are all difficult to repair later in life. In other words, the costs of not investing in children are enormous and often irreversible.

---

4 http://srsg.violenceagainstchildren.org/sites/default/files/documents/docs/A%20HRC%20 21%2025_English.pdf.

Yet, with sustained investment in prevention programmes, new opportunities arise to reduce children's exposure to violence and their involvement in criminal activities. According to recent data published in the United States, over the last two decades the number of child victims of a non-fatal crime, including domestic violence, rape and sexual assault, decreased by 68%. No less importantly, this clear drop in crime came in tandem with visible declines in teenage suicide, bullying, and physical and sexual abuse; and children report feeling safer at school and also less likely to engage in risky behaviour.

(b) *Preventing the Criminalization and Penalization of Vulnerable Children*

The second critical recommendation is that the criminal justice system cannot replace a weak or non-existent child protection system. It cannot allow the stigmatization, criminalization and prosecution of those who are the most vulnerable children in society, and who are in need of care and protection, rather than in conflict with the law.

Legislation needs to decriminalize survival behaviours and status offences, including begging and truancy; it needs to safeguard the rights of children at risk and provide the needed and appropriate support to children with mental health and substance abuse problems.

These measures need to be supported by a system of universal birth registration, still lacking for millions of children around the world, to avoid the risk of applying to children the approaches developed for the adult population.

It is equally critical to establish a legal minimum age of criminal responsibility in line with international standards; and it is vital to reduce deprivation of liberty to situations where it is truly a measure of last resort; and when such exceptional circumstances occur, for the shortest period of time possible.

Similarly, banning all forms of violence and inhuman sentencing is of utmost urgency; as is ensuring that serious consideration is given to a restorative and rehabilitative juvenile justice system that promotes alternatives to deprivation of liberty. These alternatives include mediation, diversion, probation, counselling or community service sentences.

These various measures are also critical to prevent recidivism. As noted by the UN Study on Violence against Children, recidivism among children sentenced to juvenile detention facilities is as high as 50 %, to 70 %, while recidivism rates for children placed in some community-based alternatives programs is as low as 10%. It is critical to provide second-chance opportunities for young offenders, in a safe and protective environment with genuine chances to gain life skills and support for long-lasting social reintegration.

(c)   Promoting Restorative Justice Initiatives

In many societies, restorative justice values such as healing, reconciliation and mutual respect have long served to resolve conflict and strengthen community bonds. In promoting a non-punitive approach, restorative justice seeks to address the causes and consequences of offending, helping to establish accountability for the offence and seeking to repair the harm caused by wrong-doing. Based on dialogue, negotiation and problem-solving, restorative justice helps to reconnect the offender with the community, and it guided by the best interests of the child.

Restorative justice processes can be adapted and implemented through various models, such as mediation, conciliation, conferencing and sentencing circles. They apply to children who are victims, witnesses or offenders and pro-mote healing, respect and strengthened relationships; they can be introduced at all stages of the criminal justice process; and they include the provision of services and support, including education, health care and vocational training to avoid re-engagement in risky behaviour.

Restorative justice provides an alternative to children's deprivation of lib-erty and helps to safeguard children's freedom from violence, abuse and exploitation. Children who participate in restorative programmes are more likely to stay away from gang life and less likely to become victims of armed or gang-related violence. They also demonstrate significantly lower rates of recid-ivism compared to other groups.

To be successful, however, restorative justice calls for steady action. Legislation needs to clearly provide law enforcement, prosecutors and the judiciary with options for diverting children away from the criminal justice system. Effective training on children's rights and relevant legislation needs to be promoted for all relevant actors, and supported by the development of nec-essary skills to foster dialogue, to manage emotions and conflict and secure children's safety. Moreover, guidelines and standard operational procedures are needed for all relevant law enforcement and justice actors, including the police, prosecutors, the judiciary, probation officers, lawyers, social workers, facilitators and mediators.

Coordination between restorative justice service providers and justice actors is of the essence, at national and local levels; data, research and evalua-tion of restorative justice programmes are crucial to safeguard the best inter-ests of the child, promote children's reintegration and prevent violence and recidivism; and adequate resources from national budgets and bilateral and international cooperation are needed to support restorative justice pro-grammes, invest in capacity building, consolidate evidence and promote the sharing and scaling-up of positive initiatives.

(d)   *Establishing Sound Accountability Mechanisms*

The fourth recommendation calls for strong accountability mechanisms. Oversight, monitoring and evaluation initiatives, including unannounced visits by independent institutions, are indispensable to deter incidents of violence against children, to investigate abuses and to hold to account those found responsible. Similarly, it is crucial to provide for redress and reparation for child victims.

Naturally, for all this to be effective, national legislation needs to be clear in its explicit message of prohibition of all forms of violence against children, as a form of discipline, control or sentencing. Moreover, children need to have genuine access to safe and child-sensitive counselling, reporting and complaint mechanisms, with no risk of harm or reprisals. Experience shows that these mechanisms will only be effective when steady efforts are made to ensure they are widely available and accessible, ensuring confidentiality and providing for a prompt and speedy follow-up as well as long-lasting support to child victims.

Yet, in too many countries, child-sensitive counselling, reporting and complaint mechanisms are unavailable or difficult to access. When in place, they frequently lack the resources and skills to address children's concerns and promote the healing and reintegration of child victims. Children often lack trust in existing services. They fear they will not be believed or taken seriously; and they are afraid of public exposure, stigmatization and possible reprisals if they tell their story.

According to children's own assessment and in their own words, available procedures seem useless and inadequate to meet their needs; staff in detention centres are poorly trained in how to treat children with respect and take their views into account; complaints are dismissed without the required investigation, and when they are pursued they may lead to harsh treatment for the child, including solitary confinement.

Young people are eager to enhance their knowledge of their rights and about ways of ensuring their protection. They want professionals who are ready to listen and to take their views into account, people who children can trust and who are sensitive and friendly.

The Stockholm Conference aims at unfolding the concept of child-friendly justice and at identifying ways to make it a reality for all children. Safeguarding children's rights, overcoming the challenges children face in the criminal justice system and investing in the prevention and elimination of violence against children are keys to the development of child-friendly justice and indeed of child-friendly societies. I am confident that these recommendations, together with those of the outstanding experts contributing to the

Conference, will help to advance the implementation of the sound normative foundation the international community has developed over the years,
both to ensure the realization of the rights of the child in the administration
of justice, and to secure children's protection from discrimination and
violence in all its forms.

Reflections on Child-friendly Justice*

Paulo Sérgio Pinheiro

Child-friendly justice is too often narrowly debated as being about juvenile justice, about children in conflict with the law. But when in March this year the Human Rights Council devoted its annual day on children's rights to "Access to justice for children," it provided a correct and much wider definition.

The report of the High Commissioner for Human Rights presented to that session in March[1] provided a very welcome children's-rights-focused definition: "Access to justice refers to the ability to obtain a just and timely remedy for violations of rights as put forth in national and international norms and standards, including the Convention on the Rights of the Child."

Even better, it asserted that: "The concept of access to justice for children requires the legal empowerment of all children. They should be enabled to access relevant information and to effective remedies to claim their rights, including through legal and other services...." And moreover: "Access to justice for children requires taking into account children's evolving maturity and understanding when exercising their rights."

Similarly, the Council of Europe's pioneering Guidelines on child-friendly justice[2] begin their lengthy definition: "'Child-friendly justice' refers to justice systems which guarantee the respect and the effective implementation of all children's rights at the highest attainable level..."

Let's be clear that the legal empowerment of children does not mean adults standing back and waiting in a friendly, encouraging but disengaged fashion for children to exercise and assert their rights, to go to court, to use the third Optional Protocol of the CRC.

It is mostly adults who violate children's rights and, given the dependent, disempowered status of most children and the entirely dependent status of babies and young children, it is adults who must act to secure justice for them: to ensure exposure of violations and to pursue effective remedies for them.

The children's-rights community remains far too small – a significant proportion of them assembled in Stockholm this week.

Of course I am not denying children's right to express their views and have them heard and taken seriously, and when they have the capacity to do so, to exercise their own rights, to self-advocacy. But I sometimes feel that the adult

---

* Keynote speech.

1   UN Doc. A/HRC/25/35, 16 December 2013.

2   17 November 2010.

emphasis within the Convention on children's Article 12 right is not all friendly; that it is promoted too often as an alternative to providing full respect for the entirety of children's rights. Also – and more seriously, listening to children becomes an excuse for not acting, with or without children, to end violations of their rights, just as the "best interests" right is used too often by adults and governments to trump other rights. I recall, as an extreme example, the reservation made by one Member State in ratifying the CRC, asserting that Articles 19 and 37 do not prohibit "the judicious application of corporal punishment in the best interest of the child"!

I must confess that I was a late convert to child participation in the UN Secretary General's Study on Violence against Children, which I led a few years ago. It was the first such UN Study to attempt to engage effectively with children, in particular in the series of nine regional consultations and in visits to 60 States. But the process turned me into a passionate advocate for listening to children, taking seriously what they tell us, and acting on it. Similarly, in inquiring into the tragic horrors of the conflict in the Arab Syrian Republic, it has been essential to pay special attention to children's testimony of the devastation of their childhood, in the—so far vain—hope that all parties and all States engaged directly in the conflict come to their senses and to respect for the rule of law and human rights.

The focus on children's access to justice must remain wide—as the High Commissioner's paper to the Human Rights Council asserts: "Access to justice is a fundamental right in itself and an essential prerequisite for the protection and promotion of all other human rights." But certainly a special focus is needed on children in relation to the criminal law. I am among those, including my dear friends Thomas Hammarberg and Peter Newell, who insist that we must advocate an end to the criminalisation of children altogether; no exceptions, separating entirely issues of responsibility and focusing exclusively on rehabilitation and re-integration.

It is essential, but not nearly enough, to promote the Child-Rights International Network's campaign against the persisting obscenities among these so-called "justice" systems – executions of children, life sentences still for many children, sentences of whipping or flogging for children still authorized in 39 States. As our World Report on Children and Violence proposed, children should only be detained in the very few cases where they are assessed as posing a serious danger to others, and then only as a last resort, for the shortest necessary time – and I would add, certainly not in "penal" settings.

It is easy for politicians and elements in the media to scapegoat disenfranchised children, to build on the still-persisting belief in original sin. But it is inexcusable that children's-rights advocates should be tempted into compromise, into allowing criminalisation and degrees of, if not total, retribution at age 12, or 14, or 16, intimidated from pursuing children's human rights by the heat and tone of the debate.

Wherever penal systems for children are documented accurately, their failure in terms of re-offending rates is dramatic. More tragically, when the childhoods of the children who commit serious crimes are examined in any detail, their suffering at the hands of adults and through the inadequacies of State services—education, health, mental health and welfare services—becomes visible.

It is madness, and very inhumane, rights-violating madness, to criminalize and lock up these children. We must stop criminalizing children altogether.

Best Interests of the Child

Jean Zermatten

1 Introduction: A New Status for the Child

The most spectacular innovation of the UN Convention on the Rights of the Child (CRC) is to introduce the concept that the child, in the course of his development (Article 5, the notion of evolving capacity[1]) and according to the discernment that he/she is capable of, can participate in the life of his/her family, his/her school, his/her education centre and the city, in general. He/she is not just a passive member to be taken care of, but becomes a player of his/her own existence. In effect, the CRC grants a new status to the child, who is not only the recipient of provisions or protection, but also someone whose views we should now go for and listen to, being called upon to participate in those decisions that affect him/her.

Two articles in the CRC illustrate this new status of the child as a subject of right, namely Article 12 and Article 3, para. 1. *First*, with the famous Article 12, the CRC grants to the child the right not only to express his/her views, but also to see that his/her opinion is taken into account in any decision that may in any way have an influence on his/her existence. Article 12 should not be read by itself, as it goes beyond the "technical" function of gathering the child's views; it is linked to the new rights related to the participation of the child in the Society. *Secondly*, Article 3, para. 1, (the right of the child to have his/her best interests assessed and taken as a primary consideration) puts the child at the centre of all attention and imposes to every decision maker (public or private) the obligation to weight the impact on the child (positive or negative) of the decision he has to take. In doing so, he will consider seriously the opinions of the child, expressed according to Article 12.

The two articles do not contradict each other, rather are they complementary.

2 Best Interests of the Child

In the following paragraphs, I will adapt and use one of my articles written on this theme and published in the International Journal of Children's Rights, Special issue: Children's Rights 20 years after.[2]

---

1 Landsdown, G., *The evolving capacity of the Child*, Innocenti Center, Firenze, 2004.
2 Zermatten, J., The best Interests of the Child Principle, Literal Analysis and function, 18 *International Journal of Children's Rights*, 2010, pp. 483–499.

2.1   *In General*

Article 3, para. 1 CRC is the basis for the principle of the best interests of the child; within the Convention, the concept is also mentioned in other articles, providing obligations to consider the best interests of individual children, above all in family law: Article 9: separation from parents, Article 18: parental responsibilities for their children, Article 20: deprivation of family environment, Article 21: adoption.

This principle is deriving from the Welfare System (or Protective system) from the end of XIXth, to the beginning of XXth Century and has been transformed by the CRC in a rule to examine whether the State through its decision makers has acted proportionately when considering the best interests of the child, and placing great weight on the exercise of the child's right to be heard.

2.2   *Definition*

This provision, if we analyse it as a whole, does not give any particular explanation of its application, does not fix any particular duty, nor does it state precise rules. It poses a principle:

"The best interests of the child shall be a primary consideration."

We can give two significations to this expression.

First the best interest principle is also *the fundament for a substantive right*: the right of a child that his/her best interests will be assessed and determined and that it will be taken as a primary consideration, whenever a decision is to be taken concerning a child or a group of children. This fundament for a right has been clearly explained in the title itself of the CRC Committee General Comment No. 14, but also very precisely in the para. 6 a.

A substantive right: The right of the child to have his or her best interests assessed and taken as a primary consideration when different interests are being considered in order to reach a decision on the issue at stake, and the guarantee that this right will be implemented whenever a decision is to be made concerning a child, a group of identified or unidentified children or children in general. Article 3, paragraph 1, creates an intrinsic obligation for States, is directly applicable (self-executing) and can be invoked before a court.[3]

Second, it's a *rule of procedure*: whenever a decision is to be taken that will affect a specific child or a group of children, the decision making process must

---

3   CRC/C/GC/14, para. 6 a.

go through the consideration of the possible impacts (positive or negative) on the child/children concerned and must give this impacts a primary (high) consideration in the appreciation of the different interests in play. It's a procedural rule, because Article 3, para. 1 imposes this step in the decision making process, but does not impose a solution.

Thus, the State party has the obligation to put in place the mechanism to consider the best interests, and has to legislate on the obligation made for the people who has to decide for children (judges, for example) to consider the "best interests" rule of procedure.

In addition to these two meanings, a substantive right and a rule of procedure, the General Comments gives a third meaning to the concept (threefold concept):

> *A fundamental, interpretative legal principle*: If a legal provision is open to more than one interpretation, the interpretation which most effectively serves the child's best interests should be chosen. The rights enshrined in the Convention and its Optional Protocols provide the framework for interpretation.[4]

But nobody knows what is the best interests of this child, or of these children. The best interest will be assessed by the decision maker in a process where the rule of procedure will be applied and the State party does not say what the decision maker has to decide, but just how he has to take his/her decision.

However, it's clear that the principle of best interests must respect:

· The importance of every child as an individual with his/her opinions,
· The global spirit of the CRC,
· The short, medium and long term perspective, because the child is a human being in development.

The interpretation cannot be "culturally relativist" and deny the other rights of the CRC for example to protection against traditional practices and corporal punishments.

2.3   *Child/Children*
All these considerations are valid for the individual child, as well for the children who form groups, or "children in masse." For example, we can read what the CRC Committee has written in its General Comment (GC) No. 7 "Implementing child rights in early childhood:"[5]

---

4   *Ibid.*, para. 6 b.
5   GC No. 7, Implementing child rights in early childhood, para. 13 (CRC/C/GC/7/Rev.1).

(a)   Best Interests of Individual Children
All decision-making concerning a child's care, health, education, *etc.* must take
account of the best interests' principle, including decisions by parents, professionals and others responsible for children. States Parties are urged to make provisions for young children to be represented independently in all legal proceedings
by someone who acts for the child's interests, and for children to be heard in all
cases where they are capable of expressing their opinions or preferences;

(b)   Best Interests of Young Children as a Group or Constituency
All law and policy development, administrative and judicial decision-making and
service provision that affect children must take account of the best interests' principle. This includes "actions directly affecting children (*e.g.* related to health services, care systems, or schools), as well as actions that indirectly impact on young
children (*e.g.*, related to the environment, housing or transport). GC No. 14, para. 19
    The issue of child/children has been clearly answered in the General
Comment No. 14, in particular in the paras. 21–23.[6]

(c)   Notion of Best Interests
First, it seems important to underline the plural sense of this phrase which is
used, in my opinion, as a general expression attached to the concept of "interest of the child."
    Is it necessary to attach a particular importance to the qualifier "best"? Some
criticisms were built around the use of this superlative, arguing that "the best
interests" ("supérieur" or "el interés superior del niño" according to the French
and Spanish versions) meant that in all circumstances, the interest of the child
was to precede any other interest.
    In another literal interpretation, the child is an exceptional being who, as of
the moment when he is in interference with other non-child people or other
social bodies, would inevitably always be right. This position is unbearable
because if we once again put Article 3, para. 1 in relation to Article 5 for example, we understand well that the child is not an person individualized to the
extreme, but remains a member of his family and member of the community,
and therefore a member of the State.
    We can find help also here in the new General Comment No. 14, which
explains the difficulty to understand and to apply such a complex concept "the
best interests:"

> The concept of the child's best interests is complex and its content must
> be determined on a case-by-case basis. It is through the interpretation

---

6   GC No. 14 (CRC/C/GC/14).

and implementation of Article 3, para. 1, in line with the other provisions of the Convention, that the legislator, judge, administrative, social or educational authority will be able to clarify the concept and make concrete use thereof. Accordingly, the concept of the child's best interests is flexible and adaptable. It should be adjusted and defined on an individual basis, according to the specific situation of the child or children concerned, taking into consideration their personal context, situation and needs. For individual decisions, the child's best interests must be assessed and determined in light of the specific circumstances of the particular child. For collective decisions, such as by the legislator, the best interests of children in general must be assessed and determined in light of the circumstances of the particular group and/or children in general. In both cases, assessment and determination should be carried out with full respect for the rights contained in the Convention and its Optional Protocols.[7]

In my opinion, we can also link *"Best Interests"* to the ultimate goal of the development of the child, as defined in Article 6 of the CRC.

(d)   A Primary Consideration
This general concept of best interest does not suffice on its own; it must still be imposed as a criterion for application. It is the objective of this group of phrases: grant to the best interests of the child, value of paramount consideration.

What does this expression mean? If we make a literal analysis, we realize that legislation speaks about "a" primary consideration and not "the" primary consideration.

This nuance means that in case situations where the decision maker (judicial, administrative, legislative) intends to make a decision, it must attach a particular importance to the best interests of the child, and consider first the interests of child/children and the possible impacts of the decision. But this interest will not systematically take over all the other interests (of the parents, other children, adults, or the State).

This terminology seems to mention that in a decision the best interests of the child will not always be the single, overriding interest to be considered; there may be competing other interests, for example, between individual children, between different groups of children and between children and adults (parents, caregivers, public services, State...). "The child's interests, however,

---

7   CRC/C/GC/14, para. 32.

must be the subject of active consideration; it needs to be demonstrated that children's interests have been explored and taken into account as a primary consideration."[8]

Does the article "a," used in place of "the," weaken the principle?

In my opinion, no, but it gives it its rightful place, since it establishes the obligation to consider, in all decisions, the best interests of the child; it is not a choice, but an obligation to examine this principle.

Then, this criterion enters into competition with other criteria which also have value. It is the showcasing of several interests which leads the element of the child to enter into consideration and to becoming one of the criterion in the weighing of possibly divergent interests. The fact of not systematically giving the child precedence is a factor of balance. It would not be desirable that the interest of the child be superior to all other interests and systematically have an edge. That would establish the Republic of Children, not in the sense that Korzack understood it, but in the sense that the child would be put on a pedestal, to regain an image. Such a position would have ends that oppose protection due to the child and would irremediably cause the disappearance of the rights of the child.

In the GC No. 14, the CRC Committee explains:

> The expression "primary consideration" means that the child's best interests may not be considered on the same level as all other considerations. This strong position is justified by the special situation of the child: dependency, maturity, legal status and, often, voicelessness. Children have less possibility than adults to make a strong case for their own interests and those involved in decisions affecting them must be explicitly aware of their interests. If the interests of children are not highlighted, they tend to be overlooked.[9]

and:

> However, since Article 3, para. 1, covers a wide range of situations, the Committee recognizes the need for a degree of flexibility in its application. The best interests of the child – once assessed and determined – might conflict with other interests or rights (*e.g.* of other children, the public, parents, *etc.*). Potential conflicts between the best interests of a child, considered individually, and those of a group of children or children

---

8 *Implementation Handbook for the Convention on the Right of the Child*, UNICEF 2007, p. 38.
9 CRC/C/GC/14, para. 37.

in general have to be resolved on a case-by-case basis, carefully balancing the interests of all parties and finding a suitable compromise. The same must be done if the rights of other persons are in conflict with the child's best interests. If harmonization is not possible, authorities and decision-makers will have to analyse and weigh the rights of all those concerned, bearing in mind that the right of the child to have his or her best interests taken as a primary consideration means that the child's interests have high priority and not just one of several considerations. Therefore, a larger weight must be attached to what serves the child best.[10]

But we have to mention that, in at least two particular cases, the legal provisions contain references to "the paramount consideration" or "the interests of the child shall be paramount:" Article 21 of the CRC underlines that "States Parties that recognize and/or permit the system of adoption shall ensure that the best interests of the child shall be the paramount consideration..." Article 23, para. 2 of UN Convention on the Rights of Persons with Disabilities stipulates:

> States Parties shall ensure the rights and responsibilities of persons with disabilities, with regard to guardianship, warship, trusteeship, adoption of children, or similar institutions where these concepts exist in national legislation; in all cases the interests of the children shall be paramount. States Parties shall render appropriate assistance to persons with disabilities in the performance of their child-rearing responsibilities.

In these cases, the best interests of the child becomes the sole factor to determine the solution, or as said by van Bueren "...in certain circumstances, such as adoption or for children living with disabilities, the higher standard is applicable."[11]

3   To Assess and Determine the Best Interests of the Child

3.1   *In General*
One of the recurrent critic to the best interests is that this principle is too vague and that it is difficult to implement it, without more precise guidelines. It is

---

10   CRC/C/GC/14, para. 39.
11   van Bueren G., *Child Rights in Europe, Convergence and Divergence in Judicial Protection*, Council of Europe, 2007, Pushing and Pulling in Different Directions – The Best Interests of the Child and the Margin of Appreciation of States, p. 32.

why various attempts have been made in order that this criterion be specified or supplemented, or objectify by rules for application, chosen according to the various fields where the best interests of the child must apply. For example, in Canada, the draft amendment to the "Divorce Act" requires that the child's interests be judged according to 14 elements.[12]

Trying to make things clearer, we have first to distinguish between two steps which have to be followed when a decision has to be taken:

(a) The 'best-interests assessment' consists in evaluating and balancing all the elements necessary to make a decision in a specific situation for a specific individual child or group of children. It is carried out by the decision-maker and his or her staff – if possible a multidisciplinary team – and requires the participation of the child.

(b) The 'best-interests determination' describes the formal process with strict procedural safeguards designed to determine the child's best interests on the basis of the best-interests assessment.[13]

We can also say that chronologically, determining what is in the best interests of the child should start with an assessment of the specific circumstances that make the child unique. It is when the elements of the assessment have been explored and evaluated that the decision maker will take his/her decision, according to the pertinent elements (for children in group, assessing best interests involves the same elements).

3.2   To Assess

To assess means to establish all the circumstances of life of a child (or a group of children); to do that, the person (or interdisciplinary team) in charge of the assessment has to look for all the individual characteristics of the child or children concerned, "such as, *inter alia*, age, sex, level of maturity, experience, belonging to a minority group, having a physical, sensory or intellectual disability, as well as the social and cultural context in which the child or children find themselves, such as the presence or absence of parents, whether the child lives with them, quality of the relationships between the child and his or her family or caregivers, the environment in relation to safety, the existence of quality alternative means available to the family, extended family or caregivers,

---

12   See Bala, N., "The Best Interests of the Child in the Postmodern Era: A Central but Paradoxical Concept," paper presentation at the Law Society of Canada, Special Lectures 2000, Osgoode Hall, Toronto.

13   CRC/C/GC/14, para. 47.

etc...."[14] If the Committee has enumerated these elements, this enumeration does not constitute an exhaustive list of the elements to consider, and each situation is unique and can present different specificities. There is also no hierarchical order in these elements.

How to assess and determine the best interests of the child? This is the tricky question...

(a)   Elements to be Taken into Consideration

In its GC No. 14, the CRC Committee has identified 7 elements (and contexts) to be taken into consideration when assessing the child's best interests. I will just quote these elements here, since there are developed in details in the GC No. 14 (paras. 52 to 78).

(1)   The child's views
(2)   The child's identity
(3)   Preservation of the family environment and maintaining relations
(4)   Care, protection and safety of the child
(5)   The child's vulnerability
(6)   The child's right to health
(7)   The child's right to education.

Not all elements will be relevant to every case, and different elements can be used in different ways. The content of each element will vary from child to child, and form case to case...

(b)   Procedural Safeguards

To ensure a correct implementation for the right, some child-friendly procedural guarantees must be put in place...and the Committee has also highlighted the safeguards and guarantees quoted below. I will not enter into details, since they are well explained in the GC No. 14 (paras. 88 to 98).

(1)   Right of the child to express his/her own views
(2)   Establishment of facts
(3)   Time perception
(4)   Qualified professionals
(5)   Legal representation
(6)   Legal reasoning
(7)   Mechanisms to review or revise decisions
(8)   Child-rights impact assessment (CRIA).

---

14   CRC/C/GC/14, para. 48.

I would add that the interests of the child to be supplemented with the concept of predictability, which means taking into account the best interests of the child not only at the moment when the decision must be made, but also from the point of view of the foreseeable evaluation of the situation of the concerned parties. This appears particularly important in childhood, where the situations by definition develop quickly, and where it certainly appears necessary to act immediately, while simultaneously preserving the future interests of the child.

To conclude this point, let's add the following element: in case of doubt in the difficult exercise of determining the best interests of the child during conflicts with other interests let us be humble enough to recognize that this concept, which is not objective, cannot really be established by clear elements or objectives and could then be supplanted by the opposite notion of the "least pain," or the principle of precaution. "How to cause the least amount of pain possible?" will replaces the best interest of the child and should carry the decision. Is this more objective? Perhaps not, but this approach would certainly have the advantage of being less dangerous...

4   Legislative Bodies and CRIA

The extension of States Parties' obligation to their "legislative bodies" shows clearly that Article 3, para. 1 is also to be considered in case of the adoption of any law or regulation as well as collective agreements (bilateral or multilateral trade or peace treaties which affect children).

4.1   *Legislative Bodies*
This most interesting aspect of Article 3, para.1, the addition of "*legislative bodies*" is of crucial importance and has extensive implications.

At a practical level, this means that when national, regional or municipal laws or policies are established, the Government must ensure that children are taken into account and that their best interests are balanced against other competing interests. In this way, the best interests of the child principle takes on a new function: to establish through legislative vehicles what is relevant for the child and what is not, in relation to the possible impacts (positive or negative) of the future legal instrument. "Consideration of the best interests of the child should be built into national plans and policies for children and into the workings of parliaments and government..."[15]

---

15   *Implementation Handbook for the Convention on the Rights of the Child*, UNICEF, 2007, p. 36.

The best interests of the child therefore takes on a new function of establishing what is good for the child and what is not in any legislative program.

In its General Comment No. 5 (2003) on General measures of implementation, the CRC Committee tackles this issue and asserts that: "...every State should consider how it can ensure compliance with Article 3(1) and do so in a way which further promotes the visible integration of children in policy-making and sensitivity to their rights."[16]

For the CRC Committee, it goes without saying that the best interests principle obliges State Parties to take action in order to implement this concept and transform it from rhetoric to social reality. As noted previously, the scope of the principle is wide and incorporates all State-initiated and private actions concerning children as a group. This is a crucial point to underline because there is a common misconception that this principle is limited to individual cases.

Moreover, the Committee has stressed the obligation of States Parties to take the usual measures of implementation. Since the "best interests" principle is a rule of procedure and a "passage obligé" for decision-makers, the Committee has emphasized in General Comment No. 5 the necessity to legislate and the role of the judiciary. Specifically, it states that the best interests' principle:

> ...requires active measures throughout Government, parliament and the judiciary. Every legislative, administrative and judicial body or institution is required to apply the best interests principle by systematically considering how children's rights and interests are or will be affected by their decisions and actions – by, for example, a proposed or existing law or policy or administrative action or court decision, including those which are not directly concerned with children, but indirectly affect children.[17]

4.2   CRIA

To go a step further, we have also to refer to the specific obligation of CRIA.

What is CRIA? Child rights impact assessment which:

> ...is, in the simplest terms, a tool for decision-making in the best interests of children. CRIA is a systematic process or methodology of ensuring children's best interests and the potential impacts of policy change upon them are considered in the policy-making process. CRIA involves examining a proposed law or policy, administrative decision or action in a

---

16   CRC/C/GC/5, 2003, para. 47.
17   CRC/GC/2003/5, para. 12.

structured manner to determine its potential impact on children or a specific group of children, and whether it will effectively protect and implement the rights set out for children in the Convention on the Rights of the Child. Potential impacts may be positive or negative, intended or not, direct or indirect, short or long-term. A CRIA should be undertaken whenever there are new policies, proposed legislation, regulations or budgets being adopted, or other administrative decisions at national, provincial/territorial, and local levels that can have an impact on children...[18]

It is interesting to remind that the CRC Committee in its General Comments No. 5 has used the notion of CRIA and has highlighted the importance of child impact assessments:

Ensuring that the best interests of the child are a primary consideration in all actions concerning children (Article 3 (1)), and that all the provisions of the Convention are respected in legislation and policy development and delivery at all levels of government demands a continuous process of child impact assessment (predicting the impact of any proposed law, policy or budgetary allocation which affects children and the enjoyment of their rights) and child impact evaluation (evaluating the actual impact of implementation). This process needs to be built into government at all levels and as early as possible in the development of policy.[19]

And, more specifically in the GC No. 14, the CRC Committee has developed its opinion on CRIA, in para. 99:

...the adoption of all measures of implementation should also follow a procedure that ensures that the child's best interests are a primary consideration. The child-rights impact assessment (CRIA) can predict the impact of any proposed policy, legislation, regulation, budget or other administrative decision which affect children and the enjoyment of their rights and should complement ongoing monitoring and evaluation of the impact of measures on children's rights.[20] CRIA needs to be built into

---

18   Definition by UNICEF Canada, http://www.unicef.ca/fr/discover-fr/article/what-is-a-child
      -rights-impact-assessment.
19   CRC/C/GC/5, 2003, para. 45.
20   CRC/C/GC/16, (2013) on State obligations regarding the impact of the business sector on
      children's rights, paras. 78–81.

Government processes at all levels and as early as possible in the development of policy and other general measures in order to ensure good governance for children's rights. Different methodologies and practices may be developed when undertaking CRIA. At a minimum, they must use the Convention and its Optional Protocols as a framework, in particular ensuring that the assessments are underpinned by the general principles and have special regard for the differentiated impact of the measure(s) under consideration on children.[21]

5   Conclusion

The right of the child to have his/her best interests assessed and taken as a primary consideration is probably one of the most important rights of the child; it is also one of the principle of the CRC that illuminates the new status of the child as a subject of rights.

But let's face it, this right is also one of the most complex to implement, since it uses a variety of skills, an understanding of its meaning which is not immediate and sometimes encounters interpretations that not only do not serve the interests of the child, but that could be absolutely contrary to his/her rights... This is why the exercise and to assess and to determine the best interests of the child/children is a difficult process that requires a lot of knowledge, time and availability of trained professionals. The intervention of multidisciplinary teams in the most difficult situations is an obvious necessity, but is not often practiced.

Similarly, it is important to weight the impact of policies, programs, budgets passed by parliaments and to put at the centre of the political debate the child or children who will be affected by the measures to be taken and to find solutions for best facilitate his/her/their harmonious development, because, in fact, this development is the ultimate goal sought by the Convention.

The right of the child to have his/her best interests assessed and taken as a primary consideration along with the right of the child to heard are compulsory passages for all those who have the crucial tasks of deciding on the child's future in different official (judicial and administrative) contexts, not to say in politics.

Article 3, para. 1 of the CRC is a very important tool to further respect the child as a unique person with dignity and rights, who must remain at the centre of our concerns. This is our responsibility as adults.

---

21   CRC/C/GC/14, para. 99.

Corporal Punishment, Crime and Human Rights: Lessons for Child-friendly Justice

Ashley Stewart-Tufescu and Joan E. Durrant

Introduction

Despite over 20 years of systematic research documenting the detrimental effects of corporal punishment on children, controversy remains about the rightfulness, effectiveness, necessity and social acceptance of the practice. Worldwide prevalence rates estimate that 6 in 10 children (~1 billion children) between the ages of 2 and 14 experience disciplinary corporal punishment on a regular basis, while attitudes supporting the use of corporal punishment vary widely from a low of 3% in Armenia to a high of 82% in Swaziland (UNICEF, 2014). In North America, acceptance and use of corporal punishment has declined in recent years (Bell & Romano, 2012); however it remains a significant risk factor in children's lives. In Canada in 2008, 16,179 substantiated cases of child physical maltreatment (hitting, slapping, grabbing) took place in the context of a caregiver's attempt to correct a child (Trocmé, Fallon, MacLaurin *et al.* 2010). While the attitudes perpetuating the use of corporal punishment vary widely (UNICEF, 2014), a core belief is the necessity of corporal punishment to socialize and teach children right from wrong. This belief often comes to the fore in response to mainstream media reporting on the negative effects of corporal punishment. Such reports are often followed by public uproar at the thought that corporal punishment could be anything but beneficial and even necessary for children, families and society. For example, in response to an article describing the link between physical punishment, mood disorders and substance abuse (Afifi, Mota, Dasiewicz, MacMillan & Sareen, 2012), one reader wrote:

> Assault and disciplinary spankings are two completely different things. A spanking is a punishment for an act of wrong, just like a fine or prison time. Personally, **I would rather my kids learned right from wrong from a thousand spankings, than even 1-day in prison.**
>
> Anonymous, Gabrielle Giroday, Winnipeg Free Press, April 12, 2012

Similarly, the release of a journal article documenting lessons learned from 20 years of research on physical punishment calling for a legal ban on corporal

punishment in Canada (Durrant & Ensom, 2012) resulted in intense mainstream media attention. In response to the coverage, readers commented:

> [...] Can you imagine what we could have achieved if we were not
> spanked? We could be in jail because we had no respect for rules and laws
> and thought the world was going to coddle us our entire lives and never
> have to say we were sorry or take responsibility for our actions.
>
> Dar C, Toronto Sun, February 6th, 2012

> Harper [the Prime Minster of Canada] has to **build more jails because
> the little darlings that grew up after me and where the strap was
> removed are now committing crimes** that could have been averted
> because they didn't learn how to grow up obeying rules.
>
> OldLondonGuy, Toronto Sun, February 6th, 2012

Collectively, these comments reflect a belief or sense of fear that without corporal punishment, lawlessness, violence and juvenile delinquency will be ram-
pant; and that "permissive parenting"—that is, parenting without spanking or
smacking—is to be blamed for current societal ills. Others credit their suc-
cesses in life to learning respect, values and morals from their corporal punishment experiences.

In reality, this belief could not be further from the truth. The evidence is clear
that corporal punishment is detrimental to children, families and society. Over
20 years of research, no study has ever found corporal punishment to improve
child outcomes. Conversely, it is consistently found to be a risk factor for
increased aggression & anti-social behaviour, violent crime & delinquency, and
mental health issues (Durrant & Ensom, 2012; Gershoff, 2002; Gershoff &
Grogan-Kaylor, 2013; Ma, Han, Grogan-Kaylor, Delva & Castillo, 2012). Contrary
to the beliefs of many, the elimination of corporal punishment from children's
early lives would eliminate a risk factor for their later involvement in the criminal justice system. Drawing on this research, this paper describes a theoretical
pathway leading from corporal punishment to criminality. Following this, an
argument is presented for prohibiting corporal punishment in all settings, from
the home to the prison, as one step in making the world a just one for children.

The Pathway from Corporal Punishment to Criminality

Step One: Learning Aggression
The impact of corporal punishment begins very early. Since the 1960s, we have
known that it provides a powerful model of aggressive problem solving. In the

early days of research on this issue, children shown videos of a child being physically punished became more aggressive in their play compared to children shown a video of nonviolent responses to misbehaviour (Fairchild & Erwin, 1977). Since those early studies were conducted, we have learned just how robust this relationship is. More than 30 studies have now explored the relationship between corporal punishment and aggression and each one has found that corporal punishment predicts more, not less, aggression in children (Dobbs, 2005; Gershoff, 2002, Durrant & Ensom, 2012; Taylor, Manganello, Lee, & Rice, 2010). Pain does nothing to quell aggression in anyone – and that includes children.

Learning aggression through observation or experience begins early. Children who are physically punished at one year of age are already more likely to have behavioural problems at ages 3 and 4 (Mulvaney & Mebert, 2007). In fact, the frequency of parental use of corporal punishment has been found to be the strongest predictor of children's acceptance of aggressive problem solving, above and beyond familial demographics. Most recently, researchers have begun to explore the interaction among corporal punishment, aggression and genetic vulnerabilities. Using highly sophisticated and rigorous methods, they have found that corporal punishment may actually intensify genetic vulnerabilities to aggression, particularly among males (Boutwell, Franklin, Barnes & Beaver, 2011).

Why does corporal punishment have such a powerful influence on children's aggression? The reasons are several. First, it provides a model of aggression at a time when children's brains are forming their fundamental circuitry. Physical aggression becomes encoded as an acceptable response to frustration and anger. Second, every time parents use physical punishment, they have forfeited an opportunity to teach non-violent problem solving. So the more children experience physical punishment, the stronger the encoding becomes and the less likely it becomes that they can envision an alternative way of managing conflict. This is borne out in evidence from many studies conducted in many countries that have corroborated the links between childhood experiences of corporal punishment with bullying; aggression against parents, siblings and peers; and dating violence (Cast, Schweingruber & Berns, 2006; Gershoff, 2002; Lavoie, Hébert, Tremblay, Vitaro, Vézina & McDuff, 2002; Swinford, DeMaris, Cernkovich & Giordano, 2000; Straus & Yodanis, 1996).

Step Two: Reducing Self-regulation
Moral internalization, one's sense of what is appropriate to do in a given situation, is dependent upon internal self-regulation. It is the ability to make good and right decisions even when no one is watching. Parents and caregivers often believe that spanking or smacking will actually help their children to learn

right from wrong, and to develop a strong sense of morality. But, in fact, corporal punishment is associated with *lower* levels of moral internalization, meaning that children are less able to make the right choices or decisions when parents are not present to enforce rules and dole out punishments. At least 13 studies have confirmed this finding (Grogan-Kaylor, 2005). For example, preschool boys who experience more frequent physical punishment tend to be more destructive and to have less moral regulation than boys who experience less frequent physical punishment (Kerr, Lopez, Olson, & Sameroff, 2004). Physical punishment also predicts lower levels of empathy and justice-based reasoning (Lopez, Bonenberger, & Schneider, 2001).

Why is this the case? Corporal punishment – and all forms of punishment in general – focuses children's attention on the consequences of their behaviour for themselves, rather than on the consequences of their behaviour for other people. So they learn that if they lie, for example, they will be punished, instead of learning how their lying may hurt other people. They begin to learn how to avoid getting caught, and avoiding punishment becomes the main reason to inhibit their lying. Through this process, children do not internalize why lying is wrong or how it may hurt others. The most salient aspect of the situation is the punishment and learning how to avoid it. Evidence is beginning to emerge that this learning takes place at a structural level. Physical punishment has been found to affect the development of executive functioning in the prefrontal cortex, interfering with the ability to regulate emotions and behaviours (Talwar, Carlson, & Lee, 2011; Tomoda, Suzuki, Rabi, Sheu, Polcari, & Teicher, 2009). Therefore, while corporal punishment may be seen as the quick-fix solution for minor transgressions, it actually raises the risk of anti-social behaviour over the long term, including bullying, lying, cheating, truancy, and involvement in crime (Durrant, 1999; Gershoff, 2002; Gershoff & Grogan-Kaylor, 2013; Simons, Johnson & Conger, 1994).

Step Three: Erosion of the Parent–Child Relationship

A very important unintended effect of corporal punishment is the early association of the parent with pain and fear. At least 13 studies have demonstrated that physical punishment predicts weaker parent–child relationships – and this process begins early. For example, spanking of infants predicts insecure attachment to those who spank them (Coyl, Roggman, & Newland, 2002). So, at a time when the development of trust, security and attachment is critical, these children are learning to mistrust their parents. Over time, they learn to avoid them out of fear.

By adolescence, these relationships place the child at increasing risk of becoming involved with the justice system. Not only does corporal punishment of youth predict poor family relations and weak coping skills (Lau, Liu,

Cheung, Yu, & Wong, 1999), it is one of the major reasons for children leaving home, dropping out of school, being involved in prostitution, and living on the streets (Choudbury & Jabeen, 2008). Therefore, corporal punishment is a direct cause of the actions that lead to many children's involvement in the youth justice system.

Step Four: Mental Health Issues

The impact of corporal punishment on children's trust and attachment has profound impact on their mental health. The formation of a strong, secure attachment is fundamental to psychological health and well-being throughout life. When that attachment is weakened or violated, the impact is felt in insecurity, or a sense of powerlessness and even worthlessness. At least 15 studies have confirmed the link between corporal punishment and mental health problems in children and youth, including depression, anxiety disorders, personality disorders, and alcohol and substance abuse (Afifi, Mota, Dasiewicz, MacMillan, & Sareen, 2012; Afifi, Mota, MacMillan, & Sareen, 2013; Cheng, Anthony, Huang, Lee, Liu, & He, 2011; Gershoff, 2002; MacMilian, Boyle, Wong, Duku, Fleming & Walsh, 1999). An 18-year longitudinal study conducted in New Zealand found that the more physical punishment children experienced during childhood, the more likely they were to have developed a psychiatric disorder, attempted suicide, been alcohol and/or drug dependent, or committed a criminal act (Fergusson & Lynskey, 1997).

Response of the Youth Justice System

While corporal punishment does not explain all of the behaviours that lead children into the justice system, it is undeniably a contributor in a large number of cases. And how does the justice system respond? All too often, with physical force, physical coercion and physical punishment. Corporal punishment remains an official sentence for youth crimes in 39 States' penal systems. This means that children and youth in these countries can be sentenced to caning (*e.g.*, Malaysia, Singapore); flogging (*e.g.*, Qatar, Nigeria); stoning, amputation or mutilation (*e.g.*, Saudi Arabia); or death (*e.g.*, Iran).

Corporal punishment as a disciplinary measure within penal institutions has yet to be prohibited in 72 countries, including Brazil, Ecuador, Mexico, Papua New Guinea, Peru, Russia and some US states. But even in countries where it is prohibited, physical violence by staff against young inmates can be a common feature of daily life in correctional institutions (Global Initiative to End All Corporal Punishment of Children, 2014). A 2013 report covering six

European countries (Austria, Belgium, Cyprus, the Netherlands, Romania, & the United Kingdom) revealed that many residents of juvenile detention centres experience corporal punishment by guards and other staff (Children's Rights Alliance for England, 2013). In many cases, residents reported that staff provoke violence among the youth and then respond with corporal punishment. In other cases, staff may avoid inflicting direct corporal punishment by sending young people to solitary confinement. But even more violence was experienced by young people during their contacts with police than in custody. Beatings, forced confessions, being pushed against walls and thrown to the ground were found to be typical experiences of youth at the hands of police (Children's Rights Alliance for England, 2013).

Ever more concerning are proposed changes to the ways in which children and youth are treated by justice systems in numerous States. In many countries there are political campaigns and proposals to *lower* the minimum age of criminal responsibility (MACR). In recent years Georgia, Panama and Denmark successfully led campaigns to lower the MACR. In 1999 Panama reduced the MACR from 14 to 12 years of age. Georgia lowered the MACR from 14 to 12 in 2008, but then raised it back to 14 in 2010. In the case of Denmark, in 2010 the MACR was reduced from 15 to 14 years, and most recently, in September 2014 a proposal was put forth to further reduce the age of criminal responsibility from 14 to 12, in addition to creating a separate youth court to deal with children up to 17 years of age and a separate prison system for youth (Child Rights International Network, 2014). In keeping with this trend, many other States have also put forth bills to increase criminalization of children by lowering the MACR, including Argentina, Brazil, Hungary, Mexico, Peru, the Republic of Korea, Uruguay, Russia and Spain. In the case of the Philippines, a reform bill was proposed to lower the age of criminal responsibility from 15 to 10 years of age. In 2013, that bill was defeated and the MACR remains at 15. In all cases, the Committee on the Rights of the Child has condemned States parties for these reforms towards criminalizing children (Child Rights International Network, 2014).

In Canada, proposed amendments to the Youth Criminal Justice Act have called for more stringent laws and stiffer sentences for youth 14 and older who have been charged with serious crimes. The Canadian Paediatric Society has argued against these proposed changes from a neuro-developmental perspective (Elliott & Katzman, 2014). Evolving understanding of neuroscience and developmental science provide new insight into adolescents' decision-making capacity, impulse control, assessment of risk, and susceptibility to peer influence, and the influence of drugs and alcohol on the adolescent brain (Elliott & Katzman, 2014). The message from neuroscience is clear that despite physically appearing similar to an adult, the adolescent brain, particularly the prefrontal cortex responsible for executive functions, has not yet matured to the level of an adult brain (Giedd, 2008). To put this new understanding into practice, essential changes to States' justice systems are required, including reviewing the minimum age of criminal responsibility and raising – not lowering – it; formally developing youth justice systems and youth-only prisons; considering adolescents' competency to stand trial in a developmental context; considering the long-term impact of criminalization and harsh sentencing practices for adolescent crimes, and promoting rehabilitation and alternative justice responses that support adolescents' developmental needs (Steinberg, 2009).

Beyond Research to Rights

Regardless of its impact on development or its contribution to aggression or anti-social behaviour, corporal punishment is a violation of children's rights. Both the Convention on the Rights of the Child (CRC) and the 1948 Universal Declaration of Human Rights stipulate every person's entitlement to full respect for human dignity and physical integrity. Specifically, Article 19 of the CRC obligates States to protect children against all forms of physical or mental violence. In 2006, the United Nations Committee on the Rights of the Child issued General Comment No. 8, which stated, "There is no ambiguity, 'all forms of physical or mental violence' does not leave room for any level of legalized violence against children. Corporal punishment and other cruel or degrading forms of punishment are forms of violence and States must take all appropriate legislative, administrative, social and educational measures to eliminate them" (Committee on the Rights of the Child, 2006). The Committee defined corporal punishment as "any punishment in which physical force is used and intended to cause some degree of pain or discomfort, however light." In the same year, the United Nations World Report on Violence against Children concluded that eliminating physical punishment is central to ending all violence against children (Pinherio, 2006).

But the implementation of Article 19 remains a global challenge. As of March 2015, 46 States have achieved full prohibition of all forms of corporal punishment within the home, schools, alternative care and juvenile justice settings – and this achievement should be celebrated. However, corporal punishment and other humiliating punitive practices remain widely accepted and commonly practiced by parents and caregivers in response to children's normative, and often minor behavioural transgressions (Global Initiative to End All Corporal Punishment of Children, 2014). In Canada, Section 43 of the Criminal Code provides legal justification for the parental use of physical punishment to correct a child (Durrant, 2007). Despite repeated court challenges to repeal Section 43, the Supreme Court of Canada ruled it constitutional in 2004, and defined the parameters for use of "reasonable force" against a child (Durrant, 2007). The Committee on the Rights of the Child reiterated its grave concerns that corporal punishment is allowed under Canadian law, expressing regret at the Supreme Court's decision, and concern that legalization of corporal punishment leaves children vulnerable to other forms of violence (Committee on the Rights of the Child, 2012). The Committee (2012) also recommended that the Government of Canada strengthen and expand awareness-raising for parents, children, professionals, and the public on positive discipline underlining the promotion of respect for children's rights, while raising awareness about the adverse consequences of corporal punishment. However, the Government of Canada continues to ignore all calls for repeal of Section 43 (Durrant & Smith, 2011).

This situation has played out in many countries, with governments or courts attempting to identify which children have the right to protection and which do not, based on arbitrary criteria such as the child's age, the body part struck, or the use of a hand versus an implement. Such an approach is based not on human rights standards but on adult notions of what children deserve. These laws give a green light to parents who seek justification for their actions, and place entire populations of children at heightened risk for injury and the psychological and behavioural problems that can lead them into youth justice settings.

Implications for Advocacy and Child-friendly Justice

As we celebrate the 25th Anniversary of the CRC, and look to better understand and realize child-friendly justice, we need to focus our attention on violence at all levels, from homes to detention centres. By focusing on homes and families, we can have a substantial impact on *prevention* of anti-social behaviour and criminality among youth. This strategy must have two components. First, we must advocate for law reform to abolish corporal punishment in the home and all other settings. Such laws should not be designed to punish parents and caregivers, but rather to send a clear message that all forms of physical violence against children are unacceptable and a violation of children's rights. Sweden's 1979 law—the first to prohibit all corporal punishment of children—provides the model for this approach to cultural transformation. Second, parents must be provided with universal supports and information on positive discipline – that is, discipline that promotes children's moral internalization, reduces rather than increases aggression, strengthens the parent–child relationship and promotes children's mental health. There also is a need to educate child-serving professionals about children's rights. In a recent survey in Manitoba, Canada of child-serving professionals' (teachers, social workers, early childhood educators) awareness and knowledge of the CRC, it was found that almost 50% had no knowledge of the Convention – and only 2% reported thorough knowledge of its articles. Yet these professionals make decisions about children that play a powerful role in their development (Stewart-Tufescu, Winther, Durrant, Skaftfeld, 2011). Strategic training on children's rights and the CRC for social workers, teachers, early childhood educators, paediatricians, lawyers, police officers, and staff of juvenile detention centres is critical to reducing violence against children.

Finally, all violence against children in contact with police and in custodial settings must be prohibited globally. Corporal punishment as a judicial sentence must be universally abolished. Initiatives must be undertaken to create awareness of the role of childhood violence in the pathway to the youth justice system, and professionals must be trained to understand the root causes of youth criminality. In all cases, respect for children's fundamental human rights must be a starting point for the development of effective justice system responses.

Conclusion

The evidence is clear: neither the research nor the human rights discourse supports the practice of corporal punishment. If a system of child-friendly justice is to evolve and flourish we must first create a strong foundation based on children's equal rights to protection and to dignity. As long as children can be hit and hurt with impunity, it will be exceedingly difficult to change their status in the justice system.

References

Afifi, T.O., Mota, N.P., Dasiewicz, P., MacMillan, H.L., & Sareen, J. (2012). Physical punishment and mental disorders: Results from a nationally representative US sample. *Pediatrics, 130*(2), 184–192.

Afifi, T.O., Mota, N., MacMillan, H.L., & Sareen, J. (2013). Harsh physical punishment in childhood and adult physical health. *Pediatrics, 132*(2), e333–e340.

Bell, T., & Romano, E. (2012). Opinions about child corporal punishment and influencing factors. *Journal of Interpersonal Violence, 27*(11), 2208–2229.

Boutwell, B.B., Franklin, C.A., Barnes, J.C., & Beaver, K.M. (2011). Physical punishment and childhood aggression: the role of gender and gene–environment interplay. *Aggressive Behavior, 37*(6), 559–568.

Cast, A.D., Schweingruber, D., & Berns, N. (2006). Childhood physical punishment and problem solving in marriage. *Journal of Interpersonal Violence, 21*(2), 244–261.

Cheng, H.G., Anthony, J.C., Huang, Y., Lee, S., Liu, Z., & He, Y. (2011). Childhood physical punishment and the onset of drinking problems: Evidence from metropolitan China. *Drug and Alcohol Dependence, 118*(1), 31–39.

Child Rights International Network (2014). Juvenile justice: States lowering the minimum age of criminal responsibility. London: Author.

Children's Rights Alliance for England (2013). Speaking freely: Children and young people in Europe talk about ending violence against children in custody. London: Author.

Choudhury, I. & Jabeen, S.F. (2008). *Perceptions of Children on Parenting Practices.* Save the Children Sweden, Regional Office for South and Central Asia.

Committee on the Rights of the Child. (2006). General Comment No. 8 (2006): The right of the child to protection from corporal punishment and or cruel or degrading forms of punishment (Articles 1, 28 (2), and 37, inter alia), 42nd Sess., U.N. Doc. CRC/C/GC/8. Retrieved from http://www.ohchr.org/english/bodies/crc/docs/co/CRC.C.GC.8.pdf.

Committee on the Rights of the Child. (2012). *Concluding Observations on the Combined Third and Fourth Periodic Report of Canada, Adopted by the Committee at Its Sixty-first Session (17 September–5 October 2012)*, CRC/C/CAN/CO/3-4, 2012. Retrieved from http://www.ohchr.org/EN/countries/ENACARegion/Pages/CAIndex.aspx.

Coyl, D.D., Roggman, L.A., & Newland, L.A. (2002). Stress, maternal depression, and negative mother–infant interactions in relation to infant attachment. *Infant Mental Health Journal, 23*(1–2), 145–163.

Dobbs, T. (2005). *Insights: Children & Young People Speak Out about Family Discipline.* Save the Children New Zealand.

Durrant, J.E. (2007). Corporal Punishment. In R.B. Howe & K. Covell (Eds.), *A Question of Commitment: Children's Rights in Canada* (pp. 99–125). Waterloo: Wilfrid Laurier University Press.

Durrant, J. E. (1999). Trends in youth crime and well-being since the abolition of corporal punishment in Sweden. Youth and Society, 31, 437–455.

Durrant, J.E. & Ensom, R. (2012). Physical punishment of children: lessons from 20 years of research. *Canadian Medical Association Journal, 184*(12), 12.

Durrant, J.E., & Smith, A.B. (Eds.). (2011). *Global Pathways to Abolishing Physical Punishment: Realizing Children's Rights.* Taylor & Francis.

Elliott, A.S. & Katzman, D.K. (2011, 2014). Youth Justice and Health: An argument against proposed changes to the Youth Criminal Justice Act. Ottawa, ON: Canadian Paediatric Society.

Fairchild, L., & Erwin, W.M. (1977). Physical punishment by parent figures as a model of aggressive behavior in children. *The Journal of Genetic Psychology, 130*(2), 279–284.

Fergusson, D.M., & Lynskey, M.T. (1997). Physical punishment/maltreatment during childhood and adjustment in young adulthood. *Child Abuse & Neglect, 21*(7), 617–630.

Gershoff, E.T. (2002). Corporal punishment by parents and associated child behaviors and experiences: A meta-analytic and theoretical review. *Psychological Bulletin, 128*, 539–579.

Gershoff, E.T., & Grogan-Kaylor, A. (2013). Spanking and its consequences for children: New meta- analyses and old controversies. *Manuscript under Review.*

Giedd, J.N. (2008). The teen brain: Insights from neuroimaging. *Journal of Adolescent Health, 42*(4), 335–343.

Global Initiative to End All Corporal Punishment of Children (2013). Review of research on the effects of corporal punishment: Working paper. London: Author.

Global Initiative to End All Corporal Punishment of Children (2014). Count down to universal prohibition. London: Author.

Giroday, G. (2012, July 4). Physical punishment linked to mood disorders. Winnipeg Free Press. Retrieved from http://www.winnipegfreepress.com/local/physical -punishment-linked-to-mood-disorders-161318205.html.

Grogan-Kaylor, A. (2005). Corporal punishment and the growth trajectory of children's anti-social behaviour. *Child Maltreatment, 10*, 283–292.

Kerr, D.C., Lopez, N.L., Olson, S.L., & Sameroff, A.J. (2004). Parental discipline and externalizing behavior problems in early childhood: The roles of moral regulation and child gender. *Journal of Abnormal Child Psychology, 32*(4), 369–383.

Lau, J.T., Liu, J.L., Cheung, J.C., Yu, A., & Wong, C.K. (1999). Prevalence and correlates of physical abuse in Hong Kong Chinese adolescents: A population-based approach. *Child Abuse & Neglect, 23*(6), 549–557.

Lavoie, F., Hébert, M., Tremblay, R., Vitaro, F., Vézina, L., & McDuff, P. (2002). History of family dysfunction and perpetration of dating violence by adolescent boys: A longitudinal study. *Journal of Adolescent Health, 30*(5), 375–383.

Lopez, N.L., Bonenberger, J.L., & Schneider, H.G. (2001). Parental disciplinary history, current levels of empathy, and moral reasoning in young adults. *North American Journal of Psychology, 3*(2).

Ma, J., Han, Y., Grogan-Kaylor, A., Delva, J., & Castillo, M. (2012). Corporal punishment and youth externalizing behavior in Santiago, Chile. *Child Abuse & Neglect, 36*(6), 481–490.

MacMilan, H.L., Boyle, M.H., Wong, M.Y.Y., Duku, E.K., Fleming, J.E., & Walsh, C.A. (1999). Slapping and spanking in childhood and its association with lifetime prevalence of psychiatric disorders in a general population sample. *Canadian Medical Association Journal, 161*(7), 805–809.

Mulvaney, M.K., & Mebert, C.J. (2007). Parental corporal punishment predicts behavior problems in early childhood. *Journal of Family Psychology, 21*(3), 389.

Pinherio, P. (2006). *World Report on Violence against Children*. Geneva, Switzerland: United Nations Secretary-General Study on Violence against Children.

Simons, R.L., Johnson, C., & Conger, R.D. (1994). Harsh corporal punishment versus quality of parental involvement as an explanation of adolescent maladjustment. *Journal of Marriage and the Family, 56*, 591–607.

Steinberg, L. (2009). Adolescent development and juvenile justice. *Annual Review of Clinical Psychology 5*, 47–73.

Stewart-Tufescu, A, Winther, A., Durrant, J. & Skaftfeld, E. (June, 2011). Professionals' knowledge of the CRC: An indicator of implementation in Canada. Presented at Opportunities and Challenges: Implementing the UN Convention on the Rights of the Child, Queen's University, Belfast, Northern Ireland, UK.

Straus, M.A., & Yodanis, C.L. (1996). Corporal punishment in adolescence and physical assaults on spouses later in life: What accounts for the link? *Journal of Marriage and the Family, 58*, 825–841.

Swinford, S.P., DeMaris, A., Cernkovich, S.A., & Giordano, P.C. (2000). Harsh physical punishment in childhood and violence in later romantic involvements: The mediating role of problem behaviors. *Journal of Marriage and Family, 62*(2), 508–519.

Talwar, V., Carlson, S.M., & Lee, K. (2011). Effects of a punitive environment on children's executive functioning: A natural experiment. *Social Development, 20*(4), 805–824.

Taylor, C.A., Manganello, J.A., Lee, S.J., & Rice, J.C. (2010). Mothers' spanking of 3-year-old children and subsequent risk of children's aggressive behavior. *Pediatrics, 125*(5), e1057–e1065.

Tomoda, A., Suzuki, H., Rabi, K., Sheu, Y.S., Polcari, A., & Teicher, M.H. (2009). Reduced prefrontal cortical gray matter volume in young adults exposed to harsh corporal punishment. *Neuroimage, 47*, T66–T71.

Toronto Sun (2012, February 6). Make spanking illegal. Retrieved from http://www.torontosun.com/2012/02/06/make-spanking-illegal-report.

Trocmé, N., Fallon, B., MacLaurin, B., Hélie, S., & Turcotte, D. (2010). Canadian Incidence Study of Reported Child Abuse and Neglect – 2008: Major Findings. Public Health Agency of Canada.

United Nations Children's Fund (2014). *Hidden in Plain Sight: A Statistical Analysis of Violence against Children*, UNICEF, New York.

Relational Representation: The Empowerment of Children in Justice Systems

Hrefna Friðriksdóttir

1   Introduction

The United Nations Convention on the Rights of the Child (CRC) transformed the way we view children. The CRC is founded on a vision of children as rights holders. As such it provides the standards necessary to protect their vulnerable status and to ensure their place as active members of society. The CRC has inspired numerous initiatives furthering children's rights in specific targeted areas, such as justice systems. The Council of Europe's Guidelines on child-friendly justice seek to interpret and build on the CRC in order to enhance children's access to and participation in justice.[1] The Guidelines apply to all the circumstances in which children are likely, on any ground and in any capacity, to be in contact with criminal, civil or administrative justice systems. They recall and promote the principles of the best interests of the child: care and respect, participation, equal treatment and the rule of law.[2] A growing body of research on child-friendly justice acknowledges barriers, challenges and the way forward.[3]

---

1   *Guidelines of the Committee of Ministers of the Council of Europe on child-friendly justice*, Council of Europe Publishing, 2010 [hereinafter the Guidelines]. The Guidelines also acknowledge numerous other international and regional instruments furthering children's rights in justice, among them The European Convention on the Exercise of Children's Rights, European Treaty Series (ETS) 160 (1996) [the Exercise Convention]. In addition the Committee of Ministers on 28 March 2012 adopted Recommendation CM/Rec (2012) 2 on the participation of children and young people under the age of 18 [hereinafter referred to as Rec 2012]. See also *Access to justice for children*, Report of the United Nations High Commissioner A/HRC/25/35 16 December 2013, para. 8 identifying numerous human-rights norms and standards.

2   *European Progress in Achieving Child Friendly Justice*, 2014, Council of Europe Coordination on Children's Rights, http://www.coe.int/t/dg3/children/Dubrovnik/Council%20of%20 Europe%20and%20Child%20friendly%20justicefinal.pdf.

3   See *inter alia* Peters, J.K., "How children are heard in child protective proceedings in the United States and around the world: Survey findings, initial observation, and areas for further study," 6 *Nevada Law Journal,* pp. 966–1110, 2005; O'Donnell, D., *The rights of children to be heard: Children's rights to have their views taken into account and to participate in legal and administrative proceeding,* 2009,. UNICEF Innocenti Research Centre; Podsiadlowski, A., *Practices of child participation in justice proceedings in the EU Member States: experiences of judges, lawyers, social workers and other actors involved,* 2014, http://www.coe.int/t/dg3/

This paper aims to examine broadly some of the fundamental elements that inform children's representation in justice systems and to evaluate some of the challenges and obstacles we face in ensuring children adequate representation. An analysis of children's representation requires a delicate balance of their right to be protected and their rights to participate at various levels.[4] In order to understand a child's unique position in justice it is necessary to remark on the core principles and values that enshrine children's place in society. The paper will briefly establish the status of the child, the role of parents and the intrinsic link between participation and representation. The paper then examines what characterizes children's representation in justice systems, what role parents play in that context, when a child needs separate representation and how to guarantee children the kind of representation they need. The paper argues for the need of an integrated approach to support and assistance, and suggests the use of the concept of relational representation of children in justice systems.

2   The Status of Children

Child law is based largely on the principle that all children need someone to represent their interests. The Preamble to the CRC recognizes that a child, by reason of her/his physical and mental immaturity, needs special safeguards and care, including appropriate legal protection. The Preamble also recognizes the family as the natural environment for the growth and well-being of children: children should grow up in a family environment to ensure the full and

---

children/Dubrovnik/Speeches/Dubrovnik_Astrid_Podsiadlowski_plenarysession; and Hoefmans, A., *Children's involvement in criminal, civil and administrative judicial proceedings in the EU – gaps and remaining challenges*, 2014, http://www.coe.int/t/dg3/children/Dubrovnik/Speeches/Dubrovnik_Alexander_Hoefmans_plenarysession.pdf; Yates, V., *Global Mapping of Access to Justice for Children*, 2014, http://www.coe.int/t/dg3/children/Dubrovnik/Speeches/Dubrovnik_Veronica_Yates_plenarysession.pdf; *Scheme for evaluating judicial systems*, European Commission for the Efficiency of Justice, 2012, 21 May 2013. On selected jurisdictions, see *inter alia* Brady, L. *A scoping report on advocacy services for children and young people in England,* London: Office of the Children's Commissioner, 2011; and Duqette, D.N. and Darwall, J. "Child Representation in America: Progress Report from the National Quality Improvement Center," 46 *Family Law Quarterly*, pp. 87–138, 2012.

4   General Comment No. 12 (2009) The right of the child to be heard, CRC/C/GC/12 20 July 2009 [hereinafter referred to as GC No. 12] and General Comment No. 14 (2013) on the right of the child to have his or her best interests taken as a primary consideration (Article 3, para. 1), CRC/C/GC/14, 29 May 2013 [hereinafter referred to as GC No. 14].

harmonious development of their personalities. Article 5 of the CRC acknowledges parents as, first and foremost, legally responsible for the child, and parents are thus broadly entrusted with representing their child at all levels in society.[5]

The rights and responsibilities of parents to represent their child's interests are by no means absolute. As Hodgkin and Newell (2007) note, many nations have a history of laws and customs that assume that parental rights should be exercised for the benefit of parents alone.[6] They emphasize that "the [CRC] required that current legal principles of parental rights be translated into principles of parental responsibility – the legal responsibility of parents to act in the best interests of their children."[7] The best-interests principle is a fundamental value of the CRC.[8] Article 3 gives the child the right to have her/his best interest assessed and taken into account as a primary consideration in all actions or decisions that concern her/him, in both the public and the private sphere. In furthering parental responsibility Article 18 stipulates that the best interest of the child shall be their parent's basic concern.

The Committee on the Rights of the Child has stipulated that the "concept of the child's best interests is aimed at ensuring both the full and effective enjoyment of all the rights recognized in the Convention and the holistic development of the child."[9] Among the many requirements to ensure compliance with the best-interests principle is the duty to create the necessary conditions for children to express their points of view and to ensure that their opinions are given due weight.[10] This demands careful scrutiny of the notion of children as independent holders of rights and a closer look at the meaning of participation.

---

5   This can also apply to other legal guardians in lieu of parents.

6   Hodgkin, R. and Newell, P., *Implementation Handbook for the Convention on the Rights of the Child*. Geneva: UNICEF, p. 232. Prout and James link these views to former classical socialization theory that incorporated the implicit binarism of the psychological model viewing children as immature, irrational, incompetent, asocial and acultural with adults being mature, rational, competent, social and autonomous. See Prout, A. and James, A., "A New Paradigm for the Sociology of Childhood? Provenance, Promise and problems," in James, A. and Prout, A., (eds.) *Constructing and Reconstructing Childhood: Contemporary Issues in the Sociological Study of Childhood*, 2nd edition, Farmer Press, London, 1997, pp. 12–13.

7   Hodgkin and Newell, *ibid*, p. 232.

8   The Committee on the Rights of the Child identifies four Articles 2, 3, 6 and 12 as the general principles of the CRC. See *inter alia* GC No. 14, para. 4.

9   GC No. 14, para. 4.

10   *Ibid*, para. 6.

3   Participation

One of the most fundamental achievements of the CRC is the vision of children as rights holders and active members of society. The Preamble states the conviction that a child should be afforded the necessary protection and assistance so that s/he can fully assume her/his responsibilities within the community. This can be said to foster a general notion of children as citizens.

Democratic theory argues for the necessity of an informed and active citizenry.[11] A key element of active citizenry is to encourage social commitment and to ensure the right to participate in order to affect personal and societal development.[12] Article 12 of the CRC embodies the most important formulation of how to empower children to exercise their rights through participation.[13] The article thus supports all of the substantive rights established in the Convention by ensuring that children can actively participate in interpreting, implementing and upholding their rights at every level.[14] Article 12 obliges States to assure to the child who is capable of forming his or her views the right to express those views freely in all matters affecting him/her, the views of the child being given due weight in accordance with his/her age and maturity. The concept of evolving capacities is crucial in respecting children's growing abilities to exercise their individual rights independently.[15] As mentioned before,

---

11   Flekkøy, M.G. and Kaufman, N.H., *The Participation Rights of the Child: Rights and Responsibilities in Family and Society*; Children in Charge series 4, Jessica Kingsley Publishers, London, 1997, p. 5.

12   Lister emphasizes that the recognition of children as citizens requires facilitating their participation as political and social actors. See Lister, R. "Unpacking Children's Citizenship," in Invernizzi, A. and Williams, J. (eds.), *Children and Citizenship*, Sage Publications, London, 2005, pp. 10–11.

13   GC No. 12, para. 3 and para. 79 noting child participation as a tool to stimulate the full development of the personality and the evolving capacities of the child. Roche notes how Article 12 of the CRC expresses a model of citizenship which includes children. See Roche, J. "Children: Rights, Participation and Citizenship," 6 *Childhood*, 1999, p. 484. Also de Winter, M., *Children as Fellow Citizens: Participation and Commitment*, 1997, Radcliffe Medical Press, Oxon, p. 24.

14   Rec 2012, *supra* note 1, upholds the right to be heard and taken seriously as fundamental to the human dignity and healthy development of every child and young person. Minow observes how rights discourses implicate a pattern of social and political commitment, see Minow, M., *Making All the Difference: Inclusion, Exclusion and American Law,* Cornell University Press, Ithaca, NY, 1990.

15   Lansdown, G., *The Evolving Capacities of the Child;* UNICEF Innocenti Research Centre, Florence, 2005.

Articles 3 and 12 of the CRC are inextricably linked as the best-interest principle cannot be correctly applied if the requirements of participation are not met.[16]

Various disciplines offer a steadily growing number of studies on participation in general and have firmly established the value of active participation for children in different settings.[17] Kilkely (2010) emphasizes that taking the views of children into account in decisions made about them is good, not just because of the added value it gives to the outcome, but because of the importance of the process.[18] Despite the significance attached to child participation, it has been challenging to identify what measures are needed for effective implementation. Many have identified the various levels and meanings of the concept of participation.[19] Challenges are also linked to a broad and dynamic interpretation of Article 12 of the CRC beyond the scope of what was originally foreseen.[20] In defining participation today, an emphasis is thus placed on individuals having the *right*, the *means*, the *space*, the *opportunity* and the *support*, when necessary, to freely express their views, to be heard and to contribute to decision-making.[21]

4   Participation and Representation in Justice Systems

4.1   *Justice Systems*
Justice systems play a crucial role in the exercise of individual rights and responsibilities. Rights as such may thus lay a foundation for improvement for children – it is the exercise of rights that is crucial for actual change.[22] There is

---

16   GC No. 14, para. 43.

17   *Inter alia* Lansdown, G., *Promoting Children's Participation in Democratic Decision-Making*, UNICEF Innocenti Research Centre, Florence, 2001; Friðriksdóttir, H. "Samningur um réttindi barnsins," in Thorarensen, B. *et al* (eds)., *Mannréttindasamningar Sameinuðu þjóðanna: Meginreglur, framkvæmd og áhrif á íslenskan rétt, Codex,*. Reykjavík, 2009, pp. 304–306; Thomas, N., "Towards A Theory of Children's Participation," in Freeman, M. (ed.), *Children's Rights: Progress and Perspectives,* Martinus Nijhoff Publishers, Leiden, 2011.

18   Kilkely, U., *Listening to Children about Justice: Report of the Council of Europe on Child-friendly Justice.* Council of Europe, 5 October 2010, p. 13.

19   *Inter alia* Hart, R., *Children's Participation: From Tokenism to Citizenship*, UNICEF International Child Development Centre, Florence, 1992, Friðriksdóttir, H., "Sjálfræði og réttindi barna," 50 *Úlfljótur,* 1997, pp. 731–750.

20   GC No. 12, para. 88, 133. Also Milne, B. From Chattels to Citizens? Eighty Years of Eglantyne Jebb's Legacy to Children and Beyond," in Invernizzi and Williams, *supra* note 11, p. 52.

21   Rec 2012, *supra* note 1.

22   Jane Fortin argues that "to qualify as a right, an interest has to be capable not only of definition but also of enforcement." See Fortin, J., "Children as Rights Holders," in Invernizzi and Williams, *ibid.* pp. 500–509, at p. 507.

a fundamental difference in how we on the one hand view the capacity of children to initiate legal action (*access to justice*) and on the other hand how we view their rights to participation and representation in proceedings already initiated (*children in justice*).

It is important to acknowledge the range of systems and mechanisms that play a role in delivering justice. Justice systems encompass many differing degrees of formality and procedures but are often broadly categorized as formal and informal depending on their substantive, procedural and structural foundations.[23] Formal justice systems encompass criminal, civil and administrative proceedings where all the basic elements are primarily based on statutory law. Informal justice systems on the other hand refer mainly to alternative dispute resolutions, such as mediation, where assistance or adjudication by a neutral third party is not primarily based on statutory law.[24] Within formal justice systems children may be categorized as accused, defendants, witnesses, parties, claimants *etc.* Their legal standing, implementation of their right to participate and their need for representation varies considerably within different judicial proceedings.[25] Rules on standing, participation and separate representation are for instance generally much clearer in the criminal-justice system than in civil-justice systems, especially for defendants, and in many jurisdictions also for victims. Within civil-justice systems children's right to independent access may be stronger in an administrative setting than in the courts, but the right to representation during proceedings may be weaker. In civil-court cases the concept of legal standing and the right to representation varies considerably between, for example, public-law issues, such as child-protection cases, and private-law issues, such as custody and contact disputes.[26]

---

23   GC No. 12, *supra* note 1,, paras. 50–67, notes specific obligations with regard to different types of judicial and administrative proceedings. The Guidelines, III. E. 1, *supra* note 1, emphasize the respect for due process in all judicial and non-judicial and administrative systems.

24   The difference between formal and informal justice systems is not based on a sharp set of distinctions as there are many different degrees of State recognition and guiding legal and normative frameworks. See Kerrigan, F. (ed.), *Informal Justice Systems: Charting a Course for Human Rights-Based Engagement,* UNWOMEN, UNICEF and UNDP, 2012, pp. 29–30.

25   Several instruments have been adopted to strengthen children's rights in specific areas of justice, see *supra* note 1.

26   See *inter alia* Ryrstedt, E. and Matson, T." Children's Rights to Representation: A Comparison Between Sweden and England," 22 *International Journal of Law, Policy and the Family,* 2008, pp. 135–147.

Children's access, participation and representation seem particularly precarious in informal justice proceedings.[27]

It is vital to recognize how a child is often involved in various different formal and/or informal justice systems simultaneously and to evaluate how the child's active participation and representation can reflect such complex interactions.

4.2 Access to Justice for Children

Access to justice means that children or their appropriate advocates are able to use and trust the legal system to protect their rights.[28] The CRC does not expressly recognize the child's right to claim legal redress for infringement of their rights. The UN International Covenant on Civil and Political Rights provides for the right to an effective remedy as do many regional instruments.[29] The Committee on the Rights of the Child has emphasized children's access to justice as implicit in the CRC by requiring States to establish mechanisms and procedures for complaints, remedy or redress in order to realize fully the right of the child to have his or her best interests appropriately integrated and consistently applied in all implementation measures, administrative and judicial proceedings relevant to and affecting him or her.[30] Access to justice is also emphasized by the Council of Europe in the Guidelines on child-friendly justice which underline children's rights to due process.[31]

The right of a child to an effective remedy does not necessarily ensure the child's rights to independent action. Article 12 of the CRC does not directly oblige States to award children legal standing in all matters or allow minors to exercise full legal capacity. Common restrictions are directly related to

---

27 Kerrigan, *supra* note 24, p. 8. The report represents the careful analysis of children's rights in informal justice systems, such as barriers to effective participation and representation, pp. 122–136.

28 Yates, *supra* note 3. Se also *Access to justice for children, supra* note 1, para. 4, defining access to justice as "the ability to obtain a just and timely remedy for violations of rights as put forth in national and international norms and standards, including the Convention on the Rights of the Child."

29 Article 2(3) of the ICCPR and *inter alia* Article 13 of the ECHR.

30 GC No. 5, para. 24. According to *Access to justice for children, ibid*, para. 8 "elements of access to justice for children in particular include the rights to relevant information, an effective remedy, a fair trial, to be heard, as well as to enjoy these rights without discrimination. In addition, the responsibility of States Parties to realize the rights of all children requires structural and proactive interventions to enable access to justice."

31 The Guidelines, III. E. 2, *supra* note 1, para. 5, establishes that the concept of access to justice for children requires the legal empowerment of all children.

concerns for children's vulnerability and need for protection, and traditionally children are required to take legal action through their parents, or in some specific instances other legal representatives. The Guidelines recommend that States facilitate, where appropriate, access to court for children with sufficient understanding of their rights. They also underline the need for adequate legal advice.[32] Some jurisdictions expressly recognize the child's right to initiate legal action and the right to receive assistance in bringing matters before a competent authority.[33]

4.3   *Children in Justice Systems*

Article 12 (2) of the CRC addresses the specific rights of children in justice systems by underlining that children must be provided the opportunity to be heard in any judicial and administrative proceedings affecting them, either directly, or through a representative.

The Guidelines further define participation in justice systems thus:

1.   The right of all children to be informed about their rights, to be given appropriate ways to access justice and to be consulted and heard in proceedings involving or affecting them, should be respected. This includes giving due weight to the children's views bearing in mind their maturity and any communication difficulties they may have in order to make this participation meaningful.

2.   Children should be considered and treated as full bearers of rights and should be entitled to exercise all their rights in a manner that takes into account their capacity to form their own views and the circumstances of the case.[34]

---

32   The Guidelines IV, *supra* note 1, para. 34. The Explanatory memorandum, para. 94, notes the strong link between issues of access to justice, proper legal counselling and the right to voice an opinion in court proceedings. REC 2012, *supra* note 1, recognizes the independent right of the child by requiring States to provide children and young people with effective redress and remedies through child-friendly means of making complaints and judicial and administrative procedures including access to assistance and support in using them, ensuring that these mechanisms are available to children and young people. According to Yates, *supra* note 3, CRIN's research identifies legal standing or legal capacity of children as a major issue.

33   According to O'Donnell, *supra* note 3, p. 54, a growing number of countries recognize for example children's standing to challenge custody orders or seek placement in alternative care.

34   The Guidelines, III. A. 1-2, *supra* note 1.

These provisions should be available to children regardless of whether they are implicated as perpetrators of criminal activity, victims or witnesses of crime, implicated in private family disputes or public child-protection proceedings, in immigration proceedings or other administrative proceedings.[35] GC No. 12 and the Guidelines highlight that children of all ages and capacities can express their views, perspectives and experience and that there is a range of methods and methodologies that can ensure that these are fed into the relevant decision-making process.[36] This directs attention to different types of representation for children and what mode of representation is optimal as a vehicle for active participation.

4.4   *What Do the Children Want?*

The voices of children had a direct impact on the drafting of the Guidelines. Consultation confirmed that a high majority of children feel comfortable telling someone if they are unhappy with how they are treated. It is unequivocally clear that the children's family and social circle is the single, most important source of support to them in this respect.[37] Children also expressed strong views as to how they would like their views to be heard. They overwhelmingly chose direct contact with the person making the decision before being represented by their parents, their lawyer or another adult speaking for them.[38] When asked what would have helped, most of the children identified the option of having a person of their choice with them.[39] About two thirds of the respondents confirmed that they had received explanations and that they understood decisions made. When asked who they wanted explanations from, most children chose family/parents.[40]

---

35   The Guidelines, I., *supra* note 1, para. 2.

36   GC No. 12, paras. 26–27 and Guidelines IV. D, *supra* note 1, para. 44, 47. O'Donnell, *supra* note 3, p. 53 points out how in many countries "age limits play a role in regulating children's right to be heard in legal and administrative proceedings. In most such cases, the age limits vary with the nature of the proceeding."

37   Kilkely, *supra* note 18, p. 23, confirming how "[v]irtually all other categories – including official or public persons, like health workers, teachers, youth/social workers, police officers and lawyers – fared very badly."

38   *Ibid*, p. 29.

39   *Ibid*, pp. 29–30. A significant majority acknowledged having received support but did not specify who their support person was.

40   *Ibid*, pp. 30–31. Those who explained their choices said they wanted to hear the decision from someone they trusted and believed and they wanted time to ask questions and discuss the decision.

4.5   Parental Representation

Parents as legal guardians represent their children in justice systems in many ways. They may bring a case in the child's name when appropriate, they may bring a case in their own name which may directly affect the child; and they represent their children in cases initiated by others. In fulfilling these tasks the parents must respect Article 5 of the CRC which stipulates that a parent's role is first and foremost to provide, in a manner consistent with the evolving capacities of the child, appropriate direction and guidance in the exercise by the child of the rights recognized in the Convention.[41] The more the child knows and understands, the more the parents have to transform direction and guidance into reminders and advice, and later into exchange on an equal footing.[42]

Research has identified how parent's genuine desire to protect their children from conflict and from the risks associated with involvement in justice systems can be a considerable obstacle to children's participation.[43] Allison James et al. formulate this as the tension between concepts of care and concepts of control. They illustrate how contemporary representations of childhood are actively repositioning children as both irresponsible and vulnerable, a representation that lessens their opportunities. They argue that the tension between children's rights to protection and those of participation can in reality lead to social exclusion.[44]

Many commentators have also reflected on the potential conflict of interests between the needs of the child and the interests of parents.[45] While this may in specific instances be a legitimate concern, it is important to note that

---

41   GC No. 12, para. 4 underlines that parental guidance compensates for the lack of knowledge, experience and understanding of the child.

42   GC No. 14, para. 44 and GC No. 12 para. 84. See also Recommendation Rec (2006)19 of the Committee of Ministers to Member States *on policy to support positive parenting*, para. 2 defining elements of positive parenting such as empowering, providing recognition and guidance to enable the full development of the child.

43   Kilkely, *supra* note 18, p. 15, citing *inter alia* Tomanovic, S. "Negotiating children's participation and autonomy within families," 11 *The International Journal of Children's Rights*, 2003, pp. 51–71.

44   James, A., Curtis, P. and Birch, J., "Care and Control in the Construction of Children's Citizenship," in Invernizzi and Williams, *supra* note 12, p. 85.

45   GC No. 12, para. 36 and Article 4 of the Exercise Convention. The Guidelines, IV. D, *supra* note 1, para. 37 specifically require children to have their own legal counsel and representation in proceedings where there is, or could be, a conflict of interests between the child and the parent. See also *inter alia* Freeman, M., "The future of Children's Rights," 14 *Children & Society*, 2000, pp. 277–293 and Fortin, *supra* note 22, p. 63.

discarding the notion of parental representation based on the notion of a parent-child conflict can actually compromise the complex, interwoven and reciprocal parent-child relationship. The notion of parent vs. child may exacerbate the child's vulnerability, cause the child to feel responsible for the outcome and silence him/her in the process. Herring argues powerfully that it is impossible to separate out the interests of a parent and a child as they are intertwined.[46] The child's rights should be viewed in the context of the relationship, underlining the child's *relational autonomy*.[47] This concept emphasizes the "complex coherence of responsibility and independency."[48] As a perspective it forces us to acknowledge parents as present in many elusive shapes and forms in their children's experience of justice systems.[49]

4.6   *Separate Representation for Children*

4.6.1   General Comments

Respect for children's rights to separate representation is an integral part of providing mechanisms to enable children to exercise their right to participate safely in judicial and administrative proceedings.[50] Separate representation is here defined as the appointment or role of a special person other than the parent (hereafter referred to as child advocate) with the task of advocating for or representing the interests of a child in a justice system.[51] Child advocates can contrast or complement the role of parents.

---

46   Herring, J., "Relational autonomy and family law," in Wallbank, J., Choudry, S. and Herring, J. (eds.), *Rights, Gender and Family Law*, Routledge, London, 2010, p. 262.

47   *Ibid*, p. 267. This does not diminish the dignity of the child at risk as a central aspect of relational autonomy lies in protecting people from the harm that abusive relationships can cause.

48   Kjørholt, A.T. and Lidén, H. "Children and Youth as Citizens: Symbolic Participants or Political Actors?" in Brembeck, H., Johansson, B. and Kampmann, J. (eds.), *Beyond the competent child: Exploring contemporary childhoods in the Nordic welfare societies*, Roskilde University Press, 2004, p. 83.

49   Kilkely's research with children involved in justice systems clearly shows the importance of families. See *supra* note 18. On the importance that children attach to relationships see also *inter alia* Dalrymple, J., "Constructions of Child and Youth Advocacy: Emerging Issues in Advocacy Practice," 19 *Children & Society*, 2005, pp. 3, 7, and Pithouse, A. and Crowley, A., "Adults Rule? Children, Advocacy and Complaints to Social Service," 21 *Children & Society*, 2007, pp. 201, 209.

50   The Guidelines, *supra* note 1, explanatory memorandum, para. 101.

51   Article 2(2) of the CRC defines a "representative" as "a person, such as a lawyer, or a body appointed to act before a judicial authority on behalf of a child."

O'Donnell's research indicates "that a growing number of countries recognize children's rights to legal assistance or representation in legal or administrative proceedings, although often within relatively narrow parameters or subject to discretionary criteria."[52] Many commentators have remarked on a variety of systemic pressures that impede the quality of representation, such as caseloads, limited funding and resources and inadequate training.[53]

The necessity of appointing separate representation is most often linked to conflicts of interest between parents and children. Another important justification is the need for professionalized services in view of the complexity of the proceedings.[54] Appointments based on the notions of vulnerability and complexity may reflect a concept of the child as incompetent and incapable of active direct participation or self-advocacy. The power imbalance may relate directly to children's apparent mistrust of authorities such as police and lawyers.[55] Another concern is that too strong a reliance on professionals speaking for children may actually undermine efforts to create child-sensitive proceedings and child-friendly environments and language.[56]

This all makes it of vital importance to (re)define separate representation first and foremost as a tool to enhance children's competence and self-advocacy and to empower them to make informed choices and take control.[57] This presents a very significant challenge to those working with children in any kind of official capacity with regard to developing and maintaining positive relationships of trust.[58]

---

52   O'Donnell, *supra* note 3, p. 50. Jean Koh Peters study showed that jurisdictions under the CRC that provided for a child to be heard through a representative were in a substantial minority and less than half of children worldwide involved in such proceedings had, or were slated to have, their views expressed through a representative. See *supra* note 3.

53   Duqette and Darwall, *supra* note 3, pp. 110–111; Fortin, *supra* note 22. CRIN's research also indicates that legal aid, legal representation and advice for children is limited, commonly to criminal defendants and often only available in urban areas. See Yates, *supra* note 3.

54   *Inter alia* Bilson, A. and White, S., "Representing Children's Views and Best-Interests in Court: An International Comparison," 14 *Child Abuse Review*, 2005, pp. 220–239.

55   Kilkely, *supra* note 18, p. 39.

56   Such as required by the Guidelines, IV., *supra* note 1, paras. 54–63.

57   Federle, K., "The Ethics of Empowerment: Rethinking the Role of Lawyers in Interviewing and Counselling the Child Client," 64 *Fordham Law Review*, 1996, pp. 1655–1697; and Buss, E., "Confronting Developmental Barriers to the Empowerment of Child Clients," 84 *Cornell Law Review*, 1998, pp. 895–966, noting the "growing call for child "empowerment" among those concerned with the legal representation of children." On the positive and therapeutic nature of a child's relationship with a lawyer, see also Duqette and Darwall, *supra* note 18, p. 92.

58   Kilkely, *supra* note 18, p. 24.

Who is capable of assuming such a role? A representative can be a lawyer, a social worker or another suitable person.[59] Many argue that children in general need legal representation in justice systems and the Guidelines emphasize legal counselling and free legal aid for children.[60] Duqette and Darwall argue that lawyers are experts in both substantive and procedural aspects and that without legal representation "a child has little prospect of successfully navigating the complexities of dependency proceedings."[61]

The age, capacity and intellectual development of a child require all child advocates to possess special knowledge and training.[62] The Guidelines underline the necessity of competency-based training in children's participation for all practitioners working directly with children, such as judiciary, police, lawyers, social workers and various other professionals.[63] Such training needs to account for the diversity of children's experience and needs, for example, and to be sensitive to gender, ethnicity, disability, age, religion, nationality and linguistic capacities. Child advocates especially need knowledge and training on how to facilitate communication and nurture competence. They need to be sensitive to how their role and status as professionals can diminish the child and how they can use child-centred techniques to empower the child to make decisions in an informed and fully participatory manner.[64]

Child advocates have different roles which can be conflict-filled and contentious.[65] These roles can be broadly categorized as *best-interest representation* and *child directed representation*.[66]

---

59   GC No. 12, para. 36. See also *s.c. v The United Kingdom*, Application No. 60958/00, Judgment of 15 June 2004, qualifying that a child can be represented by, for example, an interpreter, lawyer, social worker or friend.

60   The Guidelines, IV., *supra* note 1, par. 37–41.

61   Duqette and Darwall, *supra* note 3, p. 90.

62   GC No. 12, para. 36 emphasizes sufficient knowledge and understanding of the various aspects of the decision-making process and experience in working with children, and para. 134 (c) requires that adults working with children need to understand the socio-economic, environmental and cultural context of children's lives.

63   O'Donnell, *supra* note 3, p. 52 remarking on how many countries have carried out training to inform judicial and other relevant personnel and to help develop the skills needed to facilitate the participation of children in judicial proceedings.

64   Federle, *supra* note 57, p. 1690.

65   Brady, *supra* note 3, categorizes many different aspects and roles of child advocates. Federle, *ibid.*, notes the several different roles a lawyer may assume when representing a child, such as guardian ad litem, independent investigator or advocate for the child's views.

66   Duqette and Darwall, *supra* note 3, p. 94, noting how "[b]est interests models typically find greater favor with judges and lawmakers, while the preferred model among child

4.6.2   Best-Interest Representation

It is important to highlight the best-interest representation that stems from independent children's rights institutions, for example NGO s or ombudspersons established to pursue campaigns, trigger laws and policy reforms or address concerns on behalf of children. Such child advocates have frequently responded to key concerns and issues identified by children and have paved the way for significant changes in justice.

The main focus on best-interests representation relates to assistance in individual cases. The Guidelines call for the appointment of a guardian ad litem (GAL) for children in cases of conflicting interests[67] and many States require or make it possible to appoint a GAL for children in certain judicial proceedings.[68] The term has no fixed definition. A GAL's primary duty is to safeguard the interests and needs of the child and to make recommendations to courts.[69] GAL's are thought to serve the interests of children who for instance lack cognitive ability or verbal skills to articulate their views, such as the younger children involved in justice systems.[70] This model is also thought to relieve the psychological burden and responsibility some children may connect to expressing their views. Several challenges have been identified as to the duties and responsibilities of a GAL.[71] One objection is that the model is paternalistic: it substitutes the view of the advocate for the view of the child and usurps the role of the court to make a best-interest determination.[72] The multifaceted role has been identified as a problem and it has been suggested that "an optimal approach may involve having a GAL who either has or has access to the expertise and resources of attorneys, lay volunteers, and caseworkers to perform the broad range of functions and services contained in the definition of the child

---

advocates and child welfare academics is the expressed-wishes model." Also Buss, E., "'You're my what?' The Problem of Children's Misperceptions of Their Lawyer's Roles," 64 *Fordham Law Review*, 1996, pp. 1699–1762; Pithouse and Crawley, *supra* note 49, use the concepts of cause-based and individual based representation.

67   The Gudelines IV, *supra* note 1, p. 42.

68   For example Child Abuse Prevention and Treatment Act, Pub. L. No. 93–247, as amended (CAPTA) in the US, and The Children Act 1989 in UK. See further in Bilson and White, *supra* note 54.

69   The Guidelines, *supra* note 1, Explanatory memorandum, para. 105. GC No. 12, para. 37 stipulates that a representative must exclusively represent the interests of the child and not the interests of other persons, such as parents, institutions or bodies.

70   Duqette and Darwall, *supra note* 3, p. 95.

71   *Inter alia* Bilson and White, *supra note* 54.

72   *Ibid*, p. 98. See also Herring, J., *Family law.* 4th edition, Pearson Education Limited, Harlow, 2009, pp. 466–67, 641.

advocate."[73] The Guidelines argue against combining the functions of a lawyer and a GAL because of the potential conflicts of interest.[74]

Many jurisdictions appoint special independent experts that take children's views into account when formulating their expert evaluations. In some cases the child's statement is heard and presented through a trained specialist working for the authorities. Many countries have for instance taken considerable measures to reduce the adverse consequences for child victims of giving testimony in criminal proceedings, most notably child victims of sexual abuse. These measures often include the use of video-recorded statements taken by trained professionals to be used as evidence. In such cases the child may also enjoy other assistance or representation.[75]

4.6.3 Child-directed Representation

Most recent studies favour child-directed representation where the role of the child advocate is solely to represent the views of the child. This model is considered to empower children and to ensure that their concerns and wishes are considered in justice systems.[76] The model rests on a determination of the child's competence and as Duqette and Darwall point out "[d]etermining the

---

73   Aitken, S.S., Condelli, L. and Kelly, T., *Final Report on the Validation and Effectiveness Study of Legal Representation Through Guardian Ad Litem*. Report submitted to the Administration on Children Youth and Families, Department of Health and Human Services, 1993. Also Duquette, D.N., "Legal Protection for Children in Protection Proceedings: Two Distinct Lawyer's Roles are Required," 34. *Family Law Quarterly,*, 2000, pp. 441–466, arguing for two separate standards, "one for the client-directed attorney role and one for a best interests guardian *ad litem* (GAL)." He argues that both roles should be clearly established, aggressive, active, and the court should appoint either one or the other, or both, under certain circumstances. In the UK, the courts can appoint a GAL to safeguard the interests of the child (often a child welfare professional) and a lawyer, often referred to as "tandem model" since the professionals work in tandem. See Ryrstedt and Matson, *supra note* 36, p. 140. Bilson and White, *supra note* 54 call this a conflation of Articles 3 and 12 of the CRC.

74   The Guidelines, *supra note* 67, Explanatory memorandum, para. 105.

75   Prime examples of this are *Children's Advocacy Centers* in USA. Iceland was a forerunner in bringing this model to Europe in 1998 by introducing a multiagency and interdisciplinary centre for the purpose of ensuring a child-friendly response to child sexual abuse, named the "Barnahus" (Children's Houses). They have since been established in Sweden, Norway and Denmark and preparations are underway in other countries.

76   The Guidelines, *supra note* 1, Explanatory memorandum, para. 104, noting that a lawyer should "determine and defend the child's views and opinions," as in Article 10 of the Exercise Convention. See also Duqette and Darwall, *supra note* 3, p. 99; Bilson and White (2005), pp. 223, 236. Duquette, D.N., *Two distinct roles/Bright Line Test*, 6 *Nevada Law*

decision-making capacity of any particular child and the weight to be given to that child's preferences remains a difficult and elusive task." The role of a child advocate taking directions from the child is considerably different from the role of a guardian: it represents multiple challenges.[77]

4.7   Self-advocacy

While promulgating children's unequivocal right to separate representation, it is extremely important not to lose focus on the positive and powerful aspects of self-determination and self-advocacy.[78] Self-advocacy is an integral element of empowerment. It fosters critical thinking and critical expression and may help children to put judicial proceedings in a more balanced perspective.[79]

Some argue that renewed emphasis should rest on the rights and competence of the child to be present and directly involved in proceedings without having their voice moderated by a third party.[80] This does not preclude the child's advocate but calls for a new balance between their role on one hand as

---

Journal, 2006, pp. 1240–1249, proposed a strict age standard to determine which sort of representative a child is provided.

77   GC No. 12, para. 37 insists on a code of conduct for child representatives. Duqette and Darwall, *supra note 3*, pp. 106–109 articulate the role of child lawyers, such as the gathering of all relevant information, participation in all hearings, advocacy for speedy proceedings, counselling concerning the subject, the child's rights, the justice system, the proceedings and the lawyer's role. Add to this the development of a theory and a strategy of the case, recognizing issues that require the services of other professionals, formulation of requests for evaluations or independent opinions and identification of appropriate family and professional resources for the child. The lawyer must ground his representation on a deep, unbiased understanding of the situation and needs of the child and build a positive and trusting relationship with the child. To do so the lawyer needs a competency in child cognitive development and effective interviewing skills, taking into account the individual child's age, level of education, cultural context and language skills. The lawyer also needs to understand and involve the child's family and wider community and to recognize that most children wish to maintain, and benefit from maintaining, connections with their families and communities. Child advocates should also solicit feedback from clients and families as to their representation.

78   GC No. 12, para. 35. emphasizes the rights of the child to choose how to be heard and recommends that wherever possible children should be given the opportunity to be heard directly in any proceedings. Rec 2012 stipulates specifically that for a child to be able to participate meaningfully and genuinely, he or she should be offered adequate support for self-advocacy appropriate to their age and circumstances.

79   On the concept of "dynamic self-determinism," see Eekelaar, J., *Family law and personal life,* Oxford University Press, 2006, p. 157.

80   Duqette and Darwall, *supra note 3,* p. 109.

presenters or interpreters of children's views and on the other as supporters and advisors.

Promoting self-advocacy requires a careful scrutiny of all the different aspects of child participation in different judicial or administrative proceedings. There is overwhelming evidence that specialized interviewers should conduct all interviews of victims of abuse and that victims should be protected from attending court and facing their abuser. In other types of cases there is increasing discussion in a range of jurisdictions of the potential benefits of undertaking such interviews as part of the overall decision-making process; but as Kilkely points outs, "[e]mpirical research with children and young people has found that children favour speaking directly to the judge because they want their views heard by the ultimate decision-maker."[81]

4.8   *Relational Representation*

Analysis of the above shows on the one hand the development of a broad, dynamic concept of children's participation in justice systems, and on the other the growing challenges this presents for the multifaceted roles of those who represent children. It is safe to say that at first the concept of participation focused on eliciting the child's views as to the facts of a case and weighing these views in the final outcome. Now there is growing emphasis on participation not being a one-off event "but the starting point for an intense exchange between children and adults."[82] This is particularly relevant for participation in justice systems, when navigating the complex web of ongoing parallel procedures and proceedings.[83]

The dynamic concept of participation covers all elements of justice, both substantive and procedural; and the keywords to consider are – competency, information, discussion, consideration and communication – at all possible levels. This provides daunting challenges for definition and implementation of appropriate representation for children.

Children in justice systems interpret a range of different influences that affect their opinions, choices and feelings of empowerment in justice systems. They place great emphasis on respect, trust, meaningful contacts and relationships.[84] In most cases parents are undeniably present in some capacity alongside a host of non-professionals and professionals responsible for informing,

---

81   Kilkely, *supra* note 18, p. 16, argues against "settling for mediated communication between children and decision-makers, when this is not children's clear preference."

82   GC No. 12, par. 13.

83   See Rec 2012.

84   Kilkely, *supra* note 18, p. 35.

advising, listening to, evaluating, communicating, advocating or making decisions. There is a need to adopt an integrated approach and to build on the
concepts of relational autonomy this paper suggests, that children need *relational representation*. We need to accept and look closely at the child's relationships with all relevant actors responsible for, involved with or affected by
various judicial proceedings concerning the child and to construct active representation that takes account of these complex relationships. The aim of relational representation should be to build trust and respect that will empower
children.

5   Conclusions

Research clearly shows that the positive effects of allowing children to participate in justice systems are overwhelming. Knowledge also indicates that certain modes of participation can be traumatic for children.[85] It is imperative
to analyse what modalities ensure optimal balance between participation
and protection. Under-representation, over-representation and conflicting-
representation can silence the voice of the child and distort the interests of the
child in the process.

Studies indicate a lack of coherence in justice systems as to when, how and
who should inform and represent children. A judicial process is not an isolated
event in a child's life and there may be many parallel and simultaneous formal
and informal processes. Participation is not a series of separate events but an
ongoing process influenced by the many different relationships embedded in
the child's life. Respecting and empowering the child relies on mutual understanding, commitment, time and multiple resources. From the child's perspective this requires relational representation – a holistic view of representation
that recognizes and takes into account the network of persons with different
roles and capacities and the various influential factors that enhance, support
and assist the child in actively participating at all levels in justice systems.

---

85   Peters, *supra* note 3 highlights the probability that a child is at critical moments in a case
      traumatized or under great emotional stress, the complexity of personal and social issues
      surrounding the case at hand and the problems the child faces encountering an adult
      system of law and bureaucracy.

Children's Right to be Heard from Their Unique Perspectives

Ann-Christin Cederborg

Introduction

The starting point for this chapter is that children involved in legal matters have the right to be heard and understood from their unique perspectives and conditions. When countries ratified the United Nations Convention on the Rights of the Child they agreed, among other things, to follow the regulation of children's rights to be heard in all matters that concern them. Hence every official institution is expected to give children opportunities to express their opinions and experience in each specific case. However, listening to children can be a challenging task as they may lack the maturity, language and communicative skills to express their views. Children may also have various reasons for not fully reporting their experience, for example, they may try to hide information of importance when being interviewed. In addition, interviewers may lack the competence to adapt their questions to the child's level of maturity or to ask questions without influencing her or his responses. If interviewers and legal assessors are not aware of such knowledge the legal proceedings may be based on unrealistic prerequisits.

In this chapter I illuminate the importance of high-quality interviews when trying to understand legal matters from children's perspectives. I also describe possible reasons why children do not disclose information about their experience in interviews. First, I describe the importance of an open interview technique needed to elicit information that is as accurate as possible from the child. I also disucss children's abilities to express their experience. Secondly, I discuss children's disclosures and non-disclosures based on two research projects. Here I cite findings from two studies, police officers' interviews with youths exploited in the sex trade and case workers' interviews with asylum-seeking children.

Interviewers' Ability to Elicit Information

Research has shown that interviewers do not follow international recommendations on how to avoid influencing children's responses when interviewing them about their experience (se for example Cederborg, Orbach, Sternberg &

© KONINKLIJKE BRILL NV, LEIDEN, 2015 | DOI 10.1163/9789004297432_009

Lamb, 2000; Milne & Bull, 1999; Orbach & Lamb, 1999). The main problem is interviewers' extensive use of option- posing questions and suggestive questions. Option-posing questions include information not previously disclosed by the children; they are asked to confirm or reject the interviewer's option for example "Did he hit you?" or they may be asked to select an option given by the interviewers, for example, "Did this happen on either Thursday or Friday?" When posing suggestive prompts, interviewers give voice to their own opinions but also assume details not previously revealed by the child, for example, "He hit you didn't he?" These questions can influence the responses and decrease opportunities to obtain accurate detailed information (see for example Cederborg, Alm, DeSilva & Lamb, 2013; Cederborg, Danielsson, LaRooy & Lamb, 2009; Lamb, LaRooy, Lindsay, Malloy, & Katz, 2011). Repeated option-posing and suggestive utterances can also increase the risk of contaminating the reports from children (Bruck, Ceci, & Hembrook, 1998; Lyon, Malloy, Quas, & Talwar, 2008; Memon & Vartoukian, 1996). Open questions in the form of invitations and directive prompts are on the other hand less likely to influence the reports even if invitations are the most favorable question type. This is because such prompts are the least likely to contaminate responses. Invitations encourage children to freely recall their experience in a general way, for example "Tell me everything about that," or they encourage the child to elaborate further on aspects previously mentioned, for example "You said that she was very angry with you. Tell me everything about that." Directive questions proceed from information previously mentioned by the child. They ask for additional specific information using "wh"-questions, for example "Where were you when this happened?" (Cederborg & Lamb, 2008; Cederborg *et al.*, 2000; Lamb *et al.*, 1996).

Children's Abilities to Express Their Experience

Interviewing children requires not only interviewing skills but also an awareness of their capacities and motivation to report (Lamb, Hershkowitz, Orbach & Esplin 2008). The relationship between children's age and memory is complex, but they can provide reliable information about four years of age in response to open questions (Lamb *et al.*, 2003) even if developmental maturity influences what and how they are able to report (Goodman & Reed, 1986; Lamb *et al.*, 2003; Leippe, Romanczyk, & Manion, 1992). Younger children may report more briefly than older when asked open questions but their accounts can be expanded if the interviewer repeats what the child said and then ask for more information, for example "You said he slapped you. Tell me more about that slap."

Irrespective of the child's age, it is important that interviewers try to elicit information from recall rather than from recognition memory. That is achieved by using open questions before using option-posing or suggestive ones, as these two latter types of prompt risk eliciting inaccurate information (Lamb *et al.*, 2008). Children's ability to report is not just a question of how old they are. Their communicative and linguistic skills clearly influence how they report their experience as well as the interviewers' use of language (see for example Dale 1973; Dale, Loftus & Rathburn, 1978; Carter, Bottoms & Levine 1996). In addition, children may modify their reporting strategies to ensure that listeners understand what they are saying (Lamb & Brown, 2006) and they can adapt their reports according to what answer they perceive the interviewers prefer (Ceci & Bruck, 1993, 1995; Melnyk, Crossmann, & Scullin, 2007). Even children mature enough to report their experience accurately from an early age may refrain from disclosing information. If they are not mature enough to understand what they have experienced this will, of course, limit their disclosure. Other reasons for excluding information or denying experience can be that they have a secrecy pact with perpetrators or fear punishment if they tell about their experience (Cederborg, Lamb & Laurell 2009).

Interviews with Girls Exploited in the SexTrade

Well-established knowledge of how to interview children does not specifically include those exploited in human trafficking and procurement. For this reason we wanted to expand the knowledge base by analysing how children exposed to such serious crimes are interviewed and how they respond to different questions. The study reported here is part of a larger project with the overall aim of finding out how children involved in the sex trade are treated and interpreted by the Swedish legal system. Our data consists of all district-court files and the corresponding preliminary investigations including investigative interviews made by the Swedish police. We included cases with settled convictions between July 2002 and the spring of 2012 (2002 was the year during which the penal provision on human trafficking entered into force). The reason for including both trafficking and procurement was that the Ministry of Justice and the National Police Board in Sweden have noted that investigations of trafficking can lead to convictions for procurement, and that these two types of crime are difficult to distinguish legally from one another. All the children in the study reported were girls between 13–17 years of age, in total 24 adolecents who had been exposed to procurement and human trafficking for sexual purposes (Lindholm, Cederborg & Alm 2014).

In this study we explored how children in the sex trade reveal information when asked about their exposure to this serious crime. We studied how the girls responded to questions about the sex trade with respect to the quality of questions asked. The study sought to contribute to the police practice of investigative interviewing, but also to understand adolescents in the sex trade.

Results

As expected the quality of information elicited was affected by the type of question asked by the police officers. Of all the questions important for the investigation about the sex trade, over half were option-posing and suggestive prompts. These question types are not recommended since they may influence the responses given. Accordingly, the disclosures involved many yes and no responses, implying that the disclosers included few details of importance to the investigations. This interview style was evident irrespective of the police officer's gender.

On the other hand, overall the girls disclosed information nearly five times more frequently than they withheld it. However, they also avoided disclosing certain information, for example crime-specific details, their involvement in the sex trade, their relations to persons involved in the crime, and their exposure to high levels of violence and abuse and force. This type of evasiveness has been shown in previous studies concerning other types of exploitation of children (Prieben & Svedin, 2008; Schönbucher et al., 2012; Sjöberg & Lindblad, 2002; Srikantiah, 2007). Children can also feel shame, guilt and responsibility when exposed to severe sexual abuse (Cederborg et al., 2007).

These findings indicate that the girls had their own agenda and reasons for not disclosing information. Four of the girls were specifically evasive (16–38%) when asked about crime-specific details. They had been exposed to severe violence and were interviewed shortly after the police intervened. Three other girls had also suffered the same type of violent exposure but they showed much less evasiveness (1–5%). The difference was that the latter three were not interviewed directly after the exploitation had ceased (delayed 16–18 months). Ten adolescents had not been exposed to such violence and force as the previous seven. Instead, they were described as having been involved actively in prostitution. These girls were not particularly evasive (1–10%) when asked about crime-specific details and they were not interviewed within days of the intervention.

We also saw that adolescents not exposed to high levels of severe and fearful exploitation, and who deliberately and actively participated in the sex trade, can be more informative about their experience irrespective of the time elapsing since the period of exploitation ended.

In addition, seven cases involved girls who in different ways diverged from previous reported findings. In one case, the girl had been exposed to severe abuse and violence and was interviewed by the police a few days after the exploitation had ceased. However, she was not specifically evasive (5%). Another adolescent was not exposed to severe abuse and force and the interviewing started two months after the period of exploitation. Nevertheless, she produced many evasive responses (34%). Another adolescent also produced a high level of evasive responses (17%) even though she was not exposed to severe abuse and was interviewed on the day the police interrupted the exposure. This adolescent was described in the court file as having felt uncomfortable reporting about her own prostitution. Two other adolescents involved in the same case had not experienced much violence or force, either, and they were interviewed the day after the police had intervened. Their levels of evasiveness differed: one gave 15% evasive responses and the other gave 4%; but both were interviewed together with the perpetrators. They were described as not wanting to answer any questions at all. Lastly, the two remaining adolescents had not been exposed to serious violence and both had been interviewed either on the same day or the day after the interventions. They had only 2–3% evasive responses.

The police officers' use of social pressure as a strategy to obtain information was also a reason for the girls' evasiveness. Such utterances can be described as face-threatening and as such can influence informants' motivation to disclose information (Keselman, Cederborg, & Linell, 2010b).

Interestingly, the police officers' use of recommended open questions significantly increased evasive responses. These open questions (invitations and directives) are expected to reduce the risk of contaminated information and elicit more in-depth answers (Lamb *et al.*, 1996). However, open questioning of girls in the sex trade can imply that they avoid disclosing critical and important information.

Summary

Girls exposed to the sex trade may have various reasons for not disclosing crime-specific details. For example they may fear reprisals, may be under the traffickers' control, may have loyalties towards them. They can also feel guilt and shame, fear reprimands and have feelings of responsibility. Victims exposed to severe abuse and under the traffickers' control are perhaps the least likely to disclose information.

We also found that police officers' knowledge of recommended interview techniques could be criticized. This is because they extensively used option-posing and suggestive questions, resulting in vast quantities of yes and no responses or unreliable information. On the other hand the recommended open questions to this type of crime victim may result in the girls' avoiding disclosure of information of specific interest for the investigation.

These findings indicate that law enforcement needs to be aware of advantages and disadvantages with various types of treatment when seeking information from children exposed to the sex trade. If the girls are exposed to option-posing and suggestive questions, the information given may be limited but with few perhaps unreliable details. Social pressure can be perceived as face-threatening and decrease opportunities for detailed information. On the other hand, using open questions as recommended can also limit disclosure of important information even though they decrease the risk of influenced information.

Interviewing Asylum-seeking Children

The other study is also an example of the complexity encountered when one is trying to elicit information from children. It concerns unaccompanied children in asylum-seeking interviews (Keselman, Cederborg, Lamb & Dahlström 2010a) and was part of a larger project with the overall aim of highlighting aspects of participation in interpreter-mediated communication with children (Keselman, 2009).

The Swedish Aliens' Act regulates the conditions for an alien to enter, work in or reside in Sweden. Governmental directions to the Migration Board (MB) and internal MB directives influence how asylum-seeking children are received and treated. For unaccompanied asylum-seeking children to qualify for a residence permit it has to be probable that they meet the Swedish legal requirements. If they are under eighteen they receive an appointed guardian and a legal representative to safeguard their interests during the asylum-seeking process. The interviews with the children are important for the adjudication and case assessment.

The MB case workers are responsible for assuring fair treatment of the child in the asylum hearing. This involves the child's right to freely recall information of importance for the assessement of the case. The caseworker should listen and give the child opportunities to report important information, and should ask for additional information and clarification if something is unclear (Government Bill prop. 2004/05:170). Even though Sweden is considered to respect human-rights principles and the United Nations Convention on the Rights of the Child, the government, migration authorities and practitioners alike have criticized the practical implementation of Article 3 (the best interest of the child) and Article 12 (the right of the child to be heard and participate in matters that concern them) (Government Bill prop 2004/05:170; Swedish National Audit Office, 2002; Brendler-Lindquist, 2005). The criticism concerns, for example, the way children are questioned, the skills of the interviewers, the opportunities the children are given to express their views and the ways their views and best interest are taken into account in decision-making (Schiratzki, 2000; Juhlen, 2003; Olsson, 2008).

The overall project gave us insight into the ways asylum-seeking children describe their situation, but also how their reports are created (Keselman, 2009). In our first study we explored how unaccompanied asylum-seeking children from Russia were interviewed and how the information-seeking prompts used by the caseworker were rendered by the interpreter (Keselman, Cederborg, Lamb & Dahlström 2008). We found that the caseworkers relied heavily on option-posing and suggestive questions (43%) which are more likely to elicit inaccurate information. When open questions were asked, the interviewers usually used directive questions (31%) instead of invitations (5%). The most outstanding result was that about one-third of the caseworkers' questions were rendered inaccurately (33%). Almost half of the misinterpretations altered the content and one-third involved changes in the type of question asked.

With this finding in mind we further explored how the children reported information in response to the translated questions from the caseworkers, and also the accuracy with which their responses were rendered by interpreters (Keselman *et al.*, 2010). This was a quantitative analysis of interviews with 26 Russian speaking minors (6 girls and 20 boys) involving ten caseworkers who were assisted by one of 17 interpreters. The minors' stated chronological ages when interviewed ranged from 14 to 18 years of age (M = 16.0 years).

Result

Most of the renditions of minors' responses were accurate (76 %) but 16% were inaccurate and interpreters did not translate 8%. In addition, the minors distinguished themselves as active participants in the asylum hearings, as evidenced by the strategies they chose when responding to different types of question. Specifically, they were informative when asked open questions but eager to develop their responses to option-posing and suggestive questions. Overall, they seemed to recognize their obligation to be cooperative and to report facts that might inform decision-makers about their eligibility for asylum.

There was, however, some tension between the willingness to disclose and the wish to withhold specific facts, especially when asked to reveal information about identification papers, location of the smugglers, orphanages, homes, parents' identities and whereabouts, times of events that could provide information for estimating the child's age, plus smugglers' and helpers' identities.

The minors seldom gave no answers to the questions asked. Instead, they extensively elaborated their answers while attempting to explain why they did not provide the information requested. They also tried to provide alternative explanations or accounts when disagreeing with the options given by the case-workers. By so doing, they not only disagreed or refrained from responding but rather took the opportunity to reveal additional information and downplay their uncooperativeness.

The minors also elaborated upon their responses when they agreed with the options provided. By using elaborations strategically, asylum-seeking children showed the capacity to recognize the potential value of extended responses.

The interpreters typically translated the minors' responses accurately, but all inaccurate renditions were sources of concern because each could negatively affect the quality of information provided to the migration authorities. This was especially true when interpreters ignored or 'improved on' the minors' style and semantic choices.

Summary

The results show that interpreters are powerful participants who can profoundly influence the fact-finding aspects of asylum investigations. This means that migration authorities have to increase their awareness of how the minors' disclosures can be influenced by interpreters who translate the responses to questions asked. Assessments of the communicative process in asylum-seeking interviews may reduce the risk of incorrect decisions about asylum claims.

Conclusions

When children are involved in legal matters there is a need for collaboration between professionals from the behavioural sciences and the legal system.

Such interdisciplinary collaboration can clarify the knowledge necessary to increase the chance that children are understood from their unique perspectives and conditions. Workers in both disciplines agree that children involved in legal matters have the right to be heard, but psychological research shows that information is elicited and interpreted in legal contexts without the elicitor knowing the best possible prerequisites to convey children's perspectives. Such handling implies a risk that children's reports about their experience are influenced by interviewers and interpreters alike. This happens, for example, when interviewers assume children's experience and base their questions on preconceptions and beliefs about what actually happened. Such assumptions can lead to option-posing and suggestive questions that prevent accurate reports. Assessing reliability and credibility on such reports can lead to unrealistic assements as such reports are limited and influenced by the interviewers. This means that the legal assessors have to consider what the conditions were for the children in question to report accurately (Cederborg & Gumpert 2010). Instead, if children are given opportunities to report freely from open questions this can minimize the risk that legal assessment is based on inaccurate reports. However, legal assessors also have to bear in mind that narratives based on open questioning can involve evasive responses as children may have their own reasons for disclosing or not disclosing information (Keselman *et al.*, 2010a; Lindholm *et al.*, 2014).

When assessing credibility it is also important to bear in mind that children's experience and situation may vary but they are generally able to report their experience to open questions from about four years of age. In addition, how children report is influenced by their understanding of previous experience. They interpret their experience to develop unique strategies for how to manage various situations (Alanen, 1988; James & Prout, 1990; James, Jenks & Prout, 1998; Prout, 2005; Quortrup, 1997).

It is a challenging task to interview children about their experience and to assess their credibility. On the other hand, if the legal system cooperates with experts from the behavioural sciences, legal professionals can develop an understanding of children and the conditions for eliciting accurate information from them. Such collaboration can increase their right to be understood from their own perspective, and this is a crucial part of their right to be heard. Interviewers with interdiciplinary knowledge of how to interview children properly, and legal decision-makers who base their assessments of credibility on knowledge instead of only general legal classifications, can increase the chance of proper assessment procedure (Cederborg & Gumpert 2009).

References

Alanen, L. (1988). Rethinking childhood. *Acta Sociologica, 31*(1), 53–67.

Bruck, M., Ceci, S.J., & Hembrooke, H. (1998). Reliability and credibility of young children's reports: From research to policy and practice. *American Psychologist, 53,* 136–151.

Ceci, S.J., & Bruck, M. (1993). Suggestibility of the child witness: A historical review and synthesis. *Psychological Bulletin,* 113, 403–439.

Ceci, S.J., & Bruck, M. (1995). *Jeopardy in the courtroom: A scientific analysis of children's testimony.* Washington, DC: APA Books.

Carter, C.A., Bottoms, B.L., & Levine, M. (1996). Linguistic and socioemotional influences in the accuracy of children's reports. *Law and Human Behavior. 20,* 335–358.

Cederborg, A-C., Orbach, Y., Sternberg, K.J. &. Lamb M. (2000). Investigative interviews of child witnesses in Sweden. *Child Abuse and Neglect,* 24, 10, 1355–1361.

Cederborg, A-C. & Lamb, M.E. (2008). Interviewing alleged victims with intellectual disabilities. *Journal of Intellectual Disability Research.* 52, 1, 49–58.

Cederborg, A-C., Alm, C., Da Silva Nisen, D, & Lamb, M.E. (2013). Investigative interviewing of alleged child abuse victims: an evaluation of a new training program for investigative interviewers. *Police practice and research. An international journal* 14, 3, 242–254.

Cederborg, A-C., Danielsson, H., La Rooy, D. & Lamb, M.E. (2009). Repetition of contaminating question types when children and youths with intellectual disabilities are interviewed. *Journal of Intellectual Disability Research,* 440–449.

Cederborg, A-C., & Gumpert, C. (2010). The challenge of assessing credibility when the alleged victims have intellectual disabilities. *Scandinavian Journal of Disability Research, 12, 2,* 125–140.

Cederborg, A-C & Lamb, M. & Laurell, O. (2007). Delay of disclosure, minimization and denial when the evidence is unambiguous. A multi victim case. In M. Pipe., M. Lamb, Y. Orbach, & A-C Cederborg (eds,). *Child sexual abuse: Disclosure, Delay and Denial.* Hillsdale New Jersey; Lawrence Erlbaum Publishers (pp. 159–174).

Dale, P.S. (1976). *Language development: Structure and function.* New York: Holt, Rinehart & Winston.

Dale, P.S., Loftus, E.F., & Rathbun, L. (1978). The influence of the form of the question on the eyewitness testimony of preschool children. *Journal of Psycholinguistic Research, 7,* 269–277.

Goodman, G.S., & Reed, R. (1986). Age differences in eyewitness testimony. *Law and Human Behavior,* 10, 317–332.

Governement Bill prop. 2004/05:170. *Ny instans och processordning I utlännings- och medborgarskapsärenden (New system for appeals and procedures in aliens och citizenship casess).* Stockholm: Riksdagen.

James, A., Jenks, C., & Prout, A. 1998. *Theorizing childhood*. Oxford: Polity Press.

James, A., & Prout, A. 1990. Re-presenting childhood: Time and transition. In A. James & A. Prout (Red.). *Constructing and reconstructing childhood*. Basingstoke: Falmer Press.

Juhlen, K. (2003). *Separared children-a survey in Sweden*. Sweden: Save the Children.

Keselman, O. (2009). *Restricting participation. Unaccompanied children in interpreter-mediated asylum hearings in Sweden*. Dissertation. Linköping: LIU tryck.

Keselman, O., Cederborg, A-C., Lamb, M.E., & Dahlström, Ö. (2008). Mediated communication with minors in asylum-seeking hearings. *Journal of Refugee Studies. 21, 1*, 103–116.

Keselman, O., Cederborg, A-C., Lamb, M.E., & Dahlström, Ö. (2010a). Asylum seeking minors in interpreter-mediated interviews: what do they say and what happens to their responses? *Child & Family Social Work*. 15, 325–334.

Keselman, O., Cederborg, A-C., & Linell, P. (2010b). "That is not necessary for you to know!" Negotiation of participation status of unaccompanied children in interpreter-mediated asylum hearings. *Interpreting. International Journal of Research and Practice in Interpreting*. 12:1, 83–104.

Lamb, M.E., & Brown, D.A. (2006). Conversational apprentices: Helping children become competent informants about their own experiences. *British Journal of Developmental Psychology*, 24, 215–1234.

Lamb, M.E., Hershkowitz, I., Sternberg, K.J., Esplin, P.W., Hovav, M., Manor, T., & Yudilevitch, L. (1996). Effects of investigative utterance types on Israeli children's responses. *International Journal of Behavioral Development*, 19, 627–637.

Lamb, M.E., Sternberg, K.J., Orbach, Y., Esplin, P.W., Stewart, H., & Mitchell, S. (2003). Age differences in young children's responses to open-ended invitations in the course of forensic interviews. *Journal of Consulting and Clinical Psychology*, 71, 926–934.

Lamb, M.E., Hershkowitz, I., Orbach, Y, & Esplin, P, 2008: *Tell me what happened. Structured investigative interviews of child victims and witnesses*. Chichester: Wiley-Blackwell.

Lamb, M.E., LaRooy, D.J., Lindsay, C., Malloy, L.C., & Katz, C. (2011). *Children's testimony: A handbook of psychological research and forensic practice*. Chichester, West Sussex: Wiley-Blackwell.

Leippe, M., Romanczyk, A., & Manion, A. (1992). Eyewitness memory for a touching experience. *Journal of Applied Psychology*, 76, 367–379.

Lindholm, J. & Cederborg A-C. (2014). Adolescent Girls Exploited in the Sex Trade:Informativeness and Evasiveness in Investigative Interviews. *Police Practice and Research: An International Journal* (in press).

Lyon, T.D., Malloy, L.C., Quas, J.A., & Talwar, V. (2008). Coaching truth induction and young maltreated children's false allegations and false denials. *Child Development*, 79, 914–929.

Melnyk, L., Crossmann, A.M., & Scullin, M.H. (2007). The suggestibility of children's memory. In: D.F Ross, R.C.L Lindsay, M.P Toglia. & J-D Read (Eds.), The handbook of eyewitness psychology, Vol. 1: *Memory for events* (pp. 401–427). Mahwah, NJ: Erlbaum.

Memon, A., & Vartoukian, R. (1996). The effect of repeated questioning on young children's eyewitness testimony. British Journal of Psychology, 87, 403–415.

Milne, R., & Bull, R. (1999). *Investigative interviewing: Psychology and practice.* Chichester: Wiley.

Olsson, L. (2008). *Nytt system gamla brister? Barns egna asylskäl efter ett år med dem nya instans och processordningen.(New system, old flaws? Children's own grounds for asylum after one year with the new appeals and procedure system).* Sweden: Save the children.

Orbach, Y., & Lamb, M.E. (1999). Assessing the accuracy of a child's account of sexual abuse: A case study. Child Abuse & Neglect, 23, 91–98.

Prieben, G., & Svedin, C.G. (2008). Child sexual abuse is largely hidden from the adult society: An epidemiological study of adolescents' disclosures. Child Abuse & Neglect, 32, 1095–1108.

Prout, A. 2005 *The future of childhood.* London: Routledge.

Quortrup, J. (1997). A voice for children in statistical and social accounting: A plea for childrens' right to be heard. In A. James & A. Prout, (Eds.), *Constructing and reconstructing childhood.* London: The Falmer Press.

Schiratzki, J. (2000). The best interest of the child in the Swedish Aliens Act. International *Journal of Law, Policy and the Family,* 14, 206–225.

Schönbucher, V., Maier, T., Mohler-Kuo, M., Schnyder, U., & Landolt, M.A. (2012). Disclosure of child sexual abuse by adolescents: A qualitative in-depth study. *Journal of Interpersonal Violence,* 27, 3486–3513.

Sjöberg, R.L., & Lindblad, F. (2002). Limited disclosure of sexual abuse in children whose experiences were documented by videotape. *American Journal of Psychiatry,* 159, 312–314.

Srikantiah, J. (2007). Perfect victims and real survivors: The iconic victim in domestic human trafficking law. Boston University *Law Review,* 87, 157–211.

Swedish National Audit Office (2002). Ensamkommande barn-Informationsrapport 2002/03:5 (Unaccompanied children. Information report 2002/03:5). Stockholm: Riksdagens revisorer.

Children's Evidence and the Convention on the Rights of the Child: Improving the Legal System for Children

Deborah A. Goldfarb, Gail S. Goodman and Michael J. Lawler

Introduction

Article 12 of the United Nations Convention on the Rights of the Child (CRC) admirably and formidably provides children with the broad right to express their views "freely in all matters affecting" them. Included within this broad right is the children's right to have "the opportunity to be heard in all judicial administrative proceedings affecting the child." Article 12 of the Convention also protects the rights of children who desire, and so choose, to testify. For both the child who is compelled to testify and the child who chooses to testify, Article 6 requires that States ensure children's development "to the maximum extent possible," and Article 39 requires that States take "all appropriate measures to promote physical and psychological recovery and social reintegration of a child victim [of abuse]." To effectuate the Convention, legal professionals and developmental scientists must work together to determine an optimal balance for implementing these rights, thereby ensuring that the legal system provides justice without causing needless harm to children.

To help legal systems better understand how they might implement the rights provided by the Convention, in this paper we overview current legal procedures in the United States through which children's evidence is obtained, voluntarily or otherwise. We also describe current research on the presentation of evidence by children and on the potential developmental ramifications. Children who are compelled to testify—as well as children who choose to testify—are protected by the Convention and, given current research, can be shielded from further harm when providing evidence in legal settings. Yet, there is still more to be discovered about how best to obtain and present the evidence of children.

Although there are a number of instances outside of the judicial and administrative context where children should have the right to express their views, this paper focuses on the more narrow right to be heard in judicial and administrative proceedings. We also will not address Article 12's limitation that children's manner of presentation must be "consistent with the procedural rules of national law." Thus, there may be due process or other procedural concerns associated with the research discussed below. Although this paper references some of these limitations, many may go unmentioned.

With those caveats in place, we start by briefly orienting the reader to children's emotional needs after exposure to violence. We then provide an overview of judicial and administrative matters in the United States that rely on children's evidence and describe research on the implications of the presentation of this evidence. Next we turn to accommodations for children that have been implemented to better ensure accurate testimony while reducing the possibility of the legal system itself causing undue emotional harm to children. We end with a call for future research to support optimal implementation of the Convention on the Rights of the Child.

1   Children's Recovery from Violence and Abuse

Measures under the Convention to support child victims and witnesses must consider children's social-ecological context and their environment, including family and culture (Bronfenbrenner, 1989). All children need protective, supportive, and emotionally responsive relationships to thrive. Quality relationships and secure attachments serve as protective factors in the development of healthy children across cultures (Cassidy & Shaver, 2008; Dozier & Rutter, 2008; Lawler, Shaveer, & Goodman, 2011; Newland *et al.*, in press; van IJzendoorn & Sagi-Schwartz, 2008). For many traumatized children, nurturing or supportive caregiving may have been absent, resulting in compromised capacities to form new relationships or explore new environments (Bretherton, 2000; Cicchetti, 2004). These diminished capacities present unique challenges that legal procedures and interventions must consider.

Furthermore, maltreated children have more behavioral, social, relational, and emotional problems than non-maltreated children and are more likely than non-maltreated children to utilize health and mental health services (Felitti, 2002; Halfon, Mendonca, & Berkowitz, 1995; Juffer & van IJzendoorn, 2005; Lawler, *et al.*, 2011; Lawler & Talbot, 2012). Some interventions designed to protect maltreated children, such as providing evidence to law enforcement or social services, or testifying in court, can cause further trauma (Baugerud & Melinder, 2012; Block *et al.*, 2010; Quas, Goodman, *et al.*, 2005). Thus, special care must be taken with traumatized children to reduce further harm and assist in their physical and emotional recovery while also securing reliable evidence and testimony.

2   Presentation of Children's Evidence

The Convention provides broad flexibility as to how children's evidence may be presented. The Convention does not define what constitutes an opportunity to be heard. For instance, Article 12 allows a child to be heard "either directly, or through a representative or an appropriate body." Thus, children need not testify directly and, instead, another person or group of persons may speak for child witnesses. Although another speaking for children is necessary in some cases, our position is that largely, children should be encouraged to speak for themselves so as to avoid misstatement of children's experiences and opinions, and to empower children through voice. However, the conditions under which they speak must be protective of children emotionally and adjusted to account for their level of development. Examples of how children currently present evidence in court, including via representatives, are discussed below.

2.1   *Criminal Court Proceedings*
United States criminal courts operate within an adversarial system. As traditionally actualized in the United States, this system is not particularly attuned to children's abilities and needs. If evidence is considered sufficiently strong, the alleged perpetrator is charged, and an arraignment followed by a grand jury hearing or preliminary hearing is scheduled. Children may be required to testify at such hearings. However, strict Constitutional rights may not fully apply at such hearings. Thus, there can be greater flexibility for children to be protected from the stress of testifying in open court.

A prolonged discovery phase follows, permitting prosecution and defense to gather evidence to support their claims. During this time, children may be interviewed by numerous professionals about the crime, despite the documented fact that repeated interviewing can be quite stressful for children (Tedesco & Schnell, 1987). However, also during this time, most cases are resolved by confession and plea bargains, which can then save the child from having to testify at trial. If such resolution cannot be reached, a trial ensues. Trial dates are routinely continued, that is, delayed. This can make it difficult to prepare children for what they typically expect to be a stressful experience. They may arrive at the courthouse, with considerable fear and anticipation involved, only to be required to return at another time (Goodman *et al.*, 1992). During the trial, the child typically must testify face-to-face with the accused and undergo direct and cross-examination. If the case results in a guilty verdict, a disposition or sentencing hearing is held, at which time the child may again testify (Finkelhor, Cross, & Cantor, 2005; Quas & Goodman, 2012). Criminal cases in the United States involving child victims typically range from one to two years (Stroud, Martens, & Barker, 2000; Walsh, Lippert, Cross, Maurice, & Davison, 2008).

In criminal cases that result in a guilty verdict, the defendant can appeal the decision if it can be argued that the process violated her/his constitutional rights. If the decision is overturned, the case may be retried, and the children may have to testify again. Furthermore, in some instances, it may take years to apprehend the accused (McWilliams, Narr, Goodman, Ruiz, & Mendoza, 2013). Thus, although most cases are resolved within a year or two, a subset of cases lasts a decade or more.

In the United States, testifying in criminal court *at trial* requires children to face the defendant and submit to direct and cross-examination. The 6th amendment of the United States Constitution gives defendants the right to confront witnesses, including child witnesses, who testify against them. Videotaped child forensic interviews at Children's Advocacy Centers (CAC s) or police stations can be admitted as evidence, but generally only after the child has testified live in court, as pretrial videotaped interviews by authorities are considered "testimonial" (*Crawford v. Washington*, 2004), and a videotape obviously cannot be cross-examined in court. Cross-examination is widely believed to encourage truthful testimony and permit fact finders to reach the truth. However, developmental science reveals that when children testify, cross-examination actually decreases the accuracy of children's reports (Goldfarb & Goodman, 2014; Saywitz & Nathanson, 1993; Zajac, O'Neill, & Hayne, 2012). The decrement in recall results from the intimidating nature of both the questioning and the context rather than from an inability of children to recount the events in question. Children who express the greatest anxiety and negativity about seeing the defendant also experience the most difficult time on the witness stand answering prosecutors' questions (Goodman *et al.*, 1992). Moreover, child victims who served as witnesses in criminal prosecutions of child sexual abuse report that cross examination and seeing the defendant in the courtroom are particularly stressful (Goodman *et al.*, 1992). If the abuse was severe and the children are required to testify multiple times, long-term emotional damage may result (Quas *et al.*, 2005).

2.2   Civil Court Proceedings

Children's evidence can also play an important role in civil court proceedings. Here we highlight civil suits regarding equal protection (specifically, recent use of an amicus brief in a civil proceeding, permitting children to have a voice in a matter that may affect their lives), dependency court proceedings, and family court proceedings.

2.2.1   Amicus Briefs

Even when children are not themselves a party to a lawsuit, advocates can ensure that children's voices are heard. This may occur, for example, in civil court proceedings. A prominent recent example concerns children's voices in same-sex marriage cases. In 2008, California voters passed Proposition Eight, which limited the definition of marriage in California as that between a man and a woman. On May 22, 2009, Plaintiffs filed a lawsuit in the Northern District of California challenging the constitutionality of Proposition Eight. Although the definition of marriage directly affected both children of same-sex parents and lesbian, gay, and bisexual youth, for reasons outside of the scope of this paper, the children were not parties to the suit.

Plaintiffs won at the trial court and the case was eventually appealed to the United States Supreme Court (*Hollingsworth v. Perry*, 2013). On appeal to the Supreme Court, an amicus brief—a brief by an individual, group of individuals, or entity who are not parties to but have relevant information regarding the suit—was filed on behalf of children of same-sex parents and lesbian, gay, and bisexual youth. As the brief noted, "[t]he voices of children raised by same-sex parents—those who live every day within the family structure at the heart of these lawsuits—are too often unread in the debates about same-sex couples and marriage" (Family Equality Council Brief, 2013, p. 2). The purpose of the brief was thus to present "the voices of these children" (Family Equality Council Brief, 2013, p. 3).

Not only did the filing of this brief provide an avenue for the children to be heard but the emotional appeal from these young voices was clearly received by the justices. In oral argument, Justice Kennedy noted the effect denial of marriage had on children of same-sex parents and raised the question that the United Nations Convention asks of all of us, "the voice of those children is important in this case, don't you think"? (Hollingsworth v. Perry Oral Argument, 2013).

Amicus briefs are thus a potential avenue through which children can be heard in a manner that does not require them to take the stand. As in the Proposition Eight lawsuits, dependency courts frequently hear testimony regarding children's opinions about the future of the children's families, both inside and outside of the courtroom.

2.2.2   Dependency Court
In the United States, the juvenile court system typically includes a specialized court that hears cases involving child maltreatment, referred to in some states as dependency court. These cases are brought to the court's attention by child protective service agencies. Specifically, these "dependency courts" make decisions regarding children's placement (in- vs. out-of-home), safety (*e.g.* if and when it is safe for children to return home to their parents), and permanence (*e.g.* whether or not to terminate parental rights and place the child up for possible adoption) (Block, Oran, Oran, Baumrind, & Goodman, 2010; Lecklitner, Malik, Aaron, & Lederman, 1999; Quas, Cooper, & Wandrey, 2009). In principle, the dependency courts operate on the basis of children's best interests,

although in fact they often, in effect, come close to guessing as to what actually would best promote a particular child's well-being.

All too little is known from scientific research about the long-term effects of children's participation—or lack thereof—in the dependency court system or about how children's knowledge, attitudes, and anxieties about dependency court actions relate to the children's psychological adjustment as adults. Consistent with the United Nations Convention on the Rights of the Child, there is a growing trend in the United States for children to attend their dependency court hearings and to have a voice in these crucial matters that quite directly and powerfully affect their lives. This is occurring despite our country's continued lack of ratification of the Convention; most likely, our institutions and laws are affected by the Convention in any case. Scientific research makes clear that children in dependency courts want a say in dependency proceedings and that it is not harmful to them psychologically to appear and even testify (Block et al., 2010; Runyan et al., 1988; Weisz et al., 2011). They also typically want to go home to their biological parents, even if the parents are abusive or neglectful (Block et al., 2010). This poses a dilemma for the Convention's mandate for children's voices to be heard, if "being heard" means having a say in decisions made. If "being heard" has no impact on legal decisions, it becomes empty words.

The problem, of course, is that children are attached to their parents, to their siblings, their friends, their homes, and their neighborhoods, even when parents are maltreating the children (Bowlby, 1980). Some children understand that their best interest is to be separated from their parents, but some may not. When children in dependency court were interviewed, over 90% expressed a desire, often a very strong desire, to go home again and not to be placed in foster care ("Go home, and I want my mom to get herself together to get us back, and I don't want to stay in a foster home forever," "Say I could go home today or tomorrow," pp. 665). However, a small percentage of children expressed such sentiments as "To make my mommy stop beating me and send me to a foster home," and "Put my mom in jail" (Block et al., 2010, pp. 665). Society could serve such children best by greater emphasis on prevention of maltreatment in the first place; required classes starting in junior high school on nonviolent, sensitive child rearing; and on support systems for families. Countries, such as Sweden, that have banned physical punishment of children may be, at least in principle, way ahead of the United States in such regards (Gershoff, 2013).

Children who appear in dependency court have limited knowledge about the court proceedings and concepts. Even 14-year-olds lack considerable legal knowledge, both before and after attending their dependency court hearings (e.g., Block et al., 2010; Quas et al., 2009). By the time children appear in dependency court, they may understand that the social service system and judge have the power to remove them from their homes. Aside from that, young children on average often do not understand many basic courtroom concepts (*e.g.,* the lawyer's role). For such children to have a voice in the proceedings, the courts need to come down to the child's level and take the time needed for the child to play a meaningful role in any decisions reached. Giving children a meaningful voice in dependency court remains a challenge for the United States legal system.

2.2.3 Family Law Proceedings

Millions of children are affected every year by the separation or dissolution of their parents' relationship. As children are affected by custody proceedings, under the terms of Article 12, children should have an opportunity to be heard in any judicial or administrative proceedings regarding custody.

In the United States, jurisdictions are split as to whether children can and should testify regarding custody matters. Some states require the court to consider children's wishes as to their custody and residence (Texas Family Code Section 153.009; California Family Code Section 3042). California courts are required to consider children's wishes as to "granting or modifying custody or visitation" where children are of "sufficient age and capacity to reason so as to form an intelligent preference as to custody or visitation" (California Family Code Section 3042). Children older than 14 years have the right to "address the court," and courts cannot refuse to hear these children unless the courts determine denying them the right is in the children's best interest.

Vermont, in contrast, requires appointment of an attorney, and children cannot testify until the court has considered a number of factors, including whether the "evidence sought is not reasonably available by any other means" than the children's statements (15 VSA § 594). Additionally, a number of alternative dispute resolution mechanisms now specifically include children in custody discussions, some in response to prior findings that approximately 80% of custody evaluators do not include children in the decision making process (Pickar & Kahn, 2011).

Research has shown that children, on average, want a say in custody proceedings but do not want to be responsible for the final custody decision (Cashmore & Parkinson, 2007). That said, surely, some children who hold strong opinions want and emotionally need a direct say. A recent review of qualitative studies on children's participation in custody proceedings similarly found that, across a number of countries, children want a meaningful voice in the proceedings (Birnbaum & Saini, 2012). Perhaps unsurprisingly, despite wanting a say, children also expressed being upset with their involvement in the custody proceedings generally. Judicial actors thus walk a careful line in obtaining this evidence. They are not without support, however. There are a number of techniques available to interview children in custody matters to ensure that children's custody preferences are heard in a developmentally appropriate manner (Saywitz, Camparo, & Romanoff, 2010).

2.3   *Education Proceedings*

Article 28 of the Convention recognizes children's right to an education. Accordingly, any process that may deprive children of that right, such as a school suspension or expulsion hearing, falls under Article 12's requirements. Providing students with a voice at these hearings is an area of increasing concern in the United States. In 2012, in the New York City public schools alone, 69,643 children were suspended (School-Justice Partnership Task Force Report, 2013). Many leaders are concerned that these expulsions disproportionately affect minority students and students with disabilities.

New York City students, however, are not without a remedy and have, indeed, been granted many of the rights recognized in the Convention. New York City Chancellor's Regulation A-443 recognizes that children have a right not only to present their case upon being removed from a classroom but children also have a right to notice, an explanation of the evidence, and the ability to present evidence before being suspended by a principal. As with all rights, these rights are without effect if children are not aware of and empowered to exercise the rights. Child advocates throughout the United States are thus working to ensure that children have the tools necessary to guarantee that their voice is heard (see School-Justice Partnership Task Force Report, 2013).

School expulsions highlight the fact that, without an education, children will not have the tools needed for their voices to be heard in an effective manner. Article 12's goal of providing children with a voice in judicial and administrative proceedings thus also implies a right to knowledge about the proceedings.

3   The Effects of being Heard

The effects of being heard may differ from one child to the next and one case to the next. Psychological research provides some guidance to the courts, but a case-by-case evaluation in this regard may be particularly important. In the best of cases, the child will feel empowered by testifying, and a just and right outcome will emerge. In the worst of cases, children have been murdered for talking to authorities and for agreeing to take the stand. Psychological research can, nevertheless, provide important guidance.

A robust finding is that child victims who testify in criminal cases feel greater positivity about the legal case and the legal system when the defendant receives a severe sentence (*e.g.,* Goodman *et al.*, 1992; Sas, 1997). In a qualitative study of 10 children involved in child sexual abuse prosecutions in Sweden, one of the major themes in the children's narratives was the importance of a guilty verdict and the need for punishment that included imprisonment (Back, Gustafsson, Larsson, & Bertero, 2011). Apparently, children who take the stand seek being believed and achieving a fair outcome (fair in their eyes), likely just as much, if not more, than adults do.

Regarding criminal child sexual abuse prosecutions, permitting the child victim to testify predicts more positive legal attitudes for child victims later, at least when the case involves less severe abuse. Research suggests that some children need clear acknowledgment that the abuse occurred and was sufficiently wrong as to warrant public intervention. Consistent with this possibility, Henry (1997) interviewed 9- to 19-year-olds after they participated in child sexual abuse legal cases and found that 48% of the children described testifying as helpful, whereas 34% described it as harmful (the children testified in criminal or juvenile cases). Moreover, in dependency cases, foster youth are increasingly demanding to have a say in the legal decisions that affect their lives (Block *et al.*, 2010). Despite enduring some short-term distress while testifying, it may be better in the long-run for children to have their day in court.

Nevertheless, the conditions under which children testify should be carefully considered. In criminal prosecutions, Goodman *et al.* (1992) found that children who testified multiple times, who testified in cases that lacked corroborative evidence, or who testified in cases where the children lacked maternal support were at greatest risk for adverse mental health outcomes. Quas *et al.* (2005) reported that testifying repeatedly in cases involving particularly severe child sexual abuse was related to higher levels of subsequent problems even into adulthood. Whitcomb *et al.* (1991) found that hostile questioning of children predicted poorer mental health outcomes for child victims.

Discussing each of these factors in turn, it is clear that testifying multiple times proved the strongest predictor of adverse mental health outcomes. Although this may have had to do with the nature of the cases that required multiple appearances, it is also possible that exposures to multiple stressful experiences exceeded children's resilience. Another predictor of adverse mental health outcomes for child victims was lack of corroborative evidence, which can mean the case rested largely on the child victim's report. Although children may need to have a voice, when the case rests squarely on the children's shoulders, this may increase stress associated with taking the stand. Caregiver support is crucial for child victims' well-being generally, including when children testify (*e.g.*, Liang, Williams, & Siegel, 2006; Malloy & Lyon, 2006; Sas, 1997). Without caregiver support, the stress of testifying in open court while facing the defendant may simply overwhelm children's coping resources. Finally, severe abuse cases typically involved perpetrators who are closely related to the child victim and abuse that occurred over long periods of time (*e.g.*, long-term incest cases). Strong emotional conflict about the perpetrator as well as possible family pressure to recant is likely particularly great in these circumstances, making testifying an especially stressful experience (Malloy, Lyon, & Quas, 2007). Hostile cross examination is a form of questioning that can be humiliating even for adults, not to mention children, who often lack the "ego-strength" of adults, particularly when the children have already suffered abuse and trauma. As Quas and Goodman (2012) concluded, children in such cases need extra protections to ensure they are not re-traumatized by legal experiences.

A critical question in debates about legal involvement concerns whether children below a certain age should be restricted from participating. Although adverse emotional effects of legal involvement may be greater for younger than older children (Quas *et al.*, 2005), older children tend to express greater negativity than do younger ones about the criminal courts and about dependency court. Older children's greater cognitive and socio-emotional development may make them more likely to understand the implications of the court's actions (*e.g.*, a permanent separation from loved ones, being sent to a foster home) as well as the shame and guilt associated with the abuse itself.

Adolescents also know more about the legal system generally (*e.g.*, Quas *et al.*, 2009). Adolescents' increased knowledge about legal proceedings may serve as a protective factor, as such knowledge is associated with reduced distress in child witnesses (Goodman *et al.*, 1998). This increased knowledge may also underscore the seriousness of the situation for adolescent witnesses, potentially leading to greater anxiety about the case, about participating, and about the outcome.

Overall, for many children who are thrust into the legal system but lack an adequate understanding of it—which may be especially true in the dependency system—the court may seem like an arbitrary power with little discernable empathy or logic. Fortunately, children may also appreciate on some level the necessity and importance of the courts' efforts to protect them. Courts and attorneys must attend to children's needs and the circumstances that can simultaneously optimize the accuracy of children's testimony and ensure positive emotional effects of testifying.

4   Who Can be Heard under the Convention

The opportunity to be heard is limited to children "capable of forming their own views." When children are capable of forming their own views is left undefined by the Convention. It is also largely undefined in scientific psychology, although it is known that even 2- and 3-year-olds can express opinions and provide accurate statements (*e.g.*, Jones & Krugman, 1986; Price & Goodman, 1990).

In the United States, whether children are capable of forming their own views depends in part on the subject matter at issue. For instance, while the legal age of majority in the United States is 18, courts can and do consider children's views on children's desire to emancipate from their parents at a younger age (see 750 ILCS 30/3-1). As to a requirement that children form their own views prior to testifying, the closest analogue to such a requirement in the United States is the testimonial competency requirement. Given the limitations on this paper, we will focus here on this testimonial requirement. The competency requirement generally includes the "capacity to observe, remember, communicate, and tell the truth" (Goodman, 1984). When these capabilities are first present in children and whether the competency requirements are useful are sources of ongoing debate (Klemfuss & Ceci, 2012; Lyon, 2011). Given that the last prong of the competency requirement—the ability to tell the truth—is the primary focus of most jurisdictions, at least within the United States, it is also the primary focus of this section.

Countries vary as to the "test" they require of children's ability to tell the truth, with courts in the United States requiring children show they understand what truth and lie mean and affirm that they will tell the truth (Goodman, 1984). Other countries do not require these formal procedures, with some allowing children to testify unsworn and others barring any oath affirmation procedure (Lyon, 2011). These procedures assume that questioning children about the difference between a truth and a lie is a valid measure for children's abilities to differentiate between the two and that an oath secures truthful testimony from children. Each of these subjects has been studied by developmental psychologists and is discussed in turn below.

Children's ability to lie and their ability to tell the difference between a truth and a lie may follow different developmental trajectories. Most studies find that children develop the ability to lie starting around 3 years of age (Talwar & Crossman, 2012). However, children's ability to lie accurately and consistently, particularly in response to questioning about the lie, does not develop until later during the school-age years (Talwar & Crossman, 2012). Children's ability to tell when a statement by another is either right or wrong begins around

2-years-old (Lyon, Quas, & Carrick, 2013). It is not until later, however, around 3-years-old, that children can use the terms true and false and even later that children are able to understand that lying includes a knowledge component (Lyon *et al.*, 2013; Wandrey, Quas, & Lyon, 2012).

Court traditionally inquires as to whether children understand the difference between a truth and a lie. Many of these inquiries are inappropriate for children's developmental abilities. For instance, affirmations that require children to promise may be too complex for children younger than 6-year-old as research reveals that children may not fully comprehend the meaning of a promise until age 6 (Lyon & Evans, 2014). Instead, children, even 3-year-olds, better understand that the term "will" guarantees performance by the speaker and, as such, may serve as a better term for the oath (Lyon & Evans, 2014).

Developmental psychologists have additionally tested whether requiring children to take an oath or make a promise actually affects whether children subsequently tell the truth. Across preschool years to adolescence, children's rates of lying do indeed decrease when they promise that they will not lie (Evans & Lee, 2010). Thus, while judicial and administrative bodies should carefully examine the form of the affirmation required of children, to ensure that it is developmentally appropriate in its wording, the utilization of an affirmation does appear to have some effect.

For these reasons, justice is best served by ensuring that requirements that children are capable of forming their own views, including competency and oath requirements, meet children's developmental needs. In the next section, we will discuss other modifications that can be used to help protect compelled child witnesses.

5   Current Attempts to Ensure that the Presentation of Evidence becomes a Point for Amelioration Rather than Additional Harm

Child witnesses experience both pre- and post-testimony anxiety, especially when they are required to describe traumatic events repeatedly and testify in front of defendants in open court (*e.g.*, Goodman *et al.*, 1992). Concerns about secondary trauma associated with child forensic interviewing and testifying have contributed to the development of new systemic approaches to lessen trauma for child witnesses (*e.g.*, Hall & Sales, 2008; Hobbs *et al.*, 2013; Lawler, Bederian-Gardner, & Goodman, 2013; Troxel, Ogle, Cordon, Lawler, & Goodman, 2009). These approaches, including child advocacy centers, introduction of out-of-court statements as evidence, and court preparation programs, are consistent with Article 6 and Article 39 of the UN Convention on the Rights of the

Child, ensuring healthy child development "to the maximum extent possible," and taking "all appropriate measures to promote physical and psychological recovery and social reintegration of a child victim (of abuse)."

Internationally, countries vary their approach to child witnesses according to their cultural and legal balance between protecting the rights of the accused and the rights of child witness (Bussey, 2009). In recent years, progress has been made in the United States in developing alternative options for child witnesses to provide accurate statements to authorities and effective testimony outside the court or not in the presence of accused perpetrators (Bottoms, Najdowski, & Goodman, 2009; Hobbs *et al.*, 2013; McWilliams *et al.*, 2014).

5.1 *Child Advocacy Centers*

Although children's experiences within the criminal justice system vary considerably, in general, once authorities suspect a crime has occurred, an investigation ensues. For some crimes (*e.g.*, domestic violence, including homicide; child sexual assault), children's eyewitness reports constitute prime evidence. This can place considerable pressure on child victims and witnesses to provide clear, detailed information not only in the courtroom, but also well before that, in child forensic interviews.

Gathering evidence is fundamental to legal actions. In the United States, gathering children's evidence in the investigative phase increasingly occurs in Children's Advocacy Centers (CACs). These Centers employ highly trained child forensic interviewers (*e.g.*, forensic social workers) who work in conjunction with prosecutors, child protective services, and law enforcement. With an overall goal of reducing trauma associated with investigative and legal processes, CACs' core components include: providing a child-friendly setting (to put children at ease, to avoid intimidation), use of a multidisciplinary team (to share information and coordinate interviews, to limit the number of interviews), developmentally appropriate, neutral child forensic interviewing (to obtain accurate information that can withstand legal scrutiny), and videotaping of interviews (to record statements made out of court, to prove how the child was interviewed and what the child said) (Connell, 2009; Jackson, 2012; Newman, Dannenfelser & Pendleton, 2005). Some CACs also provide additional services, such as medical or mental health assessments. The CAC multidisciplinary approach is intended to reduce secondary victimization of child witnesses through collaborative services between legal and social welfare agencies (Cross, Jones, Walsh, Simone, & Kolko, 2007).

When interviewing children, many CACs now use science-based forensic interview protocols validated through developmental science. These protocols include the National Institute of Child Health and Human Development

(NICHD) Protocol (Lamb, Herschkowitz, Orbach, & Esplin, 2008; Lamb, Orbach, Sternberg, Hershkowitz, & Horowitz, 2000), the 10-Step Interview (Lyon, 2005), the Cognitive Interview-Revised for children Geiselman, Saywitz & Bornstein, the Developmental Narrative Elaboration Technique (Saywitz & Camparo, 2014), and the Stepwise Interview (Yuille, Hunter, Joffe, & Zaparniuk, 1993). These protocols rely on scientific studies showing that, like most adults, most children provide particularly accurate memory reports when positive rapport has been built with the interviewer, when given practice with task requirements (*e.g.*, narrating events), in response to free recall and open-ended questions (*e.g.*, "Tell me what happened?"), and when cued as to the type of information needed (see Goodman, Ogle, McWilliams, Narr, & Paz-Alonso, 2013; Hobbs *et al.*, 2014; Malloy, Johnson, & Goodman, 2013). But research also demonstrates that specific questions may be necessary to obtain required forensic information (*e.g.*, Saywitz, Nicholas, Goodman, & Moan, 1991).

Evaluations of the efficacy of the CAC model suggest that it decreases delays between law enforcement reports and indictment dates (Walsh, Lippert, Cross, Maurice, & Davison, 2008), increases access to medical examinations, improves the experiences of non-offending parents, and decreases the level of fear experienced by children during the interviews (Jones, Cross, Walsh, & Simone, 2007). Still to be determined are the effects of CACs on prosecution outcomes, false allegations, children's disclosure rates, and stress reduction for child witnesses (Saywitz & Camparo, 2009). Recent research suggests that CAC s do not decrease child witness credibility, at least in the eyes of mock jurors (Johnson, Shelley, Goodman-Shaver, & Goodman, 2013).

5.2   *Out of Court Testimony*
To help alleviate potential child witness trauma, United States courts permit, under certain conditions, the admission of out of court statements by child witnesses through hearsay testimony or closed circuit television (CCTV).

5.2.1   Hearsay
Hearsay evidence, a statement (1) the declarant does not make while testifying at the current trial or hearing; and (2) a party offers in evidence to prove the truth of the matter asserted in that statement (Federal Rules of Evidence 801 (c), 2014), includes out of court statements made by child witnesses to law enforcement, family, or friends. By removing the need to testify in the courtroom, hearsay evidence may help protect a child witness from secondary trauma. For instance, video-recorded child forensic interviews are a structured form of hearsay evidence that permit fact finders to directly hear out of court statements (Hobbs *et al.*, 2013). In Finland, Norway, and Sweden, child witnesses are video-recorded during

police interviews and those recordings are made available to the court for examination.

In the United States, however, hearsay statements are subject to scrutiny as they are made out of court, not subject to cross-examination, and thus may not meet the court's indicia of reliability (Goodman *et al.*, 2006). The Supreme Court decision of *Crawford v Washington* (2004) has led to increased judicial pressure for children to testify live in court in advance of any video-recorded hearsay testimony (Myers, 2011). The scientific evidence, however, does not affirm the added value of live testimony (Hobbs *et al.*, 2013). Adults' capacity, including that of various professionals (*e.g.*, legal investigators, judges), to determine truthfulness in adults and children is often not much better than chance (Aamodt & Custer, 2006; Edelstein, Luten, Ekman, & Goodman, 2006; Malone & DePaulo, 2001). Further, Goodman and colleagues (2006) found that mock jurors had difficulty discriminating between accurate and deceptive statements from child witnesses regardless of live or out-of-court testimony, including videotaped and adult hearsay testimony.

Hearsay evidence may also negatively affect perceptions of child witnesses as children testifying live are generally viewed as more truthful and credible than children who testify outside of court (Goodman *et al.*, 2006; Landstrom, Granhag, & Hartwig, 2007). In an examination of potential jurors for a child sexual abuse case, McAuliff and Kovera (2012) found that jurors thought it was easier to determine child-witness truthfulness when testimony was live in the court. Although adults who relay children's testimony are perceived as more accurate than children giving live testimony (Warren, Nunez, Keeney, Buck, & Smith, 2002), the effectiveness of this hearsay testimony may depend on the status of the reporting adult witness (*e.g.*, law enforcement, doctor) (Ross, Lindsay, & Marsil, 1999). Thus, while hearsay evidence may provide a viable alternative to live testimony there are potential negative effects on the jurors' perceptions of the child witness, at least given current expectations for witnesses to testify live in court.

5.2.2   CCTV

A number of countries (*e.g.*, Australia, New Zealand, and United Kingdom) use CCTV as an interactive tool, allowing a child witness to be in a different room while attorneys and a judge are in the courtroom. Courts in the United States are able to admit one-way CCTV under limited circumstances and generally only in child sexual abuse cases (*Maryland v. Craig*, 1990).

Confronting witnesses is commonly believed to produce more accurate testimony, but research does not support this belief. In an examination of mock jurors' perceptions of child witnesses, Goodman and associates (1998) reported that 8- and 9-year-old children generally provided more accurate information than 5- to 6-year-old children in both CCTV and open court but that CCTV was associated with less suggestibility for the younger children. Other research found that mock jurors were no better at determining truthfulness when children testified live in court or through CCTV (Orcutt, Goodman, Tobey, Batterman-Faunce & Thomas, 2001).

Researchers in many countries are concerned that out of court testimony lacks the immediacy and emotional impact of live court testimony (Landstrom *et al.*, 2007; McAuliff & Kovera, 2012). For example, Orcutt and colleagues (2001) found that children testifying through CCTV were seen as less accurate, less believable, less consistent, less confident, less attractive, and less intelligent than children testifying live in court. This bias for live testimony may be part of a "vividness effect," which suggests the closer a witness is in proximity and time, the more favorably jurors will evaluate the witness (Nisbett & Ross, 1980). McAuliff and Kovera (2012) suggest that negative evaluations of out of court child witness testimony may result from expectancy violations in which jurors expect differences in children's verbal and nonverbal behaviors as a result of the accommodations, even though those differences may not actually occur.

5.3   *Support Programs*

5.3.1   Victim Witness Assistants

Victim witness assistants are usually independent advocates appointed by the court to help a child victim witness prepare for court and overcome anxiety and potential trauma of court involvement. In the United States, victim witness assistants provide child witnesses informational and emotional support (McAuliff, Nicholson, Amarilio, & Ravanshenas, 2013). Research has documented numerous benefits to child victims of having supportive adults in the courtroom (*e.g.*, Goodman *et al.*, 1992; Goodman *et al.*, 2003), and the presence of a supportive adult, usually a mother, in the courtroom during proceedings has been found to be the most influential protective factor for child witnesses (Sas, Wolfe, & Gowdey, 1996). Whereas a well-trained, warm, emotionally supportive victim witness assistant may be increasingly influential in reducing adverse outcomes for children testifying in court, preliminary research indicates that jurors may perceive child witnesses as less trustworthy when accompanied by a support person than when they are alone (Nefas, Neal, Maurice, & McAuliff, 2008).

5.3.2   Court Preparation

Courtroom experiences can provoke a great deal of anxiety for child witnesses (Goodman *et al.*, 1992). In an examination of children interviewed in a courtroom versus a private room about a past event, Nathanson and Saywitz (2003) found that children recalled less than half the amount of information in the court room as compared to in the private room. Further, children interviewed in the private room demonstrated less stress, as measured by lower heart rates, than children in the courtroom (Nathanson & Saywitz, 2003). Based in part on these findings, the Kids Court School was developed to teach children about court processes and to reduce stress associated with court appearances (McClelland Institute, 2014). Preliminary findings suggest the Kids Court School reduces children's anxiety about participating in the judicial process (Nathanson, 2014). These findings build on previous research in Canada, which reported reduced generalized and abuse-related fears for children who were prepared with deep muscle relaxation, and cognitive restructuring and empowerment, compared to another group of children that had more standard court preparation services (Sas *et al.*, 1996).

5.4   *Holistic Model*

Saywitz and Camparo (2009) propose a promising model for effectively gathering and presenting children's evidence while also protecting against potential secondary trauma. Their proposed approach to research and practice treats children holistically, not merely as witnesses or victims of crime. In this model, forensic and clinical models share a holistic agenda, including (1) eliciting reliable and sufficient information from children to make broader decisions beyond criminal prosecution, (2) addressing children's mental health needs without compromising their reports, (3) reconciling actions when forensic and clinical goals conflict, (4) promoting children's well-being and development, and (5) implementing prevention and early intervention programs for children with health, abuse, developmental and mental health needs. A holistic model has potential to build on the extensive scientific research on child witnesses by further incorporating the United Nations Convention on the Rights of the Child and its declaration of children's rights to health and well-being.

6   Future Research

Future research should focus on how well the rights granted by the Convention are being implemented. If they are not, research can be used to identify and find ways to overcome barriers. The issue may be more complicated in the United States than in other countries given our lack of ratification of the Convention. However, even in countries that have ratified the Convention, implementation is often still lacking. Ratification may be less the issue than political will and determination to make a difference for children.

For justice to be served, child victims and witnesses, like their adult counterparts, need to participate in the legal process. Due to this fact, and the fact that researchers have identified that certain components of children's legal experiences are predictive of adverse outcomes, it is imperative that interventions to reduce such outcomes continue to be developed and tested. In this regard, future research might concentrate on identifying each country's most successful approaches for children in legal proceedings and incorporating such practices into investigations and courtrooms when children provide evidence or when children's lives will be affected.

Psychological science has enormous potential for offering social services and legal systems high quality, science-based information to better the lives of children exposed to violence or who otherwise find themselves within the jurisdiction of the courts. For example, through psychological research, we can learn how best to listen to children so that they can have a meaningful voice. Although the Convention instructs countries to give children voice in all matters that affect their lives, it does not inform countries on how best to implement that mandate. Research is needed to fill that gap. Moreover, research can examine the benefits of "what could be" rather than just "what exists" or "what has been tried."

In this regard, a crucial point is that researchers and the legal system need to work together to provide researchers with access. When investigative units, social service systems, and courts appreciate the importance of proper experimental design and open their doors to researchers, the legal system can not only ensure that the goals of the Convention are met but also help fix a nonoptimal system to prevent re-traumatization of children. For the sake of our children, let's continue to work together to right this situation.

References

Aamodt, M.G., & Custer, H. (2006). Who can best catch a liar? *Forensic Examiner, 15*(1).

Back, C., Gustafsson, P.A., Larsson, I., & Berterö, C. (2011). Managing the legal proceedings: An interpretative phenomenological analysis of sexually abused children's experience with the legal process. *Child abuse & neglect, 35*(1), 50–57.

Baugerud, G.A., & Melinder, A. (2012). Maltreated children's memory of stressful removals from their biological parents. *Applied Cognitive Psychology, 26*(2), 261–270. doi:http://dx.doi.org/10.1002/acp.1817.

Birnbaum, R., & Saini, M. (2012). A qualitative synthesis of children's participation in custody disputes. *Research on Social Work Practice, 22*(4), 400–409. doi:10.1177/1049731512442985.

Block, S.D., Oran, H.S., Oran, D., Baumrind, N., & Goodman, G.S. (2010). Abused and neglected children in court: Knowledge and attitudes. *Child Abuse & Neglect, 34*, 659–670. doi:10.1016/j.chiabu.2010.02.003.

Bottoms, B.L., Najdowski, C.J., & Goodman, G.S. (Eds.) (2009). *Children as victims, witnesses, and offenders.* New York: Guilford Press.

Bowlby, J. (1980). *Attachment and loss*. New York: Basic Books.

Bretherton, I. (2000). Emotional availability: An attachment perspective. *Attachment and Human Development, 2*, 233–241.

Bronfenbrenner, U. (1989). Ecological systems theory. *Annals of Child Development, 6*, 187–249.

Brief amici curiae Family Equality Council in support of Respondents (2013). Nos. 12–144, 12–307.

Bussey, K. (2009). An international perspective on child witnesses. In B.L. Bottoms, C.J. Najdowski, & G.S. Goodman (Eds.), *Children as victims, witnesses, and offenders: Psychological science and the law* (pp. 209–232). New York: Guilford Press.

California Family Code Section 3042.

Cassidy, J., & Shaver, P.R. (Eds.) (2008). *Handbook of attachment: Theory, research, and clinical aplications,*2nd ed., New York: Guilford Press.

Cashmore, J., & Parkinson, P. (2007). Children's and parents' perceptions of children's participation in decision making after parental separation and divorce. *Family Court Review, 46*(1), 91–104. doi:10.1111/j.1744-1617.2007.00185.x.

Cicchetti, D. (2004). An odyssey of discovery: Lessons learned through three decades of research on child maltreatment. *American Psychologist, 59*(8), 731–741. doi:http://dx.doi.org/10.1037/0003-066X.59.8.731.

Connell, M. (2009). The Child Advocacy Center model. In K. Kuehnle & M. Connel (Eds.), *Critical issues in child sexual abuse assessment* (pp. 423–449). New York: Wiley.

Crawford v. Washington, 541 US 36. (2004).

Cross, T.P., Jones,. L.M., Walsh, W.A., Simone, M., & Kolko, D. (2007). Child forensic interviewing in Children's Advocacy Centers: Empirical data on a practice model. *Child Abuse & Neglect, 31,* 1031–1052.

Dozier, M., & Rutter, M. (2008). Challenges to the development of attachment relationships faced by young children in foster and adoptive care. In J. Cassidy, & P. R Shaver (Eds.) Handbook *of attachment: Theory, research, and clinical applications* (pp. 348–365), 2nd ed., New York: Guilford Press.

Edelstein, R.S., Luten, T.L., Ekman, P., & Goodman, G.S. (2006). Detecting lies in children and adults. *Law and Human Behavior, 30*, 1–10.

Evans, A.D., & Lee, K. (2010). Promising to tell the truth makes 8- to 16-year-olds more honest, *Behavioral Sciences and the Law* 28, 801–811. doi:10.1002/bsl.

Federal Rules of Evidence 801 (c) (2014). Pub L. 93–595, 88 Stat 1926.

Felitti, V.J. (2002). The relationship of adverse childhood experiences to adult health: Turning gold into lead. *The Permanente Journal, 6*, 44–47.

Finkelhor, D., Cross, T.P., & Cantor, E.N. (2005). The justice system for juvenile victims: A comprehensive model of case flow. *Trauma, Violence, & Abuse, 6*(2), 83–102.

Geiselman, R. Saywitz, K., Bornstein, G. (2013). Effects of cognitive questioning techniques on children's recall performance. Goodman, G.S. & Bottoms, B. (Eds.) Child

Victims, Child Witnesses: Understanding and Improving Testimony. New York, NY: The Guildford Press.

Gershoff, E.T. (2013). Spanking and child development: We know enough now to stop hitting our children. *Child Development Perspectives, 7*, 133–137.

Goldfarb, D.A., & Goodman, G.S. (2014). Cross-examination's big effect on the criminal system's smallest witnesses: How the judiciary can alleviate the negative effects of cross-examination. *Chronicle of the International Association of Youth and Family Judges and Magistrates.* London, UK.

Goodman, G.S. (1984). Children's testimony in historical perspective. *Journal of Social Issues, 40*(2), 9–31.

Goodman, G.S., Ghetti, S., Quas, J.A., Edelstein, R., Alexander, K., Cordon, I., & Jones, D.P.H. (2003). A prospective study of memory for child sexual abuse: New findings relevant to the repressed memory controversy. *Psychological Science, 14*, 113–118.

Goodman, G.S., Ogle, C.M., McWilliams, K., Narr, R., & Paz-Alonso, P. (2013). Memory development in the forensic context. P. Bauer & R. Fivush (Eds.), *Handbook on the development of children's memory.* New York: Wiley-Blackwell.

Goodman, G.S., Taub, E.P., Jones, D.P.H., England, P., Port, L., K., Rudy, L., & Prado, L. (1992). Testifying in criminal court: Emotional effects on child sexual assault victims. *Monographs of the Society for Research in Child Development, 57*, i, 1–159.

Goodman, G.S., Tobey, A.E., Batterman-Faunce, J.M., Orcutt, H., Thomas, S., Shapiro, C., & Sachsenmaier, T. (1998). Face-to-face confrontation: Effects of closed-circuit technology on children's eyewitness testimony and jurors' decisions. *Law and Human Behavior, 22*(2), 165.

Goodman, G.S., Myers, J.E.B., Qin, J., Quas, J.A., Castelli, P., Redlich, A.D., & Rogers, L. (2006). Hearsay versus children's testimony: Effects of truthful and deceptive statements on jurors' decisions. *Law and Human Behavior, 30*, 363–401. doi:10.1007/s10979-006-9009-0.

Halfon, N., Mendonca, A., & Berkowitz, G. (1995). Health status of children in foster care. *Archives of Pediatric and Adolescent Medicine, 149*, 386–392.

Hall, S.R., & Sales, B.D. (2008). *Courtroom modification for child witnesses.* Washington, DC: American Psychological Association. doi: http://dx.doi.org/10.1037/11808-000.

Henry, J. (1997). System intervention trauma to child sexual abuse victims following disclosure. *Journal of Interpersonal Violence, 12*(4), 499–512. Retrieved from http://search.proquest.com/docview/619113960?accountid=14505.

Hobbs, S.D., Goodman, G.S., Block, S.D., Oran, D., Quas, J.A., Park, A., ... Baumrind, N. (2014). Child maltreatment victims' attitudes about appearing in dependency and criminal courts. *Children and Youth Services Review, 44*, 407–416. doi:10.1016/j.childyouth.2014.07.001.

Hobbs, S.D., Johnson, J.L., Goodman, G.S., Bederian-Gardner, D., Lawler, M.J., Vargas, I.D., & Mendoza, M. (2013). Evaluating eyewitness testimony in children.

In I.B. Weiner & R.K. Otto (Eds.). *The handbook of forensic psychology* (4th ed.) (pp. 561–612). Hoboken, NJ: Wiley.

Hollingsworth v. Perry, 133 S. Ct. 2652 (2013).

Hollingsworth v. Perry, Nos. 12–144, 12–307 (2013). United States Supreme Court Oral Argument Transcript.

Jackson, S.L. (2012). Results from the Virginia Multidisciplinary Team Knowledge and Functioning Survey: The importance of differentiating by groups affiliated with a child advocacy center. *Children and Youth Services Review, 34,* 1243–1250. doi:10.1016/j.childyouth.2012.02.015.

Johnson, J., Shelley, A.E., Goodman-Shaver, L., & Goodman, G.S. (2013, March). *Adults' perceptions of child victims interviewed at Child Advocacy Centers.* American Psychology-Law Society Convention, Portland, OR.

Jones, L.M., Cross, T.P., Walsh, W.A., & Simone, M. (2007). Do children's advocacy centers improve families' experiences of child sexual abuse investigations? *Child Abuse & Neglect, 31,* 1069–1085. doi:10.1016/j.chiabu.2007.04.006.

Jones, D.P.H., & Krugman, R.D. (1986). Can a three-year-old child bear witness to her sexual assault and attempted murder? *Child Abuse & Neglect, 10*(2), 253–258.

Juffer, F., & van IJzendoorn, M.H. (2005). Behavior problems and mental health referrals in international adoptees: A meta-analysis. *JAMA – The Journal of the American Medical Association, 292,* 2501–2515.

Klemfuss, J.Z., & Ceci, S.J. (2012). Legal and psychological perspectives on children's competence to testify in court. *Developmental Review, 32*(3), 268–286. doi:10.1016/j.dr.2012.06.005.

Lamb, M.E., Hershkowitz, I., Orbach, Y., & Esplin, P. (2008). *Tell me what happened.* New York: Wiley.

Lamb, M.E., Orbach, Y., Sternberg, K.J., Hershkowitz, I., & Horowitz, D. (2000). Accuracy of investigators' verbatim notes of their forensic interviews with alleged child abuse victims. *Law and Human Behavior, 24,* 699–708. Retrieved from http://www.ncbi.nlm.nih.gov/pubmed/11105480.

Landstrom, S., Granhag, P.A., & Hartwig, M. (2007). Children's live and videotaped testimonies: How presentation mode affects observers' perception, assessment and memory. *Legal and Criminological Psychology, 12,* 333–347. doi:10.1348/135532506X133607.

Lawler, M.J., Bederian-Gardner, D., & Goodman, G.S. (2013). Conclusions and next steps for researchers and practitioners. In R. Holliday & T. Marche (Eds.), *Child forensic psychology* (pp. 273–286). Hampshire, UK: Palgrave-Macmillan.

Lawler, M.J., Shaver, P.R., & Goodman, G.S. (2011). Toward relationship-based child welfare services. *Children and Youth Services Review, 33,* 473–480.

Lawler, M.J., & Talbot, E. (2012). Child abuse. In V. Ramachandran (Ed.), *Encyclopedia of Human Behavior* (pp. 460–466). London: Academic Press.

Lecklitner, G.L., Malik, N.M., Aaron, S.M., & Lederman, C.S. (1999). Promoting safety for abused children and battered mothers: Miami-Dade County's model dependency court intervention program. *Child Maltreatment, 4*(2), 175–182. Retrieved from http://search.proquest.com/docview/619404394?accountid=14505.

Liang, B., Williams, L.M., & Siegel, J.A. (2006). Relational outcomes of childhood sexual trauma in female survivors a longitudinal study. *Journal of Interpersonal Violence, 21*(1), 42–57.

Lyon, T.D. (2005). *The Ten-Step Investigative Interview.* http://works.bepress.com/cgi/viewcontent.cgi?article=1004&context=thomaslyon.

Lyon, T.D. (2011). Assessing the competency of child witnesses: Best practice informed by psychology and law. In M.E. Lamb, D. La Rooy, L.C. Malloy, & C. Katz (Eds.), Children's testimony: A handbook of psychological research and forensic practice (pp. 69–85). Sussex, UK: Wiley-Blackwell.

Lyon, T.D., & Evans, A.D. (2014). Young children's understanding that promising guarantees performance: The effects of age and maltreatment. *Law and Human Behavior, 38*(2), 162–70. doi:10.1037/lhb0000061.

Lyon, T.D., Quas, J.A, & Carrick, N. (2013). Right and righteous: Children's incipient understanding and evaluation of true and false statements. *Journal of Cognition and Development, 14*(3), 437–454. doi:10.1080/15248372.2012.673187.

Malloy, L., Johnson, J., & Goodman, G.S. (2013). Children's memory and event reports: The current state of knowledge and best practice. *Journal of Forensic Social Work, 3*, 1–30.

Malloy, L.C., & Lyon, T.D. (2006). Caregiver support and child sexual abuse: Why does it matter? *Journal of child sexual abuse, 15*(4), 97–103.

Malloy, L.C., Lyon, T.D., & Quas, J.A. (2007). Filial dependency and recantation of child sexual abuse allegations. *Journal of the American Academy of Child & Adolescent Psychiatry, 46*(2), 162–170.

Malone, B.E., & DePaulo, B.M. (2001). Measuring sensitivity to deception. In J.A. Hall & F.J. Bernieri (Eds.), *Interpersonal Sensitivity* (pp. 103–124). Mahwah, NJ: Erlbaum.

Maryland v. Craig, 497 U.S. 836. (1990).

McAuliff, B.D., & Kovera, M.B. (2012). Do jurors' get what they expect? *Psychology, Crime & Law, 18*, 27–47. doi:http://dx.doi.org/10.1080/1068316X.2011.613391.

McAuliff, B.D., Nicholson, E., Amarilio, D., & Ravanshenas, D. (2013). Supporting children in U.S. legal proceedings: Descriptive and attitudinal data from a national survey of victim/witness assistants. *Psychology, Public Policy, and Law, 19*, 98–113.

McClelland Institute (2014). http://mcclellandinstitute.arizona.edu/kids-court-school.

McWilliams, K., Goodman, G.S., Lyons, K.E., Newton, J., & Avila-Mora, E. (2014). Memory for child sexual abuse information: Simulated memory error and individual differences. *Memory & Cognition, 42*, 151–163.

McWilliams, K., Narr, R., Goodman, G.S., Ruiz, S., & Mendoza, M. (2013). Children's memory for their mother's murder: accuracy, suggestibility, and resistance to suggestion. *Memory, 21*(5), 591–598.

Myers, J.E.B. (2011). *Myers on evidence of interpersonal violence: Child maltreatment, intimate partner violence, rape, stalking, and elder abuse cases.* Alphen aan den Rijn, Netherlands: Wolters Kluwer Law and Business.

Nathanson, R. (2014). *Supporting children in legal contexts: The effects of a court education program on court-related stress.* Paper presented at the American Psychology-Law Society Meetings, New Orleans, LA.

Nathanson, R., & Saywitz, K. (2003). The effects of the courtroom context on children's memory and anxiety. *Journal of Psychiatry & Law, 31,* 67–98.

Nefas, C., Neal., E., Maurice, K., & McAuliff, B.D. (2008, March). Support person use and child victim testimony: Believe it or not. Paper presented at the Annual meeting of the American Psychology-Law Society, Jacksonville, FL.

New York City Chancellor's Regulation A-443.

New York City School-Justice Partnership Task Force Report and Recommendations (2013), reviewed at http://www.advocatesforchildren.org/sites/default/files/library/sjptf_report.pdf?pt=1.

Newland, L.A., Giger, J.T., Lawler, M. J., Carr, E.R., Dykstra, E. A., & Roh, S. (in press). Subjective well-being for children in a rural community. *Journal of Social Service Research.*

Newman, B.S., Dannenfelser, P.L., & Pendleton, D. (2005). Child abuse investigations: Reasons for using child advocacy centers and suggestions for improvement. *Child and Adolescent Social Work Journal, 22,* 165–180. doi:http://dx.doi.org/10.1007/s10560-005-3416-9.

Nisbett, R., & Ross, L. (1980). *Human inference: Strategies and shortcomings of social judgments.* Englewood Cliffs, NJ: Prentice Hall.

Orcutt, H.K., Goodman, G.S., Tobey, A.E., Batterman-Faunce, J.M., & Thomas, S.F. (2001). Detecting deception in children's testimony: Factfinders' abilities to reach the truth in open court and closed-circuit trials. *Law and Human Behavior, 25,* 339–372. doi:10.1023/A:1010603618330.

Pickar, D.B., & Kahn, J.J. (2011). Settlement-focused parenting plan consultations: An evaluative mediation alternative to child custody evaluations. *Family Court Review, 49*(1), 59–71. doi:10.1111/j.1744-1617.2010.01353.x.

Price, D.W., & Goodman, G.S. (1990). Visiting the wizard: Children's memory for a recurring event. *Child Development, 61*(3), 664–680.

Quas, J.A., Cooper, A., & Wandrey, L. (2009a). Child victims in dependency court. In B.L. Bottoms, G.S. Goodman, C. Nadjowski (Eds.), *Child victims, child offenders: Psychology and law.* Mahwah, NJ: Erlbaum.

Quas, J.A., & Goodman, G.S. (2012). Consequences of criminal court involvement for child victims. *Psychology, Public Policy, and Law, 18*(3), 392.

Quas, J.A., Goodman, G.S., Ghetti, S., Alexander, K.W., Edelstein, R.S., Redlich, A.D., Cordon, I.M., *et al.* (2005). Childhood sexual assault victims: Long-term outcomes after testifying in criminal court. *Monographs of the Society for Research in Child Development, 70*, vii, 1–117. doi:10.1016/j.soncn.2011.11.001.

Quas, J.A., Wallin, A.R., Horwitz, B., Davis, E., & Lyon, T. (2009b). Maltreated children's knowledge of and emotional reactions to dependency court involvement. *Behavioral Sciences and the Law, 27*, 97–117.

Ross, D.F., Lindsay, R.C.L., & Marsil, D.F. (1999). The impact of hearsay testimony on conviction rates in trials of child sexual abuse: Toward balancing the rights of defendants and child witnesses. *Psychology, Public Policy, and Law, 5*, 439–455. doi:http://dx.doi.org/10.1037/1076-8971.5.2.439.

Runyan, D.K., Everson, M.D., Edelsohn, G.A., Hunter, W.M., & Coulter, M.L. (1988). Impact of legal intervention on sexually abused children. *Journal of Pediatrics, 113*, 647–653.

Sas, L. (1997). Sexually abused children as witnesses: Progress and pitfalls. (pp. 248–267) Sage Publications, Inc, Thousand Oaks, CA.

Sas, L.D., Wolfe, D.A., & Gowdey, K. (1996). Children in the courts in Canada. *Criminal Justice and Behavior, 23*, 338–357.

Saywitz, K.J., & Camparo, L.B. (2014). *Evidence-based child forensic interviewing: The developmental narrative elaboration interview: Interviewer guide* Oxford University Press, New York. Retrieved from http://search.proquest.com/docview/1442382384?a ccountid=14505.

Saywitz, K.J., & Camparo, L.B. (2009). Contemporary child forensic interviewing. In B. L Bottoms, C . Najdowski, & G.S. Goodman (Eds.), *Children as victims, witnesses, and offenders* (pp. 102–127). New York: Guildford.

Saywitz, K., Camparo, L.B., & Romanoff, A. (2010). Interviewing children in custody cases: Implications of research and policy for practice. *Behavioral Sciences and the Law, 28*, 542–562. doi:10.1002/bsl.

Saywitz, K.J., Goodman, G.S., Nicholas, E., & Moan, S.F. (1991). Children's memories of a physical examination involving genital touch: Implications for reports of child sexual abuse. *Journal of Consulting and Clinical Psychology, 59*(5), 682–691. doi:http://dx.doi.org/10.1037/0022-006X.59.5.682.

Saywitz, K.J., & Nathanson, R. (1993). Children's testimony and their perceptions of stress in and out of the courtroom. *Child Abuse & Neglect, 17*(5), 613–622.

Stroud, D.D. Martens, S., & Barker, J. (2000). Criminal investigation of child sexual abuse: A comparison of cases referred to the prosecutor to those not referred. *Child Abuse and Neglect, 24*, 689–700.

Talwar, V., & Crossman, A.M. (2012). Children's lies and their detection: Implications for child witness testimony. *Developmental Review, 32*(4), 337–359. doi:10.1016/j.dr.2012.06.004.

Tedesco, J.F., & Schnell, S.V. (1987). Children's reactions to sex abuse investigation and litigation. *Child Abuse & Neglect, 2*, 267–272.

Texas Family Code Section 153.009.

Troxel, N.R., Ogle, C.M., Cordon, I.M., Lawler, M.J., & Goodman, G.S. (2009). Child witnesses in criminal court. In B.L. Bottoms, C.J. Najdowski, & G.S. Goodman (Eds.), *Children as victims, witnesses, and offenders* (pp. 150–166). New York: Guilford Press.

United Nations General Assembly, *Convention on the Rights of the Child*, Nov. 20 1989, United Nations, Treaty Series, vol. 1577, p. 3, available at: http://www.refworld.org/docid/3ae6b38fo.html [accessed 20 April 2014].

Van IJzendoorn, M.H., & Sagi-Schwartz, A. (2008). Cross-Cultural patterns of attachment: Universal and contextual dimensions. In J. Cassidy, & P.R. Shaver (Eds.) Handbook *of attachment: Theory, research, and clinical applications* (pp. 880–905), 2nd ed., New York: Guilford Press.

Vermont Statutes Annotated 15 Section 594.

Walsh, W.A., Lippert, T., Cross, T.P., Maurice, D.M., & Davison, K.S. (2008). How long to prosecute child sexual abuse for a community using a Children's Advocacy Center and two comparison communities? *Child Maltreatment, 13*, 3–13. doi:10.1177/1077559507307839.

Wandrey, L., Quas, J.A., & Lyon, T.D. (2012). Does valence matter? Effects of negativity on children's early understanding of the truth and lies. *Journal of Experimental Child Psychology, 113*, 295–303.

Warren, A.R., Nuñez, N., Keeney, J.M., Buck, J.A., & Smith, B. (2002). The believability of children and their interviewers' hearsay testimony: When less is more. *Journal of Applied Psychology, 87*, 846–857.

Weisz, V., Wingrove, T., Beal, S.J., & Faith-Slaker, A. (2011). Children's participation in foster care hearings. *Child Abuse & Neglect, 35*, 267–272.

Whitcomb, S., Runyan, D.K., DeVos, E., Hunter, W.M., Cross, T.P., Everson, M.D., *et al.* (1991). *Child victims as witnesses: Research and development program* (Final report to the Office of Juvenile Justice and Delinquency Prevention). Washington, D.C.

Yuille, J.C., Hunter, R., Joffe, R., & Zaparniuk, J. (1993). Interviewing children in sexual abuse cases. In G.S. Goodman & B.L. Bottoms (Eds.), *Child victims. child witnesses* (pp. 95–115). New York: Guilford Press.

Zajac, R., O'Neill, S., & Hayne, H. (2012). Disorder in the courtroom? Child witnesses under cross-examination. *Developmental Review, 32*(3), 181–204.

750 Illinois Compiled States 30 (Emancipation of Minors Act).

Child-sensitive Justice for Children of Imprisoned Parents

Adele D. Jones[1] and Alex Hirschfield[2]

Children of Prisoners

Worldwide, unprecedented numbers of people are being imprisoned and in many countries incarceration is on the increase (Walmsley, 2009). Indeed "more parents than ever are behind bars" (Murray *et al.*, 2012). Despite this, the psychosocial impact on children is little recognized. A meta-analysis of studies of children of prisoners synthesized empirical evidence on the associations between parental incarceration and children's later behavioural, educational and health outcomes from 40 studies involving a total of over 7,000 children of prisoners. The report of the findings states:

> Children with incarcerated parents have been referred to as the "forgotten victims" of crime..., the "orphans of justice"...and the "unseen victims of the prison boom"... They can experience multiple emotional and social difficulties during their parent's incarceration, which may develop into a range of adjustment problems in the long term.
>
> MURRAY ET AL., 2012, p. 2

A UK study of 411 boys who had experienced parental imprisonment before the age of 10 years reported double the risk for antisocial behaviour and poor mental health in adulthood even controlling for other childhood risk factors (Murray & Farrington, 2005, 2008a, 2008b), while a longitudinal study of young people in the United States found that imprisonment of mothers led to increased risks of criminal behaviour in adulthood for their children (Huebner & Gustafson, 2007; Hissel, Bijleveld, & Kruttschnitt 2011). For some children who experience these adverse outcomes, the pre-conditions were set long before, with substance misuse, domestic violence, longstanding criminogenic behaviour, poverty and social exclusion providing the backdrop to parental imprisonment in many cases (Kinner *et al.*, 2007).

This fact does not lessen the need for action, even in cases where imprisonment provides a child with some respite from these problems, for what is

---

1 Lead author.
2 Co-author.

becoming clear is that the accumulative effects of adversity are often compounded for children when their parent is imprisoned. Almost two decades ago, research by Richards and McWilliams (1996) showed that children are frequently distressed, disturbed and confused, as well as financially disadvantaged, particularly by a father's imprisonment while Philbrick (2002) found that children may suffer stigma, confusion, anger and deterioration in health, often regressing in behaviour or falling behind with their school attendance and school work. In exploring the link between parental imprisonment and children's behaviour and mental health, Murray, Farrington, Sekol and Olsen, (2009) carried out a systematic review of 16 studies and concluded:

> Theory and qualitative research suggest that parental imprisonment might contribute to child antisocial behaviour and mental health problems, because of the trauma of separation, strained child-care arrangements during parental imprisonment, loss of family income, other stressful life events such as moving home and school, and the stigma of parental imprisonment (p. 8).

For children separated from a mother because of imprisonment, the difficulties can be particularly challenging especially where the mother is the primary or sole care giver (Huebner & Gustafson, 2007).

From our review of the literature, it seems that children of prisoners can be categorized in three inter-related ways.

a   Invisible
Several reasons attest to this: statistics on children of prisoners are rarely gathered in any jurisdiction; most governments have yet to recognize that imprisonment may have adverse effects on children, so their needs are not officially recognized; stigma forces children to keep the imprisonment a secret; children's rights (CRC) are subsumed by the greater powers of the criminal justice system in most countries and this means that the specific ways in which the rights of children of prisoners can be undermined go unnoticed.

b   Marginalized
Children of prisoners are likely to face the same experiences of social exclusion that may have impacted their imprisoned parent such as poverty, alcohol and drug misuse, domestic violence, immigration restrictions, racial and ethnic discrimination (non-national children and those from ethnic minorities experience greater levels of social exclusion than other children and in many EU

countries, disproportionate numbers of adults (parents) from these populations are imprisoned).

c   *Vulnerable*
Children of prisoners are vulnerable because they are children – their developmental needs and social, emotional and economic dependence on parents may be similar to other children but the opportunity for needs to be met by parents is often undermined because of imprisonment. Although other caregivers often step in to meet children's physical needs, insecure attachment and loss due to parental imprisonment can continue to impact a child's well-being. The UN has given formal recognition to children of prisoners as one of the world's most vulnerable groups of children (UN Committee on the Rights of the Child, 2011). However, governments have yet to follow suit.

The Study

The COPING Project (Children of Prisoners, Interventions and Mitigations to Strengthen Mental Health) was established against this background. Funded by the European Union (Seventh Framework Programme, Mental Health Theme), the study (2010–2013), aimed to address deficiencies in knowledge by conducting research on the mental health needs and resilience of children of prisoners and the most promising policy and intervention responses in four countries: England, Germany, Romania and Sweden, reflecting a spectrum of different socio-cultural contexts, incarceration levels, penal systems, welfare policies and services. Led by Professor Adele Jones (University of Huddersfield, UK), the project was implemented by a consortium comprising six non-governmental organizations (NGOs) and four research institutions in England, (the University of Huddersfield and Partners of Prisoners and Families Support Group), France (Eurochips – now COPE [Children of Prisoners Europe]), Germany (Technische Universitaet Dresden and Treffpunkt e.V.), Romania (Universitatea Alexandru Ioan Cuza and Asociatia Alternative Sociale), Sweden (the Karolinska Institutet and Riksbryggan) and Switzerland (Quaker United Nations Office, Geneva).

What is distinctive about COPING is that it adopted an explicitly child-centred approach from the outset and examined some of the more subtle dimensions of parental imprisonment, including children's experiences of parental arrest and sentencing, stigma and social isolation as well as the family dynamics before, during and after parental imprisonment and the impact of these factors from the child's perspective. Utilizing mixed-methods, multi-sequential design, the study gathered evidence from around 1500 children, care-givers, imprisoned parents and stakeholders across the four EU countries studied.

The research strategy placed a clear emphasis on knowledge obtained directly from children and young people. A self-reporting survey utilizing four scientifically validated instruments including the Strengths and Difficulties Questionnaire (Goodman, 1997) and the Rosenberg Self-Esteem Scale (Rosenberg, 1965) was translated into relevant languages and administered to over 730 children, aged 7–17 and parent/carers across the four countries in order to ascertain coping strategies and mental health problems for the children surveyed.

The results of the questionnaires were compared with normative population samples for each country and further purposive sampling was carried out to identify a representative cohort of children and parents for in-depth interviews. A total of 349 in-depth interviews with children and families (161 children, 123 non-imprisoned parent/carers and 65 imprisoned parent/carers) were conducted across the four countries. In addition, simultaneously stakeholder consultations were carried out with 122 professionals/groups and a systematic mapping of interventions and services undertaken. An evaluation of fit between data on children's needs and services available concluded the field work.

Findings

The study shows that children with a parent in prison are at significantly greater risk of mental health problems than their peers in the general population. For example, at least 25% of children aged 11+ years in all four countries were identified as potentially at "high" risk of mental health problems. Children seemed at particular risk of internalizing difficulties (emotional problems), rather than externalizing problems (hyperactivity and conduct problems). The study was limited in that it was not able to control for pre-existing, confounding and mediating variables and it is therefore not possible to conclude that parental incarceration is of itself, a causal factor in children's poor mental health, nevertheless the findings support the argument that this group of children are particularly vulnerable.

Other adverse effects concerned stigma, increased financial hardship, family disruption, education, emotional and behavioural challenges. With regard to children's resilience, key factors identified were: children's innate qualities; stability of care giving, open communication with children (children informed about parental absence and able to talk about their concerns) and, the importance of sustaining and maintaining relationships with the imprisoned parent. The quality of the parents' relationship with the child prior to imprisonment was also underlined.

Despite overall deficiencies in services, the study found a wide range of good practice examples by NGOs supporting children of prisoners and their families across the four countries. The project also identified a number of important areas for future research, including: the role of grandparents in supporting children; Sweden's relatively liberal prisons' privacy policy, and its implications for other countries; the role and contribution of NGOs in supporting children of prisoners; the differential impact of paternal and maternal imprisonment on boys and on girls and, further exploration of the relative contributions of parental imprisonment and environmental factors on children's development and mental health. The main findings of COPING are summarized as follows:

1. Children with imprisoned parents as a group are at a significantly greater risk of suffering mental health difficulties than children who do not have parents in prison.
2. Key factors relating to children's resilience include: children's innate qualities; the importance of stability provided by care giving parents; the importance of sustaining and maintaining relationships with the imprisoned parent and the quality of the parents' relationship with the child prior to imprisonment. Support from other extended family members is also significant.
3. Children missed fathers in prison as much as mothers.
4. Children's resilience is closely linked to open communication systems, and opportunities for children to discuss their feelings and experiences.
5. Schools have a major role in contributing to the emotional well-being of children of prisoners.
6. Children suffer significantly from stigma.
7. Maintaining contact with the imprisoned parent is in most instances beneficial to children's mental health and well-being. Positive environments are needed for children's visits to prisons, and the importance of telephone contact was underlined.
8. While a range of services and interventions exist, these are not often targeted towards the needs of children of prisoners; services are patchy, uncoordinated and accessible by only a relatively small number of children. Nevertheless COPING found examples of good practice supporting children of prisoners and their families developed by NGOs across the four countries.

The findings showed that children's resilience is enhanced when a children's rights approach is taken into account when considering their needs; this applies to considerations within the family, within schools, within the organizations and government departments that provide services to families and, within the criminal justice system. Within families, this means that children (depending upon age and level of understanding) should be given information that is age appropriate and truthful and that they have opportunities to discuss their feelings and fears. Within schools, this means that teachers are made aware of the impact of imprisonment on children's education and development and build in non-stigmatizing ways of providing support to affected children. Within organizations, this means giving recognition to children of prisoners' vulnerability and invisibility and providing services that address their specific needs.

The recommendations from COPING centred on eight broad themes: family relationships, resilience, stigma and bullying, honesty and communication, schools, experience of the criminal justice system, contact with imprisoned parent, services and interventions. For the purposes of this paper, only those themes that are central to the establishment of child-sensitive justice approaches are presented. For the full range of recommendations see Jones *et al. "Children of Prisoners: Interventions and Mitigations to Strengthen Mental Health,"* (2013, 105920/cop.hud.2013).

Towards a Child-sensitive Justice Approach

In 2010, the Council of Europe adopted Guidelines on child-friendly justice which it defines as follows:

> Child-friendly justice refers to justice systems which guarantee the respect and the effective implementation of all children's rights at the highest attainable level...giving due consideration to the child's level of maturity and understanding and the circumstances of the case. It is, in particular, justice that is accessible, age appropriate, speedy, diligent, adapted to and focused on the needs and rights of the child, respecting the rights of the child including the rights to due process, to participate in and to understand the proceedings, to respect for private and family life and to integrity and dignity.
>
> Council of Europe, 2010, p.3

The guidelines are intended to improve children's access to and treatment within criminal justice systems and while the importance of adopting a child-friendly approach to proceedings in which children *themselves* are the primary focus cannot be overstated, the COPING research calls for the concept of child-friendly justice to be expanded in an entirely new direction: in criminal proceedings concerning *adults* who are parents. We acknowledge that the term "child-friendly" justice may not be appropriate for systems which centre on adult crime and our call is for the adoption of *a child-sensitive justice approach*. This wider concept incorporates the notion of child-friendly proceedings but goes further and argues the need for consideration of children's rights in all types of criminal proceedings in which children may be impacted whether they are involved directly or indirectly and whether the primary focus of the proceedings is a child or an adult. The specific recommendations concerning children of prisoners are as follows.

1   *Child-sensitive Justice Approach*

The evidence suggests that the welfare of the child may not be given sufficient priority by the police and criminal justice agencies. For example, prior to a parent going to prison, the attitude, behaviour and language used by the police in searching a home and making an arrest, can have a profound impact on the psychological and physical well-being of a child witnessing such events. Examples of practices that are distressing to a child include police wielding guns, doors being broken down during forced entries, drawers being spilled, teddy bears being cut open to look for drugs. The information provided concerning the arrest and how this is communicated, the proximity of the child to the parent within the home at the point of arrest and the use of handcuffs in sight of the child can all have an impact.

The UN Convention on the Rights of the Child is clear in emphasizing the right of children to be heard and to express opinions. Article 12 emphasizes the right of every child to say what they think in all matters affecting them, and to have their views taken seriously, and crucially, this includes what takes place in judicial proceedings. However, criminal justice systems across the EU provide few opportunities for children to contribute to a decision-making process, despite the fact that the judicial outcomes can have a profound effect upon the child's future. This is particularly pertinent to children whose parent is at risk of a custodial sentence and whose residence and care arrangements may be significantly altered as a result. Whilst there will always be cases in which the only appropriate sentence is one of custody, in cases when there is a choice between a custodial sentence and an alternative to prison, the impact on the child should be taken into consideration, particularly where the parent at risk of custody is the child's primary caregiver.

1.1   All governments and/or State bodies should review their arrest and search policies and procedures in accordance with the UN Convention on the Rights of the Child (CRC) giving due consideration to manner of an arrest, the delivery of a timely, age-appropriate explanation to the child at the point of arrest and the means by which the child and their family access support during and subsequent to an arrest.

1.2   All EU Member States should legislate to ensure that courts take the child's best interest into account at the time of sentencing and in decisions on imprisonment. When it falls to the courts to decide the location of imprisonment, this decision should take into account the proximity of the child's place of residence to the prison.

1.3   Consideration should be given to the adoption of Child Impact Assessments prior to sentence. The assessment should consider the status of the offender in relation to the child i.e. sole or joint carer, the current location of the child and the likely residency arrangements for the child following a custodial sentence. Where possible impact statements should consider Article 12 of the UN Convention on the Rights of the Child which stipulates that "States Parties shall assure to the child who is capable of forming his or her own views the right to express those views freely in all matters affecting the child" and that the child should be given the opportunity to be heard in "any judicial and administrative proceedings affecting the child, either directly, or through a representative or an appropriate body, in a manner consistent with the procedural rules of national law."

2   *Maintaining Contact with the Parent in Prison*

COPING's research suggests that for most children, regular contact with the imprisoned parent and maintaining the child–parent relationship was crucial for their emotional well-being and capacity for resilience. The right of a child to stay in contact with both parents is clearly stated in the Convention on the Rights of the Child. To enable a positive relationship to be maintained between a child and his/her imprisoned parent, it is also essential that the child's needs are not subordinated to the prison routine. In general, visits were less intimidating for children in lower security prisons which were more conducive to quality interaction between children and their imprisoned parent. Searches on entering prison can be daunting for children at first although the findings from COPING indicate that when handled sensitively searches do not need to be experienced as personally threatening or invasive and that children become accustomed to the procedures over time.

A balance should also be struck between the need for security in prisons (which we acknowledge is a top priority) and a child's right to maintain contact with the parent when this is in the child's best interest. In some circumstances the child's best interests might be served by not visiting (*e.g.* where relationships between the child and parent are strained, where the sentence is for an offence against the child [or any child] or doing so less frequently or by using phone calls or letters to keep in touch as an alternative. However, where direct contact is in the best interests of the child this should happen early and, if possible, within the first week of the parent going to prison.

2.1   Visits should be seen as the right of the child rather than as a privilege for good behaviour on the part of the offender.

2.2   Children should have the same right to maintain contact with an imprisoned parent who is on remand as to a parent serving a prison sentence following conviction.

2.3   Visitors should be informed about the purpose of searches.

2.4   Search procedures for visitors to a prison should be carried out in a manner which causes minimum distress to children and families.

2.5   Governments should ensure that children can visit an imprisoned parent within the first week following incarceration. This applies to both imprisonment on remand and following sentencing.

2.6   All prison security and administrative measures should be made compatible with the child's well-being and the child's right to maintain contact with an imprisoned parent. Whilst recognizing the need for heightened security in many cases, these measures must be reconciled with a child's right to maintain contact, when this is in their best interest.

2.7   Where feasible, children should be given the opportunity, on their first visit, to tour the prison, be provided with information about prison procedures and have the chance to ask questions.

3   *Promoting Continuous Quality Contact with Imprisoned Parent*

Once established, it is particularly important that quality contact is maintained between the imprisoned parent and the child both directly (face to face) and indirectly by different methods of communication.

3.1   In order to promote quality interaction between children and their imprisoned parent, prisons should provide, at least to minimum standards, welcoming and comfortable visiting environments, and ensure that security restrictions on visits, including but not limited to those on physical interaction, are kept to a bare minimum.

3.2   All prisons in all EU Member States should provide age-appropriate activities that both occupy children during visits and foster interaction between children and their imprisoned parent. Child-friendly prison-based schemes should be offered to every child visiting an imprisoned parent.

3.3   The prison and probation services should ensure that they (or an NGO) provide facilities for children to visit or visitor centres at or near the prison. This should involve easy booking procedures, information to families prior to the visit (to ensure it is best for the child) and support to child and parent/caregiver prior to and after the visit.

3.4   Prison authorities in all EU Member States should ensure that all prison staff behave in a respectful, child-friendly manner when dealing with families. Education and training modules for prison staff should introduce the child's perspective and provide guidance on how best to welcome and accompany children and families.

3.5   Consideration of the journey time for families should be taken into account by prison authorities in housing prisoners, and financial aid provided for travelling offered where necessary (as in UK).

3.6   Prisoners should be able to both make affordable outgoing telephone calls, and receive incoming calls from their family in their own language.

3.7   Modern forms of technology that permit two-way communication between prisoners and their families and facilitate quick response times should be piloted in prisons and adopted where possible.

3.8   Where it is in the child's best interests, home leave should be considered and offered to prisoners.

4   *Advice and Support to Parents, Care Givers & Children*

COPING found that children's resilience is closely related to sharing information with them openly and honestly about what has happened and the reasons for their parent's imprisonment, consistent with their age and maturity. Children of prisoners can be or feel very isolated because they do not want to tell others about their situation or having done so, lose friends, or face stigmatisation or bullying. There is real benefit in providing support and events specifically for children of prisoners to enable them to engage with peers in positive activities without having to hide their parent's imprisonment.

4.1   Parents and caregivers should be offered guidance from mental health and social welfare professionals, on what and how to tell the children in extreme cases, taking account of the child's age, individual personality and developmental stage.

4.2   The care-giving parent and the imprisoned parent should share responsibility for providing information from the start of the process to its eventual conclusion; decisions about how much children should be told should be reached in the best interests of the children (not those of parents).

4.3   Parents/caregivers and imprisoned parents should carefully consider sharing information about parental imprisonment with their children's school and wherever possible communicate this information so that schools can provide children with the support they need.

5   *Promote NGO's Role in Supporting Children and Families of Prisoners*

There was evidence that some families of prisoners were unaware of organizations specifically designed to support them. These families reported that they would have welcomed the opportunity to receive support, particularly regarding what to expect when visiting prison. Much more can be done by the police and the prisons to tell families where to find support but the NGOs need to ensure that criminal justice agencies are fully aware of their services so that they can refer families to them.

5.1   The valued role of NGOs in providing services to children and families impacted by imprisonment should be recognized by national governments.

5.2   NGOs should ensure that their support services are effectively advertized to potential service users and other relevant personnel involved in the entire criminal justice system process- from arrest to resettlement- to increase awareness of and accessibility to these services.

5.3   Criminal justice agencies should be aware of the particular needs of children with imprisoned parents and commit to publicizing information for them at all stages of the criminal justice process.

5.4   Protocols with the police service should be developed so that when a parent is arrested, the police inform the family (carer and child) about where to find support.

5.5   Prisons should ensure that standardized letters advertising the services provided for children and families of prisoners are sent to families of prisoners.

5.6   NGOs and support agencies not currently working in this area should be encouraged to expand their role to include support for families of prisoners and run activities specifically for children of prisoners.

6   *Promote the Parenting Role of the Imprisoned Parent*

COPING recognizes the potential role of the imprisoned parent as active agent in promoting children's welfare. Encouraging imprisoned parents to contribute to their children's daily lives can be problematic because they might not appreciate how hard it is for their children to deal with their imprisonment; they might not realize just how important they are in promoting their child's welfare and they may fail to see how they can possibly carry out their role as a parent from prison. Imprisoned parents need to have their awareness raised about the importance of their role, the effects on the child of the imprisonment, difficulties their children may face concerning the nature of the crime and the ways in which they can help their children.

6.1   Imprisoned parents should be offered opportunities to contribute to their children's daily lives, including being involved in their children's schooling, when feasible.

6.2   Parenting groups, workshops and other forums for sharing experience and receiving support as a parent should be widely available in prison to help them carry out their parenting role.

7   *Public Awareness and Policy Recognition*

Despite the significant numbers of children affected by parental imprisonment (estimated to be over 800,000 across the EU) support initiatives for children of prisoners in EU Member States is patchy, inadequate or lacking altogether. A major precondition to changing this is to raise the needs of children of prisoners higher up the policy agenda at both EU and national level through getting them recognized as a vulnerable group whose needs should be met regardless of the crimes committed by their parent. Whilst all States are parties to the UN Convention on the Rights of the Child there is a need for this Convention to be more closely harmonized with all areas of national law so that children have a stronger legal protection of their rights. This may help to move the focus from one concerned only with the punishment of the prisoner to one which addresses the often forgotten existence of their rights-bearing children.

7.1   An EU Framework be established for national support initiatives for children of prisoners. This Framework should define common objectives, including improving the information base about the numbers and needs of children of prisoners and the development of cross-agency support initiatives to meet these needs, to be translated into national policies according to the principle of subsidiary.

7.2   The Framework should establish common indicators against which to measure progress; require periodic monitoring; promote cooperation between relevant agencies and foster the exchange of good practice and ideas on a national level and among EU Member States.

8   *General Public Awareness-raising*

In all countries, COPING identified a need to raise the awareness of and "sensitize" media personnel to the often challenging circumstances that children of prisoners face and the impact that stereotypical or other portrayals can have on their well-being, with a view to preventing stigmatisation. Campaigners and researchers also need to be aware of possible negative repercussions of their efforts to raise the public profile of children of prisoners and a careful balance is needed between highlighting their needs and preventing further stigmatisation.

8.1   General public awareness-raising should be an on-going process across the European Union, primarily through articles in magazines for different groups of professionals and other media channels and through educational materials and sessions in schools. Content should focus on raising awareness of the existence of children of prisoners alongside other issues which create vulnerability, marginalisation or stigmatisation for children, the potential impact of parental incarceration and the need to develop effective support schemes.

8.2   Media should be sensitized as to how their reporting impacts upon children, to how stigmatisation can arise as a result of media reports about parental incarceration, and to the need to protect the dignity and anonymity of these vulnerable children.

9   *Consideration of the Perspectives of Children*

Within EU States, where national governments are implementing EU law, children are legally protected by Article 24 of the Charter of Fundamental Rights. This states that:

·   Children shall have the right to such protection and care as is necessary for their well-being. They may express their views freely. Such views shall be taken into consideration on matters which concern them in accordance with their age and maturity;
·   In all actions relating to children, whether taken by public authorities or private institutions, the child's best interests must be a primary consideration;
·   Every child shall have the right to maintain, on a regular basis, a personal relationship and direct contact with both his or her parents, unless that is contrary to his or her interests.

9.1   Decision-makers should ensure that anyone whose work impacts (directly or indirectly) on children of prisoners considers their best interests, needs, rights and perspectives, allowing for the development of support initiatives in schools, statutory agencies, the criminal justice process, and other relevant areas.

9.2   In the longer term, all Member States should seek to ensure that national law, especially in criminal matters, is more closely aligned to the Convention on the Rights of the Child.

9.3   EU legislation should be passed to ensure that Article 24 is enforceable across EU Member States in relation to the needs and rights of children of prisoners.

Conclusion

Because of the low profile attached to children of prisoners, governments and policy makers have neglected to fully consider the effects of parental imprisonment on children. This is an oversight which runs the risk of punishing innocent victims, and hence children of prisoners have been referred to as the "forgotten victims" of crime, or the "hidden victims of imprisonment." The combination of official disregard and public indifference can be situated within the current, moral and political dimensions of punishment, which tend to provoke deeply conflicting interests. As Garland noted in 1991, the institutional framework of modern penology has tended to obscure the broader social ramifications of the imprisonment of much larger numbers of offenders.

As the COPING study shows, there is no mainstream provision available to this client group, with children of prisoners often finding that they fall between a number of different government departments, such as health, the criminal justice system and child welfare services. Not only does this leave no obvious source of funding or governmental remit, but also the different organizational cultures and philosophies, and the different institutional priorities of these diverse arms of government, have acted to inhibit collaborative working arrangements. It has been left to the voluntary sector to drive the agenda for children of prisoners. However because of short term, insecure funding, NGOs have struggled to fill the gaps in provision, resulting in patchy provision which falls short of national coverage. In one country (Romania) we did not find any services being offered specifically for children of prisoners.

This chapter has discussed research on children of prisoners to argue the case for greater attention to be given to children's rights and for services for those who are vulnerable or at risk of experiencing major social and health difficulties related to parental incarceration. Prisoners are widely acknowledged as being a socially excluded group; however the idea that their children should be considered as experiencing social exclusion is a relatively new idea. As COPING shows however, this group of children, being both invisible *and* marginalized, face a high risk of social exclusion. It cannot be acceptable, that in a time when there is almost universal ratification of the CRC, the effects on children's well-being of parental imprisonment are not taken into account by criminal justice bodies or children's services.

As highlighted by the United Nations Committee on the Rights of the Child, there is urgent need for reconciliation of the interests of the State and the best interests of the child in respect of parental imprisonment (UNCRC, 2011) and beyond this child rights mandate for reform, the social and economic costs of inaction provide a critical imperative for change. This chapter has highlighted the dissonance between policy on criminal justice and that concerned with the welfare of children and argues that wide-scale adoption of a child-sensitive approach to justice would be a major step forward.

Bibliography

Committee on the Rights of the Child (2011). Report and Recommendations of The Day of General Discussion on "Children of Incarcerated Parents," http://www2.ohchr .org/english/bodies/crc/docs/discussion/2011CRCDGDReport.pdf.

Council of Europe (2010). Guidelines of the Committee of Ministers of the Council of Europe on child friendly justice, accessed 29 September 2014. https://wcd.coe.int/ ViewDoc.jsp?Ref=CM/Del/Dec(2010)1098/10.2abc&Language=lanEnglish&Ver=app 6&Site=CM&BackColorInternet=C3C3C3&BackColorIntranet=EDB021&BackColo rLogged=F5D38.

Essex, M.J., Kraemer, H.C., Armstrong, J.M., Boyce, W.T., Goldsmith, H.H., Klein, M.H., & Kupfer, D.J. (2006). Exploring risk factors for the emergence of children's mental health problems. *Archives of general psychiatry*, 63(11), 1246–1256.

Garland, D. (1991). Sociological perspectives on punishment. Crime and Justice, 115–165.

Goodman, R. (1997) The Strengths and Difficulties Questionnaire: A research note, *Journal of Child Psychology and Psychiatry*, 38, 5, 581–586.

Hissel, S., Bijleveld, C., & Kruttschnitt, C. (2011). The well-being of children of incarcerated mothers: An exploratory study for the Netherlands. *European Journal of Criminology*, 8, 346–360.

Huebner, B.M., & Gustafson, R. (2007) The effect of maternal incarceration on adult offspring involvement in the criminal justice system, *Journal of Criminal Justice*, 35, 3, 283–296.

Kinner, S.A., Alati, R., Najman, J.M., & Williams, G.M. (2007). Do paternal arrest and imprisonment lead to child behaviour problems and substance use? A longitudinal analysis. *Journal of Child Psychology & Psychiatry*, 48, 1148–1156.

Murray, J. (2005) The effects of imprisonment on family and children of prisoners. In A. Liebling and S. Maruna (Eds.) *The Effects of Imprisonment*. Uffculme Cullompton, Devon: Willan Publishing pp. 442–464.

Murray, J. (2007) The cycle of punishment: Social exclusion of prisoners and their children, *Criminology and Criminal Justice*, 7, 1, 55–81.

Murray, J. and Farrington, D.P. (2005) Parental imprisonment effects on boys' antisocial behaviour and delinquency through life course, *Journal of Child Psychology and Psychiatry*, 46, 12, 1269–1278.

Murray, J. and Farrington, D.P. (2008a) The effects of parental imprisonment on children, *Crime and Justice*, 37, 1, 133–206.

Murray, J. and Farrington, D.P. (2008b) Parental imprisonment: Long-lasting effects on boys' internalizing problems through the life course, *Development and Psychopathology*, 20, 1, 273–290.

Murray, J., Farrington, D.P., & Sekol, I. (2012). Children's antisocial behavior, mental health, drug use, and educational performance after parental incarceration: a systematic review and meta-analysis. *Psychological bulletin*, 138(2), 175.

Philbrick, K. (2002) Imprisonment: The impact on children, *Issues in Forensic Psychology*, 3, 72–81.

Phillips, S. and Bloom, B. (1998) In whose best interest? The impact of changing public policy on relatives caring for children with incarcerated parents, *Child Welfare*, 77, 5, 531–541.

Reed, D.F. and Reed, E.L (1997) Children of incarcerated parents, *Social Justice*, 24, 3, 152–169.

Richards, M. and McWilliams, B. (1996) Imprisonment and Family Ties. *Home Office Research and Statistics Directorate Research Bulletin*, Issue 38, London: Home Office.

Robertson, O. (2012) "Collateral Convicts": Children of Incarcerated Parents; Recommendations and Good Practice from the UN Committee on the Rights of the Child, Day of General Discussion 2011. Switzerland: Quaker United Nations Office. Accessed on 3.10.12 at: http://www2.ohchr.org/english/bodies/crc/discussion2011 _submissions.htm.

Rosenberg, M. (1965) *Society and the Adolescent Self-Image*, Princeton, NJ: Princeton University Press.

Rosenberg, J. (2009) *Children Need Dads Too: Children with Fathers in Prison*, Geneva: Quaker United Nations Office.

Seymour, C. (1998) Children with parents in prison: Child welfare policy, program, and policy issues, *Child Welfare*, 77, 5, 469–493.

Simmons, W. (2000) *Children of incarcerated parents. California*, California Research
    Bureau Note, 7, 2, 1–11.

The Independent, 17 September 2012. "The hidden victims of a lock 'em up culture'."
    Accessed 3.10.12 at: http://www.independent.co.uk/voices/editorials/the-hidden
    -victims-of-a-lock-em-up-culture.

Walmsley, R. (2009) *World prison population list* (eighth edition), London: International
    Centre for Prison Studies, Kings College London.

Challenges in Implementing Child Rights – A Call for Innovative Governance for Children

Trond Waage

A Perplexing Paradox

Children are universally referred to and politically advertised as the hope, promise and future of society. Child development is increasingly seen as the foundation of social and economic development. International conventions and covenants supporting children are widely endorsed.

However, a gap remains between lip service paid to children and resources budgeted for them; between commitments made to children and the lack of practical implementation of these; between declaring children's rights and making rights a reality.

The Ethos of the UN Convention on the Rights of the Child

We are celebrating 25 years with the Convention on the Rights of the Child (the Convention). As the most widely ratified human rights treaty in history, it qualifies for a celebration in itself. Lessons from the implementation of this treaty across regions and in countries with different economic, social, cultural and political contexts, provide a unique basis for reflection and an inspiration for future action. Since the nature of politics is a dynamic process that varies depending on a country's political culture and democratic maturity, no one-and-only model for implementing the rights of the child exists, though many are still searching for this universal code.

However, over the past 25 years with the Convention, children's rights have gained increasing attention at international, regional and national levels. These 25 years have been marked by a significant process of adjustment, with:

- extensive changes in national laws and policies;
- the establishment of independent institutions to voice and serve the best interests of the child;
- the setting-up of high-level governmental mechanisms to promote coordination of child-related activities;
- more and better data on children, helping to grant visibility to hidden areas of neglect and giving vulnerable children a face;

© KONINKLIJKE BRILL NV, LEIDEN, 2015 | DOI 10.1163/9789004297432_012

- the introduction of child rights in school curricula and in capacity-building initiatives of professionals working with and for children;
- international and regional initiatives promoted to consolidate standards for the protection of the rights of the child and to enhance cross-border cooperation for safeguarding children's rights; like the EU's "Agenda for Children's Rights" and the Council of Europe's "Building a Europe for and with Children."

Globally, societies are undergoing rapid socio-political transformations and are confronted with great uncertainty about the future and how inter-generational relations will continue to evolve. In the light of these developments, international standards reflect a global consensus on a set of norms and values and are able to guide countries in their undertakings to uphold the rule of law, social cohesion, and stable democracies.

The Convention emphasizes that children, as human beings, do not only have rights to protection, freedom of speech and welfare, but the right to unfold and develop their capacities; the right to master their destiny as well as to emancipate themselves. As such, the Convention emphasizes the uniqueness of every child and a child's value as a nation-builder. This is the ethos of the Convention.

Challenges in the Implementation of Child Policy

Since the Convention entered into force, States Parties have achieved significant progress in developing child rights standards and they have widely acknowledged the importance for States to invest in children. Yet, there is still limited knowledge of how the Convention can effectively be translated into child-rights practice.

Relevant questions are: How do policy makers embrace the dynamics of childhood? How do States perceive and activate the resources that children offer? How to conduct research and translate the findings into evidence-informed policy and practice?

How can policy makers be equipped and competent to manoeuvre the complex State administrations and governance structures more efficiently in the best interests of the child?

The Fragmented Policy Approach

Many of the most persistent challenges in translating child-rights standards into practice relate to structural factors. In child policy, States work traditionally through sector-specific approaches, addressing issue by issue. Although this approach may have relevance and impact, it appears as an ad-hoc policy founded on a charity approach responding to momentary needs.

There is growing recognition that policy-making and practice need to be integrated and consolidated into more systemic approaches and comprehensive implementation strategies, reflecting the indivisibility of rights and their close relation to other policy areas. In addition, policy measures often remain limited to the structures of the central State, whereas the difficulties of connecting the central, regional and local levels of the public administration still create major obstacles to the full implementation of children's rights.

Research has evidenced that this multiple fragmentation of child policy and failures to safeguard children's rights in practice, render children vulnerable in many ways. Vulnerability may adversely affect the child's development and, when widely prevalent, compromises the cohesion and development of societies and nations at large.

The Law-reform Approach

A common perception and interpretation of the Convention is that it is mainly related to legal rights and protection of children. The consequences of such an understanding have turned the implementation of the Convention into technical legal exercises, with a connotation of the law as a regulatory instrument for protection. As a result, governments, under pressure from civil society and other partners, start the hunt for child-rights indicators to be used by monitoring mechanisms, in toolkits, guidelines, national plans, reporting forms, and tick-off-boxes. At the end of the line, governments may turn into reactive accountants and protectors of the status quo. This is a risky process that leads to objectification of the child.

This development, combined with today's economic and political systems struggling to come to terms with the complexities of the 21st century, is creating growing mistrust in governments' and public institutions' ability to perform innovative governance for the future.

As an example, the international debates related to the UN Millennium Development Goals (MDGs), the post-2015 sustainable development agenda, have thus far focused strongly on designing the architecture of strategies, policies and programmes, defining objectives and measuring national and global progress in relation to these objectives. So much attention has been given to the forms and functions of institutions rather than their capability to act upon their mandates and to implement.

Nevertheless, the Convention has initiated important and necessary legal reforms to secure the rights of children worldwide. But considered from a socio-political investment perspective, the Convention offers far more than child rights standards. As a policy document, it is essential for promoting and sustaining democracy and contributes to peace and democracy building.

The Convention and the Perception of the Child

Childhood refers to both a life phase, which varies with time and space, and the social, economic, and cultural frameworks defining children's life and conditions. Children move through the framework of childhood as they grow. In the modern world, this entails moving within a framework that is constantly changing. Children are at the centre of the turbulence of modernity. They are not only being socialized in an era of uncertainty, but they are the age group living nearest the epicentre of change. Identifying the well-being of modern children is more complex than identifying the well-being of other age groups. The modern child's life conditions are rapidly changing, and rapid change implies that the models of interpretation must develop accordingly. Children's life situations today cannot be understood within the vocabulary of yesterday.

Beyond this understanding, the Convention is evolving a new perception of the child. Rather than vulnerable human beings, passive recipients of assistance and protection, children are gaining a new status as citizens and agents of change. They are increasingly being acknowledged as a resource, with their ideas, creativity, expectations, demands and an inspiring ability to influence decisions and enrich our vision of the world.

This understanding is challenging the traditional perception and accounts of childhood, as defined by the traditional theories of child development, that children are merely "adults in the making." Such a view judges children only in terms of what they will become in the future, once they have been adequately socialized. In the meantime, they are seen as inherently vulnerable, incomplete and dependent.

However, we recognize changes in the horizon. Talking *about* children and *involving* them in decision-making processes is increasingly losing the patronizing flavour of yesterday, and the investment in children is becoming perceived as a question of good governance and economics and an instrumental step for the development of society and democracy.

Need for Innovative Approaches in Child Policy

As a policy document, the Convention offers to guide public administrations towards a more holistic perception of children and the resources they offer to sustainable democracy and Nation-building. To activate the potential of the Convention as a guiding policy document, its provisions need to be understood and applied not only one-by-one, but also in their entirety.

Innovative public administrations are required to continuously improve the way they are working, on the basis of process evaluations and in relation to the dynamics of childhood. Effective linkages between the central, regional and local levels of the public administration are indispensable in this regard. Competence for strategic policy planning and implementation, combined with an innovative and entrepreneurial process is crucial to promote positive change.

Existing training and capacity-building initiatives commonly focus on knowledge and understanding of the Convention as a legislative document. They fall short of providing guidance and advice on how to ensure its effective implementation and how to translate its ethos into practice. Attaining the competence to design innovative policies is therefore a key to making existing structures and systems more effective.

Evidence-informed Policymaking

In a political environment characterized by the mantra of evidence-based policymaking, governments do encourage and stimulate the research community to conduct relevant and applied research programmes on children's situation.

Unfortunately, a gap exists between the *producers* of knowledge and the *consumers*, and research could have more impact on child policy than it has had to date. Researchers as "knowledge producers" have difficulties in understanding the resistance to policy change despite clear and convincing evidence. Policymakers as "knowledge consumers" criticize the inability of researchers to make their findings accessible and digestible for policy planning and decision-making.

There is a need for knowledge-*entrepreneurial* skills and, on both side of the table, to stimulate stronger partnership with relevant actors in the planning of the research. The translation process from research findings to knowledge-informed policy and practice will be more successful when practitioners, children, policymakers and researchers are involved in the design of the research.

This process will promote a common platform of understanding of the challenges to be addressed, as well as stimulating cross-sectorial and multi-disciplinary approaches.

Equally important, it will stimulate the research and university communities' engagement in innovative governmental processes to implement children's rights, and search for what constitutes effective child-rights governance structures.

Mechanisms in Support of an Innovative Governance Approach

To ensure a continuous focus on the best interests of the child, there are some mechanisms that can inspire and encourage governments to moving children into the center of policymaking.

1.   Ombudsman for Children an "Ombudsman for Change"

The Ombudsman for Children, with a holistic mandate from the Convention, constitutes one of the few set-ups in a society with the potential to perform the role as a strategic entrepreneur in policymaking. As a change agent the Ombudsman for Children will be a knowledge entrepreneur who acts as a catalyst for change in governance, organizational structures and mind-set. Holding this strategic position, the Change Agent must be committed, mandated and resourced to critically review and refine child policy and to pave the way for the full and holistic implementation of children's rights in practice.

A key factor for an innovative Ombudsman's role is the composition of the legislation for the Ombudsman. The balance between a strictly regulated Ombudsman's role and a more open legislation giving the official the ability to perform both in a reactive as well as in a proactive mode. To be a "children's champion" implies to hold a futuristic perspective and to perform in an innovative, creative, flexible and non-bureaucratic way.

The proactive role gives the Ombudsman for children the unique opportunity to identify and address issues that are affecting childhood in a broader way, working cross-sectorially and holistically. She or he will be the strategic entrepreneur that engages and motivates the State and local administration to implement children's rights in a perspective of "protect to enable" as well as democracy and nation-building. An Ombudsman for Change will challenge the society's perception on childhood and advocate investment policy and the shortcoming repair approach.

2. A Cross-party Child-rights Group in Parliament

A Cross-party child- rights group ensures broad support across political parties represented in Parliament. In some parliaments these groups are mobilized when special cases appear on the political agenda. Other parliaments set up a permanent "Child-rights commission." The role of these groups is to safeguard a holistic approach to children's issues debated in the parliament, to guide and monitor parliament in such a way that decisions are taken in the best interest of the child, as well as being a watchdog of government's policies.

A critical challenge has been to keep children's rights at the center of the parliamentary agenda despite the evolving political debate and the many competing national priorities the Parliament is confronted with. A cross-party child-rights group/commission may sharpen the child focus.

3. Inter-ministerial Child-rights Group in the Government

Some Governments have established an Inter-ministerial Child-rights Group with high level representation from all ministries. The cross-ministry group is mandated to coordinate and monitor government initiatives on children's issues and to serve as the central resource for children's issues within the government.

A key reason for engaging in cross-sector partnerships is to identify and embed innovations into processes, strategies and policy-making. Transformative action is inspired through the cross-sectorial coordination and the group acts as a catalyst for innovative change. Some States have engaged a Policy Managing Coordinator as a leader for the group to ensure continuity, commitment and efficiency to the cause.

4. Child-rights Observatories

In moving the child-rights agenda forward, research, knowledge production, evaluation and solid documentation are playing a reassuring role. They are capturing innovation and progress, clarifying prevailing challenges and providing evidence to ground new initiatives.

For too long, children have remained hidden in the national and international policy agenda. Diluted in statistical work, they are still poorly represented in research conducted across nations. When studied, they are frequently considered through the lens of individual technical disciplines, and rarely perceived in their value as multidimensional human beings. All too often, studies observe children, acknowledging the challenges confronting their lives but failing to appreciate their ideas, creativity and their distinct role as active informants of research. Quality data and statistics are a national identity, a national footprint, and quality statistics make the processes of change easier.

Child-rights observatories exist in a number of countries as a "social watch-dog" with the aim of monitoring and analysing the situation of children, and ensuring evidence-based advocacy for awareness-raising and influencing decision-making for the betterment of children's situation.

Quo Vadis?

After 25 years with the Convention, it is time to address the limitations of tra-ditional approaches in child policy and to initiate a practice of innovation and proactive processes of change, all with a view to generating more concrete results for children and society. Professionals involved in child policy have as yet little access to guidance and training on how to apply innovative tech-niques in their areas of work. Innovation competence may help and equip policymakers to address the challenges they are confronted with and to ensure that policy measures are not merely responsive to emerging trends but are themselves a source of innovation and looking ahead.

Respect for children's rights cannot be perceived as an option, as a question of favour or kindness to children, or as an expression of charity. Children's rights generate obligations and responsibilities that must be honoured. They need to be perceived as an expression of solidarity and partnership, empower-ing children to participate actively in the improvement of their situation and in the broader process of social change and nation building.

Childhood is not a disease that will pass – childhood lasts for lifetime and generations. As a policy document, the Convention offers to guide towards a more holistic perception of children and the resources they offer to sustain-able democracy and nation building. In order to activate the potential of the Convention as a guiding policy document, its provisions need to be understood and applied not only one-by-one, but also in their entirety.

PART 2

Children and Criminal Justice Systems

∴

It Is Not Child-friendly to Make Children Criminals[1]

Peter Newell

Introduction

We need to stop criminalizing children completely. Many are working in this direction, promoting forms of diversion and restorative justice. But many of those involved in promoting these positive approaches see them as compatible with still criminalizing (some) children.

The Convention on the Rights of the Child safeguards the rights of every human being below the age of 18 years. The suggestion that States should define an age, within the Convention's 0-18 definition of childhood, at which children can be criminalized is inevitably discriminatory and in violation of Article 2. There is nothing in the Convention which requires criminalisation and, on the contrary, it is in conflict with the Convention's requirement that the child's best interests must be a primary consideration (Article 3) and with the child's right to maximum possible development (Article 6). The Convention's Article 40 requires a distinct approach: that States shall seek to promote the establishment of laws, procedures, authorities and institutions specifically applicable to children in conflict with the law—not to some of them but to all of them up to 18 [Article 40 (3)].

Criminalizing children causes persisting harm not only to the overall development of many children but of human societies too. It encourages a spiral downwards by children into further offending and increasingly violent offending, often extending into adulthood.

Once archaic doctrines of original sin are discarded, we can see the clear evidence that the roots of serious criminality in children develop and flourish from adult—mostly parental—violence and neglect, compounded usually by a failure of the State to fulfil its obligations to support parents in their child-rearing responsibilities and to provide children with absorbing and

---

1 A version of this paper was prepared in 2012 for the Child Rights International Network – CRIN. CRIN aims to encourage a debate on juvenile justice which gets beyond pragmatism and compromise. In particular we want to provoke a new debate about the setting of minimum ages of criminal responsibility. CRIN wants to work with other organizations and human rights advocates to encourage States to design systems which keep children out of the criminal justice system altogether, systems which genuinely renounce retribution and focus exclusively on children's rehabilitation, always of course accepting the need to give necessary attention to public safety and security.

© KONINKLIJKE BRILL NV, LEIDEN, 2015 | DOI 10.1163/9789004297432_013

rights-respecting education. The more serious and extreme a child's offending is, the more certain we can be of its origins in adult maltreatment – or sometimes simply the tragic loss of parents or other key carers. Freedom of religion suggests we cannot stop people believing in original sin, but adults' freedom does not extend to justifying violence, including retributive approaches to childhood offending, any more than a belief in witches or evil spirits can justify branding children as witches or possessed by evil spirits.

Hesitant, compromised advocacy, maintaining an element of retribution while emphasizing the need for rehabilitation and re-integration, is just not working. In contrast to positive progress in some children's rights arenas, recent reports suggest that penal systems for children in many States are becoming more punitive. And let's not falsely categorize them as juvenile "justice" systems or pretend for one moment that they are "child friendly." An authoritative 2013 UN report refers to us living in a time "when public opinion expresses concern at the perceived threat posed to society by juvenile delinquency, and States around the world contemplate reductions in the minimum age of criminal responsibility and longer sentences of imprisonment..."[2]

Problems in Setting a Minimum Age of Criminal Responsibility

Regrettably, some States have tried to justify regressive moves to criminalize younger children by misusing the Committee on the Rights of the Child's unfortunate suggestion, in its General Comment No. 10 on "The rights of the child in juvenile justice," that 12 is an internationally acceptable minimum age of criminal responsibility (MACR).[3]

This was, of course, far from the Committee's intention. In its General Comment, the Committee quotes the weak assertion in the Beijing Rules (whose adoption by the UN General Assembly in 1985 preceded adoption of the CRC by four years) that the minimum age should not be fixed at too low a level. And it goes on: "In line with this rule the Committee has recommended States parties not to set a MACR at a too low level and to increase the existing low MACR to an internationally acceptable level. From these recommendations, it can be concluded that a minimum age of criminal responsibility below the age of 12 years is considered by the Committee not to be internationally

---

2 Promoting Restorative Justice for Children, Report of the Special Representative of the UN Secretary General on violence against children, New York, 2013, page 39.

3 Committee on the Rights of the Child, General Comment No. 10, Children's Rights in Juvenile Justice, CRC/C/GC/10, 2007.

acceptable. States parties are encouraged to increase their lower MACR to the age of 12 years as the absolute minimum age and to continue to increase it to a higher age level. At the same time, the Committee urges States parties not to lower their MACR to the age of 12…"[4]

But the damage was done and 12 became a sort of respectable norm. The assertion that 12 could be considered "internationally acceptable" had been arrived at by working out the median of all the known fixed ages (drawn downwards by the regrettable number of States setting seven as the age – a legacy of the British Empire). But it is hardly the role of the Committee to accept an "average" approach to respect for children's rights. There was unease among some in the children's rights community when the Committee issued this statement. There has been discussion within the Committee about revisiting it. Surely by now there has been sufficient misuse of the Committee's words to justify the current members revising this part of the General Comment in the light of the best interests of so many children?

Conventions are living instruments and General Comments must not be set in stone. The language in the Convention's Article 40 is in itself not altogether clear, urging States to seek to promote "…the establishment of a minimum age below which children shall be presumed not to have the capacity to infringe the penal law."[5] The Committee notes that "Even (very) young children do have the capacity to infringe the penal law…" And of course they do have the physical capacity to assault other children, shop lift and commit many other crimes. But the CRC drafters presumably had a broader definition of capacity in mind. In the General Comment the Committee re-interprets this provision as an obligation for States parties to set a minimum age of "criminal responsibility." But there is nothing in the Convention which prevents States establishing 18 as their minimum age for criminalization and a lot of obligations which require them to. According to a global survey of minimum ages, a very small number have done so (although close examination is required to ensure there are no exceptions, for example for serious crimes or for when adults commit crimes with children).[6]

---

4 *Ibid.*, para. 32.

5 Convention on the Rights of the Child, Article 40 (3) (a).

6 The author has been unable to find any comprehensive update of the research into minimum ages carried out by UNICEF's Innocenti Research Centre in 2002. A summary of this formed part of an early circulated draft of the Committee on the Rights of the Child's General Comment: "Regarding current State Party practices, 179 States parties have either explicit MACRs or age limits that serve in practice as MACRs. These MACRs range from the age of 6 years to the age of 18 years, while the overall average is 11.5 years, and the median is 12 years (*i.e.* an equal number of States parties have MACRs above and below the age of 12).

The Need for Uncompromising Advocacy – Moving beyond Pragmatism

Politicians and the media play on popular fears of each successive generation of children running amok if not repressed and punished, feral children out of all control. It's easy and remains popular to stigmatize in extreme terms "bad" children: the general adult voting audience is still highly receptive because adult commitment to punitive responses to children runs deep, nurtured by religious assertion of original sin and legal acceptance of violent and humiliating punishment – "for the purpose of correcting what is evil in the child:" the words of the Chief Justice of England in the still-quoted 1860 leading judgment in English common law, justifying "reasonable chastisement" of children.

Over recent decades the horrifying prevalence of legalized violent punishment of children, most commonly in their homes, has become more visible and has been recognized as a rights violation by international and regional human rights systems; simultaneously research into its very harmful impact on children has accumulated.[7] There is real progress now towards prohibition and elimination, with 46 States completely banning all violent punishment, including in the home and family by March 2015 and another 47 publicly committed to doing so. A significant majority—122—have banned it in all their schools.[8]

Enacting bans on violent punishment also runs against social norms and does not win votes: governments are having to accept their human rights obligations, listen to research and to professional views and lead public opinion. The universal prohibition and elimination of legalized violent punishment of

---

The Committee notes that these figures are significantly influenced by the large number of States parties (34) with a MACR of 7 years, virtually all of which derive their provisions from historic English common law. In the past 25 years, States parties have formed an unmistakable trend to raise their MACRs, and approximately 15 more are currently deliberating official proposals to do the same. There are very few exceptions to this general trend. From these findings it can be concluded that international MACR standards, as interpreted by current State Party practices, effectively place the norm at 12 years. Likewise, the Committee has repeatedly advised in its Concluding Observations that State parties increase MACRs that are lower than 12 years, and that States parties increase proposed MACRs (i.e. under legislative consideration) that are lower than 12 years."

Unfortunately, recent evidence collected by the Child Rights International Network – CRIN suggests the general trend is no longer all upwards.

7 For a summary of the findings of research into the impact of violent punishment on children, see www.endcorporalpunishment.org.

8 For full details see Global Initiative to End All Corporal Punishment of Children, www .endcorporalpunishment.org.

children is now in sight. For this, much credit should be given to the clear and uncompromising leadership of the Committee on the Rights of the Child. The Committee, from when it started to examine States' reports in 1993, has asserted the obvious if unpopular truth that violence, "however light," and whether or not disguised as discipline, is a violation of the child's right to respect for his or her dignity and physical integrity and its legality breaches children's right to equal protection under the law: hitting people is a crime, and children are people too. Paulo Pinheiro's rights-based comprehensive UN Study into violence against children built on the Committee's work with his assertion that "No violence against children is justifiable; all violence against children is preventable" and his priority recommendation that all violence – including explicitly all corporal punishment – should be prohibited.[9]

Progress in challenging violent punishment of children has come from making the practice and the harm it does visible and from systematically building a human rights consensus for prohibition and elimination. A similar organized approach is needed now to challenge States' violent punishment of children, the criminalisation of children. The reality of existing penal systems and their impact needs to be made ever more visible, as must the evidence that the roots of almost all serious child offending lie in adult violence and neglect. Loud, uncompromising, rights-based advocacy must insist that there is no place whatsoever for retribution. We need to move beyond the hesitant pragmatism and compromise that characterize most current debates about the future of juvenile justice. There are plenty of global, regional and national organizations working on (one could cynically say living off) the rights-violating failures of punitive systems, tinkering with but also wrongly tolerating systems which still cling to criminalization and retribution.

Separating "Responsibility" from Criminalization

We need to separate the need to identify, appropriately assess and respond constructively to children's *responsibility* for crimes from the quite distinct primitive and rights-violating urge to criminalize them. This is not an original proposal. More than 20 years ago, while the Convention was being drafted, it appears at least one State attempted to introduce an exclusive focus on

---

9 For full details of the UNSG's Study on violence against children and its report, see www .unviolencestudy.org.

rehabilitation, outside the criminal justice system. But, as the *travaux prepara-toires* record, "it became obvious that there was a total lack of consensus."[10]

A significant indication of support for not criminalizing children is in the Rome Statute establishing the International Criminal Court; the Statute excludes all people under 18 from its jurisdiction. Article 26 states: "The Court shall have no jurisdiction over any person who was under the age of 18 at the time of the alleged commission of a crime."[11]

More recently, authoritative and explicit support for stopping the criminali-sation of children has appeared which surely should have moved the debate on.

In 2003, the European Network of Ombudspersons for Children (ENOC) issued a position statement, adopted by member-institutions in 21 States who were "concerned at the tone of political and media debate and the direction of public policy and legal changes concerning juvenile offenders in many of our countries."[12] ENOC's statement argues: "We believe that current trends to reduce the age of criminal responsibility and to lock up more children at younger ages must be reversed. The treatment of young people placed in penal institutions in many of our countries is a scandal – breaching their fundamen-tal human rights." Furthermore ENOC stated "Across Europe, ages of criminal responsibility vary from as young as seven, eight and ten up to 16 in some states and 18—but with exceptions—in a few; the definition also varies. We believe that the concepts of 'responsibility' and of 'criminalisation' need to be sepa-rated. The Convention on the Rights of the Child (CRC) proposes a separate, distinct system of juvenile justice; it requires that this must be focused on respect for all the rights of the child and on the aims of rehabilitation and re-integration. This focus and these aims are not compatible with 'criminaliz-ing' child offenders." Moreover ENOC argued that "We do believe that children should be held 'responsible' for their actions in line with the concept of evolv-ing capacities and our strong advocacy for respect for children's views in all aspects of their lives. It is essential to establish responsibility for crimes. Where responsibility is disputed, there has to be a formal process to determine respon-sibility in a manner which respects the rights of the alleged offender. But this process does not have to lead to criminalizing children."

---

10   Schabas, W., Sax, H. & Alen, A., *A Commentary on the United Nations Convention on the Rights of the Child – Article 37: Prohibition of Torture, Death Penalty, Life Imprisonment and Deprivation of Liberty*, Martinus Nijhoff Publishers, 2006, p. 9.

11   Rome Statute, adopted 1998, entered into force July 1, 2002, Article 26.

12   European Network of Ombudspersons for Children, position statement on juvenile justice, 2003.

In 2009, Thomas Hammarberg, then the Council of Europe's Commissioner for Human Rights, concerned at proposals to lower minimum ages in some Member States, took up this call, issuing a "Viewpoint" which quoted ENOC's statement and concluded: "Yes, it is in all our interests to stop making children criminals. We should therefore treat them as children while they are still children and save the criminal justice system for adults."[13] He noted that the United Nations Guidelines for the Prevention of Juvenile Delinquency, adopted 19 years previously, still provide the right benchmark: "Labelling a young person as 'deviant' or 'delinquent' or 'pre-delinquent' often contributes to the development of a consistent pattern of undesirable behaviour by young people..."[14] (para. 5f). Thomas Hammarberg wants "to move the debate on from fixing an arbitrary age for criminal responsibility. Governments should now look for a holistic solution to juvenile offending which does not criminalize children for their conduct."

Then in July 2011, a report of the Inter-American Commission on Human Rights (IACHR), on Juvenile Justice and Human Rights in the Americas, prepared by Paulo Pinheiro in his role then as Special Rapporteur on the Rights of the Child to the IACHR, highlighted the incompatibility of asserting an arbitrary minimum age for criminalisation under 18 "with the right to non-discrimination enshrined in Article 2 of the CRC and the principle of the best interests of the child contained in Article 3."[15]

The IACHR report goes on to argue that "the element of retribution is not appropriate within juvenile justice systems if the objectives pursued are the reintegration and rehabilitation of the child." Paulo Pinheiro quotes Thomas Hammarberg's call for a new debate, separating the concepts of "responsibility" and "criminalisation" and ending the criminalisation of children: "Therefore, the Commission observes the need to begin a new debate, while at the same time recognizing that excluding [children] totally from the sphere of criminal justice is a complex matter which merits analysis which goes beyond that set out in this report. Removing them from the criminal justice system does not mean that they will not be held responsible for their actions, nor that they will be denied due process to determine whether allegations against them are true or false. Meanwhile, the Commission urges states

---

13   Thomas Hammarberg, Council of Europe Commissioner for Human Rights, 2009.

14   United Nations Guidelines for the Prevention of Juvenile Delinquency, para. 5f.

15   Inter-American Commission on Human Rights, Rapporteurship on the Rights of the Child, Informe sobre Justicia Juvenil y Derechos Humanos en las Américas (Report on Juvenile Justice and Human Rights in the Americas), July 2011.

to progressively raise the minimum age under which children can be held responsible in the juvenile justice system towards 18 years of age."

Despite this sort of leadership from some, we still hear the reforming organizations arguing for modest raising of the MACR, to at least 12, or 14. And many of those promoting restorative justice for children do not see it as an alternative to criminalization, more a mitigation of the worst effects, an optional alternative to *really* punitive sentencing. Among limiting conditions for pursuing restorative justice described in a recent report are that "the alleged offence must fall within the scope of offences eligible for diversion as defined by the law;" also that the consent of the victim(s) and of the offending child's parents must be obtained before diversion to a restorative process.[16]

Asserting Children's Responsibility

Children are "responsible" for many actions defined by criminal law as crimes – in so far as they did it. And many are also responsible in the sense that they did know, in one way or another, that what they were doing was wrong when they did it. It does not serve our purpose as advocates of children's human rights to deny their immediate responsibility, to belittle their evolving capacities. But we must also recognize that their Convention, recognizing their developmental status, requires a special approach, for all our sakes.

Stopping criminalizing children does not mean giving up on or giving in to children who are causing trouble and harm. Keeping all under-18s out of the criminal justice system altogether does not mean that young people who commit offences will avoid "justice" or that nothing will be done about their offending.

Nor, as some have argued, does denying all under-18s a place in the criminal justice system consequentially deny them due process, or encourage or force innocent children to accept, in the name of welfare, compulsory interventions and treatment that are as heavy as penal sanctions.

Fear of children losing their due process rights is still advanced as a reason for continuing to deal with them in a criminal justice system. But due process is not unique to criminal proceedings. It can be provided in any sort of proceedings – and Article 40 of the CRC requires it. Children must not of course lose their right to due process by being denied criminalization. And children have an explicit right in Article 12 (2) of the Convention to be heard

---

16   Promoting Restorative Justice for Children, Report of the Special Representative of the UN Secretary General on violence against children, New York, 2013, page 17.

in any judicial and administrative proceedings that affect them. So traditional due process rights, including the right to be heard, must be fully respected in the proceedings that will be needed to determine "responsibility" and in other proceedings necessary to decide on responsive action to achieve rehabilitation, prevention of future offending and possible reparation.

Others suggest that if under-18s are removed from the criminal justice system, more of them will be coerced or bribed into carrying out criminal activities on behalf of adults, noting the lack of criminal penalties for the children. Such concerns are real, but surely the necessary response to such exploitation—which is already possible whatever the age of criminal responsibility—is to step up the penalties for those adults who pursue it?

It seems these are relatively simple arguments to counter. No doubt there are others which will be aired as advocacy for genuine and complete de-criminalization of children gains weight. And there is lots of detail that needs addressing, about the design and practice of proceedings that are genuinely appropriate to the capacity of the children concerned.

As noted above, during the drafting process of the Convention, in the late 1980s, some UN agencies and NGOs did try to argue that there is no place for retribution in juvenile justice. But in the end the heaviest arguments were about trying to rule out sentences of life imprisonment for children rather than only life imprisonment without possibility of release – and even that argument was lost in the interests of consensus. Are there really human beings who still believe that sentencing a child to life imprisonment is not inhuman treatment?

In its General Comment, the Committee had another go at removing retribution:

"The protection of the best interests of the child means, for instance, that the traditional objectives of criminal justice, such as repression/retribution, must give way to rehabilitation and restorative justice objectives in dealing with child offenders. This can be done in concert with attention to effective public safety."[17] However, this statement from the Committee does not with clarity suggest stopping criminalizing children, especially when it is implied that 12 is an "internationally acceptable" minimum age of criminal responsibility.

Lowering minimum ages, as some States have done and more are considering, means stigmatizing more and younger children as criminals and responding to them in a criminal law system which in every State is still focussed

---

17   Committee on the Rights of the Child, General Comment No. 10, Children's Rights in
       Juvenile Justice, CRC/C/GC/10, 2007, para. 10.

primarily on punishment and retribution. It is absurd to suggest that this system can fulfil for children the required aims of a juvenile justice system – focussing exclusively on maximizing their overall positive development and therefore on necessary rehabilitation and reintegration.

The other reported regression is the trend to lock up more children and at younger ages. A recent report from UN agencies states: "It is estimated that at least 1 million children are deprived of their liberty worldwide, a figure that is probably underestimated. Research shows that the majority of detained children is awaiting trial, that a large proportion of these children are held for minor offences and are first-time offenders. Violence at home, poverty, structural violence and risky survival activities propel children into the juvenile justice system, and detention in the criminal justice system is often used as a substitute for referral to child care and protection institutions. There is a worrying trend for children to be placed in institutions, rather than minimizing the risk of violence against children by ensuring effective prevention. Incidents of violence occur while in custody of police and security forces, in both pretrial and post-sentence detention, as well as a form of sentencing. Violence can be perpetrated by staff, adult detainees and other children, or be the result of self-harm."[18]

All this conflicts plainly with the Convention's obligations, and Article 37 explicitly requires deprivation of liberty to be used "only as a measure of last resort and for the shortest appropriate time." Regrettably, but predictably in a human rights instrument negotiated ultimately by government representatives, there are some weasel words here: "a last resort" leaves plenty of room for punitive, retributive response by legislators and judges. And "appropriate" can be and is interpreted as making the punishment fit the crime, maintaining "proportionate" approaches to sentencing.

But, regarding the Convention as a living instrument, there is equally room for tightening the conditions on restriction of liberty in line with the child's best interests; there is also a clear prohibition in Article 9 on separating a child from his or her parents against their will unless such separation is "necessary for the best interests of the child". In a system which rejects retribution, the only justification for locking up children can be that they pose an assessed serious risk to others' safety and other ways of minimizing this risk are

---

18   *Prevention of and responses to violence against children within the juvenile justice system,*
      Joint report of the Office of the High Commissioner for Human Rights, the United Nations
      Office on Drugs and Crime and the Special Representative of the Secretary-General on
      Violence against Children on prevention of and responses to violence against children
      within the juvenile justice system, p. 7.

considered inadequate. This proposal has also had authoritative support: the World Report on Violence against Children, issued following the UN Secretary General's Study, urged governments to "ensure that detention is only used for child offenders who are assessed as posing a real danger to others, and then only as a last resort, for the shortest necessary time, and following judicial hearing, with greater resources invested in alternative family- and community-based rehabilitation and reintegration programmes."[19]

We must hope that the proposed new UN study into the restriction of liberty of children will both provide accurate, disaggregated statistics on the numbers of children whose liberty is restricted in penal and all other systems and be uncompromising in defining the very limited and short-term justifications for detaining children.[20] Hopefully, it will also authoritatively challenge the growing trend by States to privatize child detention, adding a profit motive to all the other awful motivations for locking up more children. Analysing in depth restriction of liberty of children in all systems should lead to analysis of the use of mental health detention of children. Research suggests that a majority (probably an overwhelming majority) of children currently in penal detention have mental health problems. It is surely arguable that any child who poses such a serious threat to public safety that they can justifiably be detained for a period has mental health problems? So shouldn't any such detention be in health/mental health places, not penal?

Reflections on How Separation of Responsibility from Criminalization Could Work

There is no room in this paper for a full and detailed proposal and I have been unable to find a detailed analysis of what does happen in the few States which assert that their MACR is 18.

But let us take a well-exposed and very serious crime committed by children and review how it could be treated in a system which separates the child's "responsibility" from criminalization of the child. A particularly awful (and very rare) murder of a two-year old toddler by two 10 year-olds in the north of England in 1993 seemed to put back the possibility of principled reform of justice for children by years, now decades. Media coverage of the murder of James

---

19   *World Report on Violence against Children*, published by the United Nations Secretary
      General's Study on Violence against Children, 2006, p. 218.
20   For full details of the call for a UN Study on children deprived of their liberty, see http://
      www.childrendeprivedofliberty.info/.

Bulger and the subsequent trial in an adult court went round the world, together with images of the angelic two year old. The media were also fed with the full identity of the two 10 year-old boys, named by the trial judge's very perverse interpretation of the public interest, let alone these children's best interests, in direct violation of international law. And this judge's crime has made the task of rehabilitation and reintegration of the boys infinitely more difficult – as later events have demonstrated. It also added immeasurably to the distress of their families.

Because the suspected murderers are children, under the Convention on the Rights of the Child the State has a series of inter-dependent obligations to them, including to ensure that in all actions concerning them, their best interests are a primary consideration [Article 3 (1)]; that their survival and development is ensured "to the maximum extent possible" (Article 6); that they are not separated from their parents unless competent authorities decide "that such separation is necessary for the best interests of the child" (Article 9).

And as they are children "alleged as, accused of, or recognized as having infringed the penal law," States must not only recognize their equal rights to due process, but also "to be treated in a manner consistent with the promotion of the child's sense of dignity and worth, which reinforces the child's respect for the human rights and fundamental freedoms of others and which takes into account the child's age and the desirability of promoting the child's reintegration and the child's assuming a constructive role in society" (Article 40).

There must be investigation and a hearing to determine what happened, who was immediately responsible for the crime. The victim's family has a right to know what happened. The State has an active duty to protect everyone's right to life and to respect for their physical integrity and human dignity, to protect all members of society from such crimes. This means understanding as far as possible why the crime happened – contributory factors, both direct and indirect – including in the previous lives of the two killers, and how it could have been prevented. Any broader lessons that can be learned about preventing such crimes must inform future policy.

Here, as a primitive contribution to discussion, is a first rough outline of the possible proceedings in this case, in a State which has moved on from criminalizing children:

1. A hearing to determine – beyond reasonable doubt – whether the two 10 year-olds were responsible – whether they did or did not kill the two year-old. Whether, and in what way, the 10 year olds should be involved in this investigative hearing to satisfy their due process rights would need careful assessment to determine a procedure appropriate to their individual capacities.

2. If the two boys are found responsible, then a multi-disciplinary investigation is required (extensive and detailed for such a serious crime, less so for less serious crimes – but repetition of less serious offending could signal the need for more investigation). The investigation must cover the circumstances of the crime and its antecedents, focussing on why the killing took place, including:

· Environmental and circumstantial factors, not directly related to the killers – for example levels of supervision in public places for children, effective promotion of community responsibility to protect children, *etc.*;
· Other immediate factors that may explain why the killing happened;
· Factors in the background—in the broadest sense—of the killers, which may help to understand their actions and so inform their rehabilitation.

This judicial investigation should lead to a detailed report, attributing weight to different factors, but emphasizing uncertainty, where it exists, as much as certainty.

The hearing and the ongoing investigation would need the power to require the attendance of relevant witnesses – parents, relations, friends, teachers *etc.* (with the usual rules to protect their rights). The children involved would have the right to be heard and to be represented—but here too the procedures should be appropriate to their capacity.

The Convention requires that there should be no public identification of children in juvenile justice systems (Article 40 (2) (vii). To ensure their privacy, the privacy of all involved should be protected. But the well-known dangers of entirely closed hearings suggest that factual reporting of such hearings and the publication of reports of investigations, without identifying the children involved directly or indirectly, is in the public interest.

3. Depending on the findings and on which factors have been found to have greatest weight, the investigation—perhaps with different or additional experts—would be reconvened for its second stage: to identify both how the killing could have been prevented and what forms of supervision, education, treatment and support are most likely to prevent these particular children committing further crimes, to most fully rehabilitate and re-integrate them, ensuring their maximum development. This stage of the investigation would be required to consider whether the children pose an ongoing serious risk to the public and what actions are proposed to reduce the risk to an acceptable level. The State's responsibility requires it, in fulfilling its obligations to the two murderers, to ensure that public safety is not unreasonably put at risk.

As already noted, Article 37 places very strict limits on any restriction of liberty of offending children: "No child shall be deprived of his or her liberty unlawfully or arbitrarily. The arrest, detention or imprisonment of a child shall be in conformity with the law and shall be used only as a measure of last resort and for the shortest appropriate period of time."

So in determining necessary action, the investigation will only be able to order detention "as a last resort;" that is when other possible measures have been considered and rejected as unsafe, in relation to public safety considerations. Any decision to detain requires a judicial hearing to test it and needs ongoing frequent judicial review (and also as noted above, there has to be best interests consideration of which service should be responsible for such exceptional detention).

The second stage investigation would lead to a second detailed report and plan, including proposals for necessary monitoring of the child and frequent and regular review and evaluation of the plan in the light of progress or lack of it . In line with States' obligations, the plan should have statutory force, with a statutory duty to fulfil it.

4. And what happens when a child who is being reviewed under this distinct child justice system becomes 18? The response to their offending behaviour, including necessary supervision or in a very small number of cases some form of restriction of liberty to ensure public safety, may have to continue for a period, determined by successive reviews.

There are already limitations in some States on the keeping of records of offending by children and their use in subsequent investigations. The Beijing Rules are clear that: "Records of juvenile offenders shall not be used in adult proceedings in subsequent cases involving the same offender."[21] So it seems that only the most serious considerations of public safety should allow records of responsibility for offences committed before 18 to be maintained and available to influence treatment of the person beyond 18.

✳✳✳

Surely the children's rights community now owes children strong and uncompromising advocacy to end their criminalization? Of course this is not going to be achieved easily or quickly, but without a principled and fully rights-compliant target, the various reformist moves lack a clear and logical foundation.

---

21   UN Standard Minimum Rules for the Administration of Juvenile Justice, the Beijing Rules, adopted by General Assembly Resolution 40/33, 29 November 1985, Rule 21.2.

From the Inside – Children and Young People on Life in Police Cells and in Remand Prisons

Fredrik Malmberg

You're just trying to remain in the real world.

That's how Daniel describes the effect of being held in solitary confinement. This solitary confinement is something children in Sweden are subjected to when they are deprived of liberty due to being suspected of a crime. Sweden systematically subjects children deprived of their liberty to what the UN Special Rapporteur on torture says can amount to "torture and cruel, inhuman or degrading treatment." According to the rapporteur, solitary confinement of juveniles violates article 16 of the UN Convention against Torture and article 7 of the UN Covenant on Civil and Political Rights.[1]

For a number of years, the Ombudsman for Children in Sweden has been systematically listening to children and young people in vulnerable situations. We have met children taken into social care and children who have been exposed to violence and abuse in close relationships. These children have frequently expressed disappointment that the outside world has not reacted to their signals that they need support and help. That is serious, in several ways. Those children who fall through the safety net run an increased risk of becoming alienated and turning to crime.

During 2012 the Ombudsman for Children in Sweden met with children and young people who had been deprived of their liberty in police cells and remand prisons. A recurrent criticism against Sweden from both the UN Committee Against Torture (CAT) and the Council of Europe Committee for the Prevention of Torture (CPT) regards the use of restrictions in connection with detention.[2] As children are more sensitive to being held in isolation we found it important to follow up to which degree Sweden had implemented previous recommendations from the international treaty bodies.

In international as well as in Swedish law, everyone under 18 years of age is considered a child. The Ombudsman for Children in Sweden has visited a total of 13 police cell blocks and remand prisons around the country, asking open

---

1 United Nations General Assembly. Interim report of the special rapporteur of the Human Rights Council on torture and other cruel, inhuman or degrading treatment or punishment. (2011), A/66/268. (The UN Special Rapporteur on Torture, 2011).

2 CPT/Inf (2009) 34, and CAT/C/SWE/CO/5.

questions about what happens and what a child thinks when he/she is deprived of his/her liberty. It is not possible to generalize these accounts as applying to all children who are deprived of their liberty, but they do contribute to identifying shortcomings. On the basis of the qualitative study, the Ombudsman for Children in Sweden has carried out quantitative mappings of a kind not previously done in Sweden. We sent a survey to all police authorities on what their guidelines are for children held in police cells. We also asked the courts to provide us with application for detention orders and detentions records for those children held in detention during a specific time period. Finally we requested data from police authorities on how many children were held in police cells during 2011.

Our findings and our recommendations to the Swedish Government were published in our 2013 annual report: "From the Inside – Children and Young People on Life in Police Cells and Remand Prisons."

Our report details systematic and very far-reaching shortcomings regarding the human rights of children deprived of their liberty.[3] Our position based on our findings as well as previous reports from CAT and CPT[4] is that several changes are necessary if Sweden is going to live up to its commitments under the CRC. This article summarizes our most important findings and recommendations.

Collect Data on Children in Police Cells

Sweden's latest report to the UN Committee on the Rights of the Child lacks data on the number of children held in police cells on suspicion of crimes and on the average duration of the deprivation of liberty. Swedish police authorities have not collected this type of data in the past. In 2012 the Ombudsman for Children in Sweden therefore requested data from the country's police authorities on the total number of incarcerations of persons under 18 years of age during 2011. Our accumulated data shows that there were 3,052 incarcerations of children in police cells in 2011. Our compilation provides the first national and regional picture of how many incarcerations of children in police cells occur during a year in Sweden.

Continuous follow-up of data on children deprived of their liberty is a prerequisite for upholding the human rights of children. Comparable data which

---

3   The Ombudsman for Children in Sweden: From the Inside – children and young people on life in police cells and remand prisons (2013).
4   CPT/Inf (2009) 34, and CAT/C/SWE/CO/5.

can be examined contributes to increased openness and a lower risk of judicial abuse, which in turn increases trust in the rule of law.

The Ombudsman recommends the Government to instruct the National Police Board to systematically collect data on the number of incarcerations of children in police cells and on the duration of each deprivation of liberty.

Aim at Reducing the Number of Children Deprived of Their Liberty

Figures indicate that the number of young people suspected of crimes and detained in remand prisons has grown sharply in Sweden over the past 15 years. In 1998 there were 41 children[5] a year detained in remand prisons; in 2011 that number had risen to 122.[6] This increase is notable considering that the intention of both the CRC and Swedish legislation is that children should only exceptionally be detained before trial.

In order to reduce the use of pre-trial deprivation of liberty it is necessary that the alternatives to arrest and detention, which involve adequate supervision, also are acceptable in that they fulfil the child's human rights.

The Ombudsman recommends the government to take action in order to seek other measures for children suspected of crimes, e.g. youth supervision, with the aim of reducing the number of deprivations of liberty before trial as well as the time in detention for those who do have their liberty deprived.

No Child Suspected of a Crime Shall be Held in Solitary Confinement during the Investigation

The UN Special Rapporteur on Torture defines solitary confinement as a physical and social isolation of individuals who are confined to their cells for at least 22 hours a day. When a child is placed in a remand prison or a police cell in Sweden it almost always means that the child is held for shorter or longer periods in solitary confinement according to this definition. Solitary confinement is what children perceive as the very worst treatment. Children in our study say that it takes both willpower and strength to endure the enormous mental strain that solitary confinement causes.

---

5 Svensson, L, *Häktad eller omedelbart omhändertagen? – en studie om akuta frihetsberövanden av unga lagöverträdare*, Stockholm University, Department of Social Work, 2006.

6 The Government. Sweden's fifth periodic report to the UN Committee on the Rights of the Child on the implementation of the Convention on the Rights of the Child 2007–2012. 2012.

Against the background of the serious mental harm or suffering solitary confinement can lead to for children, the UN Special Rapporteur Against Torture considers that it may amount to torture and other cruel, inhuman or degrading treatment. According to the Rapporteur, solitary confinement of young people, irrespective of its duration, contravenes Article 7 of the UN Covenant on Civil and Political Rights and Article 16 of the UN Convention against Torture and other Cruel, Inhuman or Degrading Treatment or Punishment. It is the Rapporteur's view that it should be prohibited in respect of children.[7]

In our view, no child should be deprived of his or her liberty in solitary confinement during the investigation period. The Ombudsman for Children in Sweden recommends the government to assume its responsibility for creating a justice system in which children in conflict with the law are treated in accordance with their fundamental rights.

The Ombudsman recommends the government to take urgent action to introduce an explicit statutory ban on the solitary confinement for children in remand prisons and police cells.

Introduce Time Limits

According to the UN Committee on the Rights of the Child, the law must state clearly on what grounds a child may be placed or held in a police cell or remand prison pending trial. There must be a statutory time limit for pre-trial deprivation of liberty, which must be regularly reviewed. Time limits must be shorter than those that apply to adults. The maximum time a child in Sweden may be held in a police cell is four days. The Ombudsman for Children in Sweden recommends the government to introduce a time limit of 24 hours for the time a child may be held in a police cell.

A child who has been deprived of his or her liberty pending trial shall, according to the Committee, be formally charged and put on trial within 30 days of the beginning of the deprivation of liberty. In Sweden there is no limit at all for pre-trial detention. For example one 16-year old child was recently in remand prison for nearly a year.[8]

The Ombudsman for Children in Sweden recommends the government to introduce a time limit of 30 days for pre-trial detention in order for Sweden to live up to this requirement.

---

7   The UN Special Rapporteur on Torture, 2011.
8   Sveriges domstolar, Målnummer B334-13.

No Child Shall be Placed in Police Cells in Their Current Form

The time spent in a police cell is often a frightening experience for a child. The children in our survey describe the police cell environment as unpleasant, inhuman and destructive. They compare the routines and the physical environment in the police cell with being in hell. The treatment the children describe receiving by the staff varies, but can be summarized as cold, impersonal or downright frightening. The children also describe the feeling of being worth less as a human when you have been deprived of your liberty.

Despite the rule that children who are deprived of their liberty are to be treated as children, the child rights perspective is insufficient at the country's police authorities. This emerges in the Ombudsman for Children in Sweden's survey, to which all police authorities responded. Just under a third of the police authorities replied that they had drawn up guidelines for incarcerated children.

None of the police authorities had produced information specifically for children held in police cells. In other words, there is neither specially adapted information about what rights the incarcerated children have, nor about how the judicial process proceeds. Furthermore, no police authority places any special training requirements on the police cell guards who meet children deprived of their liberty.

Locking children up in that kind of environment during the judicial process is not consistent with the child's fundamental human rights. Neither can it be considered legally certain, as the child is to be interrogated during the time he or she spends in the police cell. Today there are alternatives to the cell environment which must be used. According to the National Police Board, persons between 15 and 18 years of age should only be held in police cells when absolutely necessary. Under normal circumstances, anyone under 18 should be held under guard in an interrogation room or similar space.[9]

The Ombudsman for Children in Sweden recommends the government to ensure that no child is deprived of his or her liberty during the investigation in a cell intended for adults. If a child is arrested and for some reason cannot be held in an interrogation room or similar, he or she should be placed in a remand prison instead of a police cell.

---

9 Rikspolisstyrelsens författningssamling. Rikspolisstyrelsens föreskrifter och allmänna råd
    om förvaring av personer i polisarrest RPSFS. 2000:58.

Individualise Restrictions for Children

From our interviews with children and young people, analyses of statistics and detention records, as well as discussions with law enforcement representatives, it is clear that it is not unusual for children to have full restrictions imposed on them, both during their time under arrest and in detention, which means that their contacts with the outside world have been limited. It has even happened that young people have been held in solitary confinement in the remand prison for several months, without any contact with either their family or anyone else outside the prison. One of the most important messages from the interviewees was precisely that the lack of contact with the family can be difficult to endure. Our examination of detention records shows that restrictions were approved in all cases where the prosecutor had requested them (91 of 108 cases). In one case alone the court highlighted the suspect's young age in connection with the prosecutor's request for restrictions. Neither is it unusual for the restrictions to be maintained for relatively long periods of time.

Criticism of Sweden from both the Council of Europe Committee for the Prevention of Torture and the UN Committee Against Torture concerns the use of restrictions following detention. The UN Committee Against Torture inspected Sweden in 2008 and recommended the country to undertake measures to reduce the use of restrictions and to shorten the time restrictions lasted. Restrictions must always be based on concrete grounds, be individualised, be proportional to the crime the individual is suspected of and be removed immediately when no longer needed.

The Ombudsman for Children recommends the Swedish government to ensure that when a court decides to place a child on remand, it must make an individual assessment in each case as to which restrictions are necessary.

All Children Must Always Have Access to a Public Defence Counsel, from the First Interrogation

From the accounts we have heard it appears to be the rule rather than the exception that a defence counsel is not present at the initial police interrogation of a young person. A common reason for this is that the children themselves waive the right, since they believe that they will then be allowed to leave the police cell sooner. Children and young people we spoke to felt that they were condemned in advance even at the first interrogation, which is to say that the justice system has already decided that they are guilty. The way they are treated during the interrogation may reinforce that feeling, and thereby contribute to their giving up or saying what the chief interrogator wants to hear. In the worst case, it may lead to the young person admitting to acts he or she has not committed.

Under the CRC, every child deprived of his or her liberty shall have the right to prompt access to legal and other appropriate assistance. There must be no margin for the stakeholders of the judicial process to use pressure, threats and promises to get the child to waive these rights. Moreover, the child is already at a disadvantage due to the very form of the judicial process and therefore it cannot be regarded as acceptable, in the vast majority of situations, that the child waives that right. In most cases it is impossible for the child to foresee the consequences of such a choice, and therefore the stakeholders of the judicial process must assume their responsibility to guarantee the child his/her fundamental human rights. The circumstance that the child shall always be guaranteed public defence counsel must furthermore not mean that the duration of the deprivation of liberty is prolonged.

The Ombudsman for Children in Sweden recommends the government to ensure that all children are guaranteed fundamental rights during the judicial process. This requires society to make sure that a public defence counsel can be appointed, regardless of the time. It must also be possible to make the appointment promptly.

Provide Effective and Impartial Complaints Mechanisms and Establish an Independent Child Representative

In our interviews with children and young people deprived of their liberty it became clear that they don't always know that you can make complaints about conditions and appeal against decisions. The Council of Europe Committee for the Prevention of Torture has criticised Sweden for not informing young people of their rights. The Committee says that Sweden must ensure that all persons deprived of their liberty receive such information.[10] The Ombudsman for Children in Sweden regards it as very serious that many young people have not had a clear idea about how the system works or about the procedure for appealing against decisions. The right to information is fundamental for giving a child the ability to influence his or her situation, and a core right under the CRC.

Institutions where children are deprived of their liberty are often closed to scrutiny by the outside world. It is therefore important that every child who is deprived of his/her liberty has a right to information and access to complaints

---

10   European Committee for the Prevention of Torture (CPT/Inf [2009] 34).

mechanisms. Children must be able to turn to an independent body with any questions and complaints regarding care. Children who are deprived of their liberty and/or are subject to coercive measures must also be able to obtain redress and compensation when the authorities responsible for their care have neglected those responsibilities. These mechanisms must be known to and easily accessible to children.

The Ombudsman for Children in Sweden recommends the Swedish government to establish an independent child representative to serve as an independent instance to which children and young people deprived of their liberty can turn with any complaints about how their human rights have been upheld during the process. The representative must be entitled to represent the child in court and have the right to pursue claims in court in order to secure damages for children who are deprived of their liberty.

Conclusion

A child suspected of a crime risks being subjected to reprisals, violations of justice and harm. It is against this background that international conventions provide strong protection for the human rights of the child suspected of a crime. According to the CRC, no child shall be subjected to torture or other cruel, inhuman or degrading treatment or punishment. The arrest, detention or imprisonment of a child shall only be used as a measure of last resort, and for the shortest appropriate period of time. Every child deprived of their liberty shall be treated with humanity and respect for the inherent dignity of the human person, and in a manner which takes into account the needs of persons of his or her age.

According to the UN Committee on the Rights of the Child, a separate juvenile justice system is required for children in conflict with the law, since children differ from adults in their physical and psychological development and in their emotional and educational needs. The Ombudsman for Children in Sweden's view is that several changes are needed if Sweden is to live up to the requirements of the CRC.

"Without Resorting to Judicial Proceedings": Diversion and Mediation

The Case of Georgia

Rusudan Mikhelidze

Introduction

Article 40 (3)(b) of the Convention on the Rights of the Child (CRC) obliges the States Parties to promote measures *without resorting to judicial proceedings* in dealing with children in conflict with the law, whenever appropriate and desirable.[1] This paper analyses *diversion* as an alternative to judicial proceedings[2] in the light of the Georgian Diversion and Mediation Programme (the Programme) – a revolutionary breakthrough introduced into Georgia's criminal justice system in 2010. The paper highlights the success of the Programme and makes recommendations for its further development.

Part I

1   Overview of International Standards

1.1   *Non-judicial Alternatives to Criminal Proceedings: Relevant International Standards*

According to the Committee on the Rights of the Child, state authorities can use two types of intervention for dealing with juveniles in conflict with penal law. These are measures without resorting to judicial proceedings and measures in the context of judicial proceedings.[3] At the same time, international standards expressly recognize a non-judicial mechanism as a strongly preferred option due to its advantages for the child, for society and consequently for the State using it.

First and foremost, Article 40 (3) of the CRC requires the States Parties to promote non-judicial alternatives for juveniles in conflict with law while

---

1 UN General Assembly, Convention on the Rights of the Child, A/RES/44/25 (Nov. 20, 1989), Article 40 (3).

2 Committee on the Rights of the Child, General Comment No. 10 on Children's Rights in Juvenile Justice (2007) defines diversion as "removal from criminal/juvenile justice processing and referral to alternative (social) services."

3 *Ibid.*, p. 8.

© KONINKLIJKE BRILL NV, LEIDEN, 2015 | DOI 10.1163/9789004297432_015

ensuring that human rights and legal safeguards are fully respected. The Committee on the Rights of the Child in its General Comment No. 10 underlines that the alternative measures should have primacy over judicial proceedings as they avoid stigmatization, have good outcomes for children and society, and are cost-effective.[4]

Along with the CRC, international soft law instruments provide guidance and recommendations. Legally non-binding alternatives include Beijing Rules,[5] the Council of Europe Guiding Principles,[6] Model Law on Juvenile Justice,[7] and the UNICEF Handbook.[8]

The supremacy of alternatives to conventional criminal proceedings can be inferred from the general principles of juvenile justice enshrined in the CRC and related international documents. The cornerstone principle of juvenile justice in Article 3(1) of CRC provides that the best interests of child should be a primary consideration in all actions concerning children.[9] It is further explained in General Comment No. 10 that the best interest of a child is served only if the child is dealt with in a system that complies with international standards and norms in juvenile justice, most importantly the CRC provisions.

Another key principle, enshrined in Article 37(b) of CRC and in Beijing Rule 17 (1)(c), provides that any restriction of liberty of a child shall be a measure of last resort and that careful consideration has to be given to using it as an intervention in relation to juveniles. In exceptional circumstances when restriction of liberty is applied as a last resort, it should be used as briefly as possible.

Further, as stated in Article 40 (1) of the CRC, a child in conflict with the law should be treated in a way that promotes "the child's sense of dignity and worth" and "the desirability of promoting the child's reintegration and the child's assuming a constructive role in society."[10]

---

4   *Ibid.*, p. 9.

5   UN General Assembly, *United Nations Standard Minimum Rules for the Administration of Juvenile Justice (Beijing Rules)*, A/RES/40/33 (Nov. 29, 1985).

6   Council of Europe, *Guideline of the Committee of Ministers of the Council of Europe on child friendly justice and Their Explanatory Memorandum* (Nov. 17, 2010).

7   UN Office of Drugs and Crime, *Justice in Matters Involving Children in Conflict with the Law: Model Law on Juvenile Justice and Related Commentary* (2013).

8   UNICEF, *Toolkit on Diversion and Alternatives to Detention* (2009).

9   Committee on the Rights of the Child, General Comment No. 14 (2013). See also Committee of Ministers of the Council of Europe, *Guideline of the Committee of Ministers of the Council of Europe on child friendly justice,* p. 8.

10   Convention on the Rights of the Child, Article 40 (1).

Thus, the best interests of a child require that the least intrusive or punitive measures are applied in relation to children in conflict with the law;[11] that the least contact with the criminal justice system is ensured; and that the case of a juvenile is resolved with non-legal alternatives, diversion to social and other services, programs and activities that are best tailored to individual needs.[12]

As early as in 1985 the United Nations General Assembly in its resolution referred to as the Beijing Rules pointed out that diversion is commonly practiced in many legal systems and serves to "hinder negative effects of subsequent proceeding in juvenile justice administration (for example the stigma of conviction and sentence)."[13]

Moreover, the Beijing Rules and the related commentary give preference to diversion with no intervention at all, and consider non-intervention to be the "best response" especially when the offence is not serious and "where the family, the school or other informal social control institutions have already reacted, or are likely to react, in an appropriate and constructive manner."[14]

Nevertheless, for cases where there is a need for intervention, the said Rules provide that viable alternatives to juvenile justice processing in the *form of community-based diversion* shall be in place and applied accordingly: "Programmes that involve settlement by victim restitution and those that seek to avoid future conflict with the law through temporary supervision and guidance are especially commended."[15]

As to the *crime types* to be covered by diversion, the Committee on the Rights of the Child states that the minimum obligation of the States in promoting measures for children in conflict with the law without resorting to judicial proceedings includes, but is not limited, to providing, the possibility of diversion for "children who commit minor offences, such as shoplifting or other property offences with limited damage, and first-time child offenders."[16] However, the Committee further points out that diversion should not be limited to those children who commit minor offences.[17] The same standard can be found in the Beijing Rules: "merits of individual cases would make diversion appropriate, even when more serious offences have been committed (for example first offence, the act having been committed under peer pressure etc.)."[18]

---

11   Model Law, *supra* note 7, p. 70.
12   General Comment No. 14, *supra* note 9.
13   *Beijing Rules,* commentary to rule 11.
14   *Ibid.,* rule 11 (4).
15   *Ibid.,* commentary to rule 11(4).
16   Committee on the Rights of the Child, General Comment No. 10, p. 9.
17   Committee on the Rights of the Child, General Comment No. 10.
18   *Beijing Rules,* commentary to rule 11 (4).

Further, General Comment No. 10 clearly states the obligation for States to have in place the mechanisms for diversion and to use them as common practice in most cases: "Given the fact that the majority of child offenders commit only minor offences, a range of measures involving removal from criminal/ juvenile justice processing and referral to alternative (social) services (*i.e.* diversion) should be a well-established practice that can and should be used in most cases."[19]

As regards the *restorative justice* element in diversion, the *Vienna Guidelines* provide that whenever appropriate, mechanisms for the informal resolution of disputes in cases involving a child offender should be used, including mediation and restorative justice practices, particularly processes involving victims.[20]

In conclusion, international standards require that alternatives to traditional criminal justice measures be an integral part of any juvenile justice system. As Commissioner for Human Rights Thomas Hammarberg points out, "Diversion, whether it involves directing the child to health/social services or to informal procedures aimed at preventing further offending, should {thus} be a core objective of every juvenile justice system, and this should be explicitly stated in legislation."[21]

Hence, application of the above principles and standards in relation to juveniles in conflict with the law can only be ensured in practice if a variety of viable measures are available, alternatives that can be individualized and applied by competent authorities in observance of human rights and relevant due process guarantees.

1.2   *Standards and Requirements for Diversion*

The previous section demonstrates that application of diversion as a non-judicial disposition in a juvenile case is explicitly required in any legal system. At the same time, important human rights and due process guarantees have to be observed to bring the procedure of diversion and the measures imposed as a result into line with international standards. Diversion is an informal alternative in the administration of juvenile justice. Thus not all due process guarantees associated with the conventional justice process can or should be present when applying it. However, the CRC expressly emphasizes that human rights standards and legal safeguards are to be fully respected when applying

---

19   Committee on the Rights of the Child, General Comment No. 10, pp. 8–9.

20   UN Economic and Social Council, *Administration of Juvenile Justice* (*Vienna Guidelines*), Resolution 1997/30, II.B.15.

21   Thomas Hammarberg, "Children and Justice: Proposals for Improvement," *Commissioner for Human Rights Issue Paper*, 2009, p. 16.

alternatives to judicial proceedings.[22] Specific aspects related to the individual child and the offence shall be scrutinized when applying a concrete measure.

General principles to be taken into account when applying diversion are summarized by Hammarberg as follows: (a) Human rights must […] underpin all responses to offending, including diversion (b) the well-being of the juvenile shall be the guiding factor in the consideration of her or his case (c) when diverting a juvenile focus should be on the needs of the child rather than the criminal behaviour committed.[23]

Detailed requirements to guide state authorities when instituting diversion mechanisms are provided in General Comment No. 10. The Standards for diversion are the following:

- There should be compelling evidence that the child committed the alleged offence;
- The child should freely and voluntarily admit responsibility;
- There should be no intimidation or pressure on him/her to admit the guilt;
- Admission of guilt or any information obtained during the process of diversion shall not be used against a child in any subsequent legal proceedings;
- The child's consent to the diversionary measure should be well-informed, free, voluntary, and written; States might also consider the parents giving the consent in particular in cases of children under 16;
- There needs to be a possibility to review an authority's decision so as to protect a child from discrimination;
- The child must be enabled to seek legal or other appropriate assistance on the appropriateness and desirability of the diversion offered by the authorities and on the possibility to review this measure;
- Successful completion of the diversionary measure by a juvenile shall result in the definite closure of the case;
- No criminal record shall be attached to the diversion;
- If the information on diversion is registered for administrative and review purposes access to this information shall be given to the competent authorities only for limited periods;
- The criteria for diversion and procedure together with the competent authority shall be clearly prescribed by law.[24]

---

22   Convention on the Rights of the Child, Article 40 (3)(b).
23   Hammarberg, *supra* note 21.
24   Committee on the Rights of the Child, General Comment No. 10, pp. 9–10.

The Commissioner for Human Rights points out that States should ensure that a diversion mechanism is adequately supported, governed by a coherent legal framework and integrated into the legal system. The responsibilities of the relevant agencies must be clearly defined, all staff properly trained and supported in their work and decision-makers aware of the merits and effectiveness of diversion in order to develop and sustain confidence in the system.[25]

2   Why States Should Apply Diversion: Benefits and Efficiency

Well-shaped international standards unequivocally stress the obligation for States to seek to apply diversion in relation to child offenders. As a consequence the majority of countries have instituted alternatives to judicial proceedings for children.[26] Authoritative sources do not question the benefits of diversion. Research and analysis of practice largely support the view that the approach benefits the child and the whole of society.[27] It is believed that formal processing through the juvenile judicial system has a negative impact on a juvenile's future and is more likely to provoke subsequent delinquent behaviour than are minimum intervention and non-judicial alternatives.

A United States study shows that formal processing through the juvenile judicial system in fact harms children. Research into more than 7,300 juveniles across 29 experiments over 35 years concluded, based on the evidence, that "formal processing of juveniles appears not to control crime, but actually seems to increase delinquency."[28] There is no evidence elsewhere that traditional juvenile judicial systems effectively control crime.[29] On the contrary, traditional measures can be counterproductive to ensuring the safety of society, while diversion with restorative justice components is proved to be efficient in meeting the very objective of the criminal justice system, namely contributing to a peaceful and safe society.[30]

Stigmatization or labeling is considered to be the consequence of traditional criminal judicial mechanisms and the instigator of reoffending. Although

---

25   Hammarberg, *supra* note 21, p. 19.

26   *Justice in Matters Involving Children in Conflict with the Law, supra* note 7, p. 75.

27   Committee on the Rights of the Child, General Comment No. 10.

28   Petrosino, A., Turpin-Petrosino, C. and Guckenburg, "Formal System Processing of Juveniles: Effects on Delinquency," *Campbell Systematic Reviews* (2010):1.

29   *Ibid.*, p. 6.

30   Committee of Ministers of the Council of Europe, Recommendation N° R (99) 19 and explanatory memorandum (Sept. 15, 1999), p. 13. See also UNICEF, *Toolkit on Diversion, supra* note 8, p. 3.

some experts criticizing diversion consider that the formal juvenile judicial system can better help deter future criminal behaviour by juveniles,[31] they are very few compared to the great majority who believe that traditional measures can cause juveniles to commit more crimes, due to a "labeling" effect.[32] Interventions that lead to labeling or exposure to deviant peers may have detrimental effects on a child's development.[33] It is maintained that juveniles will more likely commit crimes as adults when labeled as delinquents. If juveniles associate with deviant groups they are also more likely to become delinquents.[34] Thus, it is crucial that minimum intervention is used in dealing with juveniles in conflict with the law and that they are handled in as non-intrusive manner as possible.

Delinquent behaviour is a characteristic of most adolescents and in most cases it is completely distinct from the personality they eventually develop. The great majority of juveniles in conflict with the law are "socio-economic victims."[35] Generally, the causes include poverty, lack of education and employment opportunities, broken homes, family problems and peer pressure. The targeted interventions, diversion to appropriate services tailored to juveniles' needs, are far more likely to deter future offending than traditional criminal proceedings are. Projects demonstrate that, depending on the quality of the program, such practices can reduce offending by up to 70%.[36]

Furthermore, court proceedings are not cheap.[37] Diversion is less costly than formal justice;[38] it thus helps save resources for cases, where formal proceedings are in fact necessary.[39]

---

31   Regoli, R.M. and Hewitt, J.D., *Delinquency in Society: a Child-centered Approach*, 2nd edition, New York, McGraw-Hill, 1994, p. 425.

32   Patrick, S. and Marsh, R., "Juvenile Diversion: Results of a Three Year Experimental Study," Boise State University, 2005; *Juvenile Justice: Modern Concepts of Working with Children in Conflict with the Law*, Save the Children, UK, 2004.

33   Petrosino, A. Turpin-Petrosino, C. and Guckenburg, S., "The Impact of Juvenile System Processing on Delinquency," *Labeling Theory: Empirical Tests*, Farrington, D.P & Murray, J. (eds.), New Jersey, Transaction Publishers, 2014, p. 114.

34   Patrick, and Marsh, *supra* note 32, p. 2.

35   *Juvenile Justice, supra* note 32, p. 11.

36   *Toolkit on Diversion, supra* note 8, p. 3.

37   *Juvenile Justice, supra* note 32, p. 90.

38   Recommendation N° R (99) 19 and explanatory memorandum, *supra* note 30, p. 8.

39   Bruce Abramson, B., "Right to diversion: Using the Convention on the Rights of the Child to Turn Juvenile Justice Rights into Reality" (2004): 9. Available here: http://www.oijj.org/en/docs/general/the-right-to-diversion-using-the-convention-on-the-rights-of-the-child-to-turn-juvenile.

Part II

3   The Diversion and Mediation Programme in Georgia

3.1   *Background: The Birth of Diversion as an Alternative to Criminal*
         Prosecution
The "zero tolerance policy" announced by the Government of Georgia in 2006
to fight large-scale criminality adversely affected the juvenile judicial system
and juveniles in conflict with the law. The prison population increased dra-
matically, placing the country in the top five of the world's prison population
rankings.[40] Incarceration rates of juveniles increased consequently as well. In
2008 the number of convicted children reached 1,166 as opposed to 459 in
2003.[41] As a part of the punitive criminal justice policy the age of criminal
responsibility was lowered from 14 to 12.

The crowded prisons lacked basic conditions for inmates; many times the
European Court of Human Rights found Georgia in violation of the European
Convention for the Protection of Human Rights and Fundamental Freedoms,
with prison conditions amounting to inhuman and degrading treatment of
prisoners within the meaning of the Convention.[42] Prisons were dominated by
the Georgian mafia, these "Thieves in Law" having huge influence on adolescents.[43] Drugs were freely available. There were no programmes or services for
inmates, and the juvenile facility was no exception in this regard. Against this
background, prosecutors guided by the zero tolerance policy, in the absence of
viable alternatives to custodial measures, would seek prison for juveniles even
for minor offences and judges would agree.

Although the special chapter on juveniles in the Georgian Criminal Code
provided for the possibility (at least for minor offences) for the courts to
impose educational measures that would not result in criminal records,[44]
these provisions remained dead letters since there was no infrastructure or

---

40   Walmsley, R., "World Prison Population List," 9thedition, International Centre for Prison
      Studies. Available at: http://www.idcr.org.uk/wp-content/uploads/2010/09/WPPL-9-22
      .pdf.
41   UNICEF, *Georgia and the Convention of the Rights of the Child – An update on the situation*
      of children in Georgia, 2011, p. 46, available at: http://www.unicef.org/ceecis/Unicef_Sitan
      _ENG_WEB.pdf.
42   *Aliev v Georgia,* Application No. 522/04, Judgment of 13 January 2009; *Ramishvili and*
      Kokhreidze v Georgia, Application No. 1704/06, Judgment of 27 January 2009; *Gorgiladze v*
      Georgia, Application No. 4313/04, Judgment of 20 October 2009.
43   *Ashlarba v Georgia,* Application No. 45554/08, Judgment of 15 July 2014, para. 24.
44   Criminal Code of Georgia, Article 80–100.

mechanism to implement them. The general policy was very punitive and the main tool to fight crime was incapacitation. The Government's overall policy for combating crime had a fascinating impact on the crime rate. It resulted in a dramatic decrease in criminality, the eradication of the impunity syndrome and the elimination of the Georgian mafia.[45] At the same time, the need for reforms in juvenile justice became self-evident. This would have been so even without the heavy criticism, pressure and urging from the international and local non-government community.

The Committee on the Rights of the Child, UNICEF, the EU and other international actors had expressed serious concern about the rapid increase in the number of children entering the criminal justice system in Georgia and, most importantly, the lack of community-based alternatives and restorative justice programs to ensure that imprisonment for juveniles was used as a measure of last resort.[46] At that time, Georgia was obviously in violation of its conventional obligations under the CRC.

A major breakthrough in juvenile justice was the introduction of diversion as a legal concept into the legal system of Georgia and the parallel process of preparing conditions for launching the diversion and mediation programme. Diversion was introduced as a part of the gradual liberalization policy proclaimed by the Government in 2009 and also reflected in Georgia's Criminal Justice Reform Strategy and its special chapter on juveniles.[47] The introduction of the mechanism that would make it possible to divert juveniles from traditional legal proceedings to non-judicial alternatives was revolutionary for the country with its criminal justice system of mandatory prosecution and its Soviet past.

3.2 The Juvenile Diversion and Mediation Programme in Georgia

Amendments to the criminal procedure legislation of Georgia in 2010 granted the prosecutor discretionary power not to prosecute first-time-offender juveniles for less serious or serious crimes. A prosecutor could now divert these offenders from the formal criminal justice system into the diversion and mediation programme.[48] Relevant legislation and guidelines provide specific

---

45 Georgia is one of the safest countries of Europe, see van Dijk, J. and Chanturia, T., "The Remarkable Case of Georgia; Secondary Analysis of the 2010/2011 Crime and Security Surveys in Georgia," University of Tilburg, 2012.

46 The Committee on the Rights of the Child, *Consideration of Reports Submitted by States Parties under Article 44 of the Convention – Concluding Observations: Georgia*, 2008, p. 18.

47 Ministry of Justice of Georgia,. "Criminal Justice Reform Strategy and Action Plan." Available at: http://www.justice.gov.ge/Ministry/Index/237.

48 Criminal Procedure Code of Georgia, Article 105.

criteria and pre-conditions (discussed in detail in the next section) for the prosecutorial decision not to initiate, or to terminate, prosecution on the grounds of non-existence of public interest in pursuing the case,[49] and for diverting a juvenile with a civil agreement of maximum duration of 12 months, known as a diversion agreement.[50]

The diversion and mediation programme introduces the important role of social worker in the administration of juvenile justice in Georgia. He or she is tasked with individual assessment of a juvenile and his/her needs (the biopsychosocial assessment). Before the Programmeme started, the traditional measures imposed on juveniles were not based on any individual assessment or needs identification. Although the legislation provided for the requirement to take into account the personal characteristics, family, environment, individual needs and circumstances of a child, there was no mechanism or instrument through which a prosecutor or a judge could apply the provision.

Importantly, interventions applied as a result of diversion are not "ordered" or imposed by competent authority through diversion orders common among the countries using alternatives,[51] but are the product of agreement among parties in the process. Measures for the diversion agreement, the combination of conditions to be observed by juveniles, are proposed by a social worker based on his or her assessment. The conditions are subsequently worked out and agreed upon by the parties and concluded in a family group conference. The diversion agreement can be a result of victim-offender mediation if the victim agrees to take part in the process.

The diversion agreement is signed by all the parties to the process, including the juvenile. Signature by a juvenile has a particular value. First, it has a symbolic meaning: by signing the agreement, the juvenile takes responsibility for his/her actions as a grown-up. Secondly, through signature he/she realizes and acknowledges the harm caused to the victim or the community and voluntarily agrees to the conditions aimed at restitution.

Pursuant to the Guidelines for Prosecutors adopted by a decree of the Minister of Justice (Guidelines for Prosecutors) the agreement may include specific obligations of the juvenile, his/her parents or the victim as well as restriction of the juvenile's behaviour and referral to specific programmes.[52]

---

49   *Ibid.*, Article 105.4.

50   *Ibid.*, Article 105.5.

51   *Justice in Matters Involving Children in Conflict with the Law, supra* note 7, p. 18.

52   Minister of Justice of Georgia, Decree N216 on "Approval of the Guiding Principles on Diversion and Mediation for Prosecution and Basic Conditions of the Agreement," Nov. 12, 2010.

The obligations under agreement typically include educational measures, sports, professional development courses and physico-social rehabilitation programmes, social responsibilities and limitations on certain activities.

Given the limited resources and lack of programmes for juveniles in Georgia, the most creative solutions are used to reinforce positive characteristics of children, increase their sense of social responsibility and shift their attention from delinquency to social activism. For example, the conditions of the diversion agreement for a "little writer" included the responsibility to help the e-book programme by digitizing literature of interest to him. As another example a dancer was hired to conduct dance classes at an orphanage.

The Programme includes victim-offender mediation through group conferencing if the victim is willing to participate. The refusal of a victim to participate, however, does not preclude the use of diversion without mediation.

The mediation process is likely to meet its objectives fully if victims and offenders meet face-to-face, express their feelings directly to each other, and develop a new understanding of the situation.[53] Thus, the mediator is mandated to work with the parties, organize their face-to-face meetings and prepare them for the concluding conference, where participants share their feelings openly, speak of the reasons and consequences of the crime and propose solutions to restore "social peace" in the community as well as repairing damage.

The social worker monitors the implementation of the agreement and subsequently reports to the prosecutor. Serious breaches of conditions may result in initiation or renewal of criminal prosecution against the juvenile. Information obtained during diversion cannot be used in subsequent proceedings. If the conditions of agreement are met, the prosecutor will terminate the case and the juvenile will have no criminal record.

In sum, the Programme is a community-based alternative with elements of restorative justice, as well as important human-rights guarantees and legal safeguards. Aimed primarily at ensuring that the best interests of a child are served, important components of the Programme are rehabilitation and social integration.

3.3   *Is the Georgian Model in Line with International Standards?*
The diversion and mediation program in Georgia is largely in line with international standards. Relevant legislation and guidelines reiterate the requirements of the international documents analysed in the first part of this paper.

---

53   UN Office on Drugs and Crime, *Handbook on Restorative Justice Programs,* Criminal Justice Handbook Series, New York, 2006, p. 18.

In the Georgian model, diversion can only be applied if there is sufficient evidence for criminal prosecution – if there is probable cause that a juvenile has committed the alleged offence, the juvenile freely and voluntarily admits responsibility with no intimidation or pressure and gives informed consent to be involved in the Programme.[54] Importantly, the relevant regulations emphasize the principles of non-stigmatization, proportionality of the measure imposed and above all the primacy of the best interests of a child.

Detailed requirements for diversion are laid down in relevant guidelines.[55] Note that diversion measures shall not interfere with the child's education and development. The juvenile's right to privacy shall be respected at all stages. To avoid harm caused to a child by undue publicity or stigma, the *principle of confidentiality* is included in the guidelines.

At any stage before signing the diversion agreement, a juvenile can refuse diversion and choose to stand trial. He/she has the right to be accompanied by parents or legal guardians at all times, provided that the presence of a particular person is not against his/her best interests. Although diversion is not a formal proceeding, a juvenile has the right to a lawyer, if so desired.

According to the guidelines, admission of guilt by a juvenile and any information received during the diversion process *cannot* be used against him/her in any subsequent legal proceedings.[56] Juveniles diverted from criminal prosecution shall not have a *criminal record.*

Nonetheless, it can be argued that the criteria for application of diversion laid down in relevant regulations are too restrictive and thus preclude wide expansion of the mechanism.

First, diversion can be applied only if a juvenile has committed less serious or serious crimes (for *certain categories only*) for the *first time* and if he/she has not taken part in the diversion and mediation program before.

Secondly, the Programme not only requires a juvenile to plead guilty but also, to be *ready to apologize* before the victim.

Further, a prerequisite is that the juvenile (his/her family) agrees to *make good the damage* caused to the victim, unless the victim waives restitution.

Lastly, even though the criteria above are fairly restrictive, there is still fair latitude for the prosecutor when deciding on diversion. In particular, the prosecutor should be convinced that the best interest of the child is being taken

---

54   Criminal Procedure Code of Georgia, Article 105.4.

55   Decree N216. *supra* note 52. There are also similar guidelines for social workers and mediators approved by relevant line Ministries.

56   Decree N216, *supra* note 52, Article 1.29.

into account and that, given the circumstances of the case, there is no public interest to pursue criminal prosecution. Moreover, the prosecutor is not required to substantiate a refusal to apply diversion and to pursue a criminal case; neither is his/her decision subject to review. Thus, the legislation leaves it to the prosecutor to apply diversion in a given case rather than setting more or less objective standards for its application.

Several aspects are worth revising in order to ensure the full compliance of the Georgian model with international standards. These include *expanding the Programme to all categories of serious* crime (omitting only especially serious crimes from its scope); considering the possibility for *repeat offenders* to benefit from the Programme; *strengthening the role of the judge* in diversion, considering the possibility to *review* a prosecutor's decision not to divert a juvenile etc. These recommendations are analysed below.

3.4   Key Challenges, Recommendations and Way Forward for the Georgian Model

The diversion and mediation program was launched as a pilot scheme on 15 November 2010 in four cities: Tbilisi, Kutaisi, Batumi and Rustavi and on 19 November the first juvenile was diverted. In fewer than three years the Programme covered the whole country. Although real results regarding the effectiveness and efficiency of the Programme are yet to be seen,[57] statistics available so far demonstrate the Programme's success. According to the official statistics, by the end of 2013, 574 juveniles had been diverted through the Programme with a recidivism rate of only 4% (24 juveniles re-offended). As of August 2014, a total of 673 juveniles had been diverted, re-offending rate 3.7%. The introduction of the Programme helped decrease the number of convicted children from 1,166 in 2008 to 456 in 2013[58] and the use of custodial sentences from 40% in 2007 to 26% in 2013.[59]

As expected, there were indeed a number of obstacles during the integration of the new concept and the new mechanism into the Georgian legal system. It was no easy task to build trust in the Programme among the legal profession in Georgia and subsequently to make the mechanism work. The professionals involved in the Programme, prosecutors, lawyers, judges, social

---

57   UNICEF is evaluating the Programme. Results are to be available by the end of 2014.
58   National Statistics Office of Georgia, "Criminal Justice Statistics," available at. http:// geostat.ge/index.php?action=page&p_id=602&lang=eng.
59   Statistics of the Supreme Court of Georgia, available at http://www.supremecourt .ge/2013yearstatistic/.

workers and mediators had to be trained.[60] In fact, mediators in criminal cases did not exist before and the profession has only emerged as a part of the new Programme.

The mechanism has unquestionably brought about a number of benefits to the criminal justice system of Georgia. Its success is undoubted. In fact since November 2010, 673[61] juveniles have been "rescued" from jails, prisons or the adverse effects of the formal criminal judicial system. Here are listed the benefits of the Programme:

– juvenile offenders can now be dealt with differently from adults, taking into account their age, immaturity and special needs;
– the likelihood of stigmatization of juveniles is much lower when involved in the Programme;
– traumatization of juveniles associated with traditional proceedings is avoided;
– the adverse effects of incarceration, with its risks of exposing juveniles to the culture of abuse, bullying and negative role modelling are diminished;
– diverted juveniles do not have criminal records;
– juveniles are encouraged and motivated to be responsible citizens accountable for their actions;
– the restorative justice element of the Programme helps juveniles to be reconciled with the victims; thus the Programme increases victim satisfaction as well;
– The needs-based services and programmes and the individual approach support the integration of juveniles into the community;
– The Programme helps improve safety – the rate of recidivism so far is very low;
– as the mechanism is less costly than traditional mechanisms, it saves the resources of the criminal justice system.

The introduction of diversion into the legal system of Georgia and the launch of the Programme that allows its practical implementation constitute a significant achievement in a country with a post-Soviet criminal justice tradition and its recently abandoned zero-tolerance policy. After almost four years of

---

60   Government of Georgia – UNICEF, *2011 – 2015 Country Programme of Cooperation*, 2014, p. 21.
61   As of August 2014.

implementation the benefits and the achievements of the Programme are being widely praised and recognized.[62]

Without questioning the success of the Programme, after almost four years of its existence important lessons have been learned and the recommendations for future development are firmly experience-based. The following recommendations should be considered:

First, the Programme needs to *grow and expand*. Although the mechanism now operates countrywide, the extent of its application in practice is still not satisfactory. It could be broadened to cover more juveniles where the eligibility criteria are met. In addition, the criteria could be expanded and the Programme extended to all categories of crime except the most serious. Obliging the prosecutor to substantiate in writing a decision not to divert a juvenile would also contribute to more objective application of diversion and its uniform expansion throughout the country. Diversion at court level should be implemented in practice.

Secondly, the Programme would benefit from simplification of procedure in order to apply lower-intensity interventions in low-risk cases and save resources for higher-risk ones. Sometimes, mere warnings may be sufficient, with no need for complex interventions. In line with international standards and the principle of minimum intervention, the procedures of the Programme could be thus revised.

In addition, the role of the prosecutor could be reduced in the whole process and the roles of the mediator and social worker enhanced. This was not possible in the initial phase of implementation of the Programme for understandable reasons – notably the predominant role of prosecutor in the judicial system.

Moreover, the culture of mediation and restorative justice has yet to grow and mature in Georgia. The profession of mediator needs support, capacity-building and development. Further, methodology for evaluation of the Programme has to be elaborated and applied. The results of evaluation should serve as a basis for further improvements. Any programme that claims to contribute to reducing offending has to stand up to evaluation.

Finally, and most importantly, for a country like Georgia with limited resources it is crucial that non-governmental organizations are stimulated through mechanisms to increase the variety and quality of the services they provide so they may serve as reliable partners in the implementation of the Programme.

It takes time indeed to develop confidence in new legal concepts and mechanisms, such as diversion. Its further expansion requires strong will and constant effort from the Government and the professionals involved.

---

62   *Georgia and the Convention of the Rights of the Child, supra* note 41, p. 46.

Children's Houses – Barnahus: Today and in the Future

Anna Kaldal and Carl Göran Svedin

1 Background

Barnahus are based on the American Children's Advocacy Center model, and have emerged in Sweden in the past ten years. The Swedish Barnahus model is a collaboration where the authorities responsible for a child who is the subject of a criminal investigation interact under one roof in a child-friendly environment. The joint investigative measures seek to optimize the quality of the investigations, interventions and treatment of the child.

Today there are about 30 Barnahus around the country. They have developed differently depending on local conditions and engagement and the variation between them is great: they differ in terms of size, organization and financing. Common to all, however, is that the target group includes victims of both physical and sexual crime, that the police and the social services are represented, that the police interview is conducted there and that the interior is child-friendly.

The overall aim of Barnahus is to let the best interest of the child be a primary consideration when a child is the subject of a police investigation, and to put the child's needs at the centre, letting the authorities adapt to the child and not the other way around. The purposes of Barnahus are thus several. First they should create a child-friendly environment where the police interview, the medical investigation, the child protection services risk assessment and psychological treatment can be done in one place. Secondly, inter-agency cooperation under one roof should optimize the conditions for better quality in the police investigations, the risk assessment and psychological treatment of the child.

2 Purpose and Questions

This article describes the activity and the ambitions of Barnahus in Sweden: Where are we today and what development is needed? Key questions are what should be required of Barnahus, if there is a need for national coordination, and whether specific legislation is needed. Another question is whether there are areas that need more and appropriate research.

© KONINKLIJKE BRILL NV, LEIDEN, 2015 | DOI 10.1163/9789004297432_016

3   Children's Rights

Through the Convention on the Rights of the Child (CRC) and the Optional Protocols, we promise to protect and promote children's rights. The CRC States that children are bearers of their own rights and that childhood is entitled to special care and assistance. Each State has a responsibility to ensure the child its rights (Article 4). Thus both Swedish and international law grant children rights based on the fact that children are vulnerable and need greater protection than adults.

A child's right to protection and safety is especially vital for children who are victims of violence and abuse. The Convention States that every child has the right to protection from all physical or mental violence, abuse, neglect or exploitation (Article 19), and a right to be protected from sexual abuse and exploitation in prostitution and pornography (Article 34). Further, the child victim of abuse or exploitation is entitled to rehabilitation and social reintegration (Article 39). These rights are closely linked to the basic principle of the CRC concerning the child's right to protection from discrimination of any kind (Article 2), the best interests of the child (Article 3), the right to life, survival and development (Article 6), and respect for the views of the child through participation and information (Article 12).

Protecting children from violence and abuse and providing them with rehabilitation is a difficult task. Criminal law is in this context in many ways limited. The standard of proof required in a criminal case is high and most police reports concerning crimes against children do not lead to prosecution.[1] Nor does conviction of an adult who committed a crime against a child automatically mean that the child is protected. Despite a conviction, a parent can still be the child's guardian and maintain custody. Criminal procedure, however, fills a number of important functions for children's ability to obtain protection and rehabilitation. The criminal investigation helps the child protection services to identify his or her need and thus provide the protection, support and rehabilitation to which he or she is entitled. The criminal procedure can also have a therapeutic function by ensuring the child its right to be heard and recognized and compensated.[2] In addition, the police investigation can also identify a potential offender and therefore future victims can be protected.

---

1   Kaldal, A., Diesen, C., Beije, J & Diesen, E., *Barnahusutredningen* 2010, Jure förlag, The Swedish National Council for Crime Prevention (Brå), A report on trends in reported assaults against children aged 0–6 years, during the period 2000–2009, BRÅ 2011:16.
2   Diesen, C., *Terapeutisk juridik*, Liber, Stockholm, 2011.

To meet children's rights to protection from violence and abuse and to rehabilitation the ability of the judicial system to adapt to the best interest of the
child is crucial. Several studies have shown poor quality in police investigations, the interview held with the child and the lack of interaction between the
police and other agencies such as the social services and the health care system. This can lead to the child's rights not being met.[3] To do so, the quality
of the police investigation, the child protection system and the health care
system (both psychiatric and somatic) needs to be adapted to the best interest
of the child. At the same time the rights of other parties must be met according
to the rule of law.

According to the Committee on the Rights of the Child, interpretation of
Article 19, investigations of all instances of violence must be undertaken by
qualified professionals with role-specific and comprehensive training. Such
investigations require a child-rights-based and child-sensitive approach.
Rigorous but child-sensitive investigation procedures will also help to ensure
that violence is correctly identified and help provide evidence for administrative, civil, child-protection and criminal proceedings. Extreme care must be
taken to avoid subjecting the child to further harm through the investigation.
To this end, all parties are obliged to invite and give due weight to the child's
views.[4] According to the "Guidelines on Justice in Matters involving Child
Victims and Witnesses of Crime" a child victim of or a child witness to a crime
must be given an opportunity to freely express her or his view.[5] According to
the Committee this means that every effort has to be made to ensure that a
child victim and/or witness is consulted on relevant matters with regard to
involvement in the case and enabled to express freely, views and concerns
regarding her or his involvement in the judicial process. This is linked to a
number of aspects: the right to be informed about issues such as availability of

---

3   Sutorius, H. & Kaldal, A., *Bevisprövning vid sexualbrott*, Norstedts juridik, Stockholm. 2003;
    Lindell, C., *Child Physical Abuse; Reports and Interventions*, Dissertation, Linköping University,
    2005; Cocozza, M., *The Parenting of Society: From Report to Support*, Dissertation, Linköping
    Universit7, 2007; Diesen, C. & Diesen, E. *Övergrepp mot kvinnor och barn: den rättsliga han-
    teringen*, Norstedts juridik, Stockholm, 2009; Kaldal, A., *Parallella processer – En rättsvetens-
    kaplig studie av riskbedömningar i vårdnads- och LVU-mål*, Jure, Stockholm, 2010; Leviner, P.,
    Rättsliga dilemman i socialtjänstens barnskyddsarbete, Jure, Stockholm, 2011; Forsman, M.,
    Rättsliga ingripanden vid föräldrars våld och övergrepp mot barn, Norstedts juridik, Stockholm,
    2013; Svensson, B., *Barn som riskerar att fara illa i sin hemmiljö: Utmaningar i ett förebyggande
    perspektiv*, Dissertation, Karlstad University, 2013.
4   CRC/C/GC/13 para. 51.
5   United Nations Economic and Social Council resolution 2005/20, in particular Articles 8, 19
    and 20.

health, psychological and social services, the role of a child victim and/or witness, the ways in which "questioning" is conducted, existing support mechanisms for the child when submitting a complaint and participating in investigations and court proceedings, the specific places and times of hearings, the availability of protective measures, the possibilities of receiving reparation, and the provisions for appeal.[6]

The Council of Europe has expressed the importance of adapting the legal proceedings to the child's needs. Its Guidelines for Child-friendly Justice recommend treatment of suspected child victims that is consonant with that of the Children's Houses, Barnahus.[7]

4   Barnahus

As mentioned above the purposes of Barnahus are several. The activities in a Barnahus function in four different "rooms" where each meets a different need. The four activities are criminal investigation, child protection, the child's physical health and the child's mental health. Different agencies are responsible for the various rooms. The fact that all authorities are represented leads to interdisciplinary collaboration between professionals from the various agencies.[8] One example, and also the core of Barnahus, is the multi-professional consultation meetings concerning coordination of the investigations, examinations and the child's psychological and social needs.

Barnahus can also be described by following the child's pathway through the system:[9]

· Police report: How does suspicion that the child is a victim of crime come to the authorities' attention?
· Pickups: Some children come to Barnahus with a guardian while others are picked up and accompanied by a special legal representative or by the social services.
· First child questioning and medical examination: The child is initially interviewed by police with the prosecutor, social services, the special legal

---

6 CRC/C/GC/12, para. 63 and para. 64.
7 https://wcd.coe.int/ViewDoc.jsp?Ref=CM/Del/Dec(2010)1098/10.2abc&Language=lanEnglis h&Ver=app6&Site=CM&BackColorInternet=C3C3C3&BackColorIntranet=EDB021&BackCo lorLogged=F5D383.
8 Landberg, Å, & Svedin, C-G., *Inuti ett Barnahus*. Rädda Barnen, Stockholm, 2013.
9 *Ibid.*

representative and sometimes health professionals following the interview from another room. Some children are medical examined at the site.

- Drop off: After visiting Barnahus some children are placed in custody, but most go home again. Many return home to a parent who is suspected of a crime against the child.
- Continued investigation by police and social services: Many children are heard only once by the police, others repeatedly. The majority are investigated by social services and will be interviewed again.
- Crisis support and treatment: Different forms of crisis support and treatment can be initiated based on the information from the first multi-professional consultation, the police interview and the mental health evaluation. These can be given at Barnahus but also elsewhere, by child and adolescent psychiatry and/or the social services.
- Decisions on prosecution, trial and sentencing: Children are involved to varying degrees in subsequent legal proceedings, depending on their age. For some children the police investigation is closed down shortly after the police interview. When prosecuted the legal process can take a considerable time.

In 2009 the Swedish Prosecution Authority, the National Police Board, the National Board of Forensic Medicine and the National Board of Health and Welfare launched national guidelines for Barnahus and similar activities. Accordingly the core of Barnahus is inter-agency collaboration under one roof with the child's best interests in focus during the process. The goal is to assure suspected child victims legal security, good treatment and support and, where necessary, immediate crisis and therapeutic treatment. The child should be informed of the investigative measures which concern him or her, and enabled to express views and opinions to the extent and in the manner his or her maturity allows. The inter-agency cooperation appears through multi-professional consultation meetings where the professionals discuss investigative measures and the child's need for protection and treatment. Audibility from another room during the police interview is emphasized, where the interview can be observed by representatives of the police and prosecution, the defence lawyer, the child's legal advocate and the child's social worker. The aim is to facilitate coordination of the parallel investigations and to assess the child's need for protection, treatment and support. The importance of access to specialized prosecutors, police and social workers is pointed out. Child psychiatry, paediatrics, gynaecology and forensic medicine should also be represented in Barnahus.[10]

5   Previous Research

As mentioned above, the model for the Swedish Barnahus, is the Children's Advocacy Centers, which have existed in the u.s. since the 1980s. They were comprehensively studied during 2001–2003 by a research group at the University of New Hampshire Crimes Against Children Research Center.[11] The study included 1,500 children from four locations with well-established and certified Children's Advocacy Centers and four locations without correspond-ing facilities. The Children's Advocacy Center was found to be better for the kids. The police and prosecutors were involved in more cases, cases were coor-dinated better and more children underwent a medical examination than in locations without Children's Advocacy Centers. More children were referred to child psychiatry and more were taken into custody. The study also showed that parents were more satisfied. The study did not detect that the Centers' activi-ties contributed to an increase in prosecutions.[12] Other studies, however, dem-onstrated a correlation between a shorter time from the police report to prosecution, especially in more severe cases, and that Children's Advocacy Centers did contribute to more cases resulting in prosecution.[13]

The Swedish Barnahus have been studied in three national evaluations. The first was by the Sociology of Law Department at Lund University. The study included the first six Barnahus (2005–2007) and was presented in March 2008. Although the evaluation found that Barnahus were not sufficiently advanced in their establishment, making the evaluation difficult, it was concluded that the situation was better for the children in Barnahus than in an ordinary police investigation. The children were treated in a thoughtful and positive manner in

---

10   Rikspolisstyrelsen (2009), *Delredovisning av regeringsuppdrag avseende gemensamma natio-nella riktlinjer kring barn som misstänks vara utsatta för brott och kriterier för landets Barnahus.*

11   Walsh, W.A., Lippert, T., Cross, T.E., Maurice, D.M., & Davison, K.S., "How long to prosecute child sexual abuse for a community using a children's advocacy center and two compari-son communities?" 13 *Child Maltreatment,* 2008, pp. 3–13; Miller, A., & Rubin, D., "The contribution of children's advocacy centers to felony prosecutions of child sexual abuse," 33 *Child Abuse & Neglect,* 2009, pp. 12–18.

12   *Juvenile Justice Bulletin*e, August 2009, *Evaluating Childrens'Advocacy Centers'Response to Child Sexual Abuse,* www.ojp.usdoj.gov.

13   Walsh *et al., supra* note 12; Miller & Rubin, *supra* note 12.

a child-friendly environment and more had access to some form of crisis support. More police interviews were conducted with children, more children underwent medical examinations, and it was more common that a special legal representative or legal counsel was appointed. It was noted, however, that child and adolescent psychiatry, forensic medicine and paediatrics were not fully involved in Barnahus in all locations. However, there was no support for the notion that collaboration in Barnahus led to better prosecution or shorter processing times for police and prosecutors. The evaluation included interviews with 12 children, all but two teenagers. The children described an overall positive picture.[14]

The thesis *Right, power, and institutional change – A critical analysis of the authorities' cooperation in Barnahus* was based on the material from the evaluation, mentioned above.[15] The material consisted primarily of surveys of and interviews with the interaction operators, and observations of multi-professional consultation meetings. The study concluded that there was an inherent duality in the work in Barnahus. This duality was described as a tension between a social system characterized by the idea of holistic treatment and thinking and a legal system characterized by an ideology of formal justice. The two pervasive ideas with Barnahus are to protect and support children (processing logic) and to streamline the legal system (criminal logic). The author, Johansson, observed that criminal logic took precedence over processing logic, which led to a general process of juridification. Examples of this were that the child protection services awaited the police interview with children before doing their risk assessment and talking to the child or contacting the parents, thus allowing criminal logic priority. Meanwhile the child could keep on living in a dangerous environment.

The second evaluation was conducted by the Department of Law at Stockholm University in 2009–2010. The aim was to investigate whether the activity in Barnahus was better for children than regular police investigations and child protection in communities where there were no Barnahus. The study included 1,000 criminal investigations from eight locations with Barnahus and four locations without and 500 child protection investigations concerning the children who were investigated by the social services in parallel with the criminal investigation. The study found that none of the Barnahus fully lived up to the national criteria. Some including the Barnahus in Linköping, Gothenburg and Lund met

---

14   Rejmer, A. & Åström, K., *Det blir nog bättre för barnen*, Rättssociologiska Institutionen, Lunds Universitet, 2008.

15   Johansson, S., *Rätt, makt och institutionell förändring, En kritisk analys av myndigheters samverkan i barnahus*, Rättssociologiska Institutionen, Lunds Universitet, 2008.

the basic criteria. In many places, for example, health care was not represented by either paediatrics or child- and adolescent psychiatry. In some Barnahus the prosecutor was present at the child interview but not at the consulting meeting and vice versa.[16]

Also in this latter evaluation it was noted that a Barnahus that meets the basic criteria was better than ordinary investigation forms. The evaluation showed that there was more cooperation between the authorities involved in locations with Barnahus. This applied particularly to the contact between the social services and the police, the number of medical examinations of the child related to the criminal investigation, and the number of psychosocial interventions for the child. In communities with Barnahus the social services reported more crimes to the police (it is not mandatory for the social welfare to report to the police in Sweden) and more information concerning the child was exchanged between the police and the social services. Even though few children in the population as a whole underwent a medical examination, the involvement of paediatric experts was greater in Barnahus; and the participation of paediatrics in the consultations meetings led to more medical examinations. While the study demonstrated no correlations in individual cases, the prosecution rate appeared higher in places where there were more medical exams than in other locations. Although the children in Barnahus were not receiving psychosocial interventions to the extent that was expected, more children got treatment and support in places with Barnahus. The study included a survey aiming to examine how children experienced the visit in Barnahus. They were in most cases pleased with the hospitality they received.

The report identified weaknesses in the documentation of both the police investigations and the social service investigations. In the former, one weakness concerned the lack of documentation of which professional representatives were following the police interrogation from another room. Another weakness related to a lack of documentation regarding the directives given by the prosecutor. Other measures were documented clearly, such as decisions about enforcement and the appointment of a special legal representative or legal counsel for the child. The documentation in the social services' child welfare investigations was often incomplete and unclear. The line between investigative measures and psychosocial interventions was often unclear and only certain actions, such as compulsory foster care, were consistently and coherently documented. Documentation of action taken in Barnahus concerning the child and his/her family had several flaws. One explanation was uncertainty about how far documentation of activities that were neither a part of

---

16   Kaldal *et al.*, *supra* note 1.

the police investigation nor the child protection investigation was allowed. Since some of the activities could be both or neither, some information was missing. The lack of documentation and registration concerned the core of Barnahus such as consultation meetings, parallel listening and therapeutic support to the child. The report therefore highlighted a need for regulation concerning documentation and registration in Barnahus of the individual child and the family. The report stressed the importance of Barnahus living up to the criteria required for higher quality.[17]

A third assessment and report, *Inside Barnahus*, was presented in June 2013 in collaboration between Linköping University and Save the Children. The report looked at how far the Swedish Barnahus meet the national criteria for being a Barnahus. The quality evaluation was intended to result in a Swedish quality manual for Barnahus. The analysis was done from the child's perspective on the basis of the CRC. The review followed twelve criteria, against which each activity was assessed and rated. The report describes Barnahus activities in four different "rooms," each meeting a different need of the child.

The Barnahus included in the study were classified based on how far operations were conducted in the four different rooms. The overall conclusion from the performance review was that Barnahus had come to stay and were a step in the right direction to ensure that children and adolescents experiencing different types of abuse and crime receive good treatment. Several Barnahus were considered to maintain very high quality. However, there still existed a lot of flaws and weaknesses in many Barnahus. Of the 23 Barnahus surveyed, four met all the criteria for being a full Barnahus with operations in all four rooms. The other 19 Barnahus lacked activity in one or both rooms for physical and/or mental health. One area for development highlighted in the quality review was, again, the need for more effective documentation. Such a system should ensure that the child's way through Barnahus would be possible to follow. This would allow further evaluation and development and guarantee the child's need for and right to information and participation.[18]

6   The Situation Today and Identified Needs

In the light of the national guidelines for Barnahus, and the results and recommendations from the report *Inside Barnahus* and the two earlier national evaluations, a consensus on basic criteria for an activity to constitute a

---

17   *Ibid.*
18   Landberg & Svedin, *supra* note 8.

Barnahus has been reached. These criteria are reflected in the activities in each "room:" criminal investigation, child protection investigation and inventions, the child's physical health and the child's mental health. The environment should be child-friendly and safe. All the agencies that are responsible for the child shall be represented in the Barnahus and all shall participate in for example the multi-professional consultation meetings. Each Barnahus shall be able to meet the child's mental and physical needs with crisis support, treatment and medical examination. Barnahus have in several respects improved many children subjected to criminal investigation To achieve sustainability there shall be a co-operation/collaboration agreement among the authorities plus staff to coordinate activities. In addition the child's right to information and to express his or her views must be observed.

As pointed out, there are still shortcomings. Despite the overall consensus many Barnahus do not meet these basic criteria, and despite developments observed, the research shows that difficulties remain and that there is a need for continuous development. Although the interaction and cooperation between the authorities involved were greater in areas with Barnahus, the treatment, support and interventions related to the child's physical and mental health were inadequate in many places/cases. The quality of the police investigations was often poor, which could lead to too few prosecutions, but also to justifiable investigative measures not being implemented. The documentation was often incomplete, rendering the child's pathway through Barnahus impossible to follow. This made it difficult if not impossible to comprehensively evaluate whether each child got the right help or activities within Barnhahus as such. It was also unclear if not to say impossible to evaluate whether the child's right to information and to express his or her views was handled satisfactorily.

7   The Future and Development Needs

The idea behind Barnahus is to adjust the judicial process to the best interest of the child. This is achieved by giving the child protection and rehabilitation, at the same time improving the quality of police investigations to ensure that the rights that children are guaranteed under the CRC are met. As noted above, there is a consensus that Barnahus makes it better for children as long as the basic criteria are being met. The variation among Barnahus in Sweden is, however, great. Thus in many places only the police and social services are represented, and many Barnahus do not offer crisis support. The number of medical examinations varies and a common problem for all is ambiguity as to how the child's progress through Barnahus is documented and how his or her right to participation through information and expression of his/her view is met.

Lacking national coordination or funding, the different Barnahus have been established and developed depending on local initiative and commitment. A child's ability to get rights and needs met when the child is a subject of a criminal investigation depends not only on whether there is a Barnahus, but also on how the Barnahus is conducted. One question is whether the large variation throughout Sweden means that we are not living up to the requirement that all children have a right to be treated equally.

According to Article 4 of the CRC, it is a national responsibility to undertake the appropriate legislative, administrative measures for implementing the rights recognized in the Convention. This raises the question whether there is a need for national coordination of Barnahus in Sweden to meet the requirement of non-discrimination. National coordination should reflect the responsibility for Barnhus' certification, continuous monitoring and quality assurance. It should also function as a national knowledge centre. National joint responsibility for the authorities involved would also strengthen and bring sustainability to the Barnahus and therefore also to the rights of the child. National coordination could also play a role in the need to follow up the previous national investigations/surveys to develop activities and to correct deficiencies that have emerged. This is of great importance for the quality assurance of Barnahus but not least for the individual child.

The evaluations mentioned above pointed out areas that require changes in legislation. One is the need of documentation of all activities related to a child and its family in Barnahus. This is of importance for the child's right to trace back their way through Barnahus. A Lex Barnahus would also facilitate the function of a coordinator to have insight into all investigations connected to a particular child. Today this function collides in certain aspects with existing confidentiality legislation.

Given that previous research has concentrated mainly on Barnahus that do not fully live up to the basic criteria, there is also a need for research on those Barnahus which do meet the basic criteria, so as to study more specific questions. Results from previous evaluations can make a valuable contribution to future research. The problem areas identified earlier can be followed up for further analysis and development, and areas not highlighted earlier can be studied. Earlier research thus provides the prerequisites for studying constraining and promoting factors for good quality concerning all aspects of Barnahus.

One conclusion from earlier research is that collaboration does not always automatically lead to achievement of all the goals envisaged. The research has demonstrated that constraining and promoting factors of interaction can be found in both the regulations and the organization in the role the parties adopt. The reasons why greater interaction does not necessarily mean better investigations – both police and child protection and psychosocial support to the child – still needs further investigation.

One shortcoming is the ambiguity concerning how the child's right to participation in information and right to express views are handled in Barnahus. The lack of regulation or policy concerning participation is probably one reason for this. Clarification of who has the responsibility for this right is needed. Closely linked here is the role of the child's legal representative. The representative plays a central role in meeting the child's rights as a victim of crime. In short, the role of the child's legal representative is in some aspects unclear and needs to be clarified and strengthened.

The rights of the child are being given a more central role in both international and national legislation and society at large. The importance of bringing in and observing the child's own perspective is therefore of great importance. As stated above, children have a right to be heard regarding issues that concern them. The basic tenet is that children are the ones who best can describe their conditions, and how their needs can be met. Put simply, the child's best interests cannot be met unless the child's own views and perspectives are taken into account in the future development of Barnahus, To examine how children perceive and understand social activities targeted at them it is therefore essential for society to meet children's rights and live up to the CRC requirements.

Child Victims and Witnesses of Crime in India

Asha Bajpai

1 Children in India – The Paradigm Shift

India is a multicultural, multi-ethnic and multi-religious country. It is home to the largest number of children in the world: around 440 million of the one-billion-plus Indian population. The law, policy and practice of child welfare have undergone significant changes. Before 1839, the approach was authority and control. Earlier, the wellbeing of children depended on traditional Indian notions of welfare based on *daya* (pity), *dana* (charity), *dakshina* (charity), *bhiksha* (what you receive as charity), *and tyaga* (sacrifice), towards recipients of welfare measures. The 1950 Constitution of India, which is the basic law of the land, provides special status and protection to children in various provisions in the directive principles and fundamental rights.[1] It guarantees fundamental rights to all children in the country and empowers the State to make special provision for them. The Directive Principles of State Policy specifically guide the State in securing children from abuse and ensuring that they are given opportunities and facilities to develop in a healthy manner in freedom and dignity. Thus the State must ensure that childhood is protected from exploitation and moral and material abandonment.[2] In 1992 India ratified the

---

1 The Constitution of India was adopted by the Constituent Assembly on 26 November, 1949 and came into force on 26 January 1950.

2 Provisions in the Constitution of India relating to children:

Article 15(3) stipulates that the State can make special provisions to prohibit discrimination against children;

Article 21A provides for free and compulsory education for all children aged 6–14 years in such manner as the State may by law determine;

Article 23 prohibits trafficking of human beings;

Article 24 says no child below 14 can work in any hazardous occupation or industry;

Article 39(e) &(f) establishes State policies that are directed towards securing children;

Article 45 stipulates that the State shall endeavor to provide early childhood care and education until they complete the age of six years;

Article 51A states that it shall be the fundamental duty of parents and guardians to provide opportunities for education of their children or wards between the age of six and fourteen years.

Judicial interpretation has caused many of the directive principles to become enforceable through legal action before the Courts.

United Nations Convention on the Rights of the Child (CRC)[3] and the two optional Protocols to the CRC.[4] Other related international instruments ratified by India include the Declaration of the Rights of the Child, the Universal Declaration of Human Rights and its Covenants, the United Nations Convention on the Rights of Persons with Disabilities, the United Nations Convention against Transnational Organized Crime, the Protocol to Prevent, Suppress and Punish Trafficking in Women and Children, the Hague Convention on Protection of Children and Cooperation in Respect of Inter-country Adoption, and the Convention on the Elimination of All Forms of Discrimination against Women.

According to the 2013 National Policy for Children, the State shall promote child- friendly jurisprudence, enact progressive legislation, build a preventive and responsive child-protection system, including emergency outreach services, and promote effective enforcement of punitive legislative and administrative measures against all forms of child abuse and neglect. The policy commits the nation to promote and strengthen legislative, administrative and institutional redress mechanisms at national and State levels for the protection of child rights.[5]

The constitutional mandates and judicial interventions, along with commitment to international norms and standards, have prompted a paradigm shift in the approaches to children. The focus has changed from needs to rights, from welfare to development and empowerment, from treating a child as a beneficiary and recipient to treating him or her as a participant and partner; and from isolation to inclusion and mainstreaming. These changes in approach have been incorporated in the law, policy and practice relating to children. The Government has also striven to incorporate the spirit and the articles of the Constitution of India, the CRC and other international instruments while developing various laws and policies related to children.

---

3   The CRC requires the State Parties to undertake all appropriate national, bilateral and multilateral measures to prevent (a) the inducement or coercion of a child to engage in any unlawful sexual activity; (b) the exploitative use of children in prostitution or other unlawful practices and (c) the exploitative use of children in pornographic performances and materials.

4   Optional Protocol to the Convention on the Rights of the Child on the sale of children, child prostitution and child pornography (2000). Optional Protocol to the Convention on the Rights of the Child on the involvement of children in armed conflict (2000) Ratified by India on 30 November 2005.

5   National Policy for Children, 2013, Government of India, Ministry of Women and Child Development, adopted 26 April 2013.

2   Offences against Children

Children can be victims in relation to any offence under the legal system. For example, as victims they may have been abused sexually or physically by adults or assaulted by other children. In addition, children can be victims of and witnesses to domestic violence, sexual abuse and physical abuse and witnesses in family court proceedings relating to marriage, divorce, custody, guardianship.

The 2007 Ministry of Women and Child Development study on Child Abuse in India produced the first national database on the subject. It highlights the serious issue of child abuse and neglect in the Indian context.[6] The study included nationwide empirical data on the nature and extent of child abuse in different settings and recommended immediate and appropriate responsive action that could be undertaken by families, the community, government, and civil society organizations. The study included a sample of 12,447 child respondents, young adults and other stakeholders across 13 states of India. It covered children aged five to 18 years and young adults from between 18 and 24. It has a fair representation across gender, mother tongue, caste and religion. The children in the sample came from five different evidence groups: children in family environment but not in school, children in school, in institutions, at work, and on the streets. The study highlighted various forms of abuse experienced by the children including physical, sexual, and emotional abuse. It also covered the neglect experienced by girls. The study indicated a phenomenal percentage of abuse experienced by Indian children.[7]

---

6   Study on Child Abuse: India, Ministry of Women and Child Development, Government of India, 2007, wcd.nic.in/childabuse.pdf.

7   Some of the major findings:

Physical abuse: (i) Two out of every three children were physically abused, (ii) of 69 per cent of physically abused children in 13 sample states, 54.68% were boys, (iii) The states of Andhra Pradesh, Assam, Bihar and Delhi almost consistently reported higher rates of abuse in all forms as compared to other states, (iv) Of those children physically abused in family situations, parents were responsible in 88.6% of cases, and (v) 65% of schoolchildren reported facing corporal punishment.

Sexual abuse: (i) 53.22% of children reported having faced one or more forms of sexual abuse; (ii) Andhra Pradesh, Assam, Bihar and Delhi reported the highest percentage of sexual abuse among both boys and girls; (iii) 21.90% of child respondents reported facing severe forms of sexual abuse and 50.76% experienced other forms of sexual abuse, while 5.69% cent reported being sexually assaulted; and (iv) 7.50% of abusers were persons known to the child or in a position of trust and responsibility in the child's life.

According to the Report on Crime in India, cases in which children are victimized and abused can be categorized under two broad sections:[8]

(i)   Crimes committed against children which are punishable under Indian penal code (IPC).

(ii)   Crimes committed against children which are punishable under special and local laws (SLL).

i.   **Crimes against Children Punishable under the Indian Penal Code (IPC) are:**[9]

(a)   Murder (302 IPC).

(b)   Feticide (Crime against a foetus) IPC Sections 315 & 316.

(c)   Infanticides (Crime against new-born child, 0 to 1 year) Section 315 IPC.

(d)   Abetment to suicide (abetment by other persons for commitment of suicide by Children) Section 305 IPC.

(e)   Exposure & abandonment (Crime against children by parents or others to expose or to leave them with the intention of abandonment): Section 317 IPC.

(f)   Kidnapping & abduction.

ii.   **Crimes against Children Punishable under "Special and Local Laws,"** *i.e.*

(a)   the Immoral Traffic Prevention Act, 1956 (minors abused in prostitution),

(b)   the Child Labour (Prevention & Regulation) Act, 1986.

The table below lists crimes against children 2010–2012.[10] According to the Crime in India Report 2012, a total of 38,172 cases of crimes against children

---

Emotional abuse and girl neglect: (i) Every other child reported emotional abuse; (ii) Equal percentages of both genders reported this; (iii) In 83% cent of the cases, parents were the abusers; and (iv) 48.40% of the girls wished they were boys.

8   National Crime Records Bureau, Ministry of Home Affairs, Government of India, Chapter 6, 2011. See www.ncrb.in visited on May 1, 2014.

9   National Crime Records Bureau, Ministry of Home Affairs, Government of India, Chapter 6, 2011. See www.ncrb.in visited on May 1, 2014.

10   *Crime in India, 2012,* National Crime Records Bureau, Table 6.1, Ministry of Home Affairs, Government of India, 2012 www.ncrb.in.

Sr. No.	Crime Head	Year			% Variation in 2012 over 2011
		2010	2011	2012	
(1)	(2)	(3)	(4)	(5)	(6)
1	Murder	1,408	1,451	1,597	10.1
2	Infanticide	100	63	81	28.6
3	Rape	5,484	7,112	8,541	20.1
4	Kidnapping & abduction	10,670	15,284	18,266	19.5
5	Foeticide	111	132	210	59.1
6	Abetment to suicide	56	61	144	136.1
7	Exposure & abandonment	725	700	821	17.3
8	Procuration of minor girls	679	862	809	−6.1
9	Buying of girls for prostitution	78	27	15	−44.4
10	Selling of girls for prostitution	130	113	108	−4.4
11	Other crimes (including under Prohibition Of Child Marriage Act 2006)	7,253	7,293	7,580	3.9
	Total	26,694	33,098	38,172	15.3

were reported during 2012 as compared to 33,098 cases during 2011, suggesting an increase of 15.3%.[11] The actual cases may be higher.

Victims are in general reluctant to come forward in filing complaints against those who have violated their rights, or to testify in court. The national conviction rate for these crimes stood at 29.0%.[12] This poor rate is mostly due to lack of protection for victims and their families, especially where children are involved. Another reason for a large percentage of acquittals in criminal cases is witnesses turning hostile as they find the criminal justice system intimidating, particularly the courtroom experience. Under these circumstances, a vulnerable witness—i.e. a child—provides weak testimony and contributes less information than should have been elicited. Further, the lengthy and complex process of navigating the formal and adversarial criminal justice system can

---

11   National Crime Records Bureau, Ministry of Home Affairs, Government of India, Chapter 6, 2011. See www.ncrb.in, visited on May 1, 2014.

12   *Ibid.*

affect the vulnerable witness's psychological development and leave a long-term impact of trauma. Many offences against children were neither specifically provided nor addressed before the POCSO Act was passed in 2012.[13]

3 Child Victims and Witnesses and the Indian Legal System

The legal system has traditionally given child witnesses little support and preparation. In the courtroom children used to be subjected to harassing, intimidating, confusing and misleading questioning. In addition, court buildings do not provide privacy for the child or promote his or her safety outside the courtroom. Hence children are frequently traumatized by their court appearance. The abuse many children suffered was compounded by the abuse perpetrated by the legal system itself. The interests of the child both as victim and witness were not adequately provided for.

Under the Indian Evidence Act, 1872, that deals with witnesses, all persons shall be competent to testify unless the court considers that they are unable to understand the questions put to them, or to give rational answers, for reasons of their tender years, extreme old age, disease, of body or mind, or any other similar cause.[14] To determine the competency to appear as a witness,

---

13   Section 375, defining rape. Other IPC provisions invoked relate to unnatural practices are in Section 377. This is generally invoked when boy children are sexually abused. Although forcible sex with a boy is an act of rape, the rape law of the country under the IPC does not cover it. Outraging the modesty of a woman or a girl is dealt with in Section 354. Insulting the modesty of woman is handled in Section 509. Obscenity and pornography are dealt with under the Young Persons (Harmful Publications) Act, 1956. A young person means a person under the age of 20 years. It is an offence to sell, let, hire, distribute or publicly exhibit harmful publications. Under Section 67 of the Information Technology Act, 2000, publication and transmission of pornography through the internet is an offence.

    The ordinary criminal laws were totally inadequate to protect child victims of sexual abuse. The above sections do not include the common forms of child sexual abuse or their impact on the children. The restrictive interpretation of "penetration" in the Explanation to Section 375 is an obstacle to cases of child sexual abuse. The Explanation to Section 375 does not treat forced sexual intercourse by a husband against his wife (above 15 years) as an offence. There is no provision to deal with the trauma of the child. The testimony of the child victim is not recorded sensitively by the police/judge/prosecutor magistrate. The recording of child victims' statements need a special provision in the 1973 Criminal Procedure Code (CrPC), at present lacking.

14   Section 118, Indian Evidence Act, 1872, Chapter 9, Government of India –118. Who may testify: All persons shall be competent to testify unless the Court considers that they are prevented from understanding the questions put to them, or from giving rational answers

the legislature has underlined the basic requirement that a person must understand the obligation to speak the truth and to give an accurate impression, and possess the mental capacity at the time of the occurrence concerning which he has to testify and also to have received an accurate impression of it, especially in the case of children. An assessment by the court of the competency of a child who is to appear as a witness on these issues is essential.[15] As far as this competency is concerned, Indian courts have relied on the proposition formulated by Justice Brewer in *Wheeler v United States*,[16] that the evidence of a child witness need not be rejected *per se*, but the Court, as a rule of prudence, considers such evidence with close scrutiny. Only on being convinced about the quality and reliability of such evidence can the Court record conviction based on it. Reservations relating to the testimony of a witness are based on apprehensions that children may be vulnerable and susceptible to what others tell them; and the child witness can be easily tutored. Therefore their evidence must be evaluated carefully and with greater circumspection.[17] In *Rameshwar v State of Rajasthan*,[18] the court ruled that it was desirable that the judge or magistrate should always record their opinion as to whether the child understands his duty to speak the truth or also state when they think that the credibility of the witness would be so seriously affected that in some cases it may be necessary to reject the evidence altogether.

The treatment of child victims and witnesses in the legal system leads to further secondary victimization of the child. The courtrooms in court buildings are normally crowded places, with all kinds of petty and hardened criminals as well. The courtroom environment is unfamiliar and definitely unfriendly to a child who is required to testify as a witness. If the child witness is also a victim as well, the trauma is only further aggravated.[19] An already apprehensive child in an unfriendly atmosphere is in difficulty even in recounting his or her experience. Such nervous testimony is then exposed to being shredded by an insensitive defines lawyer out to prove the child a "liar." The defines strategy of repetitive and aggressive questioning and shouting out loudly regarding

---

to those questions, by tender years, extreme old age, disease, whether of body or mind, or any other cause of the same kind. Explanation: A lunatic is not incompetent to testify, unless he is prevented by his lunacy from understanding the questions put to him and giving rational answers to them.

15   *State v Allen*, 70 Wn, 2d 690,424 P.2d 1021 (1967).
16   159 US 523 (1895).
17   *Panchhi v State* of U.P. MANU/SC/0530/1998, Criminal Law Journal (CriLJ), 1988, 4044.
18   AIR 1952 SC 54.
19   *Virender v The State Of Nct Of Delhi*, The High Court Of Delhi – Crl.A.No. 121/2008 Date of decision: 29th September, 2009.

details of the occurrence so as to secure varying interpretations given by him/her and make them appear inconsistent with her allegations leads to further victimization.[20]

India is a country where several languages are spoken. The Constitution of India recognizes several of these while the number of dialects prevalent and in use in different areas runs into hundreds. Against this background, communication with the child witness has added concerns. First, it is difficult to get a translator or interpreter who understands the child's language or dialect. Secondly, the court has to ascertain not only the child witness's comprehension but also the extent of his or her vocabulary before recording a deposition. Thirdly, in many instances, the same word may have different connotations and meanings in different languages and regions. Fourthly, the child is also being called upon to make a deposition with regard to events which may be way beyond her/his knowledge and comprehension.[21]

To prevent secondary victimization of the child witness, the Supreme Court has repeatedly ruled that there is no rule of practice that the evidence of a child witness needs corroboration: it has stated that conviction can be based on it. Only as a rule of caution and prudence may the court find it desirable to have corroboration from other dependable evidence.[22] In the landmark judgment of *Sakshi v UOI & Ors*,[23] the Supreme Court gave the following direction regarding trials of offences involving child sexual abuse and/or rape:

(i)   The mere sight of the accused may induce extreme fear in the mind of the victim or the witnesses, or a state of shock. He or she may then be unable to give full details of the incident, and this may result in miscarriage of justice. Therefore, a screen or some such arrangement can be made where the victim or witnesses do not have to undergo the trauma of seeing the body or the face of the accused.

(ii)   Often the questions put in cross-examination are purposely designed to embarrass or confuse victims of rape and child abuse. The object is that shame or embarrassment may prevent the victim from speaking out or giving details of certain acts committed by the accused. It will, therefore, be better if questions by the accused in cross-examination are given in

---

20   *Ibid.*

21   *Ibid.*

22   *Dattu Ramrao Sakhare & Ors. v State of Maharashtra*, MANU/SC/1185/1997 : (1997) 5 SCC 341; *Suryanarayana v State of Karnataka*, MANU/SC/0001/2001, CriLJ, 2001, 705.

23   *All Indian Report* (AIR) 2004 SC 3566.

writing to the Presiding Officer of the Court, who may put the same to the victim or witnesses in language which is not embarrassing.

(iii)   The victim of child abuse or rape should be given sufficient breaks as and when required.

In another judgment by the Supreme Court, recording of evidence by way of video conferencing as per Section 273 of the 1973 Criminal Procedure Code[24] has been held to be permissible.[25] Directions relating to child witnesses were also given in *State of Punjab v Gurmit Singh & Ors.*[26] The Courts held that courts should examine the broader probabilities of a case and not get swayed by minor contradictions of a non-fatal nature or insignificant discrepancies in the statement of the prosecutor, to throw out an otherwise reliable prosecution case. Some other directions included:

·   Trial of rape cases *in camera* should be the rule and open trial in such cases the exception.
·   The anonymity of the victim of the crime must be maintained as far as possible throughout.
·   If possible lady judges should try a case of sexual assault of a female to provide some ease for the victim and, for the system, an improved quality of evidence and proper trial.

The Court in this case also hoped and observed that "...the Parliament will give serious attention to the points highlighted by the petitioner and make appropriate legislation with all the promptness which it deserves."

In the case of *The Director, Tamil Nadu State Judicial Academy v State of Tamil Nadu,*[27] the High Court of Madras gave various directions to different

---

24   Criminal Procedure Code, Sec 273: Evidence to be taken in presence of accused. Except as otherwise expressly provided, all evidence taken in the course of the trial or other proceeding shall be taken in the presence of the accused, or, when his personal attendance is dispensed with, in the presence of his pleader.

25   The whole inquiry before a Court being to elicit the truth, it is absolutely necessary that the victim or the witnesses are able to depose about the entire incident in a free atmosphere without any embarrassment. Section 273 CrPC. merely requires the evidence to be taken in the presence of the accused. The Section, however, does not say that the evidence should be recorded in such a manner that the accused should have full view of the victim or the witnesses. *State of Maharashtra v Dr. Praful B Desai*, MANU/SC/0268/2003:2003 CriLJ2033.

26   AIR 1996 SC 1383 : (1996) 2 SCC 384.

27   Writ Petition.No.36807 of 2006.

authorities, including those to judicial magistrates, juvenile justice boards and legal services authorities:

- Trials of cases of trafficking should generally be *in camera* and the Magistrate/Board should avoid disclosing the name of the prosecutrix and their orders, to save embarrassment to the victim, and anonymity of the victim of the crime should be maintained throughout.
- The evidence of the child should be taken *in camera*, as per Section 327 of the CrPC.; and translators should be provided if the child is from another State and does not speak the local language. Ensure that the Special Courts/Boards have a child friendly and supportive atmosphere while taking the child's evidence. Preferably, an elder woman who inspires the confidence of the child may be present.

The case of *Sheeba Abidi v State and Another*[28] laid down the following:

(i)   Permitted use of a videotaped interview of the child's statement by the judge (in the presence of a child-support person).
(ii)   Child allowed to testify via closed-circuit television or from behind a screen to obtain a full and candid account of the acts complained of.
(iii) Cross-examination of a minor should only be carried out by the judge based on written questions submitted by the defence upon perusal of the minor's testimony.
(iv)   Whenever a child is required to give testimony, sufficient breaks should be allowed as and when required by the child.

4   Special Laws for Child Victims and Witnesses

In keeping with the Constitutional mandate given in Article 15(3), there are special laws and legal institutions relating to child victims and witnesses:

i   *Commission for the Protection of Child Rights Act 2005 (CPCR Act)*
Section 25 of the Commission for the Protection of Child Rights Act, 2005, provides for speedy trial of offences against children or of violation of child rights. This states that "the State Government may, with the concurrence of the Chief Justice of the High Court, by notification, specify at least one Court in the State

---

28   *Sheba Abidi v State*, National Capital Territory (NCT) of Delhi & Anr. =113(2004) Dehli Law Times.

or specify, for each district, a Court of Session to be a Children's Court to try the said offences." The Section further provides an exception that where a Court of Session is already specified as a Special Court, or a Special Court is already constituted for such offences under any other law for the time being in force, Section 25 will not apply. Children's Courts have been notified of this in some states e.g. Delhi, Karnataka, Mumbai, Tripura, Goa, and Kerala. However, it is yet to become functional in any State except Goa. In Goa, the existing Children's Court under the Goa Children's Act has been notified as the Children's Court under the CPCR Act.[29]

ii   *The Protection of Children from Sexual Offences (POCSO) Act, 2012 (POCSO 2012)*

The Protection of Children from Sexual Offences (POCSO) Act, 2012 is a special law to protect children from sexual abuse and exploitation.[30] It provides protection to children below the age of 18 years from offences of sexual assault, sexual harassment and pornography, plus a child-friendly system for the trial of these offences. The Act provides for stringent punishment, graded as per the gravity of the offence.

POCSO has consolidated the various Supreme Court and High Court guidelines and directions relating to child victims and witnesses and strengthened the legal provisions for the protection of children from sexual abuse and exploitation. It incorporates child-friendly mechanisms and procedures for reporting, medical examination, recording of child statements, during investigation and trial in courts to maintain respect for and dignity of a child victim and ensure him or her care and protection at every stage of the legal process.[31]

Any person (including the child) who has an apprehension that an offence under the POCSO Act is likely to be committed, or has knowledged that such an offence has been committed, has a mandatory obligation to report the matter.[32] An express obligation has also been laid upon media personnel, staffs of hotels, lodges, hospitals, clubs, studios, or photographic facilities, to report a

---

29   Report of Judicial Colloquium on Children's Court Organized by the Centre for Child and the Law, National Law School of India University, Bangalore in collaboration with Law Commission of India with the support of UNICEF India Country Office, New Delhi, 26 February 2012.

30   The Act along with Rules came into effect from 14 November 2012.

31   Raha, s. and Sajjanshetty, G., *Frequently Asked Questions on the Protection of Children From Sexual Offences Act*, Center for Child and Law, National Law School of India University, Bangalore, India, 2012.

32   Section 19, POCSO Act 2012.

case if they come across materials or objects that are sexually exploitative of children.[33] Failure to report is punishable with imprisonment for up to six months or fine or both. This penalty is, however, not applicable to a child. The Act also makes it an offence to report false information, when such a report is made other than in good faith.[34]

A case must be reported to the Special Juvenile Police Unit (SJPU) or the local police. The police or the SJPU must then record the report in writing, with an entry number, read the report over to the informant for verification, and enter it in a book. A FIR[35] must be registered and its copy handed to the informant free of charge.[36] If a case is reported by a child, it must be recorded in simple language so that the child understands what[37] is being recorded. If it is being recorded in a language that the child does not understand, a qualified translator or interpreter must be provided.[38]

Some significant provisions under POCSO Act are as follows:

· Establishment of Special Courts. A Sessions Court in every District to be designated as SC by the State Government in consultation with Chief Justice that will keep the best interest of the child as of paramount importance at every stage of the judicial process.[39]
· Special Court (SC) to take cognizance of offences without accused being committed to it for trial.[40]
· Special Public Prosecutor to be appointed.[41]
· Ensure that the child's identity is not disclosed at any time during investigation or trial. Disclosure with SC's permission if found to be in the child's interest.[42]
· Before medical examination, consent by or on behalf of child must be obtained. Medical examination irrespective of whether a FIR/complaint

---

33   Sec 20, POCSO Act 2012.
34   Section 21, POCSO Act 2012.
35   A FIR stands for first information report. It is a document providing the basic information that a cognizable offence has been committed. It should be noted that FIR is not a conclusive proof that a person has committed an offence. FIR is the starting point of the investigation in a particular offence.
36   Section 19, POCSO 2013.
37   Section 28 POCSO Act 2013.
38   Section 19(3) POCSO Act 2013.
39   Section 28 POCSO Act 2013.
40   Section 33 POCSO Act 2013.
41   Section 32 POCSO Act 2013.
42   Section 33(7) POCSO Act 2013.

has been filed under Section 27 POCSO Act. The privacy of child must be respected and the examination conducted in the presence of a trusted parent/guardian/other. If such is not available, the examination must be conducted in the presence of a woman nominated by the head of medical institution. A girl victim must be examined by a woman doctor.[43]

· The police must record the child's statement at the child's residence or where child usually resides, or a place of the child's choice; as far as practicable by woman police, not below the rank of sub-inspector, in plain clothes. The statement to be recorded in simple language so that child comprehends what is recorded. Assistance of translator or interpreter if the child does not understand the language in which the statement is recorded. In the case of mental or physical disability, assistance of a special teacher, and a person familiar with the manner of child's communication, or other expert. During examination, police personnel to ensure that prevent contact in any way with the accused.[44]

Wherever possible, the statement should also be recorded by audio-video electronic means.[45]

• Recording of statements by Magistrate under Section 164 CrPC: the Magistrate must record the statement as spoken by child. The presence of the accused's advocate not required when a statement is being recorded electronically.

• An *in camera* trial has to be in the presence of a family member, guardian, relative or friend in whom child has trust or confidence. The child should not be called repeatedly to testify. To ensure a speedy trial the Special Public Prosecutor and the accused's advocate shall communicate questions to be asked of the child to the Special Court, which shall in turn put them to the child. No aggressive questioning or character assassination. The child's dignity to be maintained.[46] Frequent breaks must be given to the testifying child, when found necessary. His or her evidence should be recorded within 30 days of cognizance being taken by the Special Court, i.e., final report being filed. In cases of delay, the Special Court is to record reasons. The trial is to be completed [as far as possible] within one year of cognizance. The Special Court must ensure that the child is not exposed "in any way to the accused at the time of recording of the evidence." The accused should be

---

43   Section 27 POCSO Act.
44   Section 24(3) POCSO Act.
45   Section 24 POCSO Act.
46   Section 34 POCSO Act.

able to hear the child's testimony and communicate with a lawyer. The evidence of a child may be recorded through video-conferencing, one-way mirror, curtain or any other device.[47]

iii   *Implementation of POCSO*

Since the Act is still at an early stage of implementation, any conclusion is premature. For effective and better implementation, on the directions of the WCD Ministry at various levels, the State Governments/Union Territories have initiated action to set up the special courts/children courts. As a result so far, eighteen States/UTs have designated Special Courts/Children's Court to try offences under the Act.[48]

The National Commission for Protection of Child Rights (NCPCR) and the State Commissions for Protection of Child Rights (SCPCR) have been designated the role of monitoring authority under the Act. Thus the Ministry has been following up with State Governments to expedite the formation of SCPCRs in their States. As a result, SCPCRs have been set up in 26 States/UTs.

Section 39 of the POCSO Act requires the State Government to prepare guidelines for use of NGOs, professionals and experts or persons to be associated with the pre-trial and trial stage to assist the child. At the request of several State Governments, model guidelines have also been issued to all the State Governments/UT Administrations which can be adopted or adapted by them for better implementation of the Act.

There is a need for greater awareness and sensitization among law-enforcement officials. POCSO does not offer support to e.g. counsellors to the child victim and the family at the police stations. At present, the child has to be produced before a Child Welfare Committee (CWC) which will then offer the victim a support person. A victim-protection scheme needs to be included in POCSO. The Act needs to be amended to reduce the age of consensual sexual act to the former sixteen years, as the present provision could be misused against teenagers. As a result, sexual interaction or intimacies among or with children below the age of 18 years will constitute an offence. Many Court rooms continue to be formidable with the judge on a high podium and the small child witness far below where her or his voice is barely audible to the judge.

---

47   Section 36 POCSO Act.
48   http://www.dnaindia.com/analysis/editorial-dna-edit-the-c-in-pocso-1949876 dated January 13, 2014.

5   Some Initiatives for Child Victims and Witnesses

There have been several initiatives and best practices relating to child victims
and witnesses.

i   *Vulnerable Victims and Witness Courts in Delhi*[49]
Delhi has now become the first city in the country to have its own "Vulnerable
Witness Deposition Complex," designed "to provide protection, privacy, confidentiality and comfort to vulnerable witnesses in an in-camera atmosphere" in
cases of sexual offences. Delhi has also laid down guidelines for recording the
evidence of vulnerable witnesses.[50] The objectives of the guidelines are:

· securing best interests of the child;
· eliciting complete, accurate and reliable evidence;
· minimizing harm or secondary traumatization of witnesses;
· ensuring the rights of the accused to fair trial.

ii   *Special Children's Court in Goa*[51]
In Goa, matters related to sexual abuse are dealt with *in camera* so as to protect the victim from the alleged offender. The atmosphere in the court room
is free and informal, that the president does not wear a black coat or a gown,
and advocates and police appear in civilian dress. The Court has the power to
award compensation to child victims. The victims and witnesses are helped
in getting familiarized with the court settings, to be comfortable with the
court proceedings and are also informed about the roles by key persons in
the Court namely, the judge, defence lawyer, prosecutor etc. The Court
ensures that the questioning is short and clear so as to not confuse child witnesses. Child witnesses below eight years are permitted to respond to leading
questions facilitated by social workers. Aggressive questioning of child witnesses during cross-examination is avoided and permission to ask direct
questions to children below ten years in cross-examination is denied. Such

---

49   http://www.indianexpress.com/news/city-anchor-a-courthouse-to-allow-child
      -witnesses-to-depose-without-fear/1003530.
50   Delhi High Court Delhi Committee.
51   Report of Judicial Colloquium on Children's Court Organized by the Centre for Child and
      the Law, National Law School of India University, Bangalore in collaboration with Law
      Commission of India with the support of UNICEF India Country Office, New Delhi,
      26 February 2012.

questions are asked through the presiding officer or a person with whom the child is comfortable. The views of child witnesses may be heard and respected, their privacy is respected, and inconvenience to them is minimized. The president ensures that the child is prepared for the testimony and is capable as a witness. The prosecutor is given sufficient time to prepare the child witness and adjournment is granted when the child is found to be uncomfortable. The child's testimony is recorded soon after charges are framed; and the identity of the victim is protected.

The challenges in the Goa courts are:

· the need to change the negative mindset of the presiding officer, prosecutor, police, advocates and parents of child victims;
· effective protection of child victims, lack of infrastructure, no space for child to sit with family till testimony is recorded, no place for witnesses to sit till they are called in the Court, no regular presiding officer to conduct the matter, and the presiding officer and the prosecutor lack training.

iii   Intellectually Challenged Children before the Criminal Justice System as Victims and Witnesses – The Chunauti[52] Project

Children with mental or other developmental disabilities in institutions are perfect targets for neglect, sexual abuse and assault. A sexual assault is a severe, heinous breach of trust and faith for the mentally deficient child victim, by persons who are their "caregivers." At Kavas, Kaylan and Mama Homes and other homes throughout the State of Maharashtra in India, there was an abdication of responsibility and dereliction of duty by those responsible including the State, the Department of Women and Child Development, the Child Welfare Committees, the Inspection Authorities, the State advisory Boards and other carers of the most vulnerable and marginalized unfortunates of our society, namely our mentally deficient children. It was a collective failure of the structures and system. The children saw the institution as a "place of refuge." They put complete faith and trust in the "Babas," "Pappas and Mummies," but it resulted in abuse, starvation and also death.

This all came to light when on August 23, 2010 the Mumbai Mirror reported that five children had died of malnourishment. Some were sexually abused and more would have died if they had not been shifted because of the report. The report disclosed the unsanitary conditions in which the children had been housed and the lack of basic facilities. It noted that the Child Welfare

---

52   Chunauti means challenge.

Committee (CWC) of Thane District and the District Women and Child Welfare Department (DWCD) officer had failed to do their mandatory duty of inspection and take adequate remedial steps. The news report raised fundamental questions about the denial of human rights to mentally challenged children. It also questioned the apathy and neglect of those running the institution and of public functionaries vested with statutory powers under the Juvenile Justice (Care and Protection) Act, 2000 (amended 2006).

The High Court of Mumbai took *suo motu* cognizance of this article and public interest litigation was initiated (PIL 182/2010.).[53] The Court stated that "the case highlights the plight of children desperately in need of care and protection. Their needs have been ignored in years of neglect. Their right to life under the Constitution has been brazenly infringed. The solemn covenants of the Convention on the Rights of the Child have remained an unachieved illusion. The Court has had to act *suo motu* because the mentally challenged are unable to secure the protection of their human rights or access to justice. The Court is constrained to intervene to ensure that those who are under a public duty act in accordance with law."

A civil-society committee was formed to study the homes and while doing so came across another case of abuse in Panvel. Nineteen girls were rescued from the Panvel home and on medical examination all of them were found to have been sexually abused. But there were no legal provisions for the rehabilitation and reintegration of these victims and witnesses so the Chunauti Project was started. It is a field action project working for the rehabilitation and reintegration of 93 victims of abuse in the MDC Home, Mankhurd. The Project is a unique partnership project between several stakeholders. Its activities include:

- Assessment of the children's immediate needs and provision of services
- Counselling to address trauma and behavioural issues
- Life skills education
- Therapeutic inputs – dance therapy
- Provision of therapeutic toys
- Vocational inputs – gardening and mehendi
- Occupational therapy
- Sending children to a regular school through SSA
- Special education
- Developing care plans

---

53   The present author has been appointed amicus curiae to assist the court in this PIL 182/2010, Bombay High Court.

- Regular monitoring and reporting to the High Court
- Staff capacity building
- Advocacy for policy changes

After two years of these interventions the children have calmed down and settled into the home. They are slowly overcoming their traumas and negative experience of the past. These victims and witnesses gave evidence in court during criminal proceedings. This was a landmark event, setting a precedent for mentally-challenged, hearing- and speech-impaired children to give evidence.

On March 31, 2013, six accused were convicted. The death sentence was passed on the founder of the orphanage for murder of an inmate and gang rape of five mentally-challenged girls, including three minors. The others were sentenced to imprisonment ranging from life to seven years.[54] On Dec 6, 2013, the Thane judgment was given. Six accused were held guilty of charges ranging from rape, sodomy, attempted murder and culpable homicide to torture and neglect. Their sentences range from five years to life in prison. Delivering the judgment, the Principal Sessions Judge said: "The children were subject to such forms of torture that they could not raise their voice against the people torturing them. This sentence should send a correct message to society."[55]

The children are gradually coming out of the trauma. They have expressed their interests in the areas of education and vocational skills. This has led to the Chunauti project developing further links to provide children with these skills.

6   Conclusions and Recommendations

We have a long way to go to further improve the status of child victims and witnesses through law in keeping with constitutional mandates and international law. In fact it is time for reform. We need to review the adversarial legal system in India itself as far as child victims and witnesses are concerned. Many children of varying ages, different intellectual and physical abilities, speaking different languages or not able to speak at all are victims and witnesses of crime and have to go through the traumas occasioned by our adversarial system. They should no longer have to give evidence or be cross-examined in

---

54   See more at: http://www.mid-day.com/articles/panvel-orphanage-founder-gets-death
      -sentence-in-girls-gang-rape-case/205292#sthash.zO8EJISc.dpuf.

55   http://ibnlive.in.com/news/kavdas-orphanage-case-six-convicted-two-acquitted/
      437997-3-237.html.

court. Advances in video technology could also be exploited to spare victims of sexual offences the ordeal of appearing in a courtroom. Their physical presence itself in a criminal trial and subjection to forensic procedures must be dispensed with.

The child victim of crime being an important player in the whole process of criminal justice, much attention needs be given to his or her rights, privileges and protection. Since the testimony of the victim is a very important piece of evidence in the criminal trial, it is essential that the victim should be able to give his/her testimony freely and without fear or pressure for the purpose of securing the ends of justice. There is a need for legislative, procedural and even constitutional reform for child victims and witnesses.

References

Constitution of India.

National Crime Records Bureau 2011.

Criminal Law (Amendment) Act, 2013.

Criminal Manual (2013), Universal Law Publishing Co. Pvt. Ltd., New Delhi.

Levy, E., *Examination of Witnesses in Criminal Cases*, Thompson Professional Publishing Ontario, 1991.

Daruwala, M. (ed), *Fair Trial Manual: A Handbook for Judges and Magistrates,* Commonwealth Human Rights Initiative, New Delhi, 2010 http://www.humanright sinitiative.org/publications/police/fair_trial_manual.pdf.

"India: Building a Protective Environment for Children," Ministry of Women and Child Development (2006):, http://wcd.nic.in/.

Study on Child Abuse: India 2007, wcd.nic.in/childabuse.pdf.

"Rights of the Child: Report of the Independent Expert for the United Nations study on Violence against Children," United Nations, 2006, www.violencestudy.org.

"Report of the Consultation on Child Abuse Prevention," World Health Organization, 1999, http://www.who.int/violence_injury_prevention/violence/neglect/en/ – (2002).

"Child Abuse and Neglect by Parents and Other Caregivers," *The World Report on Violence and Health*, 2003, www.who.int/violence_injury_prevention/violence/world report/en/.

The UN Convention on the Rights of the Child (CRC), 1989.

United Nations Standard Minimum Rules for Administration of Juvenile Justice (The Beijing Rules), 1985.

United Nations Guidelines for the Prevention of Juvenile Delinquency (The Riyadh Guidelines), 1990.

The UN Model Law on Justice in Matters involving Child Victims, Juvenile Justice (Care and Protection of Children Act), 2000 as amended in 2006.

Juvenile Justice (Care and Protection of Children) Model Rules, 2007/ Applicable Juvenile Justice Rules (If State Government has notified its own Rules).

Victims and Witnesses of Crime, the United Nations Office on Drugs and Crime, Vienna, 2009.

Report of Judicial Colloquium on Children's Court Organized by Centre for Child and the Law, National Law School of India University, Bangalore in collaboration with Law Commission of India with the support of UNICEF India Country Office, New Delhi, 26 February, 2012.

Raha, S. and Sajjanshetty, G., *Frequently Asked Questions on the Protection of Children From Sexual Offences Act,* Centre for Child and Law, National Law School of India University, Bangalore, India, 2012.

Evidential Difficulties in Criminal Proceedings Concerning Alleged Child Sexual Abuse against Children with Neuropsychiatric Disorders

Katrin Lainpelto

Introduction

Child neuropsychiatry can be defined in several ways and includes at least the categories of Attention Deficit/Hyperactivity Disorder (ADHD), autism spectrum disorders (ASD), mental retardation, and the spectrum of tic disorders. Children with neuropsychiatric disorders are a particularly vulnerable group. International research has shown a significant correlation between these disorders and different types of abuse[1] – especially sexual abuse.[2] Also, the perpetrators are more often found within the family and the children are exposed to recurring and more severe incidents of abuse.[3] However, the incidents often go unreported.

One reason could be that the perpetrators are often family members, and children with neuropsychiatric disorders are more dependent on their parents and other relatives than other children of the same age are. Another aspect of this increased vulnerability is difficulties in communicating the experience, highlighted by the fact that there is often no direct evidence alongside the child's statements. Further, knowledge and experience among the actors in the justice system might be inadequate to elicit correct statements. In the light of the increased vulnerability and the difficulties that may occur during a criminal investigation, it is imperative that children with neuropsychiatric disorders receive special attention in research.

In Sweden, during the past ten years, an increasing proportion of police reports regarding physical and sexual abuse concerns abuse against children

---

1 See for example Sullivan, P.M. and Knutson, J.F., "Maltreatment and Disabilities – A Population-Based Epidemiological Study," 24 *Child Abuse and Neglect*, 2000, pp. 1257–1273 at p. 1261 f.; Briscoe-Smith, A.M and Hinshaw, S.P., "Linkages Between Child Abuse and Attention-Deficit/Hyperactivity Disorder in Girls – Behavioral and Social Correlates," 30 *Child Abuse and Neglect*, 2006, pp. 1239–1255 at p. 1247; and UNICEF, *The State of the World's Children: Children with Disabilities*, 2013, p. 44.

2 See Sobsey, D., *Violence and Abuse in the Lives of People with Disabilities – The End of Silent Acceptance?*, Brookes, Baltimore, 1994.

3 Hershkowitz, I. Lamb, M.E. and Horowitz, D., "Victimization of children with disabilities," 77 *American Journal of Orthopsychiatry*, 2007, pp. 629–635 at p. 629.

© KONINKLIJKE BRILL NV, LEIDEN, 2015 | DOI 10.1163/9789004297432_018

with neuropsychiatric disorders (approximately 15 per cent of all police reports in Stockholm County). However, prevalence figures show that approximately eight per cent of all children in Sweden receive a neuropsychiatric diagnosis before or during their first years of school.[4] Also, none of the police reports in the studied county in 2006 led to prosecution or an order for summary punishment, although the alleged perpetrator confessed in one-third of the cases. These figures indicate, first, a strong correlation between neuropsychiatric disorders and different types of abuse also in Sweden and, secondly, that children with these types of disorder do not receive adequate legal protection.

This paper presents some preliminary findings of the research project *"The Swedish Criminal Justice System's Response to Victimized Children with Neuropsychiatric Disorders"* – in particular how Swedish courts argue when a child with a neuropsychiatric disorder has allegedly been sexually abused and to what extent the judgments are based on the involvement of experts.

Perceived Credibility and Negative Stereotypes

Historically, persons with cognitive and intellectual disabilities have been regarded as less credible witnesses. This due to the belief that their memory systems are inherently defective and the assumption that they are susceptible to suggestibility and lack the skills to report events accurately.[5] However, modern research has begun to challenge these negative assumptions. Even if children with intellectual disabilities generally provide less detailed information,[6] they are capable of accurately reporting events, and their accuracy is generally high.[7] Memory in individuals with ASD may under certain conditions be more accurate than in those without. Moreover, individuals with ASD are able to discriminate false memory items from true ones significantly better than control subjects

---

4   Gillberg, C., *Sexuella övergrepp mot barn: Expertrapport – Neuropsykiatriska aspekter*, The National Board of Health and Welfare, 2000, p. 10.

5   Perlman, N.B., Ericson, K.I., Esses, V.M. and Isaacs, B.J., "The Developmentally Handicapped Witness – Competency as a Function of Question Format," 18 *Law and Human Behavior* 1994, pp. 171–187 at p. 171.

6   Henry, L., Ridley, A., Perry, J. and Crane, L., "Perceived Credibility and Eyewitness Testimony of Children with Intellectual Disabilities," 55 *Journal of Intellectual Disability Research*, 2011, pp. 385–391 at p. 385.

7   Henry, L.A. and Gudjonsson, G.H., "Eyewitness Memory and Suggestibility in Children with Mental Retardation," 104 *American Journal on Mental Retardation*, 1999, pp. 491–508 at p. 491 ff.

can.[8] However, children with intellectual disabilities can be more suggestible in response to closed misleading questions than children without disabilities.[9] Evidence for acquiescence (yes-saying) can be caused by many factors, such as a desire to please and an increased submissiveness, but also over-complex questions.[10] Among persons with high-functioning autism, researchers have found no increased risk of suggestibility. However, these individuals might be more eager to please or be more inclined to avoid conflict and confrontation and may therefore be more prone to responding compliantly to requests or demands.[11] For this reason, repeated questions should be avoided. ADHD is not correlated to the ability to accurately report events nor to an increased risk of suggestibility, although comorbidity may imply altered prerequisites.[12]

Despite the research on competence and credibility, an accurate statement can be unpersuasive if negative stereotypes towards children with neuropsychiatric disorders affect the evaluation of the statement. Previous studies have analysed individuals' attitudes toward different groups of children. For example, evaluations of the labels "gifted children," "normal children," and "physically handicapped children" were significantly more positive than the evaluations of the labels "mentally-retarded children," "learning-disabled children," and "emotionally-disturbed children."[13] As part of this research project, the perceived credibility of children with neuropsychiatric disorders was tested among Swedish law students during 2013.[14] All participants were presented with the same forensic interview with an 11-year-old girl who had

8   Beversdorf, D.Q., Smith, B.W., Cruciand, G.P., Anderson, J.M., Keillor, J.M., Barrett, A.M., Hughes, J.D., Felopulosi, G.J., Bauman, M.L., Nadeauk, S.E. and Heilman, K.M., "Increased Discrimination of 'False Memories' in Autism Spectrum Disorder," 97 *Proceedings of the National Academy of Sciences* 2000, pp. 8734–8737 at p. 8734.

9   Henry and Gudjonsson, *supra* note 7, p. 491.

10   Finlay, W.M. and Lyons, E., "Acquiescence in Interviews with People Who Have Mental Retardation," 40 *Mental Retardation*, 2002, pp. 14–29 at p. 14.

11   North, A.S., Russell, A.J. and Gudjonsson, G.H., "High functioning autism spectrum disorders – An investigation of psychological vulnerabilities during interrogative interview," 19 *Journal of Forensic Psychiatry and Psychology*, 2008, pp. 323–334 at p. 323.

12   Lindblad, F. and Lainpelto, K., "Sexual Abuse Allegations by Children with Neuropsychiatric Disorders," 20 *Journal of Child Sexual Abuse*, 2011, pp. 182–195 at p. 190.

13   Parish, T.S., Dyck, N. and Kappes, B.M., "Stereotypes concerning normal and handicapped children," 102 *The Journal of Psychology*, 1979, pp. 63–70 at p. 68 f.

14   See Lainpelto, K., "Är en barnneuropsykiatrisk funktionsnedsättning detsamma som en processuell funktionsnedsättning? – Om objektivitet, saklighet och rättstrygghet," in: Cederborg, A-C. and Warnling-Nerep, W (eds.), *Barnrätt – en antologi*, 2014, Norstedts Juridik, Stockholm, pp. 268–281.

allegedly been sexually abused by her father. Fifty-four students (35 females; 17 males; 2 not reporting gender) were presented the case with the information that the girl had ADHD and high functioning autism and fifty-three students (42 females; 10 males; 1 not reporting gender) were presented the case without diagnostic information. After reading the forensic interview, the participants rated the child's credibility and the statements' reliability. The students who had not been informed about the diagnosis rated higher on the four 10-score items: credibility of the victim ($p < 0.001$), that her narrations were self-experienced ($p < 0.001$), that they were detailed ($p = 0.029$), and that the accounts were veracious ($p < 0.001$). In a general linear model, adjusted for gender and group-gender interactions, the associations – that students who had not been informed about a diagnosis rated higher – remained.

The result of the Swedish study differed from previously conducted studies in the United States, where no negative correlations between diagnosis and perceived credibility have been confirmed. In a mock-trial study conducted by Bottoms *et al.* (2003), the participants watched videotaped excerpts from an actual trial concerning sexual assault. When the victim was portrayed as "mildly mentally retarded" instead as "having average intelligence," jurors were more likely to vote guilty and considered the victim to be more credible.[15] Similar results have been shown in two previous studies by Podell *et al.* (1994;1996).[16]

The American results have been explained by the theory that persons with disabilities, like young children, are judged negatively in terms of intellectual capacity but positively in terms of trustworthiness and honesty – traits that are generally more important than cognitive ability in child sexual abuse cases and traits that lead to increased perceived credibility. Also, like young children, disabled children and even disabled teenagers, might be considered sexually naive in ways that could preclude the fabrication of false accusations. Thus, teenagers with disabilities might be perceived as more credible than non-disabled teenagers based on the assumption than non-disabled teenagers have the cognitive capacity and sexual knowledge to fabricate sexual abuse charges.[17] This theory is confirmed by a study by Henry *et al.* (2011), which explored how mock

---

15   Bottoms, B.L., Nysse-Carris, K.L., Harris, T. and Tyda, K., "Jurors' Perceptions of Adolescent Sexual Assault Victims Who Have Intellectual Disabilities," 27 *Law and Human Behavior*, 2003, pp. 205–227 at p. 216 ff.

16   Podell, D.M., Kastner and J., Kastner., S., "Mental Retardation and Adult Women's Perceptions of Adolescent Sexual Abuse," 18 *Child Abuse and Neglect*, 1994, pp. 809–819; Podell, D.M., Kastner, J. and Kastner, S., "Adolescents with Mental Retardation – Perceptions of Sexual Abuse," 66 *American Journal of Orthopsychiatry*, 1996, pp. 103–110.

17   Bottoms *et al., supra* note 15, p. 207 f.

jurors perceived free recall transcripts of children with intellectual disabilities and age-matched children without disabilities in the absence of knowledge of group membership. The participants rated the testimonies of children with intellectual disabilities as less credible than the testimonies of the comparison group.[18] The above suggests that non-judicial factors affect jurors when they have knowledge of the neuropsychiatric disorder.

It can be discussed why the results of the Swedish study differ from those of the American studies. First, note that the Swedish study examined the perceived credibility among law students and not mock jurors. This is because instead of a jury, which is characteristic for the common-law tradition, Swedish courts have both lay judges and legally qualified judges and the latter participate in the rulings. Even if there is some support in the research that lay judges and legally qualified judges evaluate evidence differently,[19] the Swedish study does not present enough support for this conclusion. Secondly, the American studies analysed the perceived credibility of children/teenagers with mental retardation/intellectual disabilities, whereas the Swedish study analysed the perceived credibility of a child with ADHD and high functioning autism. Mental retardation often implies significant limitations of cognitive ability, which ADHD and high-functioning autism do not. The theory described above might therefore gain increased significance.

In sum, there is no support for the assumption that children with ADHD and/or high-functioning autism lack the skills to report events. The results of the Swedish study may therefore indicate that the participants were affected by non-judicial facts and negative stereotypes concerning neuropsychiatric disorders. Consequently, these findings *highlight the need for forensic experts in cases where children with neuropsychiatric disorders are alleged victims.*

Forensic Experts

In a criminal case, a forensic expert can be appointed by the court *ex officio* according to the *Swedish Code of Judicial Procedure* (Chapter 40, Section 1). The purpose of such an appointment is to provide the court with expertise and

---

18   Henry, 2011, *supra* note 6, p. 388 f.

19   See Kalven, H. and Zeisel, H., *The American Jury*, Little, Brown and Company, Boston, 1993; Heuer, L. and Penrod, S., "Trial Complexity – A Field Investigation of Its Meaning and Its Effects," 18 *Law and Human Behavior*, 1994, pp. 29–51; and Eisenberg, T., Hannaford-Agor, P.L., Hans, V.P., Waters, N.L., Munsterman, T.G, Schwab, S.J. and Wells, M.T., "Judge-Jury Agreement in Criminal Cases – A Partial Replication of Kalven and Zeisel's The American Jury", 2 *Journal of Empirical Legal Studies,* 2005, pp. 171–206.

knowledge beyond that of the average person. The decision to involve an expert lies within the discretion of the court and an expert could be appointed ex officio if, for example, the experts appointed by the parties have conflicting opinions, or if an expert appointed by one of the parties is less reliable or if one party has not appointed an expert at all.

Even if modern research has shown that historical presumptions concerning the competence and credibility of children with neuropsychiatric disorders are mostly unfounded, several other challenges may arise during forensic investigation which call for the involvement of an expert (even during the police investigation[20]). For example, an increased frequency of sexual behaviour has been seen in patients with Tourette's syndrome and developmental problems.[21] On the other hand, sexually inappropriate behaviour is more common in children who have experienced sexual abuse.[22] This might indicate a potential forensic dilemma, *i.e.* there is a risk of over-evaluation of the child's statements if the symptoms are wrongly misinterpreted as symptoms of abuse. On the contrary, there is also a risk of under-evaluation if possible abuse symptoms are wrongly misinterpreted as symptoms of the disorder. Another possible forensic dilemma is the overlap of symptoms between ADHD and posttraumatic stress disorder (PTSD) and the comorbidity between these disorders. This dilemma is also reflected in the increased risk of ADHD in sexual-abuse victims.[23] Problems may also arise during the forensic investigation due to interaction and communication dysfunctions.

Cases and Methods

All District Court cases from 2010 (n = 269) concerning alleged sexual abuse (sexual harassment excluded) against child (< 15 years of age) were identified through criminal registers and requested from each separate District Court (n = 48).

Fourteen cases (5 per cent) concerned alleged sexual abuse of children with neuropsychiatric disorders (nine females; four males; one unknown gender).

20   The Swedish Prosecution Authority, *Handläggning av ärenden gällande övergrepp mot barn: Handbok*, Utvecklingscentrum, Göteborg, 2012, p. 35.

21   See Comings, D.E. and Comings, B.G., "Sexual Abuse or Tourette Syndrome?" 38 *Social Work*, 1993, pp. 347–350.

22   McCurry, C., McClellan, J., Adams, J., Norrei, M., Storck, M., Eisner, A. and Breiger, D., "Sexual Behavior Associated With Low Verbal IQ in Youth Who Have Severe Mental Illness," 36 *Mental Retardation*, 1998, pp. 23–30 at p. 23.

23   Lindblad and Lainpelto, *supra* note 12, p. 183 with references.

The children's mean age was 13.15 years. The diagnostic groups were: mental retardation (eight cases), ASD (two cases), ADHD (two cases), ASD/ADHD (one case), and ASD/ADHD/Tourette's syndrome (one case). In 10 cases the allegations concerned intercourse (vaginal, anal, oral, or a combination of these) and four cases concerned less severe forms of abuse.

The alleged perpetrators (n = 14) were: unacquainted with the victims (six cases), an acquaintance (three cases), a partner (two cases), a parent/step-parent (two cases), and a brother (one case). Nine of the alleged perpetrators denied the allegations (64 per cent) and five confessed to the allegation (36 per cent). Nine of the alleged perpetrators were convicted by the District Court (64 per cent) and five were acquitted (36 per cent). Eight of the cases were appealed against (57 per cent) and five judgments were affirmed. Two of the earlier convicted perpetrators were acquitted by the Court of Appeal and one earlier acquitted perpetrator was convicted by the Court of Appeal. After binding judgment, nine of the perpetrators were convicted (64 per cent) and five were acquitted (36 per cent).

All information about the cases was collected from the written sentences of the courts and the material was examined to elucidate the ways in which courts evaluated the credibility of the alleged victims. Also, 14 randomly chosen cases concerning sexual abuse against children with no disabilities were compared to the 14 cases presented above. These randomly chosen cases are not presented in detail in this paper.

Results

In five of the 14 cases, arguments related to the disorder were applied by the court – this without the involvement of an expert. In most cases the courts entered into complicated analyses of the statements of the victims without clarifying the significance of the neurodevelopmental considerations for these statements. Also, in some cases the courts discussed the behaviour of the victim without including the implication of the neuropsychiatric disorder in the behavioural analysis. In one case the District Court stated that the absence of emotions on behalf of the victim during the interview was "peculiar." The victim was diagnosed with mental retardation. In another case concerning alleged abuse of a victim with ASD, the perpetrator was convicted by the District Court which in the written sentence stated:

> According to the court the interviews,[...], have been performed in an exemplary manner. No leading questions have occurred. NN has been

given plenty of time to answer the questions. NN has been eager to object and to correct the information when a misunderstanding has surfaced. NN has reported on details in a way that makes him credible. [...] The court arrives at the conclusion that NN's statement contains such details that it must reflect a self-experienced event.

The case was taken to the Court of Appeal and the same videotaped police interview with the victim was shown to the court without reference to new evidence or expert evidence. The defendant was now acquitted and in the written sentence the Court of Appeal stated:

NN is during a predominant part of the interviews hiding his face and he is sparing of words. The statement contains few details and cannot be viewed as spontaneously related.

Expert evidence was presented in five of the 14 cases. Two expert witnesses (psychologists) appeared in court and three written expert reports from *Child and Adolescent Psychiatry* were presented. All of the expert evidence was referred to by the prosecutor; thus, the courts did not appoint any of the expert evidence. The expert evidence was concerned with the general credibility of the child and not an evaluation of the child's cognitive prerequisites, such as capacity to correctly perceive and interpret events, memory functioning, conceptual and intellectual development, or communicative ability. Questions concerning neurodevelopmental issues were handled by the courts on their own or were not identified at all. Also, the interpretation of psychiatric symptoms was handled by the courts on their own. Notably, in four of the five cases where expert evidence was referred to by the prosecutor, the alleged perpetrator was acquitted (of the five acquittals in total).

According to established practice, based on precedents from the Swedish Supreme Court since the 1980s, Swedish courts have long relied upon the conceptual frameworks of Statement Reality Analysis (SRA) and Criterion-Based Content Analysis (CBCA) when evaluating children's credibility.[24] Statements are often evaluated against factors such as richness of detail, contextual embedding, unusual details, subjective experience, and reproduction of

---

24   See Gregow, T., "Några synpunkter på frågan om bevisprövning och bevisvärdering i mål om sexuella övergrepp mot barn," *Svensk Juristtidning*, 1996, pp. 509–523. Judgment of the Supreme Court of Sweden, 23 December 1980, *Nytt Juridiskt Arkiv* 1980:137; and Judgment of the Supreme Court of Sweden, 2 July 1992, Case No. B 1673–92, *Nytt Juridiskt Arkiv* 1992:67.

speech. Credible statements should for example be coherent, clear, detailed, and should not contain information that is difficult to explain or information that raises doubt concerning the alleged events.[25] Also, there should be no obvious motive for false accusations. Only in two of the 14 cases did the courts not evaluate the victims' accounts against the above-mentioned criteria. This indicates that statements from children with neuropsychiatric disorders are expected to have the same clear characteristics as statements by alleged victims without disabilities, to be viewed as credible. The richness of detail was the most commonly mentioned criterion in the ten cases studied. In six, the statement was deemed inadequate in details, but only in one did the court discuss the neuropsychiatric disorder as a cause of the deficit (still the defendant was acquitted). Thus, courts do not seem to take neurodevelopmental aspects into account when deficits concerning the above-mentioned criteria are detected. The evaluation seems to be concerned predominately with the victims' motives for the accusations and the nature of the relationship between the victims and the alleged perpetrators.

Compared to the 14 randomly chosen cases concerning sexual abuse of children with no disabilities, 12 of the alleged perpetrators were convicted (86 per cent) compared to the nine (64 per cent) convictions where the victim had a neuropsychiatric disorder.

Discussion

The aim of this paper was to present some preliminary finding of the research project *"The Swedish Criminal Justice System's Response to Victimized Children with Neuropsychiatric Disorders"* – in particular how Swedish courts argue when a child with a neuropsychiatric disorder has allegedly been sexually abused and to what extent the judgments are based on the involvement of experts. All district court cases from the year 2010 concerning alleged sexual abuse against a child were identified, gathered, and qualitatively analysed. Fourteen of the 269 cases concerned alleged sexual abuse of children with neuropsychiatric disorders. Cognitive impairment (mental retardation and autism) was the dominating diagnosis among the alleged victims.

The analysis of the 14 cases led to three reasons for concern. First, arguments related to the neuropsychiatric disorder were applied by the courts in

---

25   See Cederborg, A-C., Lamb, M.E., "How Does the Legal System Respond When Children
       with Learning Difficulties are Victimized?" 30 *Child Abuse and Neglect*, 2006, pp. 537–547
       at p. 539.

only a few of the cases. Secondly, children with neuropsychiatric disorders were expected to provide the same sort of statements as children without disabilities. Thirdly, expert evidence was appointed (by the prosecutor) in only a few of the cases.

The statements were evaluated without trying to clarify the significance of the neurodevelopmental considerations. This is also shown in previous studies by Cederborg and Lamb (2006) and Lindblad and Lainpelto (2011).[26] Also, in some of the cases the behaviour of the victim was discussed without including in the evaluation the implication of the neuropsychiatric disorder. Instead, a majority of the courts entered into quite complicated analyses of the victims' statements, resting heavily on the conceptual frameworks of SRA and CBCA. This criteria-based evaluation has been availed of in the practice of the Supreme Court since the beginning of the 1980s, and is still used, even though the methods have been disputed by modern research.[27] Thus, children with neuropsychiatric disorders are expected to provide the same sort of statement as children without such difficulties in order to be deemed as credible. In sum, the courts' judgments were made in ignorance of the capabilities and limitations of the children.

The results indicate that the courts lack adequate knowledge to assess the competence and the credibility of children with neuropsychiatric disorders. By seeking expert evidence, the courts can gain knowledge of these children's abilities and limitations – knowledge that could strengthen the decision-making. To minimize the risk of judgments being based on ignorance, stereotypes, and uncertainty, the courts need to apply more thorough assessments of children's abilities and of the implications of the disorders. Unfortunately, such assessments have not been applied by the courts. In a few cases expert evidence was referred to by the prosecution, but the courts did not seek such evidence in these cases. This confirms the results in two previous studies, *i.e.* that Swedish courts generally evaluate statements of children with neuropsychiatric disorders without the help of experts.[28] The reason for the courts' general reluctance to appoint psychological/psychiatric expert evidence ex officio is probably that such experts are not viewed as sources of useful information by the Swedish justice system,[29] especially concerning sexual

---

26   Cederborg and Lamb, *supra* note 25, p. 539 ff. and Lindblad and Lainpelto, *supra* note 12, p. 187 f.

27   See Schelin, L., *Bevisvärdering av utsagor i brottmål*, Norstedts Juridik, Stockholm, 2007.

28   Cederborg and Lamb, *supra* note 25, and Lindblad and Lainpelto, *supra* note 12.

29   See the Judgment of the Supreme Court of Sweden, 2 July 1992, Case No. B 1673–92, *Nytt Juridiskt Arkiv* 1991:67.

abuse cases. However, the precedents from the Supreme Court are not clear, and lower courts may have misinterpreted the opinion that courts should make decisions independently of psychological experts. Also, the Swedish courts strive for objectivity where appointment of an expert might jeopardize this objective, which is why the responsibility to appoint experts has been laid on the parties.

In four of the five cases where expert evidence was referred to by the prosecutor, the alleged perpetrator was acquitted, which means that the courts had ruled against the assessments of the experts. This might be explained by the low mean quality of professional statements.[30] If an expert report is poorly written or prepared by an expert who lacks the necessary skills, the courts are left to rely on their own assumptions and knowledge. Also, as in the study by Lindblad and Lainpelto (2011), expert evidence was sought regarding the general credibility of the child.[31] Expert evidence concerning neurodevelopmental issues and the interpretation of psychiatric symptoms was not sought, or not provided by experts. As discussed by Cederborg and Lamb (2006), there might be discrepancies between the type of information requested by the legal system and the type of information experts can provide. Forensic psychologists cannot assess credibility reliably, although a predominant part of the requests to psychologists concern such assessments.[32]

Finally, the number of court cases where the victim has a neuropsychiatric disorder represents five per cent of all the cases concerning alleged child sexual abuse in Sweden in 2010. This can be compared to two percent in 2004 and 2006 respectively.[33] However, prevalence figures show that approximately eight per cent of all children in Sweden receive a neuropsychiatric diagnosis. Moreover, approximately 15 per cent of all police reports regarding alleged child abuse in Stockholm County concern abuse of children with neuropsychiatric disorders. This indicates, first, a strong correlation between neuropsychiatric disorders and abuse and, secondly, that children with these types of disorder do not receive adequate legal protection. This is highlighted by the fact that 86 per cent of the control cases concerning sexual abuse of children

---

30   See Gumpert, C.H., Lindblad, F., Grann, M., The Quality of Written Expert Testimony in Alleged Child Sexual Abuse – An Empirical Study, 8 *Psychology, Crime and Law*, 2002, pp. 77–92.

31   Lindblad and Lainpelto, *supra* note 12, p. 189.

32   Cederborg and Lamb, *supra* note 25, p. 543.

33   Lindblad and Lainpelto, *supra* note 12, p. 192. However, the figures from 2004 and 2006 are based on the number of victims and the figures for 2010 are, up till now, based on the number of cases. Therefore, the percentage for 2010 will probably decrease when based on the number of victims.

with no disabilities led to conviction while the corresponding number of convictions in cases concerning sexual abuse against children with neuropsychiatric disorders was 64 per cent. However, the sample is too small to draw any far-reaching general conclusions.

Conclusions

To minimize the risk of judgments based on insufficient knowledge and inaccurate assumptions the Swedish courts have to involve experts in the decision-making when the alleged child victim has a neuropsychiatric disorder—a point of view that can be put forward on behalf of both the victims and the defendants. Also, the expert evidence should not concern the general credibility of the child, but an evaluation of the child's cognitive prerequisites. Therefore the courts should formulate distinct neurodevelopmental questions for the experts.

PART 3

Children and Civil and Administrative Justice

∵

Justice for the Migrant Child: The Protective Force of the Convention on the Rights of the Child

Mary E. Crock

1 The Challenge of Migration

The process of leaving one country and establishing a home in another can be an intrinsically dangerous enterprise for children. The physical frontiers to be crossed pose obvious challenges, especially where children are travelling alone or as irregular migrants. However, migrant children also face a myriad of less visible barriers to gaining admission and acceptance into the society of a host nation. As a general rule, most migrate with at least one parent or responsible adult – not that this is a guarantee of safety or access to rights. Within any flow of forced migrants, however, a sizeable percentage[1] travels as unaccompanied minors or as children traveling with a guardian but separated from family. Children can be victims of trafficking or other abuse; they can move in search of asylum or economic advancement. Children can be abandoned in a foreign land or they can be born stateless because of the status of migrating parents. Citizen children born to mothers who are irregular migrants can face abandonment in their birth country or constructive deportation upon their mother's removal.[2] Children can be vulnerable by virtue of their age alone, and/or they can face particular challenges because of the circumstances surrounding their movement.[3] Much will depend on how and why a child comes to migrate – and on the child's legal entitlements.

---

1 Overall statistics are difficult to obtain, but one measure of migration by unaccompanied and separated children is the number of applications lodged by those children in industrialized countries: for these statistics, see United Nations High Commissioner for Refugees, Global Trends 2012 (UNHCR, 2013). The number of applications lodged by unaccompanied or separated children in 2012 was the highest number on record since UNHCR started collecting such data in 2006.

2 *E.g. ZH (Tanzania) v Secretary of State for the Home Department* [2011] UKSC 4. Compare the decision of the European Court of Human Rights in *Nunez v Norway* – Application No. 55597/09, Judgment of 28 June 2011.

3 Office of the High Commissioner for Human Rights, "Study of the Office of the UN High Commissioner for Human Rights (OHCHR) on challenges and best practices in the implementation of the international framework for the protection of the rights of the child in the context of migration" Human Rights Council, 15th session, 5 July 2010, Agenda Items 2 and 3, UN Doc A/HRC/15/29, para. 7.

© KONINKLIJKE BRILL NV, LEIDEN, 2015 | DOI 10.1163/9789004297432_019

There are many aspects of domestic immigration and citizenship laws that impact directly on children. These laws operate together as a legal mechanism to determine which persons are accepted into the community in both formal and informal senses of membership. State laws confer legal statuses that correspond to a hierarchy of legal rights and benefits such as rights of residence and access to government services. Young migrants can find themselves excluded in matters as fundamental as access to primary health care, social security and education. Linguistic, cultural and religious differences can deepen the divide between the newcomer and societal insiders.

Under international law, child migrants have suffered from a form of double institutional blindness born of their minority and status as non-citizens. As Chetail documents,[4] migrants were seen traditionally through the lens of States' rights and responsibilities, a lens that provided little scope for recognizing agency in non-citizen adults, let alone children. It is only in recent times that human rights have emerged to transform understanding of the place of the individual in international law.[5] If international law was slow to acknowledge children as rights bearers, migrant children have suffered particular neglect. This article explores the Convention that has operated—or should be operating—as game-changer for these children.

The United Nations Convention on the Rights of the Child—the most subscribed of all the UN human rights treaties[6]—enjoins States Parties to treat *all* children as rights bearers, irrespective of citizenship or immigration status.[7] Article 22 goes so far as to accord *asylum seeker* children the same rights and entitlements as *refugees* – whatever their actual status under the Convention relating to the Status of Refugees and its related Protocol. As the United Nations

---

4   Chetail, V., "The Transnational Movement of Persons under General International Law: Mapping the Customary Law Foundations of International Migration Law," in Chetail, V. and Bauloz, C. (eds.), *Research Handbook on International Law and Migration*, Edward Elgar, 2014.

5   On this evolution, see generally Kamminga, M.T. and Scheinin, M. (eds.), *The Impact of Human Rights Law on General International Law*, Oxford University Press, 2009; Meron, T., *International Law in the Age of Human Rights*, Martinus Nijhoff, 2004; and Reisman, M., "Sovereignty and Human Rights in Contemporary International Law," 84 *American Journal of International Law*, 1990, p. 866.

6   United Nations Convention on the Rights of the Child (adopted 20 November 1989), entered into force 2 September 1990, 1577 UNTS 3 (CRC). As 25 April 2014, 194 states are parties to this Convention.

7   CRC Art 22; compare Convention relating to the Status of Refugees, opened for signature 28 July 1951, entered into force 22 April 1954, 189 UNTS 137 as amended by the Protocol relating to the Status of Refugees, opened for signature 31 January 1967, entered into force 4 October 1967, 606 UNTS 267 (Refugee Convention) Chapters II–V.

High Commissioner for Human Rights explains, this means children "appear in the universal protected group of 'children'"[8] no matter what classifications— legal or illegal, regular or irregular migrants—States choose to superimpose on them. The CRC is designed to apply to all children, at all times, wherever they may be.

The two most critical achievements of the CRC are what have become known as the "best interests" principle and the notion that children should have the right to participate in all decisions affecting their future. As explored in Part 2, these matters require some un-packing in the immigration context. However, the 54 articles of the CRC and the Convention's three Protocols cover a huge range of issues, creating both qualified and absolute rights in children and obligations to similar effect in States Parties. Together, these operate as a super human rights convention for children. It is well to recall moreover that many of the provisions of the CRC adopt or build on protections enshrined in other instruments, all of which are normative in their effect. At an international level these include (but are not limited to) the UN Convention and Protocol relating to the Status of Refugees; the International Covenant on Civil and Political Rights;[9] the Convention against Torture and Other Cruel, Inhuman, or Degrading Treatment or Punishment;[10] the Convention on the Rights of Persons with Disabilities;[11] the International Convention on the Protection of the Rights of All Migrant Workers and Members of Their Families;[12] various Conventions of the International Labour Organization (ILO);[13] the Convention

---

8   OHCHR, *supra* note 3, para. 18.

9   International Covenant on Civil and Political Rights, opened for signature 19 December 1966, entered into force 23 March 1976, 999 *UNTS* 171 (ICCPR).

10   Convention against Torture and Other Cruel, Inhuman or Degrading Treatment or Punishment, opened for signature 10 December 1984, entered into force 26 June 1987, 1465 *UNTS* 85 (CAT).

11   Convention on the Rights of Persons with Disabilities, opened for signature 30 Mar 2007, entered into force 3 May 2008, 2515 *UNTS* 3 (CRPD).

12   International Convention on the Protection of the Rights of All Migrant Workers and Members of Their Families, opened for signature 18 December 1990, entered into force 1 July 2003, 2220 *UNTS* 3 (CMW).

13   See, for example, Convention Concerning Forced or Compulsory Labour, opened for signature 28 June 1930, entered into force 1 May 1932, 39 *UNTS* 55; Convention Concerning the Abolition of Forced Labour, opened for signature 25 June 1957, entered into force 17 January 1959, 320 *UNTS* 291; Convention Concerning Discrimination in Respect of Employment and Occupation, opened for signature 28 June 1958, entered into force June 15, 1960, 362 *UNTS* 31; Convention Concerning Minimum Age for Admission to Employment, opened for signature 26 June 1973, entered into force June 19, 1976, 115 *UNTS* 298; Convention the Prohibition and Immediate Action for the Elimination of the Worst Forms of Child Labour, opened for

on the Reduction of Statelessness;[14] and Protocols to combat Trafficking[15] and Smuggling of migrants,[16] which supplement the UN Convention against Transnational Organized Crime. To these must be added regional instruments that protect the rights of migrant children.[17]

Against the background of this rich source of normative provisions, this article explores the extent to which the CRC can assist in addressing the vulnerability and precariousness of the migration process for children. A discussion of the protective function of the Convention begins in Part 2 with an examination of the best interest provision contained in Article 3(1). This has been described by the Committee on the Rights of the Child as a "right, a principle and a rule of procedure"[18] The Committee notes that there is no hierarchy of rights in the CRC: all rights are deemed to embody the notion of best interests. This is a point that is made also in the CRC General Comments – most particularly General Comment No. 6 relating to unaccompanied and separated

---

signature 17 June 1999, entered into force November 19, 2000, 233 *UNTS* 161. See Lenzerini, F., "International Trade and Child Labour Standards," in Francioni, F. (ed.), *Environment, Human Rights and International Trade*, Hart Publishing, 2001.

14   Convention on the Reduction of Statelessness, opened for signature 30 August 1961, entered into force 13 December 1975, 989 *UNTS* 175.

15   Protocol to Prevent, Suppress and Punish Trafficking in Persons, Especially Women and Children, Supplementing the United Nations Convention against Transnational Organized Crime (Palermo Protocol), opened for signature 15 November 2000, entered into force 25 December 2003, 2237 *UNTS* 319.

16   Protocol against the Smuggling of Migrants by Land, Sea and Air, Supplementing the United Nations Convention against Transnational Organized Crime, opened for signature 15 November 2000, entered into force 28 January 2004, 2241 *UNTS* 507.

17   African Charter on the Rights and Welfare of the Child, opened for signature 1 July 1990, entered into force 29 November 1999, OAU Doc CAB/LEG/24.9/49, Article 4; European Charter of Fundamental Rights, adopted 18 December 2000, entered into force 1 December 2009 with the Treaty of Lisbon, *Official Journal of the European Union* C83/391, Article 24; The League of Arab States Revised Arab Charter on Human Rights, opened for signature 22 May 2004, entered into force 15 March 2008, 12 *International Human Rights Reports* 893, Article 33(3); The American Convention on Human Rights, opened for signature 22 November 1969, entered into force 18 June 1978, 1144 *UNTS* 143, Article 17(4); see further International Association of Refugee Law Judges, *2011 World Conference – Vulnerable Persons Working Group Workshop Discussion Paper*, OHCHR, 2012, http://www.ohchr.org/Documents/HRBodies/CRC/Discussions/2012/Submissions/InternationalAssociation RefugeeLawJudges.pdf.

18   See Committee on the Rights of the Child, General Comment No. 14 on The Right of the Child to Have His or Her Best Interests Taken as a Primary Consideration (Article 3, para. 1), 62nd session (29 May 2013), UN Doc CRC/C/GC/14, para. 21.

asylum seeker children.[19] Indeed, the CRC is constructed as a seamless web. The concept of best interests underpins the whole instrument,[20] but so too does Article 12 with its injunction to involve children in all matters affecting their interests. It is this provision that embodies the move from the outmoded paternalistic "welfare" approach to children to one that treats children as rights bearers.

In the parts that follow, the article examines four contexts of particular concern: the identification of migrant children at risk; guardianship and care; family unity; and the significance of the right to participate. The article concludes with some comments on the legality of deterrence measures that target non-citizen children. While the CRC is often honoured more in the breach than in the observance, I argue that the Convention does indeed operate as a legal game-changer for child migrants.

2   The Best Interests Principle and the Unique Precariousness
         of Childhood

The best interests principle enshrined in Article 3(1) of the CRC creates a substantive right insofar as it obliges States Parties to make the best interests of children within their care a matter of primary concern.[21] The revolution in the provision is that it relegates the rights of parents and other responsible adults to second place,[22] identifying the child as rights-bearer. The problem for the migrant child is that this over-arching principle does not create an absolute right. States have been quick to note that the use of the pronoun "a" in the phrase "a primary consideration" reflects the understanding that the interests of the child are not given absolute priority – they can be overridden.[23] This

---

19   Committee on the Rights of the Child, General Comment No. 6 on Treatment of
      Unaccompanied and Separated Children outside Their Country of Origin, CRC, 39th ses-
      sion (1 September 2005), UN Doc CRC/GC/2005/6.
20   This point is made by Philip Alston and Bridget Gilmour-Walsh in *The Best Interests of the
      Child: Towards a Synthesis of Children's Rights and Cultural Values*, UNICEF, 1996, p. 1.
21   Committee on the Rights of the Child, *supra* note 19.
22   *Secretary, Department of Health and Community Services v JWB and SWB* (1992) 175 CLR 218
      (*Marion's Case*) [13].
23   *Minister of State for Immigration & Ethnic Affairs v Ah Hin Teoh* (1995) 183 CLR 273 ("Teoh's
      case"). In that case, Mason C.J. and Deane J. observed that Article 3 "is careful to avoid
      putting the best interests of the child as the primary consideration; it does no more than
      give those interests first importance along with such other considerations as may, in the
      circumstances of a given case, require equal, but not paramount, weight" (at [31]).

much is acknowledged by the CRC Committee.[24] Article 3(1) may not create a right for children in all situations. The point made by the Committee is that in becoming party to the Convention, States undertake to consider the issue of children as a first order priority. Moreover, there is a raft of other protective provisions in the CRC that do place absolute obligations on State Parties to extend a protective veil over children in their care or under their control.

The "best interests" requirement invites reflection on how children are affected by the process of crossing borders. As we have argued in the context of children seeking asylum alone,[25] there are three ways in which child migrants can experience hardship. First, child migrants can be vulnerable in ways that are tied to their status as children. Children can be subjected to sale, trafficking or bartering for the purposes of illicit adoption, child marriages or other form of exploitation.[26] Second, children can be vulnerable in the same ways as adults. Immigration can be a stressful and disorienting experience for any person. Separation from family and friends can be a source of grief, depression and vulnerability to harm. The process of migrating can be attended with economic deprivation. However, and this is the third point, there are aspects of the migratory process that can be common, yet uniquely harmful to children. Examples are the devastating impact on children of separation from family; of prolonged periods in immigration detention; and of failure to secure adequate housing and nutrition. The economic privations of moving countries can also result in a diminution of educational opportunities. For children, denial of education can have lifelong consequences, reducing the prospects of successful integration into a host society.

A careful reading of the CRC suggests that the drafters of this instrument were alive to the situations where children are uniquely vulnerable to harm. Noteworthy are two contexts in which the CRC does make the best interests of a child *the* paramount factor to be considered: adoption (Article 21) and separation of a child from their parents against their will (Article 9).[27] Both contexts are of critical importance to migrant children. The CRC also

---

24   Committee on the Rights of the Child, *supra* note 19, para. 39.

25   Bhabha, J. and Crock, M., *Seeking Asylum Alone: Unaccompanied and Separated Children and Refugee Protection in Australia, the UK and the US*, Themis Press, 2007.

26   One example that springs to mind are the children used as jockeys in camel races. See Houbara Bustard Hunting, "Camel-Jockeys;" and Alam, S., "We Should Not Let Their Dreams Die," available at: http://www.iearn.org.au/clp/archive/write93.htm.

27   On the recognition of this in the context of Australia's child welfare laws, see Parker, S., "The Best Interests of the Child – Principles and Problems," 8 *International Journal of Law and the Family*, 1994, pp. 26–41, at pp. 27–28. See also Alston, P., "The Best Interests Principle: Towards a Reconciliation of Culture and Human Rights," in Alston, P. (ed.), *The Best Interests of the Child: Reconciling Culture and Human Rights*, UNICEF and Clarendon Press, 1994, at p. 4.

contains provisions that are mandatory in their effect. One example is Article 6 that speaks to the child's "inherent right to life." It reads: "State Parties shall ensure to the maximum extent possible the survival and development of the child." Another is Article 11(1) which provides:

> States Parties shall take measures to combat the illicit transfer and non-return of children abroad.

Article 19 directs States Parties to take "all appropriate legislative, administrative, social and educational measures" to protect children from "all forms of physical or mental violence, injury or abuse, neglect or negligent treatment, maltreatment or exploitation, including sexual abuse." This provision is reinforced by Article 20 which deals with the protection of children temporarily or permanently deprived of their family environment, as well as by articles that deal expressly with situations which render a child vulnerable.

In addition to the special protections mandated for "refugee" children (Article 22), the CRC requires recognition of a child's right to be protected from economic exploitation (Article 32), and from the harms caused by illicit drugs (Article 33). A series of mandatory provisions address the issues of the sexual exploitation of children (Article 34); trafficking and sale of children (Article 35) and "all other forms of exploitation prejudicial to any aspects of the child's welfare" (Article 36). The CRC's Optional Protocol on the sale of children, child prostitution and child pornography and the Optional Protocol on the involvement of children in armed conflict are also worthy of special mention in this context. Both make provision for the protection of children in the context of migration and are mandatory in their language.

Reading these provisions together, it is difficult to see that the CRC leaves States Parties much room at all to argue that migrant children have fewer rights to protection than their citizen counterparts. The issue, rather, is what the provisions require in terms of concrete actions on the part of States.

3   The Identification of Migrant Children at Risk

Although somewhat counter-intuitive, one of the first challenges facing States charged with the protection of child migrants can be the identification of children at risk. The problems here are twofold. The first relates to the correct determination of the age of children: the protection entitlements of the CRC apply only to persons aged less than 18 years (see CRC Article 1). The second involves a more serious genus of institutional blindness. Even where no doubts arise about a child's status as a minor, officials can fail to pick up that the child is at risk of exploitation or abuse. As the Special Rapporteur on the human rights of migrants has observed, this reflects a fundamental problem in States' approach to migrant children: a failure to make distinctions between adult and child migrants, and following from that a failure to include in public policies on children the specific needs and protection to be afforded to the child in the context of migration.[28]

Age Assessments

The *Seeking Asylum Alone* research uncovered problems in the mechanisms used to determine the age of migrant children in two of the three countries studied.[29] This was (and is) important because of the legal and procedural entitlements that attach to minority. In the United Kingdom, for example, asylum seekers identified as children are diverted into the care of child protection authorities. Assessed to be at risk, they can nominally be placed in care for the duration of their childhood. For children seeking asylum alone in Australia and the United States, minors are also diverted into special programs for care and processing. The primary tools used by US and Australian officials in the *Seeking Asylum Alone* study were oral examinations of the children who (like many asylum seekers) presented without identity documentation of any kind. Estimates appear to have been made on the basis of appearance or, in contested cases, on the basis of bone scans or other rather invasive examinations of the individuals involved. In contrast, the UK provided an example of good practice, using much more holistic methodologies. These involved age assessments by a range of professionals charged with evaluating physical, cognitive and psycho-social development indicators.[30] While there is no common approach to age determinations in European countries, there is now a considerable amount of case law on this subject both at EU level and at country level. Here there does seem to be a consensus favouring the use of experts, taking an holistic approach to a child's state of development.[31]

---

28 Bustamante, J., *Report of the Special Rapporteur on the Human Rights of Migrants*, Human Rights Council, 11th Session Agenda Item 3, A/HRC/11/7, para. 24.

29 See Crock, M., *Seeking Asylum Alone: A Study of Australian Law, Policy and Practice Regarding Unaccompanied and Separated Children*, Themis Press, 2006; and Bhabha and Crock, *supra* note 25.

30 Compare Australia: Department of Immigration and Border Protection, Procedures Advice Manual 3: Protection Obligations Evaluation Manual (2013) [9.3] Age determination and a person's claimed age.

31 See Office of the High Commissioner for Human Rights, Regional Office for Europe, Judicial Implementation of Article 33 of the Convention on the Rights of the Child in

Guidelines published by the UN High Commission for Refugees (UNHCR)[32] suggest that the following principles should be observed in assessing the age of refugee or migrant children:

(a) Assessments should take into account not only the physical appearance of the child but also his/her psychological maturity;
(b) When scientific procedures are used in order to determine the age of a child, due allowance should be made for a margin of error. Such methods must be safe and respect human dignity; and
(c) The child should be given the benefit of the doubt if the exact age is uncertain.

Making Children Visible

When children travel across borders, most do so in the company of a responsible adult. Absent the institution of special measures, migrant children at risk of all kinds of exploitation can pass through immigration controls without being detected. As the researchers discovered in the course of the *Seeking Asylum Alone* project, few States question the authority of apparently responsible adults traveling with children in their care.[33] Children are rarely interviewed unless obviously traveling as unaccompanied minors. The vast majority of migrant children will pass unscrutinised through the entire immigration process from application through to immigration "clearance" (border control) as "accompanying family." An example of good practice was the program established by the UK to sensitize immigration officials to issues around the trafficking or smuggling of children. Using profiling and statistical data from law enforcement, immigration and other sources, officials in that country were trained to identify child migrants at risk. The scheme targeted both point of entry and other operations within the country where officials interacted with migrant children.[34]

The invisibility of children is reflected in the failure of many States to collect and maintain basic statistical information about migrant children. An exam-

---

Europe: The case of migrant children including unaccompanied children, OHCHR and UNICEF, 2012, Chapter II.

32   UNHCR *Guidelines on Policies and Procedures in Dealing with Unaccompanied Children Seeking Asylum*, UNHCR, 1997, Section 5.

33   Bhabha and Crock, *supra* note 25.

34   See *Paladin Child: The Safeguarding Children Strand of Maxim Funded by Reflex: A Partnership Study of Child Migration to the UK via London Heathrow* Reflex, Metropolitan Police, the United Kingdom Immigration Service, Association of Directors of Social Services, NSPCC, London Borough of Hillingdon, 2004.

ple is the statistical responses given to Australian researchers on the *Seeking Asylum Alone* project in 2006. Requests for information on the experience of trafficking in Australia met with what could only be called an incredible response – namely that Australia has seen only one child trafficked into the country (in 1994). This has not just been an issue in Australia, however. The failure by States to collect data on migrant children has been the subject of criticism by various UN organs.[35]

Perhaps as a result of dramatic increases around of the world of children traveling alone in search of protection, many governments appear to have become responsive to calls for more transparency in the processing of these children.

4   Caring for Child Migrants

The Guardianship of Unaccompanied and Separated Children
General Comment No. 6 deals specifically with issues surrounding children who migrate without the protection of a responsible adult. The Comment calls for the identification and registration of such children as soon as possible after entry into the host country. Thereafter, taking into consideration the views of the child, the appointment of a (trained) guardian and appropriate care arrangements for the child should be first order priorities.[36] While States are quick to acknowledge and respond to the needs of abandoned citizen children, the response to migrant children traveling alone is often much more complex and nuanced. In many cases the children are seen first as migrants, subject to stringent controls. In Australia, care arrangements for unaccompanied asylum seeker children are compromised by legislation that appoints the Minister for Immigration as guardian of certain unaccompanied minors who arrive in Australia without a parent or relative over 21 and with the intention to permanently reside. Yet the same person is charged with mandating the detention and removal of unauthorized arrivals.[37] In a system that requires undocumented asylum seekers arriving by boat to be transferred to Nauru or Papua New Guinea's Manus Island for processing and resettlement,[38] the conflict of interest in the Minister as guardian is obvious. In 2013–14 conscious decisions were made to include unaccompanied children amongst the transferees – as a

---

35   See OHCHR, *supra* note 3, para. 7 and note 10.
36   Jorge Bustamante, *supra* note 28, paras. 35–36.
37   *Immigration (Guardianship of Children) Act* 1946 (Cth).
38   *Migration Act 1958* (Cth) s 198AB.

message to deter others from sending their children on the perilous boat jour-
neys to Australia. These practices place Australia obviously in breach of its
obligations under the CRC. In contrast, there are now many States where the
identification of unaccompanied migrant children triggers appropriate care
and guardianship responses.

Anti Trafficking

The CRC and its first Optional Protocol—together with the more recent
Protocols to the UN Convention against Transnational Organized Crime—
provide important safeguards where children fall victim to trafficking or other
forms of transnational organized crime. These instruments reinforce the dictates of considering the best interests of these children by stressing that the
children should be cared for and viewed through the lens of child protection –
not criminal law. In practical terms protection should not be predicated on a
child co-operating in operations to target smugglers or traffickers.[39] The obligations enshrined in these instruments reinforce and are reinforced by international instruments controlling inter-country adoptions.[40]

Detention

An area where many States find themselves in flagrant breach of the CRC is in
the detention of children presenting as undocumented or irregular migrants.
Sometimes children can be placed in detention as an alternative to appropriate care arrangements. The fate of children consigned to places of incarceration that involve gross abuses of their human rights is well documented.
Children can be subjected to physical and sexual abuse, deplorable living conditions, inadequate nutrition and lack of medical care. The experience of
migrant children detained for long periods in Australia demonstrates that even
"humane" incarceration can have a devastating effect on a child's psycho-social
and even physical development.[41]

---

39   See also Bustamante, *supra* note 27, para. 36.
40   See for example the International *Convention on Protection of Children and Cooperation in*
      Respect of Inter-country Adoption, signed at The Hague on 29 May 1993. For a full list of
      the Hague conventions relating to the protection of children, see http://www.hcch.net/
      index_en.php?act=conventions.listing.
41   For one example of the now-extensive literature on the psychological effects of detention
      on children, see Mares, S., Newman, L., Dudley, M. and Gale, F., "Seeking Refuge, Losing
      Hope: Parents and Children in Immigration Detention," 10 *Australian Psychiatry*, 2002,
      pp. 91–96; see further Everitt J., *The Bitter Shore*, Pan McMillan, 2008.

The international law on this matter is clear and should be beyond dispute.[42] Article 37 of the CRC provides that children should only ever be detained as a last resort and for the shortest possible period of time. Detention must always be provided for in the law; it should be for a finite period; and children should have a right to challenge their incarceration in a court of law. The Special Rapporteur on the human rights of migrants has made it clear that detention is never in the best interests of children, reinforcing the CRC Committee's call that children not be detained on the basis of their immigration status or mode of entry into a country.[43] The European Court of Human Rights has also criticized detention policies.[44] Yet in Australia, detention for immigration reasons has been set apart from the general protections offered to children. In 2003 a majority of the Full Family Court made history by deciding that its welfare jurisdiction[45] and injunction powers[46] enabled the Court to make orders for the welfare of children held in immigration detention.[47] The High Court allowed an appeal from the decision, holding that the legislation empowering the court to make orders for the best interests of children did not extend to children in immigration detention. The ongoing importance of this case is not only because it comprehensively excluded the jurisdiction of the family court over the welfare of children in immigration detention, but also because of the qualifications placed on rights for migrant children.

Migrant Children and Access to Basic Services

While universality and equality of children's rights may be correct as a matter of law and theory, the rights embodied in the CRC do fall into something of a natural hierarchy. At the apex must be the child's right to life, aligned with other rights that go to the child's ability to subsist. Thereafter, the transient nature of childhood dictates that a child's health and wellbeing must include those elements necessary for growth and development, namely food, shelter, housing, health services and education. Yet as the International Organization for Migration has observed – of regular and irregular migrants, accompanied and unaccompanied children – during the migration process children are at

---

42   See ICCPR, Arts 9 and 10; CAT Article 16; CRC Article 37(b) and (d); CRPD, Articles 14 and 17. See also Refugee Convention, Article 31.

43   Committee on the Rights of the Child, *supra* note 19, para. 61.

44   *Rahimi v Greece*, Application No. 8687/08, Judgment 4 May 2011; *Popov v France*, Application No. 39472/07, Judgment 19 January 2012.

45   *Family Law Act* 1987 (Cth) s 67ZC.

46   *Family Law Act* 1987 (Cth) s 68B.

47   See *B & B v Minister for Immigration & Multicultural & Indigenous Affairs* MIMIA (2003) 199 ALR 604, (2003) 173 FLR 360, [2003] FamCA 451 (19 June 2003).

particular risk of having their social rights violated and they often face discrimination when trying to access necessary basic services.[48]

The recently-revised EU Reception Directive echoes the CRC in demanding
that best interests be a primary consideration, and goes on to stipulate that
"Member States shall ensure a standard of living adequate for the minor's
physical, mental, spiritual, moral and social development."[49] These rights are
recognized also in the International Covenant on Economic Cultural and
Social Rights as well as other key human rights treaties. In the European context, these rights are given force through mechanisms that allow States to be
held to account where there is a failure to abide by the dictates of the law.[50]
Demonstrating the value of supra-national supervisory institutions, the
European Committee of Social Rights has found that a French restriction on
access to healthcare to migrant children was contrary to the charter (unless
they had been in France for a fixed period or were in a life threatening situation). So too were policies in The Netherlands that linked housing entitlements
to residence status.[51]

5   Migrant Children and Family Unity

The Dissonance in Sponsorship Rights between Adults and Children

The central importance of family in the development of children is given recognition in various aspects of international and regional human rights law.[52]
In fact this principle is one of the oldest and most consistent statements of the
rights that inhere in human society. The problem is that the principle of family
unity is compromised too often by a tendency to link the rights of migrant
children to the *immigration* status and rights of adults.

---

48   Written Contribution of the International Organization for Migration to the Commit-
      tee on the Rights of the Child 2012 Day of General Discussion 28 September 2012,
      OHCHR, 2012.

49   Directive 2013/33/EU of the European Parliament and of the Council of 26 June 2013, lay-
      ing down standards for the reception of applicants for international protection (recast),
      180 *Official Journal of the European Union* pp. 96–116 at p. 107.

50   OHCHR, *supra* note 31.

51   *International Federation of Human Rights Leagues (FIDH) v France, European Court of
      Social Rights*, Complaint No. 14/2003; *Defence for Children International v The Netherlands*,
      European Court of Social Rights, Complaint No. 47/2008.

52   See, for example, ICCPR, Article 23. A child's right to family life is established in the CRC
      in the Preamble and Articles 3, 7, 8, 9, 10, 16 and 18. The CMW also recognizes the right to
      the protection of the family in Article 44, but only in the context of regular migrants.

At its worst, there is an enduring tendency to see migrant children as the commodities of parents and adult relatives. This is seen most starkly in the discrepancies between the visa entitlements of adults and children. On the one hand, adults wishing to either travel with or to sponsor children enjoy expansive rights. On the other, children can face serious obstacles in their efforts to sponsor family members or to prevent the removal of non-citizen parents.

For example, no limits are placed on the number of dependent children[53] and orphaned relatives[54] that migrant parents can sponsor upon settlement in Australia.[55] In contrast, minor children cannot sponsor parents of working age from within Australia[56] and strict quotas apply. The "contributory" parent visa2 scheme allows priority for wealthy children who can afford the sponsorship fees.[57] Children from disadvantaged backgrounds face waits in excess of 15 years in the "non-contributory" stream.[58] A "balance of family" test requires nominated parents to have more children permanently resident in Australia than in any other country.[59] This causes particular problems for unaccompanied refugee children and youth from large families who are typically the only family member to have been sent abroad.

Until August 2012, concessions were made for unaccompanied children granted protection in Australia as refugees to allow them to sponsor family to join them in Australia. With the steep increase in the number of children arriving on boats from Indonesia after 2008,[60] however, the government became increasingly concerned about encouraging refugee families to use their

---

53   *Migration Act*, s 87(1) and (2); and the discussion at Crock, M. and Berg, L., *Immigration, Refugees and Forced Migration: Law, Policy and Practice in Australia*, Sydney, Federation Press, 2011, Section 8.03.

54   *Migration Regulations* 1994, sch 2, subcll 117 and 837, discussed in Crock and Berg, *ibid.*, Section 8.21ff.

55   See also Crock and Berg, *ibid.*, Section 8.2; and Crock, M., Kenny, M.A. and Allison, F., "Children and Immigration and Citizenship Law," in Monaghan, G. and Young L. (eds.), *Children and the Law in Australia*, Sydne, Lexis Nexis, 2008, pp. 238–255.

56   *Migration Regulations* 1994, Sch 2, subcl 103; and Crock and Berg, *supra* note 53, at Section 8.3.

57   *Migration Regulations* 1994, Sch 2, subcl 143; and Crock and Berg, *ibid.*, Section 8.34.

58   Crock and Berg, above n 41, Section 8.32.

59   *Migration Regulations* 1994, reg 1.05; Sch 2, subcll 103.213, 143.213; and Crock and Berg, *supra* note 53, Section 8.35.

60   Statistics provided by the Department of Immigration and Citizenship in November 2012 suggest that the number of arrivals went from 8 in 2008 to 848 in 2012. Document provided to the author on 27 November 2012, available on request.

children as "anchors" to achieve migration outcomes. It recognized that unaccompanied refugee children could face permanent separation from their families. However it claimed that the amending regulations[61] did not infringe
Australia's international legal obligations because Australia had taken no positive action to separate the families in question. The only relevant actions had
been those taken by the families themselves when sending their children
across the seas in search of protection.[62]

An even harsher approach is taken by the United States government in its
"Special Immigrant Juvenile Status" (SIJS) program.[63] It operates to grant
unaccompanied migrant children who have suffered abuse a direct path to
permanent residence. The application must be completed before the child turns
21 and the child must remain unmarried.[64] SIJS children face a life time ban on
sponsoring family for migration to the US.[65]

Family Unity and Child Protection

Even where unaccompanied children are able to negotiate the restrictions
on family sponsorship outlined earlier, Australia provides an example of
how measures designed to protect children can be used to frustrate a child's
right to family reunification. In *Tahiri v Minister for Immigration and
Citizenship*[66] the Plaintiff was a young Afghani national who had come to
Australia by boat as a 17 year old unaccompanied minor. Granted asylum in
Australia, he sponsored his mother and four (minor) siblings under the
"split-family" scheme then in operation. His mother's visa was refused on

---

61   See http://www.immi.gov.au/legislation/amendments/2012/120928/lc28092012-01.htm.
62   Explanatory Statement to Migration Amendment Regulation 2012 (No. 5), Select
      Legislative Instrument 2012 No. 230 issued by the Minister for Immigration and Citizenship
      under the Migration Act 1958.
63   See 8 USC § 1101(a)(27)(J); Section 101(a)(27)(J) of the *Immigration and Nationality Law
      Act*. The first version of the statute required that the child had no parent available; in
      2008, the statutory language was amended to protect children if reunification with one or
      both parents was not viable. The *Trafficking Victims Protection and Reauthorization Act*
      (TVPRA) of 2008, Public Law 110–457, 122 Stat 5044.
64   For a recent critique suggestion improvement in the processing of applications for SIJS
      status, see the report of the Ombudsman for US Citizenship and Immigration Services at
      http://www.dhs.gov/xlibrary/assets/Citizenship-and-Immigration-Services-Ombudsman
      -Recommendation-Special-Immigrant-Juvenile-Adjudications.pdf
65   For a discussion of this aspect of US immigration law, see Bhabha, J. and Schmidt, S.,
      *Seeking Asylum Alone: Unaccompanied and Separated Children and Refugee Protection in
      the US*, 2006, at pp. 51–54.
66   *Tahiri v Minister for Immigration and Citizenship* [2012] HCA 61; (2012) 293 ALR 526.

the basis that she could not satisfy the prescribed "Public Interest Criteria" (PIC) embodying the Hague Convention rules on the trans-national custody of children. The relevant provisions required the Minister to be satisfied that the admission into Australia of any child be permitted by the law of the child's home country; that relevant permissions for the child's removal had been obtained; and that the grant of the visa would be consistent with any Australian child order in force.[67]

The Plaintiff's problem was that his mother had travelled to Pakistan from Afghanistan with her children in 2003 after the disappearance of his father. Mrs Tahiri was unable to prove that she had lawful custody of her children. She was also unable to obtain the consents required under Afghan law from a male relative of her husband for the removal of her children to Australia. The High Court found no legal error in the delegate's ruling that these requirements applied even where there was a strong presumption that the Plaintiff's father was dead.

Children Left Behind

Another context in which a child's right to family is frequently tested is in the context of citizen children whose parent or parents face deportation or removal from a host country. These children suffer what Bhabha calls a "citizenship deficit" insofar as their citizenship has been found not to prevent the removal of a noncitizen parent and therefore, sometimes, their own removal too.[68]

The very first case in which Article 3 of the CRC was considered by Australia's High Court involved a father and sole carer of seven citizen children who was threatened with deportation on criminal grounds.[69] A majority of the Court ruled that Australia's signature and ratification of the CRC created procedural rights in Mr Teoh, even if he could not invoke a substantive right to have the interests of his children given primacy.[70] This ruling met with some resistance – and was somewhat down-played as a precedent in Australia.[71]

---

67   See *Migration Regulations 1994* (Cth), Schedule 4, PIC 4015; and Schedule 2, cl 202.228.
68   Bhabha, J., "Arendt's Children: Do Today's Migrant Children Have a Right to Have Rights," 31 *Human Rights Quarterly*, 2009, pp. 410–451.
69   *Teoh's Case* (1995) 183 CLR 273.
70   *Ibid.* at 291.
71   See Administrative Decisions (Effect of International Instruments) Bill 1995, s 5 which would have expressly over-ridden the decision (it was never passed into law). See also the comments made in *Re Minister for Immigration and Multicultural Affairs; Ex parte Lam* (2003) 214 CLR 1 at [102]; and Taggart, M., "Legitimate Expectation and Treaties in the High Court of Australia," 112 *Law Quarterly Review*, 1996, at p. 54; and Lacey, W., "A Prelude to the

In other countries, however, the fate of citizen children either "left behind" or at risk of "constructive deportation" has received considerable attention. An example of good practice is *ZH (Tanzania) v Secretary of State for the Home Department*.[72] In that case the UK Supreme Court found that Art 3 of the CRC was a binding obligation in international law. Writing for the Court, Lady Hale ruled that it would not be in the best interests of two British citizen children for their Tanzanian mother to be deported. The mother had made three unsuccessful applications for asylum.[73]

6   Migrant Children and Participation Rights

Hearing the Migrant Child

Article 12 of the CRC recognizes the right of the child to have a voice in all administrative proceedings affecting the child, a right that finds expression also in the ICCPR and the CRMW. A CRC and rights-based approach recognizes that children take an active part in the migration process, and sees them as agents rather than merely "objects" or "victims" of circumstance. The centrality of Article 12 to the due process rights of children was acknowledged by the CRC Committee in its General Comment No. 12. For migrant children this provision operates as a directive to States to make administrative processes accessible to children. Put another way, the CRC should operate to require States to involve all children in the processes relating to their entry or stay in a host country. Children should be informed of their rights; and they should be consulted before decisions are made on their future. Most importantly, due process must involve the provision of assistance for children so that they can both understand what is occurring and articulate their views.

In practical terms the international instruments deliver a minimum of 10 "due process guarantees."[74] In respect of proceedings affecting the child, these are rights to: a hearing; adequate interpretation; legal representation; speak,

---

Demise of *Teoh*: The High Court Decision in *Re Minister for Immigration and Multicultural Affairs; Ex parte La*," 26 *Sydney Law Review*, 2004, pp. 131–156.

72   [2011] UKSC 4.

73   Contrast *Nunez v Norway, supra* note 2.

74   See Committee on the Rights of the Child, 2012 Day of General Discussion: The Rights of All Children in the Context of International Migration, Background Paper, August 2012, Office of the High Commissioner for Human Rights http://www.ohchr.org/Documents/HRBodies/CRC/Discussions/2012/2012DGDBackgroundPaper.pdf Part IV(e).

be heard and considered; appeal; consular assistance; and a guardian or legal representative. In addition, children should have the following rights in respect of any proceedings involving a parent or responsible adult: to be heard and participate; to be informed; and to have access to justice and effective remedies.

Sadly, the reality in most countries is that the voices of migrant children are rarely heard. Children are included as "accompanying family" or as "dependants" in applications made by adults and their fate is generally tied to those adults. Such systems have the adult parents as active rights holders and decision makers and children as subject to parental control. In its 2012 Concluding Observations on Australia, the CRC Committee expressed its concern that Australian law does not provide for compulsory separate interviewing of children so as to ensure that they are heard.[75]

For many children whose cases are uncomplicated and who immigrate without incident, this paradigm may seem relatively unimportant. In instances where the experience of the children is significant, however, problems arise. While children can make their own claims for protection, in practice, children are often not interviewed to see if they have a separate claim that could be considered.[76] This can result in the failure to appreciate claims that might operate to the advantage of a family group as a whole. An example of good practice is the situation in New Zealand where legislation mandates the separate consideration of claims made by all persons, irrespective of age. As far as practicable, children must be given an opportunity to express their views on the matter, whether personally or through a responsible adult.[77] New Zealand Immigration officers are directed to give due weight to those views, taking into account the child's age and level of maturity and understanding.

---

75   Committee on the Rights of the Child, Concluding Observations on Australia, CRC, 60th session, 28 August 2012, UN Doc CRC/C/AUS/CO/4, paras. 31 & 80.

76   The Department of Immigration *Protection Visa Manual* states at [181.5]: "Decision-makers should not assume that a child cannot have a claim for protection independent of their parents. If a parent/s does not appear to have an approvable claim, the decision-maker should enquire into the child's case even though the child may be dependent on the claims of their parent and might not have made claims in their own right. As importantly, the fears and experiences of the child might help to enhance the strength of the parent's claim for protection." It should be noted that even in this instance the manual only speaks about Department officers speaking to a child if the parent does not have a strong claim.

77   *Immigration Act 1987* (NZ) s 141D.

Citizenship and Birthright

Perhaps the most fundamental obstacle to participation for the migrant child is the absence of a legal identity. For children born to irregular migrants, the CRC, the ICCPR and the CMW enshrine the right to be registered immediately after birth; and the rights to acquire a name and nationality.[78] These are rights that are supposed to inhere in children, regardless of the immigration status of their parents. Children who are denied their civil right to be registered at birth are self-evidently vulnerable to the denial of most of the rights associated with membership in a community – civil, political, social, economic and cultural.

In an attempt to deter irregular or "chain" migration, some States have diminished the opportunities that migrant children have to obtain citizenship in their host countries.

In a case involving two girls born to ethnically Haitian mothers in the Dominican Republic, the Inter-American Court of Human Rights found that migratory status (or lack of official status) can never justify depriving a person of a right to nationality. Accordingly, a person born on the territory of a State must be citizen of that state if they would otherwise be stateless. In that case the Dominican Republic had interpreted its restriction on granting citizenship to people "in transit" as applying to all persons of Haitian descent. Importantly, the Court also found that the migratory status of a child is not "transferred" from their patents.[79]

Education

One further issue that is critical to ensuring the development and participation of migrant children is access to education. Article 28 of the CRC states that primary education should be free and available to all and that States should encourage different forms of secondary application that are accessible to all children. The importance of education as a development tool for children is reinforced by similar provisions in Article 30 of the CRMW. It is of critical importance because of the opportunities it creates for a child's access to gainful employment and because knowledge is fundamental to basic health and wellbeing. The denial of education can render a child more susceptible to poverty, physical and psychosocial abuse, trauma and exploitation. Children can be drawn into criminal enterprises, with girl children at particular risk of harm of sexual exploitation and abuse. Although access to education been an issue

---

78 See CRC, Article 7; ICCPR, Article 24; and CMW, Article 29. See also the Convention against Statelessness.

79 *Case of the Yean and Bosico Children v The Dominican Republic*, Inter-American Court of Human Rights, 8 September 2005.

in many States across the world, the area with the most encouraging jurisprudence and general good practice is in the UK and the more progressive members of the European Union. States highlighted by UNICEF and OHCHR as
worthy of mention include Belgium, France, Italy, Spain and the Netherlands.[80]

7 Child Migrants and Deterrence Measures

For refugee children admitted through regular (humanitarian) intake programs, the regimes for the education and resettlement of these children in
Australia are also as good as anywhere in the world. It is the children entering
as irregular maritime arrivals who suffer deprivation and exclusion. The ratio-
nale provided by Australia for its policies serve to highlight what may be one of
the great challenges facing migrant children around the world. The discourse
of Australia's Conservative politicians makes little attempt to mask distaste for
any kind of irregular migration: as former Prime Minister John Howard proclaimed: "We will decide who comes to this country and the circumstances in
which they come."[81] In more recent times, however, the discourse has shifted
subtly to actually embrace the ethics of child protection. "Australians," our
politicians tell us, "have to be cruel to be kind." We have to "take the sugar off
the table" so as to deter parents from embarking on the perilous step of irregular travel in search of asylum in Australia. This country's decision to send asylum seeker children to Nauru and to seek out other poor countries where the
child will be at risk of every type of deprivation stands as one of the most
extreme examples of deterrent policies.

The irregular movement of migrant children is indeed a challenge for governments around the world. In the United States, the number of unaccompanied children presenting as asylum seekers stood at between five and six
thousand when we embarked on the *Seeking Asylum Alone* project in 2004.
One decade later, the statistics suggest a tenfold increase, with 60,000 such
children reported in 2014.[82]

The reality is that children can present as the most vulnerable of migrants,
most especially when traveling without the protection of a responsible adult.

---

80   OHCHR, *supra* note 31, Chapter IV.
81   John Howard, quotation from speech delivered at the Federal Liberal Party Campaign
      Launch, Sydney, 28 October 2001, reported Australian Broadcasting Corporation, "Liberals
      accused of trying to rewrite history," *Lateline* 21 November 2001 (Sarah Clarke).
82   See Center for Gender and Refugee Studies/Kids in Need of Defense *A Treacherous
      Journey: Child Migrants Navigating the US Immigration System*, February 2014, ii.

What is absolutely objectionable about Australia's response, and similar policies designed to discourage irregular migration, is that they harm the embodied child in the name of protecting the putative child – the child who might otherwise be taking to the high seas in search of safe haven.[83] It is at the very heart of the CRC that States Parties should see, hear, respect and protect the children on their territory and within their care and control. The rights of those children inhere because they are children. They should apply regardless of citizenship, ethnicity or immigration status.

---

83   For a fuller exposition of this argument, see Crock, M., "Of Relative Rights and Putative Children: Rethinking the Critical Framework for the Protection of Refugee Children and Youth," 20 *Australian International Law Journal*, 2013, pp. 33–54.

Unaccompanied and Separated Asylum-seeking Minors: Implementing a Rights-based Approach in the Asylum Process

Rebecca Thorburn Stern[*]

Introduction

By the end of 2013 some 51.2 million people had been forcibly displaced world-wide.[1] Almost 17 million of them were refugees and about 1.2 million were asylum seekers.[2] The United Nations High Commissioner for Refugees (UNHCR) estimates that approximately half of the forcibly displaced people in the world today are under eighteen and are therefore children, according to the definition of childhood in Article 1 of the Convention on the Rights of the Child[3] (CRC).[4] Refugee and asylum-seeking children are vulnerable because of their need for protection and owing to the fact that they are outside their countries of origin and beyond the normal protection presumed to be provided by citizenship. A particularly vulnerable category is that of unaccompanied and separated children, who lack not only the protection presumed to be provided by their own States but also of parents or legal guardians. It is therefore of the utmost importance to establish and implement norms and practices that meet the needs of such children by safeguarding and respecting their rights.[5] At international level the CRC and the Convention relating to the Status of Refugees[6] (the Refugee Convention) together provide separate yet interconnecting normative frameworks for their protection, addressing procedural as well as substantive aspects.

The focus of this chapter is on unaccompanied and separated children claiming international protection but whose status has not been determined—that is, asylum-seeking children. Definitions of "unaccompanied" and "separated"

[*]   The research for this project has been generously supported by the Swedish Research Council.
1   UN High Commissioner for Refugees (UNHCR), UNHCR Global Trends 2013: *War's Human Cost*, 20 June 2014, p. 2.
2   *Ibid.*
3   United Nations Convention on the Rights of the Child (adopted 20 November 1989, entered into force 2 September 1990) 1577 *UNTS* 3. As of April 2014, 194 States were parties to this Convention.
4   *A Framework for the Protection of Children*, UNHCR 2012, p. 7.
5   CRC Committee General Comment No. 6, Treatment of Unaccompanied and Separated Children outside of Their Country of Origin, CRC/GC/2005/6, para. 13.
6   Convention relating to the Status of Refugees, opened for signature 28 July 1951, 189 UNTS 137 (entered into force 22 April 1954).

children are provided by the Committee on the Rights of the Child[7] in its General Comment on treatment of unaccompanied and separated children outside their countries of origin.[8] *Unaccompanied children,* according to the General Comment, are "children, as defined in Article 1 of the Convention, who have been separated from both parents and other relatives and are not being cared for by an adult who, by law or custom, is responsible for doing so."[9] *Separated children* are "children, as defined in Article 1 of the Convention, who have been separated from both parents, or from their previous legal or customary primary caregiver, but not necessarily from other relatives. These may, therefore, include children accompanied by other adult family members."[10] The same definition is applied by the UNHCR in its 2009 Guidelines of International Protection on child asylum claims.[11] However, the vulnerability of asylum-seeking children, unaccompanied and separated children in particular, as emphasized both in the General Comment and the Guidelines, is in many cases less visibly acknowledged in domestic practice.[12] Rather than being viewed primarily as children exposed to risks they are considered first and foremost as migrants – a category upon which suspicion, resentment and policies of immigration control often fall.[13] Asylum-seeking children are thus put at risk of not having their vulnerability properly taken into account and of being denied their rights, or even treated as criminals.[14] With that in mind this chapter will focus on the

---

7   The monitoring body of the Convention on the Rights of the Child.

8   CRC/GC/2005/6.

9   CRC/GC/2005/6, para. 7.

10   CRC/GC/2005/6, para. 8.

11   UN High Commissioner for Refugees (UNHCR), *Guidelines on International Protection No. 8: Child Asylum Claims under Articles 1(A)2 and 1(F) of the 1951 Convention and/or 1967 Protocol relating to the Status of Refugees,* 22 December 2009, HCR/GIP/09/08, para. 6.

12   As pointed out in *e.g.* Pobjoy, J.M., "A Child Rights Framework for Assessing the Status of Refugee Children," in Singh Juss, S. & Harvey, C. (eds.), *Contemporary Issues in Refugee Law,* Cheltenham, Edward Elgar Publishing, 2013, pp. 91–137, at p. 93.

13   See *e.g.* Pobjoy, *id.,* p. 93 with references; Bhabha, J., "Arendt's Children: Do Today's Migrant Children Have a Right to Have Rights?" 31 *Human Rights Quarterly,* 2009, pp. 410–451, at pp. 420–423; and Heaven Crawley in the ILPA policy paper *Child First, Migrant Second: Ensuring That Every Child Matters,* ILPA/Heaven Crawley, February 2006. See also Study of the Office of the United Nations High Commissioner for Human Rights on challenges and best practices in the implementation of the international framework for the protection of the child in the context of migration, A/HRC/15/29, 5 July 2010, para. 9.

14   See *e.g.* judgments by the European Court of Human Rights in *Rahimi v Greece* Application No. 8687/08, judgment 5 April 2011 and *Mayeka and Mitunga v Belgium,* Application No. 13178/03, judgment 12 October 2006.

assessment of asylum claims and discuss the importance of applying a rights-based and child-sensitive perspective to the matter of unaccompanied and separated asylum-seeking children, and to consider how the general principles of the CRC can best be employed in this process.

Normative Framework

The Convention on the Rights of the Child

The main human rights treaty on the human rights of children[15] is the UN Convention on the Rights of the Child. Adopted in 1989, it is one of the core human rights treaties and the one most widely ratified. The Convention has been described as "international law's response to the paradigm shift in thinking about children largely engineered by modern sociological thinking,"[16] moving from a welfare-based to a rights-based perspective, and placing the rights of children permanently on the global agenda. The CRC both strengthens already existing rights in relation to children and introduces rights specific to children. For asylum-seeking children, key articles of the CRC include the four general principles outlined in Articles 2 (the right to non-discrimination), 3 (the best interest of the child), 6 (the right to life and development) and 12 (the right to be heard and have one's views taken into account) and in Articles 4 (implementation), 9 (separation of children from parents/carers), 10 (family reunification), 20 (children in temporary care), 22 (refugee and asylum-seeking children), 37 (prohibition of torture/inhuman/degrading treatment or punishment and deprivation of liberty) and 38 (children in armed conflict). It will be noted that the needs of refugee children were recognized from the beginning of the CRC drafting process.[17]

Moving on to tools of interpretation, particular mention should be made of three General Comments adopted by the Committee on the Rights of the Child. By its previously mentioned 2005 General Comment on unaccompanied and separated children the Committee sought to provide clear guidance to States on their obligations relating to this particular group of children.[18] The

---

15   In my view, a term preferable to "children's rights" as we are not referring to a separate framework of rights, rather to how the universal human rights can and should be applied to children.

16   Freeman, M., "The Value and Values of Children's Rights," in Invernizzi, A. & Williams, J. (eds.), *The Human Rights of Children: From Visions to Implementation*, Farnham, Ashgate 2011, pp. 21–36, at p. 27.

17   Pobjoy, *supra* note 12, pp. 106–107 with references.

18   CRC/GC/6, para. 4.

General Comment clarifies the interrelation between the CRC and international refugee and asylum law with regard to refugee status and complementary protection.[19] In the two General Comments adopted so far on the general principles of the CRC, the needs of asylum-seeking children are highlighted both in relation to the right to be heard and to have one's views taken into account (General Comment No. 12 on Article 12)[20] as well as the best interests of the child (General Comment No. 14 on Article 3.1).[21] The Committee, moreover, in its expression of concern over how such children are treated, recurrently comments on the situation of unaccompanied and separated children in its Concluding Observations to various State Parties.[22]

The Refugee Convention and Related Instruments

The Refugee Convention and its 1967 Protocol relating to the Status of Refugees[23] are the primary instruments in international refugee law, setting international standards for refugee status determination and for the rights of refugees. Article 1A(2) establishes who is a refugee in the context of the Refugee Convention: this is a person who

> owing to well-founded fear of being persecuted for reasons of race, religion, nationality, membership of a particular social group or political opinion, is outside the country of his nationality and is unable or, owing to such fear, is unwilling to avail himself of the protection of that country; or who, not having a nationality and being outside the country of his former habitual residence as a result of such events, is unable or, owing to such fear, is unwilling to return to it.

"Persecution," a key concept in the refugee definition, is commonly explained as grave violations of human rights.[24] A link between refugee law and human rights law is thereby established, since in order to identify what constitutes persecution one must understand both the content of a certain right and what would be a grave breach of that right. The Refugee Convention and the Protocol

---

19   *Ibid.*, paras. 74–78.

20   CRC/C/GC/12 (2009).

21   CRC/C/GC/14 (2013).

22   See *e.g.* the CRC Committee's comments on Australia 2012 (CRC/C/AUS/CO/4) and Sweden 2009 (CRC/C/SWE/CO/4).

23   Protocol relating to the Status of Refugees, opened for signature 31 January 1967, 606 *UNTS* 267 (entered into force 4 October 1967).

24   James C. Hathaway, in his seminal *The Law of Refugee Status* (1st ed.), Butterworths, 1991, advocated this approach, which since has become mainstream in the refugee law discourse.

apply to all people irrespective of age and contains no specific references[25] to children apart from that of the rights of parents in relation to religious education in Article 4 (certain rights such as the right not to be treated less favourably than nationals with respect to elementary education (Article 22) are, however, particularly relevant to minors).

The fact that children are not particularly mentioned in the key instruments of the international refugee protection regime has not, however, prevented the guardian[26] of the Refugee Convention, the UNHCR, from addressing the matter. Most likely as a result of growing awareness in international law of the need to deal with the specific wants and rights of children in various ways the UNHCR Executive Committee made its first reference to refugee children in 1986,[27] noting that this category of refugee required special attention. It published its first Conclusion on refugee children in 1987.[28] Since then, the Executive Committee has commented on refugee children on a number of occasions, emphasizing the need for particular attention to be paid to their special protection requirements. Its most recent comment was the 2007 Conclusion on Refugee Children,[29] which made reference to the importance of viewing children as active subjects with rights, and that the application of a rights-based perspective was fundamental to child protection. This demonstrated evidence of the impact of the rights-based approach permeating the Convention on the Rights of the Child.[30]

In addition to the statements of the Executive Committee, the UNHCR has issued various guidelines and policies on refugee children. The first was the 1988 version of the Guidelines on Refugee Children,[31] the most recent (at the time of writing) being the 2009 Guidelines on child asylum claims.[32] The 2009

---

25   Pobjoy on recommendation B, *supra* note, 12, pp. 102–103.

26   On the UNHCR, see *e.g.* Lewis, C., *UNHCR and International Refugee Law: From Treaties to Innovation*, Oxon, Routledge, 2012.

27   UN High Commissioner for Refugees (UNHCR), Executive Committee General Conclusion on International Protection No. 41 (XXXVII) – 1986.

28   UN High Commissioner for Refugees (UNHCR), Executive Committee Refugee Children, 12 October 1987, No. 47 (XXXVIII) – 1987.

29   UN High Commissioner for Refugees (UNHCR), Executive Committee Conclusion on Children at Risk No. 107 (LVIII) – 2007.

30   *Ibid.*, preamble para. b(x).

31   UNHCR Guidelines on Protection and Care, UNHCR 1988, amended in 1994.

32   UNHCR, HCR/GIP/09/08, *supra* note 11.

Guidelines cover all child asylum seekers (including unaccompanied and separated children) who may have individual claims to refugee status[33] and attends to both procedural and substantive matters such as assessment of asylum claims. Mention should also be made of the 1997 Guidelines on Policies and Procedures in Dealing with Unaccompanied Children Seeking Asylum,[34] and the 2008 UNHCR Guidelines on Determining the Best Interest of the Child.[35] These both address the rights codified in the CRC. Summing up, the impact of the CRC and the approach expressed in the treaty is obvious in UNHCR documents and policies on refugee children.[36] This is particularly visible in what Pobjoy calls the "alignment phase," which refers to the period during which international bodies such as the UNHCR began promoting the CRC as being essential to conceptualizing the special needs of refugee children and the succeeding "operational phase" where the UNHCR and the Committee on the Rights of the Child seek to provide guidance on how the CRC can be applied in the context of refugee status determination.[37]

Complementary protection is not covered by the Refugee Convention. Complementary protection is protection that might be available for a person who falls outside the refugee definition but is still at risk of serious harm—for example, due to persecution on a non-convention ground or to armed conflict. Such protection, however, can be granted based on human rights treaties or regional instruments of asylum law, such as the EU Qualification Directive.[38] As with the Refugee Convention, interpretation and implementation of these instruments is influenced by the child rights discourse, even going as far as including direct references to the best interest of the child and child-specific persecution.[39]

---

33   HCR/GIP/09/08, para. 6.

34   UN High Commissioner for Refugees (UNHCR), *Guidelines on Policies and Procedures in Dealing with Unaccompanied Children Seeking Asylum*, February 1997.

35   UN High Commissioner for Refugees (UNHCR), UNHCR Guidelines on Determining the Best Interests of the Child, May 2008.

36   Pobjoy, *supra* note 12, pp. 110–115.

37   *Ibid.*

38   Directive 2011/95/EU of the European Parliament and of the Council of 13 December 2011 on standards for the qualification of third-country nationals or stateless persons as beneficiaries of international protection, for a uniform status for refugees or for persons eligible for subsidiary protection, and for the content of the protection granted (recast).

39   See *e.g.* the EU Qualification Directive preambular, paras. 18–19 and Article 9.2(f).

A Rights-based Approach

The instruments and policy documents referred to above thus seem to embrace a "rights-based approach" or a "rights-based perspective," exemplifying how this course has gradually become the mainstream in relation to human rights and refugee law. The concept of children having rights in the first place, however, remains controversial in many contexts – perhaps in particular where rights-based approaches are to be implemented in practice. One major obstacle for effective implementation is the still prevailing view that children are human "becomings" rather than "beings," a position instrumental in denying them rights considered self-evident for adults.[40] Freeman has somewhat pessimistically commented that "the majority opinion is still...that the only right that children have is to autonomous parents."[41]

Whether or not children are considered to be rights holders depends on how "rights" are interpreted. Should such a definition be based on a legal or moral perspective?[42] As far as *legal* rights are concerned, it appears simple. Children undeniably have rights under the law in both international legal instruments and in many national jurisdictions, the CRC being the landmark international instrument. The difference, however, between possessing rights on paper and having access to rights in practice is obvious. This is a distinction of great importance, not least to asylum-seeking children having rights on paper they know nothing about because they are not informed of them.[43] For the system to work, legal rights obviously have to be implemented on the ground and considered by those in power to be relevant at every level. This in turn requires that rights are taken seriously. In practice, however, this requirement can encounter numerous obstacles. One such barrier is that the validity of a right in practice – the effect it is accorded – can be argued to be dependent on the cultural legitimacy of a particular society.[44] Moreover, the normative framework and the way in which it is formulated must be relevant for those to whom

---

40   The child rights literature is vast. On the development of the child rights discourse, see *e.g.* Archard, D., *Children, Rights and Childhood*, 2nd ed., Routledge, 2004; Freeman, *supra* note 16. For a critical perspective on children as rights-bearers, see *e.g.* Guggenheim, M., *What's Wrong with Children's Rights*, Cambridge MA, Harvard University Press, 2005.

41   Freeman, M., "Human Rights of Children" 63 *Current Legal Problems*, 2010, pp. 1–44, at p. 2.

42   Archard has described the relationship between legal and moral rights not as being different sets of rights but rather distinctions between how rights are understood. Archard (2004), *supra* note 40, p. 53.

43   Bhabha, J., "Arendt's Children: Do Today's Migrant Children have a Right to Have Rights?" 31 *Human Rights Quarterly*, 2009, pp. 410–451.

44   Kaime, T., *The Convention on the Rights of the Child. A Cultural Legitimacy Critique*, Amsterdam, Europa Law Publishing, 2011.

it is intended to be applied: the CRC, for example, has been criticized for not sufficiently concentrating on the varying conditions and situations of children living without a family or otherwise not fitting into its preconceived notion of who is "a child."[45] Furthermore, at the core of the issue of the legitimacy and applicability of the legal rights of children lies the debate on moral rights and whether children can be rights holders at all – and if so, to what extent.[46] This is neither the time nor place to explore arguments on the theoretical under-pinning of children as rights holders. I will, however, briefly call attention to the fact that a grasp of these different understandings of "rights" is necessary in relation to how the decision-maker, the judge, the government official, the teacher, the parent or anyone else in a position to exercise power over a child perceives children as rights holders and influences how their legal rights (if any) are understood, respected and implemented in practice.

The Rights-based Approach of the CRC and Unaccompanied and Separated Asylum-seeking Children

The rights-based approach to asylum-seeking children established in the instruments and documents referred to above refers to *legal* rights based on the Convention on the Rights of the Child and general human rights law. The moral element, however, is also present by way of the emphasis placed on the importance of applying a rights-based approach – presented, as it is, as "the right thing to do." The legal and moral aspects of rights are thereby intertwined.

---

45 See *e.g.* Freeman, *supra* note 16; Ennew, J., "Why the Convention is Not About Street Children," in Fottrell, D. (ed.), *Revisiting Children's Rights: 10 Years of the Convention on the Rights of the Child*, The Hague, Kluwer Law International, 2009; Bourdillon, M. & Musvosvi, E., "What Can Children's Rights Mean When Children are Struggling to Survive? The Case of Chiweshe, Zimbabwe," in Twum-Danso Imoh, A. & Ansell, N. (eds.), *Children's Lives in an Era of Children's Rights. The Progress of the Convention on the Rights of the Child in Africa*, Oxon, Routledge, 2014.

46 See *e.g.* the references in note 40 above and also Archard, D. & Macleod, C.M., *The Moral and Political Status of Children*, Oxford, Oxford University Press, 2002; Eekelaar, J., "The Importance of Thinking That Children Have Rights," 6 *International Journal of Law and the Family*, 1992, pp. 221–235; Hunt Federle, K., "Rights Flow Downhill," 2 *International Journal of Children's Rights*, pp. 343–368; Freeman, M.D.A.(ed.); *Children's Rights* Vols. I & II, Aldershot, Ashgate, 2004; Freeman, M., "Why It Remains Important to Take Children's Rights Seriously," 15 *International Journal of Children's Rights*, 2007, pp. 15–23; Freeman, *supra* note 41, 2010; and McCormick, N., "Children's Rights: A Test-Case for Theories of Rights," 62 *Archiv für Rechts-und Sozialphilosophie*, 1976, pp. 305–316.

For a child seeking asylum with his or her family, being recognized as a rights-holder is essential. This prevents the child from being seen primarily as part of the family unit (an object) rather than as an individual (a subject) having a specific claim for protection to be addressed separately and not subsumed by the family (or, as is often the case, the adult members of the family).[47] For unaccompanied and separated children who lack the (presumed) protection provided by a parent or equivalent, to be considered an active subject of rights—someone with the right to exercise influence over his or her own destiny—rather than an object of protection and care essentially dependent on the goodwill of the State, is crucial in order to prevent and avoid protection gaps identified in relation to this category of children, including discrimination, abuse, detention and child labour.[48]

In what follows the spotlight will be on the rights-based approach as expressed in the four general principles of the CRC and how they relate to the particular needs of unaccompanied and separated children.[49] The focus on the general principles is explained by the fact that they represent core rights permeating the interpretation and implementation of the Convention as a whole and children's rights in general.

An overarching right for all children, asylum-seeking or not, is the *right to non-discrimination* in accordance with Article 2 of the CRC. Implementation of this article prohibits any discrimination on the basis of the status of a child as being unaccompanied or separated, or as being a refugee, asylum seeker or migrant.[50] In relation to unaccompanied and separated children this means, for example, that the child in question cannot be treated less favourably than an accompanied asylum-seeking child with regard to legal representation and protection of interests. An unaccompanied child must also be offered the same quality of treatment in every sphere that the host State accords its "own" children. This applies to health care, education, the right to information, institutional care and detention.[51] The article moreover prohibits children from being treated less favourably than adults in their not being considered eligible for refugee or other protective status because it is not

---

47   See *e.g.* HCR/GIP/09/08, 2009, para. 2.

48   CRC/GC/6/2005, para. 3.

49   The general principles were identified by the CRC Committee in General Comment No. 5, CRC/GC/2003/5, para. 12.

50   CRC/GC/2005/6, para. 18.

51   Bantekas, I., "Unaccompanied Children and Their Protection under International Refugee Law," in Juss, S. (ed.), *The Ashgate Research Companion to Migration Law, Theory and Policy*, Farnham and Burlington, Ashgate, 2013, pp. 347–362, at pp. 358–360.

considered possible for them to be persecuted or put at risk of serious harm in the same way as adults. The article further states that children should be protected against discrimination on account of the status of their parents, legal guardian or family members.

The *best interest principle* of Article 3(1) of the CRC is relevant in all aspects of the asylum process. The article refers to "interests" rather than "rights," implying that a broader concept than rights is sought.[52] The best interests of the child must, however, be understood in light of the rights and principles provided for by the Convention as a whole, thus making the connection to "rights" clearer.[53] The CRC Committee in its General Comment on Article 3(1) stated that individual decisions by asylum authorities must "be assessed and guided by the best interests of the child, as for all implementation measures"[54] and that the child's vulnerable position as an asylum seeker must be taken into account when determining what is in the best interests of the child. The Committee further stated that "a determination of what is in the best interests of the child requires a clear and comprehensive assessment of the child's identity"[55] and that "the principle must be respected during all stages of the displacement cycle."[56] For unaccompanied and separated children the best interest principle has particular significance both in relation to the procedural/practical aspects of seeking asylum *and* in the assessment of protection claims and the possibilities of a safe return to the country of origin. The best interest of the child should also override other interests, including any conflicting provisions of migration policy.[57]

Given that the best interest of the child is an overarching principle in the interpretation and understanding of all the rights included in the CRC, the principle is highly relevant when determining whether a child is persecuted within the meaning of Article 1A(2) of the Refugee Convention or is eligible for complementary protection. When assessing the validity of claims for protection, it is imperative that any possible future harm is assessed from the child's perspective, a prognosis in which child-specific rights,[58]

---

52   van Bueren, G., *The International Law on the Rights of the Child*, Dordrecht, Martinus Nijhoff Publishers, 1995, p. 47.

53   Freeman, M., *A Commentary on the Convention on the Rights of the Child Article 3: The Best Interests of the Child*, Martinus Nijhoff Publishers, 2007, p. 5 with references.

54   CRC/C/GC/14, para. 30.

55   "Identity" includes the child's nationality, upbringing, ethnic, cultural and linguistic background, particular vulnerabilities and protection needs. CRC/GC/2005/ 6, para. 20.

56   *Ibid.*, para. 19.

57   A/HRC/15/29, *supra* note 13, para. 24.

58   See HCR/GIP/09/08, 2009, paras. 13–14, listing a number of CRC provisions.

child-related manifestations of persecution[59] and child-specific forms of persecution[60] are all taken into account. Essential guidance in the understanding of these concepts is provided by the CRC.

On complementary protection it has been argued that the CRC can give rise to an independent source of protection.[61] There are two elements to this claim. One is founded on the principle of non-refoulement as expressed in the CRC in its third general principle, the *right to life and development* in Article 6, and also in Article 37. On the principle of non-refoulement and unaccompanied and separated children, the CRC Committee asserted that "States shall not return a child to a country where there are substantial grounds for believing that there is a real risk of irreparable harm to the child, such as, but by no means limited to, those contemplated under Articles 6 and 37 of the Convention."[62] What constitutes "irreparable harm" must thus be considered within the context of all the Convention's provisions. The non-refoulement aspect of the CRC from these statements appears uncontested. (To what extent it is applied in individual cases, however, is difficult to assess without making an extensive empirical study of case law.) Secondly, it has been suggested that Article 3(1) creates a complementary base for international protection, based on the fact that the best interests of the child introduces additional elements to the assessment of future risk given that such interests are to be considered a primary consideration in all actions concerning children and (as underlined by the CRC Committee) a "return to the country of origin shall in principle only be arranged if such return is in the best interests of the child."[63] The CRC Committee insists that if on return to the country of origin there is a reasonable risk that the fundamental rights of the child would be violated, then return is not an option.[64] The consequence would then be that the child is offered some kind of complementary protection. In situations of what is referred to by the Committee as "lower level risks" such as the child being affected by the indiscriminate effects of armed violence "such risks must be given full attention and balanced against other rights-based considerations."[65] The Committee concluded: "in this context, it must be

---

59   HCR/GIP/09/08, paras. 15–17.

60   *Ibid.*, paras. 18–36.

61   See *e.g.* Chapter 5 in McAdam, J., *Complementary Protection in International Refugee Law*, Oxford, Oxford University Press, 2006 and Pobjoy, 2013 *supra* note 12.

62   CRC/GC/2005/6 para. 27.

63   CRC/GC/2005/6 para. 84.

64   CRC/GC/2005/6 para. 82.

65   *Ibid.*

recalled that the survival of the child is of paramount importance and a pre-condition for the enjoyment of any other rights."[66]

The conclusion to be drawn with regard to this argument is that the best interest principle could play an important part in the assessment of protection needs and in cases where neither the Refugee Convention nor the principle of non-refoulement apply, thereby creating a new category of protected persons eligible for complementary protection.[67] In a world where one of the main reasons for forced migration is that of some kind of armed conflict, the opening up of these grounds of protection and their further exploration should not be underestimated. For example, the conflict in Syria, which is laying waste a whole generation of children, could well be argued to represent such a situation where both the best interest of the child and the principle of non-refoulement based on the provisions of the CRC could constitute independent grounds for protection.[68]

On the fourth general principle of the CRC, *the child's right to be heard and have his or her views taken into account* as established in Article 12 (also described as the right to participation), the CRC Committee stresses that "children who come to a country [...] as refugees are in a particularly vulnerable situation [...] For this reason it is urgent to fully implement their right to express their views on all aspects of the immigration and asylum proceedings [...] In the case of an asylum claim, the child must additionally have the opportunity to present her or his reasons leading to the asylum claim."[69] However, for the child merely to be interviewed in the asylum process is insufficient to meet the provisions of Article 12. What the child says, bearing in mind age and maturity, must also be taken into account.[70]

The above mainly refers to the part played by Article 12 with regard to the procedural aspects of seeking asylum. It could additionally be argued that Article 12 is also relevant when assessing the substantive nature of a protection

---

66   *Id.* See also the enumeration of situations that could constitute threats to life and devel-opment in Nowak, A.M., *Commentary on the Convention on the Rights of the Child Article 6 The Right to Life, Survival and Development*, Martinus Nijhoff Publishers, 2005.

67   Pobjoy, *supra* note 12; McAdam (2006), *supra* note 61.

68   On the situation for children in Syria, see *e.g. Syria's Children: A Lost Generation? Crisis Report March 2011–March 2013*, UNICEF March 2013, and *The Future of Syria: Refugee Children in Crisis*, UNHCR November 2013.

69   CRC/C/GC/12, para. 123.

70   On what is required for Article 12 to be implemented in a satisfactory way, see *e.g.* Stern, R., *The Child's Right to Participation. Reality or Rhetoric?* Uppsala, Uppsala University, 2006; Parkes, A., *Children and International Human Rights Law. The Right of the Child to be Heard*, Oxon, Routledge, 2013.

claim. While this is not a path explored to any great extent it is nevertheless not impossible to conceive circumstances where a wholly blatant denial of opportunity of expression of the child's views and having them properly taken into account (that is, to be able to exercise an influence over one's own life and the decisions affecting it) could constitute discrimination and if sufficiently severe, persecution. Analogies could be drawn with unacceptable limitations of the right to freedom of expression.[71] But given the fact that children in so many parts of the world are daily denied this right without its causing any particular uproar, it is difficult to imagine the success rate of such a claim in the foreseeable future.

Final Reflections

The fact that both the Refugee Convention and the CRC are relevant for the status determination of an asylum-seeking child, as Pobjoy reminds us, is not news.[72] That the child rights discourse could and should inform both procedural and substantive aspects of the asylum process for children is also well accepted. The CRC, not least in its general principles, provides several ways where this can be achieved, both in terms of providing tools for child-related interpretation of key concepts such as "persecution," "grave harm" and "non-refoulement" and in creating independent grounds for subsidiary protection. When interpreting these concepts and assessing the risk of persecution or other serious harm perpetrated on the child it is important to adopt an open mind as to what can be covered by a particular right, such as the right to non-discrimination, the right to development or the right to participation, and to assess the extent to which the denial of such human rights could constitute grounds for international protection for the asylum-seeking child. In addition, the weight to be accorded to the best interest of the child must be constantly borne in mind, as must the fact that this principle cannot be disregarded in favour of non-rights-based arguments such as migration control or State sovereignty.[73] For unaccompanied and separated children the rights-based approach is perhaps of particular importance. This can ensure that the child's claim for asylum is treated on an equal footing with an adult, while simultaneously

---

71   On the relationship between the right of the child to express his or her views and having them taken into account and freedom of expression in general, see CRC/C/GC/12, paras. 80–81.

72   Pobjoy, *supra* note 12, p. 115.

73   See *e.g.* CRC/C/GC/5, paras. 20, 84 and 86.

ensuring that the child is treated as a child with the additional safeguards that this entails. When such an approach is applied to all aspects of the asylum process the asylum-seeking child can be regarded as "child first, migrant second," without the traditional view of the child as primarily an object of protection being returned to, in order for the child's particular vulnerability as an asylum-seeker to be taken into account. In essence, children's rights need to be taken seriously for the same reasons that rights should be taken seriously for adults: the best protection against violations is to be considered a rights holder, as someone with a right to have rights.[74]

---

74   Freeman, *supra* note 16, p. 33 and Freeman, *supra* note 46.

The Child's Right to Protection of Private Life and Family Life

Elisabeth Gording Stang

Introduction

According to the 1989 UN Convention on the Rights of the Child (CRC) Article 16, no child shall be subjected to arbitrary or unlawful interference with his or her privacy, family, home or correspondence, nor to unlawful attacks on his or her honour or reputation. The wording of Article 16 is taken from the International Covenant on Civil and Political Rights of 1966 (ICCPR) Article 17. A similar human-rights provision can be found in The European Convention for the Protection of Human Rights and Fundamental Freedoms (ECHR), Article 8 stating that everyone has the right to respect for his private and family life, his home and his correspondence.

During the negotiations for the adoption of the ICCPR, several representatives claimed that the inclusion of family was unnecessary because home and privacy already covered the idea of the family.[1] This is an interesting comment in the light of the case-law of The European Court of Human Rights (the Court) on Article 8—the notion of private life. In connection with child abuse and maltreatment, the Court has developed a case-law based on an interpretation of private life covering the Member States' obligation to secure the child's right to protection of his or her moral and physical integrity. If the abuse or maltreatment is committed by the child's parents or other family members, as is often the situation, a strict human-rights protection of the family as a unit might exclude the child from protection of integrity.

This paper aims at analysing and discussing the child's right to family and family life on the one hand, and to privacy and private life on the other; and the tension between these rights. I connect the provisions of the CRC to the ECHR and its case-law given the important interaction between the two human-rights instruments. On this basis, I argue that the child does not merely have a right to family life as such, but to a family life that reaches a certain level of quality: the child has a right to a family life.

---

1 Detrick, S., *A Commentary on the United Nations Convention on the Right of the Child*, Martinus Nijhoff Publishers, 1999, p. 272.

In the first part of this article, I explore the notion of family and family life. I describe the kinds of close relationship between the child and his or her carers which can amount to protection under ECHR Article 8. The second part of the article contains a similar discussion of private life. In the concluding remarks, I will draw lines from case-law and synthesize it into a child-sensitive definition of family life that might serve as a relevant argument in assessments of the child's best interests.

During the past 20 years the Court has developed an interesting approach to the CRC by actively utilizing some of its fundamental principles and provisions in the legal argumentation according to the ECHR. The Court has consequently contributed to strengthening the legal status of the CRC – within the European jurisdiction at least – as well as increasing our awareness of children as legal subjects under the ECHR provisions. The areas in which the CRC has been included in the Court's assessments consist mainly of issues like physical punishment and abuse (Articles 3 and 19), juvenile justice (Articles 3, 37, 40), immigration cases/cases of expulsion (Articles 3, 9 cf. 16) and cases concerning child protection and visitation rights after divorce (Articles 3 and 9 cf. 16). It has been noted that "[b]y using the detailed and comprehensive child-specific provisions of the CRC to interpret the ECHR in accordance with its highly successful system of individual petition, it is possible to maximize the potential of both treaties to protect and promote children's rights."[2]

States Parties to the CRC have chosen different levels of implementation. Some of them, such as Norway, have incorporated the Convention into domestic law. However, for the European States Parties that have ratified it without incorporation in national law, the importance of using the CRC as a tool to interpret the ECHR cannot be underestimated.[3]

The Child's Right to Protection of Family and Family Life

The Notion of Family
The notion of family has changed over the years, and is continuously changing, along with the development of new family arrangements in different cultures and communities. In the preamble to the CRC the family is recognized as "the fundamental group of society and the natural environment for the growth and well-being of all its members and particularly children." The preamble

---

2   Kilkelly, U., "'The Impact of the Children's Convention on the European Convention on Human Rights," in Fottrell, D. (ed.), *Revisiting Children's Rights: Ten Years of the UN Convention on the Rights of the Child*, Dordrecht, Kluwer Law International, 2000, p. 88.

3   *Ibid.*, p. 100.

highlights the importance of necessary protection and support to enable the family to assume fully its responsibilities in the community. The preamble further states that the child should grow up in a family environment—"in an atmosphere of happiness, love and understanding"—to enable the full and harmonious development of the child's personality.

Articles 9 and 16 of the CRC provide for the child's right to legal protection against arbitrary or unlawful interference with his or her privacy, family and family life, home or correspondence. The term "family" is to be given a broad interpretation, and includes a range of family structures. There is a close connection between Article 16 and Articles 5 and 18. While Article 18 highlights the shared responsibility for the child by both parents and/or legal guardians, Article 5 describes who may be considered as carer of a child, with the responsibilities, rights and duties to provide "appropriate direction and guidance in the exercise by the child of the rights recognized in the Convention…in a manner consistent with the evolving capacities of the child." The persons legally responsible for the child are defined as "parents or, where applicable, the members of the extended family or community as provided for by local custom." The broad definition of family in the Convention reflects the wide variety of kinship and community arrangements within which children are brought up around the world.[4]

During a general Day of Discussion in 1994, the UN Committee on the Rights of the Child asked whether it would be "possible to favor a perspective where only under certain conditions would children be given the opportunity to enjoy rights which, in fact, are inherent to the dignity of their human nature?"[5] The answer follows from the Convention's Article 2 (1), stating the following grounds of discrimination (which are not exhaustive due to the wording "such as"): the child's or his or her parent's or legal guardian's race, colour, sex, language, religion, political or other opinion, national, ethnic or social origin, property, disability, birth or other status. The latter alternative covers family status.[6]

Adults choose the family arrangement; children are born and grow up under circumstances they have not been able to choose, and they cannot separate from their parents by themselves. Thus the words "other status" offers quite large scope for appreciation and dynamic development of the non-discrimination principle applied to children's different family situations. In the future will probably see a range of different family constellations appear.[7]

---

4 Hodgkin, R. and Newell, P., *Implementation Handbook for the Convention on the Rights of the Child*, UNICEF, revised edition, 2007, p. 76.

5 CRC/C/34 1994, para. 190. General discussion on the role of the family in the promotion on the rights of the child.

6 Detrick, *supra* note 2, pp. 75–76.

7 I am thinking for example of families created—legally or illegally—through surrogacy. Some children born from a surrogate mother are de facto born stateless, which consequently is a violation of the CRC Articles 2 and 7.

Protection of Family Life

Article 8(1) of the ECHR states that everyone has the right to respect for his private and family life, his home and his correspondence. Article 8(2) delineates the exceptions: Interference in private or family life can only take place in accordance with the law and when such interference "is necessary in a democratic society in the interests of national security, public safety or the economic well-being of the country, for the prevention of disorder or crime, for the protection of health or morals, or for the protection of the rights and freedoms of others."

As both children and their parents (or other close relatives or carers) are legal subjects in relation to Article 8, and as their interests might conflict, the right to protection of family life must be analysed from different angles. How do the parents versus the child experience their mutual family life, and in whose interests will it be to protect it? In most cases children and parents will share a common interest in protecting their mutual family life. But if family life becomes harmful to the child's health and development, the parent's might nonetheless argue their right to protection under Article 8, while the consideration of the best interest of the child might lead to a limitation of contact or full protection against that very family life. In the CRC Article 9(1) the conflict of interests is made explicit where it is stated that separation might be necessary for example in cases of abuse and neglect.

Clearly, it is not only the biological nuclear family, based on marriage, that deserves the full protection of Article 8. An increasing number of relationships enjoy the automatic protection as family life under Article 8, and the Court maintains a flexible approach to the notion of family.[8] The core element of family life is repeated in a number of cases concerning the relation between parents and children:

> According to the Court's well established case-law, 'the mutual enjoyment by parent and child of each other's company constitutes a fundamental element of family life' and domestic measures hindering such enjoyment amount to an interference with the right protected by Article 8.[9]

As to what kinds of the child's relationships to carers constitute family life, the Court's case-law shows that Article 8 automatically applies to the child's relationship with the biological mother. Children living together with their biological parents will normally be said to enjoy family life, irrespective of

---

8 Kilkelly, U., "The Right to Respect for Private and Family Life. A Guide to Implementation of Article 8 of the European Convention on Human Rights," *Human Rights Handbooks*, No. 1, Council of Europe, 2001, p. 16.

9 *McMichael v The United Kingdom 1995*, para. 86.

marriage.[10] Marriage will nonetheless strengthen the possible protection under Article 8, but long-lasting co-habitation may, equally, serve as marriage in the sense of mutual commitment: "During the relevant period taken as a whole they were living together and leading a joint 'family life'..."[11]

The child's relationship with grandparents, siblings and aunts/uncles may also fall into the scope of family life in Article 8, which protects the bonds between near relatives:

> In the Court's opinion, 'family life', within the meaning of Article 8, includes at least the ties between near relatives, for instance those between grandparents and grandchildren, since such relatives may play a considerable part in family life. 'Respect' for a family life so understood implies an obligation for the State to act in a manner calculated to allow these ties to develop normally...[12]

Adoptive parents will normally enjoy protection under Article 8 on equal terms with biological parents, and the legal bond will in some cases serve as a biological bond even where no de facto family life is established yet.[13]

The child's relationship with a carer living together with the child's biological parent and functioning as a social parent to the child may also be protected under Article 8: "[T]he existence or non-existence of 'family life' is essentially a question of fact depending upon the real existence in practice of close personal ties..."[14]

In line with the Court's flexible approach to "family," transsexual and same-sex relationships are included. In the case *X, Y and Z v the United Kingdom* 1997, X was a female-to-male transsexual. He had lived in a permanent and stable union with Y who was the biological mother of the child Z born as a result of artificial insemination by an anonymous donor. X thus had no biological connection to the child. English law defined a person's sex by reference to biological criteria at birth and did not recognize that it could be changed by surgery. As a result of this, a female-to-male transsexual was not permitted to

---

10   Kilkelly, 2001, p. 16.

11   *McMichael v The United Kingdom* 1995., para. 90.

12   *Marckx v Belgium 1979*, para. 45. See also *e.g. Bonda v Italy 1998*, para. 51, *Olsson 1 v Sweden 1988*, paras. 81 and 84.

13   Kilkelly 2001, pp. 16–19.

14   *K.T. v Finland 2001*, para. 150.

marry a woman and could not be regarded or registered as the father of a child (para. 20). The Court postulated:

> When deciding whether a relationship can be said to amount to 'family life', a number of factors may be relevant, including whether they have demonstrated their commitment to each other by having children together or by any other means... In the present case, the Court notes that X is a transsexual who has undergone gender reassignment surgery. He has lived with Y, to all appearances as her male partner, since 1979. The couple applied jointly for, and were granted, treatment by AID [artificial insemination by donor] to allow Y to have a child. X was involved through that process and has acted as Z's 'father' in every respect since the birth (...). In these circumstances, the Court considers that de facto family ties link the three applicants together.[15]

Despite the de facto family life ascertained in this case, the Court concluded that there had been no violation of Article 8 by denying X formal status as a father. One reason seemed to be the lack of case-law and legislation in the field, and consequently the Court gives room for extended margin of appreciation:

> The Court observes that there is no common European standard with regard to the granting of parental rights to transsexuals. In addition, it has not been established before the Court that there exists any generally shared approach amongst the High Contracting Parties with regard to the manner in which the social relationships between a child conceived by AID and the person who performs the role of the father should be reflected in law... Since...the law appears to be in a transitional stage, the respondent State must be afforded a wide margin of appreciation...[16]

The Court does not explicitly refer to the best interest principle in Article 3 (1) of the CRC. Nevertheless, an underlying argument appears to be that general knowledge of what will be in the child's best interests in cases concerning artificial insemination is uncertain; morally and legally there is a lack of consensus that makes the Court resist from imposing "any single viewpoint:"

---

15   Paras. 36–37.
16   Para. 44.

It is impossible to predict the extent to which the absence of a legal connection between X and Z will affect the latter's development. As previously mentioned, at the present time there is uncertainty with regard to how the interests of children in Z's position can best be protected...and the Court should not adopt or impose any single viewpoint.[17]

On the other hand it is hard to see how it might not be in the best interest of the child to have a regulated relationship to the one of her parents, including the father's name on her birth certificate, inheritance rights *etc.* It is tempting to propose that lack of knowledge is a covering argument for not imposing any legal binding viewpoints concerning a very sensitive political issue: sexual identity and diversity.

16 years later, in 2013, the Court handled a case with many similar aspects, and came to a clear conclusion. In the case of *X and Others v Austria 2013*, two women were living together in a stable relationship. One of the women had a son born outside of marriage; the father had recognized paternity, but the mother had sole custody of the boy. The two women made an agreement whereby the boy would be adopted by the woman who was not his mother, to "create a legal relationship" between the future adoptive mother and the boy "corresponding to the bond between them." The Court concluded that there was a difference in treatment in national law and from the national authorities concerning heterosexual versus homosexual partnerships, which amounted to a violation of the non-discrimination principle set out in Article 14, and that this difference "was inseparably linked to the fact that the first and third applicants formed a same-sex couple, and was thus based on their sexual orientation."[18] The Court also found that the two women and the boy constituted a family unit and enjoyed the protection of Article 8, and that rejecting adoption would lead to a violation of Article 8:

> The Court reiterates that the relationship of a cohabiting same-sex couple living in a stable de facto relationship falls within the notion of 'family life' just as the relationship of a different-sex couple in the same situation would ...They have been cohabiting for many years and the second applicant [the boy] shares their home. His mother and her partner care for him jointly. The Court therefore finds that the relationship between all three applicants amounts to 'family life' within the meaning of Article 8 of the Convention.[19]

---

17   Para. 51.
18   Para. 130.
19   Paras. 95 and 96.

As the case-law reveals, a series of different relationships between the child and his or her care-takers may enjoy protection under Article 8. Nevertheless, a de facto family life is not always necessary to establish protection under Article 8. On the other hand, a lived family life will not always be enough to establish protection under Article 8 (see below *Görgülü v Germany 2004*).

In the case of *Ericsson v Sweden 1988* the child was taken into care shortly after birth and placed in a foster home. Several attempts from the mother to terminate the care order failed. Later the care order was lifted, and replaced with a prohibition of removal with restrictions of access for the mother to her daughter. As a result, mother and daughter were prevented from developing a relationship. The child had developed a full attachment to the foster-parents. The Court remarked:

> In cases like the present, a mother's right to respect for family life under Article 8 includes a right to the taking of measures with a view to her being reunited with her child... [S]he was in fact denied the opportunity to meet with her daughter to an extent and in circumstances likely to promote the aim of reuniting them or even the positive development of their relationship.[20]

In the case of *Boughanemi v France 1996* a (biological) father was prevented from establishing a family life with his child as a consequence of a deportation decision. The Court underlined the fact that "the concept of family life on which Article 8 is based embraces, even where there is no cohabitation, the tie between a parent and his or her child..." (para. 35).

In the case of *Keegan v Ireland 1997* a non-married father experienced that the child's mother signed for adoption shortly after birth, as their relationship broke down. The Court highlighted that a child born out of such a relationship is "ipso iure part of that 'family' unit from the moment of his birth and by the very fact of it. There thus exists between the child and his parents a bond amounting to family life even if at the time of his or her birth the parents are no longer co-habiting or if their relationship has then ended..."[21].

The bond referred to in the quotation above is presumably to be understood as the biological bond. Nevertheless, as the Court's case-law reveals, other carers than biological parents might develop close personal ties to the child, and vice-versa, which can amount to family life based on a documented de facto family life, at least in cases where there are no "competing" biological bonds. In the case of *Görgülü v Germany 2004*, the biological father had at no time lived together with his eight-year old son who was placed in a foster home.

---

20   Para. 71.
21   Paras. 44–45.

The boy's attachment to his foster-parents was well documented, as well as the risk of a possible removal to the father. The Court let the biological bond be the paramount argument:

> [B]earing in mind that the applicant is Christofer's biological parent and undisputedly willing and able to care for him, the Court is not convinced that the Naumburg Court of Appeal examined all possible solutions to the problem... [T]he Court of Appeal apparently only focused on the imminent effects which a separation from his foster-parents would have on the child, but failed to consider the long-term effects which a permanent separation from his natural father might have on Christofer."[22]

Considering the character of the relationship between Christofer and his foster-parents on the bases of the Court's case-law discussed above, one might very well conclude that the emotional and social bonds qualify for the objective criteria for protection under Article 8 – as the development of a close personal tie, a de facto family life *etc*. The Court would nonetheless probably have been unable to interpret Article 8 so as to protect the emotional ties between the boy and the foster-parents without jeopardizing the whole of case-law. Repeatedly, the Court has highlighted that public care must be regarded as a temporary measure, and that the ultimate aim is reunification with biological parents.[23] On this point, Norwegian child protection legislation, policy and practice over the past 15 years has moved towards a weakening of the biological principle – and a corresponding strengthening of the child's right to adequate care and stability, in cases where the best interests of the child contradict those of the parents. An interesting question, even though hypothetical, is whether Christopher's actual everyday life with his foster-parents would have been recognized as protectable under Article 8 if the foster-parents had been Christopher's relatives. There is a tendency in child protection practice, at least in Norway (and also in Denmark and Sweden) to look more actively for foster-parents among the child's own relatives, and some studies show that family placements, in certain ways, seem to be more "successful," bearing the potential of "the best of both worlds."[24]

---

22   Para. 46

23   See *i.e. Johansen v Norway 1996*, para. 78 (also referring to *Olsson (no. 1) v Sweden 1988*, p. 36, para. 81).

24   Tørnblad, R., 2011, Holtan 2002, Moldestad, B. 2003, Backe-Hansen, E. og Havik, T 2013.

The Child's Right to Protection of Privacy and Private Life

The Notion of Privacy

"Privacy" in Article 16 of the CRC refers to the child's personal sphere, but has not been defined in details in the *travaux préparatoires*. In its observations, the Committee has referred to subjects like personal and body search, personal information and the gathering and holding of personal information about the child, confidential advice and counselling for children and adolescents, privacy in institutions and juvenile justice.[25] Article 16 thus raises issues concerning the physical environment in which the child lives, the privacy of his or her relationships and communications with others. The protection of the child's personal sphere in the sense explained above, is closely connected to the protection of the child's personal integrity. The link to the Articles 3 and 19 is obvious.

While the child's right to protection of his or her privacy refers to the child's personal sphere in a quite indefinite way, the child's right to protection of his or her private life will specifically encompass his or her physical and moral integrity according to Article 8 of the ECHR and the Court's case-law. Protection of a child's integrity while in the hands of parents or other carers is first and foremost a responsibility for the adults in charge.[26] Only when the parents fail in exercising their parental responsibility in a manner to ensure the child the protection and care necessary for his or her well-being (Article 3 no 2) does protection of the child's integrity become an obligation for the public authorities.

Protection of Integrity

I now turn to the child's right to protection of his or her integrity, on the basis of the Court's case-law. It is interesting that in many cases concerning child welfare measures, abuse, neglect or violence, Article 8 of the ECHR is merely argued by parents in connection with a possible violation of the their right to family life, while the Court tends to conclude with a violation of the protection of private life on behalf of the child involved. In these decisions, the Court regularly refers to Articles 3, 19, or to 37 of the CRC in very serious cases of cruel, inhuman or degrading treatment or punishment. The case-law reveals the fine balance between the child's and his or her parent's mutual interest in protecting their family life and the specific interest of the child to be protected from a harmful family life.

---

25   Detrick, *supra* note 2, p. 273, Hodgkin and Newell, *supra* note 5, pp. 203–210.
26   Cf. Articles 3, 5, 18 and 19 of the CRC.

Some of the case-law refers to breaches of children's integrity amounting to a violation of Article 3 of the ECHR—the prohibition of torture or other cruel, inhuman and degrading treatment or punishment. In several of those cases, the Court underlines the importance of State obligations also when children, or other vulnerable persons, are exposed to such ill-treatment committed by private individuals.

In the case of *A v the UK 1998*, a nine-year-old boy was mistreated by his stepfather who had hit him with a stick, amounting to a violation of Article 3 of the ECHR: "[T]he applicant, who was nine years old, was found...to have been beaten with a garden cane which had been applied with considerable force on more than one occasion... The Court considers that treatment of this kind reaches the level of severity prohibited by Article 3."[27]

The Court referred to the CRC in the case, and stated:

> States [are required] to take measures designed to ensure that individuals within their jurisdiction are not subjected to torture or inhuman or degrading treatment or punishment, including such ill-treatment administered by private individuals... Children and other vulnerable individuals, in particular, are entitled to State protection, in the form of effective deterrence, against such serious breaches of personal integrity..., see also the United Nations Conventions on the Rights of the Child, Articles 19 and 37."[28]

This case illustrates how the Court empowers the CRC in its argumentation, strengthening the child's position as a holder of rights under the ECHR. The Court assesses the level of severity in relation to Article 3. Interestingly, the Court takes a child-sensitive approach by underlining that this assessment is relative, based on "all the circumstances of the case, such as the nature and context of the treatment, its duration, its physical and mental effects and, in some cases, the sex, age and state of health of the victim."

The Court's consideration of individual factors determining the severity of the actions is linked closely to vulnerability as a human-rights approach. Morawa argues for vulnerability as a separate legal category deserving "a higher level of human rights protection in their favour," and that such a higher level of protection is "required from States."[29] The argumentation is quite similar to the spirit and principles set out in the preamble to the CRC: "Bearing in mind

---

27   Paras. 20–21.

28   Para. 22.

29   Morawa, A.H.E., "Vulnerability as a Concept of International Human Rights Law," 6 *Journal of International Relations and Development*, 2003, p. 150.

that...the child, by reason of his physical and mental immaturity, needs special safeguards and care, including appropriate legal protection..."

In the case of *Z. and Others v the UK 2001* four siblings were awarded compensation for having been exposed to severe, long-term neglect and abuse during their childhood, with the local welfare authorities knowing, but not acting. The four children lived under conditions described by the medical expert as "horrific." The children were stealing food at night, locked outside the house for hours, locked into their filthy bedrooms; they would frequently appear with bruising on their faces, neighbours reported screaming at the children's home. *Z and Others* is the first case where the Court interprets Article 3 as to covering fundamental neglect. It has had a significant impact on later case-law:

> The...children had been subject to appalling neglect over an extended period and suffered physical and psychological injury directly attributable to a crime of violence (...). The present case, however, leaves no doubt as to the failure of the system to protect these applicant children from serious, long-term neglect and abuse."[30]

The cases of *A v the UK 1998* and *Z and Others v the UK 2001* may serve as examples of "the red line." The Court establishes a clear responsibility for Member States to take active steps to protect children living under conditions that amount to a violation of Article 3.

In the case of *Bensaid v the UK* 2001, which concerns the use of forced treatment in mental health care, the Court stresses the impact of serious breaches of integrity, on mental health and the right to development and identity:

> 'Private life' is a broad term not susceptible to exhaustive definition. The Court has already held that elements such as gender identification, name and sexual orientation and sexual life are important elements of the personal sphere protected by Article 8... Mental health must also be regarded as a crucial part of private life associated with the aspect of moral integrity. Article 8 protects a right to identity and personal development, and the right to establish and develop relationships with other human beings and the outside world.[31]

The Court describes the limit of Article 8, and discusses whether the treatment was proved to have had "sufficiently adverse effects on physical and moral

---

30   Paras. 74–75.
31   Para. 47.

integrity," and concluded with a violation of Article 8. This is especially important to children who, per definition, are under constant development and totally dependent on their carers.

According to the case-law, Article 3 may cover issues like physical punishment, sexual abuse, severe neglect of children and forced medication and treatment in mental care.[32] One important criterion for the State's responsibility concerning domestic abuse and neglect is that local authorities knew, or were to blame for not having known, that the abuse/neglect/mistreatment was going on. Strong evidence (convincing reason) is required. In *D.P. and J.C. v the UK 2003* the Court denied compensation because of lack of evidence for that knowledge, although the child welfare authorities had been in close contact with the family for several years, with different assisting measures, and several signs and symptoms of neglect and sexual abuse were well documented. The abuse was kept a secret within the family, and even the children did not talk about it with each other because "it was almost accepted that it happened." The children did not dare to tell the social worker, for fear for being punished by the parents. One of the children told her mother once, during a row, about the abuse in the presence of her stepfather, and the response from the parents was to beat all the children.[33] The social report, though, considers the stepfather as "such a caring figure in the house"[34] The Court states:

> While the seriousness of the abuse and its effects of the applicants are not in doubt, the Court found above, in context of Article 3 of the Convention, that the social services were not aware, and were not in a position that they ought to have been aware, that their stepfather was abusing them sexually.[35]

The Court seems to set an extremely high threshold for evidence – in cases where evidence often is the largest challenge. It follows from the nature of sexual abuse that there are rarely any witnesses or other "hard core" proof. Requiring a high standard for documenting knowledge may render children without necessary protection (or compensation when the abuse is revealed).

---

32   *I.e. E and Others v UK 2002*, para. 89 and *Z and Others v UK 2001*, para. 74.
33   Para. 58.
34   Para. 22.
35   Para. 118.

Concluding Remarks

As the case-law shows, the child has a right to protection of his or her family life with carers the child is attached to, emotionally, socially or biologically, the latter in spite of no established family life. The tension between the broad definition in both the CRC and the European Court case-law of family and family life, and the fact that the very existence of biological bonds amounts to protection of a future family life, leaves us in a paradoxical and unresolved legal situation. It will be interesting to follow the case-law in the future, to see whether the principle of biology will uphold its position in the Court's argumentation.

The Court interprets private life to include the child's moral and physical integrity. Consequently, serious breaches of the child's integrity caused by parents or other carers might amount to a violation of Article 8 of the ECHR, and in extremely severe cases, to Article 3. Some of the cases mark an absolute limit – a "red line." By crossing "the red line," we move from protecting the child's family life to protecting the individual child against a harmful development through serious breaches of the child's integrity. As stated in *Adele Johansen v Norway 1996*, parents "cannot be entitled under Article 8 of the Convention to have such measures taken as would harm the child's health and development."[36]

There is no consensus among the different national legal systems of the contracting parties to the ECHR or the CRC on the notion of children's private life or private sphere – for example the content or extension of it. Probably on the contrary, taking the diversity of cultural, political and socio-economic factors into account. The child's position in the family varies among communities and States, as does the child's position in society as a holder of individual rights. There will continue to be a strong need to enlighten and strengthen the child's right to protection of his or her private life, with a focus on moral and physical integrity, especially in the child's own family where most of the violence against children takes place.

To conclude, the child's right to family life is assumed to consist mainly of three elements. The first is *the right to a family life experienced by the child as safe and caring*, with carers to whom the child is attached by psychological, social and/or biological bonds. The second element is *the right to protection of the child's physical and moral integrity*, as well as other elements of the child's *private* life, which is first and foremost the parents' or other carer's

---

36   Para. 78.

responsibility. The third element may be defined as *the right for the child to develop identity and personality in a harmonious and fruitful way*. The child has a right not only to family life, but to a *good* family life. As a consequence of children's vulnerability and total dependency of adults, they must be entitled to a higher level of human rights protection in their favour – also with regard to other human rights instruments than the CRC.

The Right to a Fair Trial from a Child's Perspective – Reflections from a Comparative Analysis of Two Child-protection Systems

Pernilla Leviner

Protecting children from abuse and neglect is an international obligation according to the UN Convention on the Rights of the Child (the Convention). Its Article 19 prescribes that the signatory States are to take all appropriate measures to protect children from all forms of abuse and neglect while they are in their home environments. However, States also have an obligation to respect other interests, such as parental autonomy, as stemming from the Convention and other international conventions.[1] Any decision regarding the protection of children from harmful home environments involves balancing the child's right to protection against parental rights and also the fundamental right to private and family life, for example, as set out in Article 8 of the European Convention for the Protection of Human Rights and Fundamental Freedoms ("European Convention"). Interference with this latter right must always be in accordance with the law, and also be necessary in a democratic society, for the protection of the rights and freedoms of others (for example, the child in child-protection cases). This means that the least intrusive intervention for securing the child's safety and wellbeing is always to be chosen, and limited to what is necessary and reasonable under the circumstances, *i.e.* the interference must be proportionate to the aim pursued.[2] Further, decisions by authorities to protect and place a child out-of-home, are always to be tried and reviewed by an independent and impartial court.[3] This is a fundamental requirement in line with fair-trial principles set out in Article 6 of the European Convention and numerous other declarations throughout the world.[4]

---

1   For example, the International Covenant on Civil and Political Rights (ICCPR), the International Covenant on Economic, Social and Cultural Rights (ICESCR) and the European Convention for the Protection of Human Rights and Fundamental Freedoms (European Convention).

2   White, R.C.A. & Ovey, C., *The European Convention on Human Rights*, 5th edition, Oxford University Press, 2010, p. 325.

3   Despite variations in wording and placement of the fair-trial rights, international human-rights instruments define the right to a fair trial in broadly the same terms.

4   See for example Article 10 of the Universal Declaration of Human Rights (UDHR) and Article 47 of the Charter of Fundamental Rights of the European Union.

© KONINKLIJKE BRILL NV, LEIDEN, 2015 | DOI 10.1163/9789004297432_022

Without doubt, protecting children from abuse and neglect is a legal question that encompasses a complex balancing between at times opposing interests,[5] and interventions are encircled by several rule-of-law principles. By tradition, these principles have primarily focused on guaranteeing that unlawful and illegitimate measures are not taken, and they have had a parental or adult perspective. This article focuses on the requirements on child-protection processes, from the perspective of judicial proceedings guaranteeing that illegitimate interventions are not taken, but also that authorities *are* intervening when needed to protect children. The overall objective is to analyze the meaning of the right to a fair trial in these processes from a child's perspective, and with respect to the best interest of the child as well as the right of the child to be heard. Thus the article seeks to evaluate the requirements needed to create a well-working, just and child-friendly child-protection system.

Different States have chosen different ways of organizing and regulating their child-protection systems, including the interpretation and implementation of the right to a fair trial.[6] The analysis here draws on a comparative analysis made in a previous study,[7] in which the child-protection systems in Sweden and Australia, specifically the state of Victoria, were contrasted with a focus on the different roles and functions of the courts in child-protection cases. That study showed that, although largely based on the same principles and rights (children's right to protection, the respect for private and family life, the right to a fair trial, best interest of the child, *etc.*), the role and function, as well as the organization, of the courts in these two systems differ greatly. The analysis and conclusions on the differences in this regard raised several questions, one of which focuses on the closer meaning of the right to a fair trial and how the specific needs of children involved in child-protection cases are to be handled

---

5 Child protection is fundamentally a balancing between Article 3 (the prohibition of torture or inhuman or degrading treatment or punishment) and Article 8 (the right to private and family life) of the European Convention. A clear and often cited case from the European Court of Human Rights is *Z and others v United Kingdom* (Application No. 29392/95, Judgment of 10 May 2001). This case clarifies that Article 3 entails a responsibility for States to act in order to protect children from indefensible life circumstances in their home environments.

6 The differences in these aspects most probably depend on many factors, historical, cultural and, but not the least, financial; but also on the legal culture and traditions in the country, what role the courts have in different systems and also what overall approach or ideology the child protection system is based on.

7 Leviner, P., "Domstolens funktion i LVU-ärenden – behov av specialiserade barndomstolar?" (The Function of the Court in Child Protection – A Need for Specialized Children's Courts?), in *Nordisk socialrättslig tidskrift*, 2012, pp. 85–132.

according to this fundamental due-process principle. The objective of the present article is to address and discuss this question further.

The article begins with a short overall description of the right to a fair trial, as commonly interpreted, and also child-specific requirements as to child-friendly justice set out under international law. Thereafter the two systems, Sweden and Victoria, will be fairly simply described and compared. The aim is to give an understanding of how differences relating to the role and function of judicial proceedings can play out in different child-protection systems. Although neither system is specifically "un-child-friendly," both have a limited focus on children and their specific needs with regard to fair process. This raises the question of whether the right to a fair-trial principle should be more clearly defined from a child perspective in order to enable reforms with a substantive-rights-based approach regarding specific needs of children in child-protection processes.[8] This will be discussed in the concluding section of the article where aspects to consider in order to create a fair and child-friendly child protection system will be raised. The goal is not to discuss which system of Sweden and Victoria is the "better" in this respect, nor to give specific answers to what the right to a fair trial means from a child's perspective. Rather, the article discusses questions relating to what the right to a fair trial can and/or should mean from a child's perspective, and what the role and function of the courts should be in a child-friendly child-protection system.

I   The Right to a Fair Trial in Child Protection Cases

Generally, removing a child from a home and dictating the terms and conditions of an individual's private and family life are among the most invasive measures a public authority can take. Consequently, high requirements must be placed on these authorities and courts with respect to such measures. As

---

8   A substantive-rights-based approach has been used as *one of six* in a classification of approaches to children's rights. See Tobin, J., "Judging the Judges – Are Judges Adopting the Rights Approach in Matters Involving Children," in 33 *Melbourne University Law Review*, 2009, pp. 579–625 and Tobin, J., "Children's Rights in Australia – Confronting the Challenge," in Gerber, P. & Castan, M. (eds.), *Contemporary Perspectives on Human Rights Law in Australia*, Thomson Reuters, Sydney, 2013, pp. 275–299. Tobin analyses factors that can undermine a substantive impact of children's rights on social and policy debates concerning children. It is argued that many reforms have an (1) invisible, (2) incidental, (3) selective, (4) superficial and/or (5) rhetorical approach to children's rights which tend to marginalize or misuse the notion of children as rights-bearers. Instead, reforms should have an approach that gives substantive effect to children's rights – (6) a substantive-rights-based approach.

stated above, the requirement that such measures be taken under the law acts as a guarantee that they are not taken without legal support. Another important safeguard against illegitimate interventions is the principle of proportionality, requiring that interventions must always be *necessary* under the circumstances. In a rule-of-law State, it is also fundamental that the legality and proportionality of actions by public authorities involving civil rights, such as child-protection cases, must always be reviewed in a fair court proceeding.

A fundamental element of the right to a fair trial – the most-cited right before the European Court of Human Rights – is that the individual is given the opportunity to appear before the court: "access to justice." That a proceeding before a court is fair is secondary to whether the individual has the opportunity to initiate a court process.[9] Although the principle of the right to a fair trial is very complex, it is commonly stated as entailing the requirement that the individual be guaranteed a fair and public proceeding within a reasonable time before an impartial court that is constituted by law.[10] Regarding the requirement of an independent and impartial court, this is primarily combined with the guarantees against conflicts of interest and subjectivity, circumstances that generally can be seen as undermining confidence in the courts.[11]

The right to a fair trial does not enshrine child-specific entitlements,[12] and has not been thoroughly and explicitly interpreted in the context of child protection. However, with regard to the Convention and a modern view of children as individual rights bearers, it is clear that the right to a fair trial also comprises children and that a fair process must be guaranteed in any case involving civil rights, such as child-protection cases.[13] But what does this actually mean and how should the right to a fair trial be interpreted from a child's perspective in such cases?

---

9   White & Ovey, *supra* note 2, p. 254.

10   For a more comprehensive account of the right to a fair trial and case law from the European Court of Human Rights, see *ibid.*, Chapter 12 and Danelius, H., *Mänskliga rättigheter i europeisk praxis – en kommentar till Europakonventionen om de mänskliga rättigheterna* (Human Rights in European Case-Law), 4th edition, Norstedts Juridik, Stockholm, 2012, Chapter 9.

11   White & Ovey, *ibid.*, pp. 266–269 and Danelius, *ibid.*, pp. 199–216.

12   Article 6.1 of the European Convention, however, specifically notes that the press and public may be excluded from all or part of a trial, *i.e.*, an exemption from the requirement of public proceedings, in criminal cases concerning juveniles.

13   Van Bueren, G., *Child Rights in Europe – Convergence and Divergence in Judicial Protection*, Council of Europe Publishing, Strasbourg, 2007, p. 104.

II Child-specific Requirements as to the Right to a Fair Trial under Public International Law

International discussion on the fairness of processes from a child's perspective, and also a general discussion on how to create a more child-friendly justice system, have led to the drafting of some recommendations and guidelines.[14] The discussions have often focused on children in the criminal justice system, *i.e.*, juvenile offenders and child victims and witnesses of crime; but some of the guidance given is also relevant to child-protection processes. Fundamental in any proceedings involving children, affecting the right to a fair process from a child's perspective and emphasized in such international document, is of course children's right to participation according to Article 12 of the Convention. This includes a right for children capable of forming views to be allowed to express these freely in all matters affecting them and that these views are to be given due weight in accordance with the child's age and maturity.[15] Central here is also Article 3 of the Convention, stating the best-interest-of-the-child principle which underlines that all actions concerning children must have the child's best interest as a primary consideration. The UN Committee on the Rights of the Child has underlined that Article 12 obliges States Parties to ensure that mechanisms are in place to solicit the views of the child. This is most important in guaranteeing a fair process for children.[16] The Committee also stresses that the realisation of the right of the child to express her or his views requires that the child be informed about the matters, options and possible decisions to be taken and their consequences.[17]

As to fair and child-friendly proceedings, the UN Committee on the Rights of the Child has further emphasized that although due process must always be respected, the protection and further development of the child must form the primary purpose of decision-making in court proceedings involving children

---

14   See, for example, UN Committee on the Rights of the Child, *The Guidelines for Action on Children in the Criminal Justice System*, 1997, the United Nations Guidelines on Justice in Matters Involving Child Victims and Witnesses of Crime, ECOSOC Res. 2005/20, 2005 and European Council, *Guidelines of the Committee of Ministers of the Council of Europe on Child Friendly Justice*, 17 November, 2010.

15   According to UN Committee on the Rights of the Child, General Comment No. 12, *The Right of the Child to be Heard*, 2009, paragraph 32, the right to be heard applies to all relevant judicial proceedings affecting the child, without limitation, including, for example care and adoption, *i.e.* child protection.

16   *Ibid.*, para. 19.

17   *Ibid.*, para. 25.

needing protection from abuse and neglect.[18] In order to adjust judicial involvement in cases involving children in need of protection from harmful home environments, the Committee has also stressed that in line with Article 19 of the Convention, it is recommended that States organize an integrated, cohesive, interdisciplinary and coordinated child-protection system. Specialized courts and units within the police and judiciary for handling child victims of violence are pointed out as important measures. The need for specific interdisciplinary training on the rights and needs of children of different age groups, as well as on proceedings adapted to children, are also underlined as being very important.[19]

More specific aspects as to child-friendly proceeding are also outlined in the 2010 Guidelines of the Committee of Ministers of the Council of Europe on child friendly justice. These guidelines aim to ensure that children's rights such as the right to information, representation, participation and protection, are fully respected. The Guidelines further emphasize that the rule of law should apply fully to children as it does to adults and that important elements of due process, such as the right to a fair trial and the right to access to courts, should be guaranteed for children as they are for adults, and should not be minimized or denied under the pretext of the child's best interest.[20]

In line with the above recommendations and guidelines, States clearly need to include specific considerations in the organization and development of child-protection systems. This should also affect how the court proceedings are set up. However, the international recommendations in this regard are fairly non-specific and not focused on the special circumstances at hand in child-protection cases. States can without too much problem argue that they do fulfill the requirements set out in these recommendations. However, it must be emphasized that a judicial assessment in child-protection cases is very complex. First of all, this process involves a balancing act between children's right to protection and the right to private and family life. Further, assessment of the legality and proportionality of different measures and interventions in most cases requires knowledge of risk and protective factors and the multifaceted relationship between them. Arguably, more specific requirements must be placed on child-protections systems and courts in order for these processes to be fair from a child's perspective.

---

18   UN Committee on the Rights of the Child, General Comment No. 13, *The Right of the Child to Freedom from all Forms of Violence*, 2011, para. 54.

19   *Ibid.*, para. 56.

20   Council of Europe, *Guidelines of the Committee of Ministers of the Council of Europe on Child Friendly Justice*, 2010, Sections I and III(E).

In the following, the child-protection systems in Sweden and Victoria will be described and compared, with the aim of giving a deeper understanding of how differences relating to the role and function of judicial proceedings can play out in different systems, including how these two systems handle the right to a fair trial from a child perspective. Although the two different systems and models are considered to be fairly child-friendly and in many aspects in line with the recommendations and guidelines described above, they both have a problematically limited focus on children's needs and rights. The need for reform will be discussed in the concluding section.

III   The Two Child-protection Systems

The two systems compared in this article differ but there are also similarities. To begin with, both Sweden and Australia are signatories to the Convention, and therewith bound by its Article 19 prescribing a responsibility to protect children from all forms of abuse and neglect in their home environments. Despite differences in how the welfare systems dealing with children and families are constructed and organized (in Australia there are also differences between the states and territories), and taking into account that comparisons between different systems in themselves encompass many challenges, similar ambitions can be seen in the two countries for schools, health care and social welfare for children and their families.[21] Another similarity regarding the

---

21   Both countries are considered as rich/wealthy, and comparative UNICEF studies show that the number of children that die as a cause of abuse and neglect, a common welfare indicator in different countries, is relatively low in both Sweden and Australia. UNICEF, *A League Table of Child Maltreatment Death in Rich Nations*, Innocenti Report Card Nr. 5, Innocenti Research Centre, Florence, 2003. In Esping-Andersen's influential and often-cited typology of welfare States – in which a distinction is drawn between liberal, conservative and social-democratic models – Australia belongs to the liberal model while Sweden belongs to the social-democratic one. See Esping-Andersen, G., *The Three Worlds of Welfare Capitalism*, Princeton University Press, Princeton, 1990. Even if Sweden and Australia are perceived as different models, they have been invoked as relevant and adequate objects of comparison, not least regarding social work, see *inter alia* Healy, K., Lundström, T. & Sallnäs, M., *A Comparison of Out-of-Home Care for Children and Young People in Australia and Sweden – Worlds Apart?* Australian Social Work, vol. 64, 2011, focusing on child protection systems in Sweden and Australia. This study compares these countries with respect to the frequency of placing children and youths, plus similarities and differences with respect to age and reasons for such placements.

actual child protection systems addressed here is that both systems have been more or less constantly criticized and reformed during the past few decades, with Victoria leading this competition with more than ten relatively significant reforms during the past thirty years.

The Swedish and Victorian systems dealing with protecting children differ as to type. The systems in Western countries are often divided into family support systems and systems with a child-protection approach.[22] In *family-support systems*, of which Sweden is an example, the focus is on family relationships and risk situations are viewed as the result of dysfunctional relationships rather than directly harmful parental behavior. Central to a family-support system is working for change through consensual support to the family. In contrast, *child-protection approach systems*, as adopted for example in the USA, the UK and the Australian states and territories, emphasize individual rights and focus on protecting children from abuse and neglect. The potential for coercive interventions and the removal of a child from a family is therefore present in this latter approach at an earlier stage of investigation and work with families.[23]

The two systems also differ organizationally. While the courts in Sweden dealing with child-protection cases are general administrative courts, a specialized court in Victoria, the Children's Court, deals with child protection and juvenile justice. Overall, the countries also represent two types of legal system into which Western legal systems are most commonly divided. In the often-used classification of legal systems, Victoria is described as a common-law system while Sweden belongs to the Nordic legal family, often referred to as a third way different from both common-law and civil-law systems.[24]

---

22   Gilbert, N., Parton, N. & Skivenes, M. (eds.), *Child Protection Systems – International Trends and Orientations*, Oxford University Press, 2011.

23   *Ibid.*

24   Countries such as the United States, the United Kingdom and Australia, are common-law systems and many European States, among others France and Germany, are civil-law systems. The Nordic countries in Europe (Sweden, Denmark, Norway, Finland and Iceland) are often described as something in between, or different, comprising the Nordic legal family. Common-law systems emphasize case law and are sometimes described as relying heavily on judge-made law. The Swedish system, and civil-law systems, is instead perceived as strongly bound by legislation. Sweden however lacks complete codifications such as the Code Civil in France or the BGB in Germany. Generally, cases from the highest courts are accorded more importance in Sweden than in civil-law systems but the perception of the role of the courts is more or less the same in Sweden as in civil-law systems. The courts are only to determine the intent of the legislator when

All in all, both the legal and the child-protection systems in Sweden and Victoria differ in many ways, although certain similarities make them an interesting and comparable couple. The similarities and differences in the two systems offer a valuable contrast and a basis for analysis of what the role and function of courts and judicial proceedings in child-protection cases can and should be, including an analysis of the meaning and potential of the fundamental right to a fair trial when challenged from a child's perspective.

IV The Judicial Process and Function of the Courts in Two Child-protection Systems[25]

In both the systems compared, social workers (in the Social Services in Sweden and in the Department of Human Services (DHS) in Victoria) have the primary responsibility and authority to act in child-protection cases. In both Sweden and Victoria, institutions and professionals meeting with children and families, such as schools and health-care facilities, have a duty to report concerns about children to the Social Services/DHS, and the majority of child-protection cases are initiated based on such reports in both systems. The threshold to report is lower in Sweden and a wider group of professionals are required to report, as compared to Victoria. There is also a different threshold as to what the responsible child-protection authority is to investigate. In Sweden, all

applying the law, and do not "make law" as in common law systems. See Zweigert, K. & Kötz, H., *Introduction to Comparative Law*, 3rd edition, Clarendon, Oxford, 1998; and Carlson, L., *The Fundamentals of Swedish Law*, 2nd edition, Studentlitteratur, Lund, 2012. It should be noted that classifications like the above are simplified with many differences within the groups of legal systems, and also similarities between States belonging to different groups.

25   The description and analysis in this section is based largely on my previous study, Leviner, P., *Domstolens funktion i LVU-ärenden*, 2012. For more information and analysis of the two child-protection systems, see for Victoria Sheehan, R., "Deciding the Best Interest of the Child – Legal Responses to Child Protection Concerns," in Sheehan, R., Rhodes, H. & Stanely, N. (eds.), *Vulnerable Children and the Law – International Evidence for Improving Child Welfare, Child Protection and Children's Rights*, Jessika Kingsley Publishers, London, 2012, pp. 333–346; Mathews, B., "Protecting Children from Abuse and Neglect," in Monahan, G. & Young, L. (eds.), *Children and the Law in Australia*, LexisNexis, 2008; and Cummins, P., Scott, D. & Scales, B., *Protecting Victoria's Vulnerable Children Inquiry*, Melbourne, 2012. For Sweden, see for example Leviner, P., "Child Protection under Swedish Law – Legal Duality and Uncertainty," *European Journal of Social Work*, 2013, pp. 206–220, and Cocozza, M. & Hjort, S., "The Dark Side of the Universal Welfare State? Child Abuse and Protection in Sweden," in Gilbert, *et al.*, *supra* note 22.

reports in theory are to be investigated, whereas in Victoria a screening process leaves only the more serious cases to be investigated. Another difference is that in Sweden there is strong emphasis on voluntariness and support in the investigative phase, and the focus is on consensus and motivation rather than on finding facts about possible risk exposure. Victoria, on the other hand, the emphasis identifying risks and problems, screening and investigation. As can be noted, this is in line with the above-described different overall approaches – family-support versus child-protection approach.

There is also a difference in that the courts are involved at different stages of the process in the two systems. Swedish courts are not involved until the Social Services have decided to remove a child due to serious deficiencies in the home environment and when the removal cannot be reached with parental consent. Decisions to remove a child can be made either by the Social Welfare Board in emergency cases with a judicial review within one week, or by the court after an application by the same board (in both situations on the proposal of a Social Services official). In contrast, Victorian courts are involved earlier in that the issue does not necessarily need to be a removal sought by the DHS. Also, decisions to remove a child in an emergency situation need to be reviewed by the court within 24 hours (compared to one week in Sweden). Swedish courts can only decide whether to remove a child, but in Victoria, there are different protection orders, from interim and supervision orders where the child stays with the parents, to custody and guardianship orders where the court decides where the child is to be placed and for how long, *etc*. The Victorian court can also decide on different conditions connected to the different orders, for example parental drug testing. Comparing the legal prerequisites for intervention and the removal of children is very difficult, not least because of linguistic differences. But in both systems a removal requires that one or several environmental factors, for example assault, abuse and/or neglect in care, be ascertained; and it has to be shown that these factors represent a tangible risk to the child's health and development.

Another difference already touched upon is that courts dealing with-child protection in Sweden are general administrative courts also handling everything from planning and building, taxes and social benefits to child protection. In Victoria, as already mentioned a specialized court—the Children's Court— deals only with juvenile justice and child protection. Swedish judges working with child protection cases are not specialized and there are no specific requirements as to training and knowledge regarding risk factors and other psychological and medical issues involved. Involvement of expert witnesses is very rare in the Swedish system. In Victoria on the other hand, the judges working in the Children's Court are specialized, dealing only with child protection and juvenile justice. Connected to the court is a clinic with experts in relevant fields such as psychology, psychiatry and social work—the Children's Court Clinic. The clinic is responsible for assessments and recommendations to the court. The judges in the Children's Court are offered training regarding risk assessments, *etc.*, though this is not compulsory. It has been observed in both systems that the judges' knowledge in this regard is limited.[26]

The roles of the courts in the two systems are also very different in that the Swedish court more or less only reviews a case and decides whether a removal is lawful. It is a kind of all-or-nothing concept—is the child to be removed or not? There are no mediation mechanisms once a protection application has been made by the Social Welfare Board. There is only one court hearing in each case, which normally lasts at the most for three-to-four hours.[27] Apart from considering whether the prerequisites of the law are fulfilled (environmental factors + tangible risk), the Swedish courts also consider whether the placement and care proposed by the Social Services can be given on a voluntary basis. The application can be dismissed on the ground that parental consent, given as late as in the actual court hearing, is viable. If so, no decision will be made about out-of-home-placement by the court, and it is up to the parents and the Social Services to agree on whether and how placement and care are to be organized, *etc.* This "consent-construction" leads to a highly conflicted climate in the court proceedings. The Social Services have to convince the court that the parents do not understand the needs of their children, and even if they consent to support, that this consent should not be viewed as viable.

In Victoria, court orders as a main rule are also needed in cases where parents consent to the child being placed in out-of-home-care. Most cases go through mediation and alternative dispute resolution processes with the aim of working for a court order to which the parents can consent. The Children's Court in Victoria has a sort of case manager role, compared to the Swedish court where the focus is more or less only on reviewing and deciding whether the

---

26 This is noted for Victoria by Sheehan in Sheehan, *supra* note 25, p. 343 and for Sweden by, for example, Alexius, K., "RÅ 2009 ref. 64 – något om tvångsvårdsbedömningar rörande ett barn till en utvecklingsstörd förälder" (Yearbook of the Supreme Administrative Court, Case No. 64 – Reflections on assessments in a child-protection case with an intellectually disabled parent) *Nordisk socialrättslig tidskrift*, 2011, 25–51 and Svensson, G., "Högsta förvaltningsdomstolen och LVU" (The Supreme Administrative Court and the Care of Young Persons Act), *Nordisk socialrättslig tidskrift*, 2011, pp. 53–94.

27 Hollander, A., Jacobsson, M.. & Sjöström, S., "Defender, Spokesperson, Therapist – Representing the True Interest of the Client in Therapeutic Law," in 16 *International Journal of Social Welfare*, 2007, pp. 373–881.

proposal by the Social Welfare Board is to be accepted. In the Victorian system, there are many court hearings during the process combined with "out-of-court" mediation. If the parties cannot agree during this process, there will be a contested hearing that can be compared to the only court hearing normally held in the Swedish system. Contested hearings in the Victorian system can be described as highly conflicted and can last for many days and even weeks.

When it comes to legal representation, in Sweden both parents and children are always legally represented. Legal representatives (private lawyers) are appointed and paid by the State. The cost to parents is not means-based, which means that all parents will be represented. In Victoria, legal representation is means-based and it is not unusual that parents not entitled to legal aid will be unrepresented during the process. Children in the Victorian system are entitled to representation on a direct basis, *i.e.*, if they are mature enough to give instruction (normally from the age of seven years old). Only in exceptional circumstances are younger children represented and in those cases on a "best-interest basis," not on instructions. In contrast, the Swedish system has representation for all children. If a child is under 15, the representative will present both the child's view (if applicable) and their own view as to the best interest of the child, whereas if the child is over 15, the representation is based on instructions from the child, *i.e.*, the lawyer will not present best interest considerations in those cases.

v   Concluding Comparison – Different Yet Similar Problematic End Results and Limited Focus on Children

As can be seen from this brief overview, the systems differ in many ways. The courts are organized differently, a general court vs. a specialized court, and their role and function also differ. The courts in Sweden have more of a reviewing role (whether a decision/proposal to remove a child is legitimate and needed), whereas the court in Victoria has a "case-manager" function with a strong focus on finding consensual solutions. The information on which the courts in these different jurisdictions base their decisions also differs. Investigation by the Swedish Social Services in the majority of cases is the main source of facts for the court, apart from what parties bring forward orally at the single court hearing. This has been observed as a problem in the Swedish system in that the courts often base decisions on limited information that also uncritically points towards a removal.[28] In Victoria on the other hand, if a case

---

28   Friis, E., *Sociala utredningar om barn – en rättssociologisk studie av lagstiftningens krav, utredningars argumentationer och konsekvenser för den enskilde* (Social Investigations on

goes as far as a contested hearing (*i.e.*, if it has been impossible to find a solution) the parties may bring forward experts, witnesses and documentation supporting their claims. The court in many cases will also request an assessment from the Children's Court clinic. On the one hand, this can lead to a case being thoroughly documented and assessed, but on the other hand, all the information brought before the court might create an "information-overload-situation." The court in many cases tends to decide in line with the court clinic's suggestion.[29] In both systems, issues arise as to the power relations among judges/the law and experts/other fields of sciences, and the question of who is most suited to decide in child-protection cases, and with what knowledge base, especially if judges lack the knowledge to evaluate what the experts are saying.

In addition, both systems focus on consensus, motivation and mediation but as seen above, during different phases and in different ways. For Sweden, the risk has been identified of the Social Services "doing nothing" in the grey-zone between voluntariness and coercion (in other words, between reports and removals), referred to as the "consensus paradigm,"[30] in which conflicts, risk and problems are hidden. The focus is on motivating the parents rather than investigating risks and the needs of children. Services might be offered to families and will be provided if parents agree to them. This creates a situation where investigations by the Social Services are rather a motivational process with a limited focus on children and their needs and risky situations. Interventions and removals are done when this is really the only option, and the shift in focus can then in many cases come as a sudden surprise to parents and children possibly unaware of the seriousness of the investigation. In Victoria, there is also a (different) contradiction in the system. On the one hand, the process focuses on problems and risks but at the same time, there is a strong focus on finding voluntary agreements with parents in the very highly conflicted climate that child-protection cases many times encompass. The earlier court involvement (compared to Sweden) probably gives greater legal clarity, but at the same time it seems that the judicial focus might increase the conflict, even if ADR and mediation are invoked. In both systems, the focus on

---

Children – A Sociology of Law Study of Legislative Requirements, Argumentation and Consequences for the Individual), Dissertation, Lund University, Lund, 2003, and Edvardsson, B., *Kritisk utredningsmetodik – begrepp, principer och felkällor* (Critical Methodology of Investigation – Terms, Principles and Sources of Error), 2nd edition, Liber, Stockholm, 2003.

29   Cummins, *supra* note 25, pp. 103 and 448.

30   Leviner, P., *Rättsliga dilemma i socialtjänstens barnskyddsarbete* (Legal Dilemmas Inherent in the Child Protection Work of the Social Services), Dissertation, Jure förlag AB, Stockholm, 2011.

consensus can also be viewed as problematic from an overall perspective. Regardless of when in the process the focus is on motivation/mediation (in the investigative phase within the Social Services as in Sweden or during the court involvement as in Victoria), it can be questioned whether the agreements sought are truly voluntary, and maybe more importantly from a child's perspective, in line with what the child actually needs. Instead, it might be that solutions and agreements focus rather on points of possible agreement.

Another difference of relevance here is the different models of legal representation of children. Children in Sweden are, as described above, always represented (up to 15 years old on a best-interest-model and between 15 and 18 on instruction) whereas in Victoria children in most cases are represented only when over seven years old when they are assumed to be able to give instructions. From a child's perspective, it seems obvious that representation, regardless of age, is crucial; and this has been emphasized by both the UN Committee on the Rights of the Child and the European Council (see above). However, it is not evident which model is preferable, best-interest-model or instructions-model, and from what age either is ideal from a child's perspective. Another crucial question is when a legal representative is to be appointed. In the Swedish system, children (and parents) are represented only when the Social Services have already deemed it necessary to remove a child. This can be compared to Victoria where the courts as well as legal representatives in many cases are involved and appointed at an earlier stage during the investigative phase.

All in all, the systems differ in many ways and both face challenges, some different and some similar. One main challenge permeating both systems is their limited focus on children and on truly proactive solutions. This naturally leads to the question of how fair these processes really are, from a child's perspective. This question is returned to in the following concluding sections.

VI   Aspects to Consider for a Fair and Child-friendly Child-protection System

The right to a fair trial is clearly fundamental, important and relevant also for children. In addition, specific requirements need to be fulfilled for a child-protection system to be fair and just from a child's perspective. Although different in many ways, the systems in Sweden and Victoria have in common a limited focus on children and their needs, and limitations on how fair processes are from a child's perspective. These problems are probably shared with many other systems. Even if the systems in Victoria or Sweden are not viewed as specifically "un-child-friendly," there is a need for further development of the right to a fair trial so as to create more child-friendly and just child-protection systems in the two States (and probably most other States as well). When doing so, the recommendations and guidelines from the UN Committee of the Rights of the Child and European Council referred to above, can serve as a starting point.

However, in order to go from what has been described by John Tobin[31] as problematic, invisible, incidental, selective, superficial and/or rhetorical approaches to children's rights, reforms should be guided by a substantive-rights-based approach, which would have a fundamental effect on children's needs and interests in child protection proceedings.[32] In moving towards such an approach Tobin suggests that the following should be considered; (a) conceptualisation of the issues in terms of the rights of children; (b) procedures to be adopted for the determination of these issues; (c) the meaning to be given to the content of the rights in question; and (d) the substantive reasoning by which to resolve the issues and balance the competing interests. Such considerations are anything but easy, yet necessary in order to contribute to the resolution of complex issues involving children and their rights.

In analysing the child-protection systems in Sweden and Victoria, four aspects have emerged as being specifically important to consider in order to respond to the challenges facing the right to a fair trial from a child's perspective, and thereby moving towards a substantive-rights approach and systems that are fair and just from a child's perspective as well as child-friendly.

1   *Access to Justice*

Children observed by authorities to be at risk have the interest in and right to a judicial assessment and review of whether interventions and out-of-home-placements are in fact needed and in line with the child's right to protection. In addition, from a child's perspective, the right to access to justice demands also that decisions *not* to intervene (and decisions during the investigative phase) should be judicially assessed and reviewed. Children have a right to protection and interventions must be guaranteed when needed. The child might also have a general interest in judicial oversight as to the carrying out of measures, *i.e.,* what happens after out-of-home placement and when re-unification with parents is considered. Access to justice in this sense can be specifically important in systems with a strong focus on parental motivation rather than investigation of risk factors. It might be that striving for consensual solutions hides the needs of children, which in itself is an area of further analysis.

---

31   Professor at the Melbourne Law School, Victoria, Australia.

32   See Tobin, "Children's Rights in Australia – Confronting the Challenge," *supra* note 8.

2   *Children's Needs in the Problem-Solving/Mediation/Motivation*
       Process

While consensual solutions in many cases are most probably in the best interests of the child, guarantees are needed for a focus on children's needs and risk
factors in these problem-solving processes, regardless of whether these be conducted by the Social Services during the investigative phase as in the Swedish
system or in the court setting, as in Victoria. There need to be mechanisms to
ensure that the child's independent interests and rights are also on the negotiating agenda. This is closely connected to the questions of independent representatives for children, the entire journey through the child protection process,
i.e., from reports, or at least from the beginning of the investigative phase, to
out-of-home placements and also reunification.

3   *Independent (Legal) Representation*

Connected to the aspects pointed out in points 1 and 2 above is the need for
children to be independently represented, *i.e.*, not simply have their interest
and rights considered only by their parents and the child-protection authorities, who might have conflicting interests. Being represented is not only
important when authorities have decided to remove a child, but also prior to
such decisions, in the investigative phase. It is also critical for children with
out-of-home-placements and in situations where reunification is considered,
to be represented. Representation can, as described above with regard to both
systems, be very differently set up with different age limits and models, *i.e.*,
best-interest or instruction models. From a child's perspective, it is always
crucial to be represented, and the question is how to set up a model that guarantees children's participation and balances the need for representation by an
individual who is to consider the child's best interest without limiting the
child's own capacity for decision.[33]

4   *Requirements as to the Competence and Knowledge of Judges*
       Rendering Decisions

An issue that arises with respect to an analysis of the right to a fair trial from
the perspective of a child is the requirement that decisions from courts shall be
reasoned and materially correct. As seen above, both the UN Committee on the

---

33   Section D2 of the Guidelines from the European Council states that "[c]hildren should be
     considered as fully-fledged clients with their own rights and lawyers representing chil-
     dren should bring forward the opinion of the child." However, it might be that lawyers at
     times, irrespective of the child's age, should also bring forward a best-interest consider-
     ation from their viewpoint as representatives.

Rights of the Child and the European Council have emphasized the importance of interdisciplinary work and multidisciplinary approaches so as to obtain a comprehensive understanding of the child's situation. Interdisciplinary training for those professionals working with child protection is also stressed. Neither Victoria nor Sweden has compulsory training for judges, and the multidisciplinary approach is limited and problematic. In line with the right to a fair proceeding, it should arguably be required that judges need specific knowledge on risk and protective factors and other questions relevant in child-protection cases. This would be in line with the best interest of the child in that an assessment of what this actually *is* in an individual case needs to be based on knowledge and proven experience as well as on what the child expresses as his or her wish. The least that can be expected is that judges have knowledge enough to consider whether more information is needed in order to make a reasoned and correct decision, regardless of whether this is to intervene or not.

VII   A Call for Proactive and Holistic Considerations of the Right to a Fair Trial

To conclude, a child's right to protection entailing intervention, in the same manner as protection against unlawful interventions, ought to be embraced by the same mechanisms as to guarantee intervention by society when such is called for. Considerations of the kind described and suggested above would facilitate a move towards a substantive-rights-based approach needed in reforming child-protection systems around the world. However, a truly fair and child-friendly system also needs proactive mechanisms. Overall, the right to a fair trial has to be seen from a broader perspective. A process arguably is not fair if it illegitimately interferes in family life, *i.e.*, with interventions and separations from parents and families that could have been avoided in the first place. From a legal perspective it is natural and "easy" to focus on the role of the courts and the right to a fair trial from a somewhat limited viewpoint. However, it must be emphasized that the ultimate main focus should not be on judicial assessment and review at all – the law, lawyers and courts can only do so much.

The aspects pointed out in the section above, would in fact lead to increased judicial involvement and therefore a "juridification" of the system. No matter how important the questions discussed above is, it must be underscored that the focus should really be on how society can prevent children from being at risk and how authorities proactively can support parents so that children will not risk harm to begin with. This of course raises other questions, legal as well as political. But these questions need to be raised in the search for a more per-fect and proactive child-protection system, which should be the next point on the agenda for politicians, international organizations and researchers. It is time to focus on how to protect children and reform systems accordingly, so that they have the potential of being truly fair and child-friendly, even if this means that children's rights trump other rights and interests.

PART 4

Child-friendly Justice: Continental Perspectives

∴

SECTION 1

Europa

∴

Children and Justice

Nils Muižnieks and Françoise Kempf

Introduction

The UN Convention on the Rights of the Child (hereinafter CRC), to which all Member States of the Council of Europe are party, requires States to develop juvenile justice policies that ensure protection of the rights of children coming in contact with judicial authorities, whether as offenders, victims and witnesses of crime, in order to seek redress for rights infringements, or to safeguard their interests.

Juvenile justice should be built around the core CRC principle of the best interests of the child. This implies that reintegration and rehabilitation of juvenile offenders should prevail over repression. It also means that children, as full bearers of rights, must have access to justice to seek remedies when their rights are violated.

Moreover, a child-friendly justice system should, according to the relevant Council of Europe Guidelines, be "accessible, age appropriate, speedy, diligent, adapted to and focused on the needs and rights of the child."[1] It should take duly into account the evolving capacities of the child.

Building effective juvenile justice systems based on these key principles has been an important objective for the Member States of the Council of Europe, as epitomized by the large number of texts adopted around this topic over the last 40 years.[2] At global level, the United Nations have also produced important work and guidance, complementing the CRC provisions.[3] Juvenile justice is a high-ranking issue in both the Council of Europe and the European Union's strategies to advance children's rights.[4] My Office has also repeatedly taken

---

1 Guidelines of the Committee of Ministers of the Council of Europe on child friendly justice, adopted on 17 November 2010, see Section II.A.c.

2 See, *inter alia*, European Convention on the Exercise of Children's Rights (1996, STE No. 160). For a comprehensive list of texts adopted by the Council of Europe, see: http://www.coe .int/t/dghl/standardsetting/childjustice/Related_texts_and_documents_en.asp.

3 For a comprehensive list of UN documents on juvenile justice, see: http://www.unicef.org/ ceecis/protection_7704.html. See in particular UN Committee on the Rights of the Child, General Comment No. 10 on children's rights in juvenile justice, 2007.

4 Council of Europe Strategy for the Rights of the Child (2012–2015); Communication from the Commission to the European Parliament, the Council, the European Economic and Social Committee and the Committee of the Regions, An EU Agenda for the Rights of the Child, 15 February 2011.

positions on juvenile justice, including through the publication in 2009 of an Issue Paper on children and juvenile justice by my predecessor.[5]

It is therefore perplexing that, after almost four decades of producing far-reaching and in-depth guidance, so much remains to be done to achieve effective and human-rights compliant juvenile justice systems. In some countries, there is still resistance to the very idea of having specialized justice in order to address the needs of children in contact with the law.[6] Several mutually reinforcing factors converge to build such resistance: the belief that juvenile justice may result in undue State interference with the parents' rights to educate their children; lack of awareness that children are bearers of rights, on an equal footing with adults, and that adequate safeguards must subsequently be put in place by the authorities to protect these rights; and more generally, lack of understanding of the substance of the rights enshrined primarily in the CRC, but also in other international human rights instruments, including the European Convention on Human Rights and the European Social Charter.

In other countries where juvenile justice systems have been put in place, the same lack of consideration for children as fully-fledged rights holders has led to incomplete reforms, which have not brought about adequate protection of children's rights in practice. Finally, in a number of countries with long-established juvenile justice systems, public discourse around the need to tackle more severely an actual or perceived increase in juvenile misconduct has led to the resurgence of punitive approaches, by which children in conflict with the law tend to be considered as adults. Furthermore, the economic crisis and subsequent austerity measures have had a negative impact on the functioning of juvenile justice systems in Europe.

At the same time, a large number of children continue, throughout the continent, not to have effective access to justice to remedy violations of their rights.

This paper will first review some of the persisting gaps and challenges in the functioning of justice with regard to children in the Council of Europe Member States. It will highlight the negative consequences for children's rights of punitive approaches applied to juvenile offenders (Part I) and address some of the main obstacles preventing effective access by children to justice and redress for rights' violations (Part II). In Part III, some key principles and best practices that States should follow in order to remedy existing shortcomings will be recalled.

---

5   Council of Europe Commissioner for Human Rights, Children and juvenile justice: proposals for improvements, Issue Paper by Thomas Hammarberg, doc. CommDH(2009)1, 19 June 2009.

6   See Novosti, R., *Western-Style Juvenile Justice Not for Russians*, 8 February 2013.

1   Justice and Children in Conflict with the Law

Juvenile justice should aim at promoting the reintegration into society of children in conflict with the law and helping them to assume a constructive role in society. However, a number of Member States which have committed to these obligations as parties to international treaties such as the CRC, continue to favour a punitive approach over prevention, diversion (measures aimed at avoiding resorting to judicial proceedings to deal with children in conflict with the law) and reintegration.

1   *Treating Children as Adults and Criminalising*
         Youth-specific Conduct
Punitive policies have long been applied in a limited number of Member States, which continue to treat juvenile offenders as adults and to apply heavy sanctions, including detention, for a range of offences, even petty ones.[7] Moreover, in the last decade, a number of States have modified their legislation with a view to imposing on juvenile offenders sanctions similar to those imposed on adults, notably on those aged 16–18.[8] Other measures taken include the lowering of the age of criminal responsibility and the lifting of the maximum length of detention for children.

Other countries have opted for defining and sanctioning youth-specific conduct, often understood as "anti-social" conduct, as part of policies aimed at toughening the response to real or perceived youth delinquency. Such measures, which have often been taken in response to alleged pressure from the public, include measures such as "Anti-social behaviour orders," which can result in imprisonment.[9] Additionally, in a number of Member States, conduct

---

7   See, *inter alia,* UN Committee on the Rights of the Child, *Concluding Observations on the Russian Federation*, 23 November 2005, §84–86. See also, Open Democracy, *Russia and beyond, Children in Prison*, 28 May 2010.

8   See for instance UN Committee on the Rights of the Child, *Concluding Observations on France*, 11 June 2009, §94. See also *Concluding Observations on Denmark*, 7 April 2011, §65–66.

9   See *Memorandum* by Thomas Hammarberg, Commissioner for Human Rights of the Council of Europe, following his visits to the United Kingdom (5–8 February and 31 March–2 April 2008), CommDH(2008)27, 17 October 2008, Chapter II.d. See also *Letter* from the Council of Europe Commissioner for Human Rights to the UK Lord Chancellor and Secretary of State for Justice, Kenneth Clarke, about the system of juvenile justice in the United Kingdom, CommDH(2012)17, 15 March 2012. Similar provisions have been adopted in France (a 2003 provision criminalizes "gatherings in lobbies and stair cases of buildings hindering the circulation of persons," see CRC Committee, *Concluding Observations on France, ibid.*)

such as vagrancy, roaming in the streets or running away from home, which does not constitute criminal offences in the case of adults, has been criminalized when the author is a minor. These "status offences" discriminate against children and, even more so, against disadvantaged children, such as street children.

Such measures are at variance with the principles of the CRC, as repeatedly stressed by the UN Committee on the Rights of the Child (hereinafter: CRC Committee). At the same time, while their effectiveness in reducing offending and re-offending rates is not established, their stigmatising effect on youth is quite apparent.

Additional measures, such as the systematic taking of DNA samples, fingerprinting and practices consisting in providing the public with information on young offenders (known as "naming and shaming") have often been taken as part of repressive approaches. They have led to violations of the right of children to respect for their private life.[10]

2 *Detention*

Detention is rarely in the best interest of a child. Unfortunately, it is often the main response given to youth crime, including petty criminality, in the context of punitive policies. Despite the fact that a number of Member States have been developing alternatives to detention for children who must serve custodial sentences, detention remains common across the Council of Europe Member States. It involves detention in police, pre-trial and post-trial facilities. According to a 2013 EU study on the implementation of juvenile justice standards in the 28 Member States,[11] over 8 700 children were detained in custodial institutions in the 21 Members States in which data was available. The CRC has also highlighted constant, and in some countries, growing numbers of children

---

and in some Belgian municipalities (see CRC Committee, *Concluding Observations on Belgium*, 18 June 2010).

10   See *Memorandum* by Thomas Hammarberg following his visit to the United Kingdom, *ibid*. See also European Court of Human Rights, *S. and Marper v the United Kingdom* , Application. No. 30562/04 and 30566/04, Grand Chamber judgment of 4 December 2008, in which the Court reiterated the need for the protection of privacy of minors at criminal trials and called for particular attention to be paid to the protection of juveniles from any detriment that may result from the retention by the authorities of their private data following acquittals of a criminal offence.

11   European Commission, DG Justice, Summary of contextual overviews on children's involvement in criminal judicial proceedings in the 28 Member States of the European Union, 29 November 2013, pp. 3–4.

being detained, including in pre-trial and police custody.[12] In some countries in which juvenile justice has recently been established, prisons for children continue to exist even though detention was abolished and children are held in the same institution now labelled as educational centres.[13] In contrast, in a number of countries of the former Soviet Union, including Armenia, Azerbaijan, Georgia, Moldova and Ukraine, rates of detention of children have substantially decreased in the last decade, although they remain substantial.[14]

According to Article 37 of the CRC detention should be a measure of last resort and for the shortest possible length of time. However, not all Member States have yet enshrined this principle in their legislation.[15]

That detention has long-standing negative consequences for the development of children has been amply demonstrated. In addition, rather than preventing recidivism, it often forms the bedrock for reoffending, especially in the absence of reintegration policies.

Ill-treatment of children in detention continues to be a source of deep concern.[16] The CRC and the Committee for the Prevention of Torture (CPT) have also widely reported about these long-standing problems in their country monitoring work. Children held in police custody and pre-trial detention, sometimes for a long time, are especially vulnerable to all sorts of abuses, including intimidation, attempts to force confessions and psychological and physical ill-treatment, which can amount torture.[17] Other serious children's rights violations include solitary confinement, detention together with adults,

---

12 See European Council for Juvenile Justice, Measures of Deprivation of Liberty for Young Offenders: How to Enrich International Standards in Juvenile Justice and Promote Alternatives to Detention in Europe? by Ursula Kilkelly, November 2011, pp. 35–38.

13 *Report* by Nils Muižnieks, Council of Europe Commissioner for Human Rights, following his visit to Romania, from 31 March to 4 April 2014, doc. CommDH(2014)14, 8 July 2014.

14 See UNICEF, *Juvenile Justice in the CEE/CIS Region: Progress, Challenges, Obstacles and Opportunities*, 2013, p. 5.

15 European Commission, DG Justice, Summary of contextual overviews, *supra* note 11, p. 48.

16 See *inter alia Report* by Nils Muižnieks, Council of Europe Commissioner for Human Rights, following his visit to Albania, from 23 to 27 September 2013, §111, 114, 117, 144, 148, 162. See also European Council for Juvenile Justice, Measures of deprivation of liberty for young offenders, Kilkelly, *supra* note 12, pp. 39–43, and Joint Report of the Office of the High Commissioner for Human Rights, the UN Office on Drugs and Crime and the Special Representative of the Secretary General on Violence against Children on Prevention and Responses to Violence against Children within the Juvenile Justice System, 27 June 2012.

17 See, *inter alia*, UNICEF, *Torture and Ill-Treatment in the Context of Juvenile Justice: The Final Report of Research in Armenia, Azerbaijan, Georgia, Kazakhstan, Kyrgyzstan, Republic of Moldova, Tajikistan, and Ukraine*, 2013.

inhuman and degrading detention conditions and lack of adequate education and reintegration programmes.[18]

The European Court of Human Rights (hereinafter: the Court) has repeatedly found breaches of the Convention in cases concerning the detention of children. In a recent judgment (*Coselav v Turkey*),[19] the Court found Turkey in violation of Article 2 of the ECHR, protecting the right to life, in connection with the suicide of a teenager who was detained together with adults and deprived of any specific medical and other support.

Given the cost of detention,[20] the case for its extensive use in respect of children, including the building of more and larger facilities, is even more difficult to make in the current context of economic crisis. Moreover, in such a context it is doubtful whether sufficient means will be available to implement, in detention facilities, measures to prevent re-offending and promote successful reintegration.

3   *Prevention and Reintegration Policies*

A growing number of Member States have set up specialized juvenile justice systems. Nonetheless, many of the existing systems still lack two key features that should be part of any human-rights compliant juvenile justice policy, namely effective policies to prevent offending and reoffending[21] and measures to support reintegration into society. This is not only the consequence of a lack of means, but also of understanding of the goals of juvenile justice.[22]

Austerity measures have had a particularly detrimental impact on prevention and reintegration programmes.[23] In countries like Spain, Portugal and Greece which have implemented stringent austerity policies, families with children have been particularly affected by cuts in social policies and programmes, including social benefits. The proportion of children at risk of poverty has risen substantially in some countries.[24]

---

18   CPT *Standards*, CPT/Inf/E(2002) rev. 2013, pp. 83–89.

19   ECtHR, *Coselav v Turkey*, Application No. 1413/07, judgment of 9 October 2012.

20   See European Council for Juvenile Justice, Save money, protect society and realize youth potential, improving youth justice systems during a time of economic crisis, by Marianne Moore, 2012, pp. 9, 63.

21   Recommendation CM/Rec(2008)11 of the Committee of Ministers to Member States on the European Rules for Juvenile Offenders Subject to Sanctions or Measures, 5 November 2008.

22   See UNICEF, Juvenile justice in the CEE/CIS region, 2013, *supra* note 14, pp. 7, 10.

23   *Ibid.*

24   See *Report* by Nils Muižnieks, Council of Europe Commissioner for Human Rights, following his visit to Spain from 3 to 7 June 2013, doc CommDH(2013)18, 9 October 2013. See also

While we may have not yet seen the full extent of the impact of austerity measures on children, massive cuts in educational budgets are likely to have seriously negative consequences, especially for children from a disadvantaged social background, children with disabilities and children belonging to ethnic minorities. Diminishing support provided to these children in mainstream education could increase drop-out rates and the vulnerability of children who have not completed their studies and are not likely to find a job.[25]

Entire areas of social work, pertaining to public services, such as child protection services, or programmes implemented by NGO s, can hardly be maintained in the face of budgetary cuts. Activities which are crucial for juvenile crime prevention, such as youth work, community policing, mental health services for youth and programmes to combat substance abuse, have been stopped. Budgetary restrictions have also reduced the services offered in institutions in which children are detained.[26]

Budgetary measures have furthermore resulted in cuts in staff employed in juvenile justice, leading to excessive caseloads with increasingly limited means available. In some countries, specialized juvenile courts or sections are not in place throughout the territory.[27] Inter-agency work, which is key to providing individualized support to young offenders from the moment of offending until reintegration, is threatened by staff reductions, including among child justice professionals, and the closing down of a number of state agencies. The same applies to the effective availability of alternatives to detention and reintegration programmes.

II   Access of Children to Justice

For children to enjoy their rights in practice, it is crucial that effective remedies are available in case these rights are violated. Just like adults, they should be able to seek and obtain redress for human rights violations.[28] However, in practice, substantial gaps continue to prevent many children from accessing justice

---

Report by Nils Muižnieks, Council of Europe Commissioner for Human Rights, following his visit to Portugal from 7 to 9 May 2012, doc. CommDH(2012)22, 10 July 2012.

25   *Ibid.*

26   See, *inter alia*, La Vanguardia, JSM critica los « peligrosos recortes » en los centros de menores, 11 August 2012.

27   See European Commission, DG Justice, Summary of contextual overviews, *supra* note 11, pp. 7–8.

28   See in particular UN Human Rights Council, *Resolution* on access to justice for children, adopted on 25 March 2014.

in Europe. They often lack awareness of existing remedies and face substantial obstacles when trying to access such remedies Moreover, the outcomes of justice are not always fair to children as a result of their best interests not being adequately considered.

1 *Awareness about Children's Rights and Existing Remedies*

Efforts have been made by a number of Member States to disseminate knowledge about children's rights, notably as part of the implementation of the CRC, which requires States Parties to raise awareness about the rights protected therein. However, information about rights, and even more so about existing remedies at national level, does not reach all children and their parents/educators.

In fact, the children who are most exposed to risks of human rights violations tend to be precisely those who are least likely to have access to information about remedies for rights violations: street children, victims of human trafficking, unaccompanied migrant children, children living in slums, those placed in institutions, children with disabilities, children belonging to disadvantaged minority groups such as the Roma, and others. During visits to Roma settlements in several countries of the Western Balkans, for instance, I found that many children and their parents were not aware of the consequences of having no birth certificate and identity documents or were unaware about proceedings to undertake in order to obtain the required documents.[29] Children victims of domestic violence may also often not be aware that such violence is a violation of their rights.

Furthermore, in a number of Member States, children and their families, especially those coming from disadvantaged and discriminated groups, lack trust in the police and the courts, due to a lack of independence of the judiciary, widespread corruption and other related problems affecting the administration of justice.[30] They do not seek redress because they do not expect that state institutions will provide it.

Lastly, new challenges have appeared in connection with development of the Internet, on which children are increasingly present and, therefore, exposed to human rights violations, such as violations of their right to privacy. Internet is also used by predators to contact children under a false identity with a view to abusing them, including sexually, and even to recruit them for

---

29   See for instance Commissioner for Human Rights, *Report* by Nils Muižnieks, following his visit to "the former Yugoslav Republic of Macedonia," from 26 to 29 November 2012, doc. CommDH(2013)4, 9 April 2013.

30   See for instance Commissioner for Human Rights, Report following his visit to Albania, 2013, *supra* note 16.

trafficking purposes. Adequate remedies to such rights violations are not always in place or, if available, known to children and their educators.[31]

2   Access to Effective Remedies

The right of children to be heard, as protected under Article 12 of the CRC, and the possibility for them to make legal representations in judicial proceedings, are not guaranteed in all Council of Europe Member States. In a number of States, children do either not have a legal standing or the possibility to initiate a complaint is limited to children beyond a certain age. While such limitations aim at protecting children, they can also prevent redress for rights violations.

A number of additional barriers affect the access of certain categories of children to justice, as my country work has also shown. Unaccompanied minor migrants, for example, are sometimes deprived of access to judicial and non-judicial remedies and even sometimes barred from accessing asylum procedures, due to deficiencies in the system of appointment of guardians and/or legal representatives.[32] The situation can be aggravated by the lack of access to legal aid and interpretation services.

Children with intellectual and psycho-social disabilities, particularly those living in institutions, also frequently face obstacles in accessing justice, due to a lack of adequate information and advice, ineffective guardianship systems and, in general, restrictive legal capacity legislation. In September 2013, I intervened as a third party before the Court in a case concerning the treatment of a young man of Roma origin, suffering from a severe mental disability and HIV positive, who died in a psychiatric institution.[33] He was an orphan and did not have any legal representative. Although the applicant was 18 at the time of his death, this case raises important questions for the access to justice of children detained in psychiatric institutions. The fact that they are often abandoned by their family and relatives and the absence of effective guardianship systems often deprives them of access to any remedy, even though they are highly vulnerable to a wide range of abuses, including violations of their right to life and their right not to be subjected to inhuman and degrading treatment.

---

31   See Commissioner for Human Rights, Human Rights Comment on: *Protecting Children's Rights in the Digital World: An Ever-Growing Challenge*, 29 April 2014.

32   See *Report* by Nils Muižnieks, Council of Europe Commissioner for Human Rights, following his visit to Greece, from 28 January to 1 February 2013, doc. CommDH(2013)6, 16 April 2013, §147–148.

33   European Court of Human Rights, *Center of Legal Ressources on behalf of Valentin Câmpeanu v Romania*, Application No. 47848/08, judgment of 14 July 2014.

Should national remedies be ineffective, children can seek redress before international bodies. Several cases have been brought to the European Court of Human Rights by children through their representatives.[34] The Court has even considered that children could be represented by persons who were not able to do so under domestic law, in order to ensure effective access to the Court.[35]

Similarly, the entry into force on 14 April 2014 of the third Protocol to the CRC on individual communications is an important step forward in promoting access for children to justice at international level.

Finally, non-judicial remedies, such as children's ombudsmen and other national human rights institutions, constitute valuable alternatives to judicial proceedings. They often prove more accessible than courts and can provide adequate responses to certain categories of rights violations, notably of social and economic rights. Several children's ombudsmen have set up specific help lines through which children can directly report abuses and ask for information and advice. It is therefore worrying that some of these institutions, including specialized children's ombudsmen, have had their budgets tightened while at the same time they have witnessed a steep increase of complaints connected with the impact of austerity measures. Some institutions have even been closed down.[36]

3   Child-friendly Proceedings

Even where specialized juvenile justice systems exist, justice systems in Europe are not yet as child-friendly as they should be and often do not adequately reflect the principles contained in the Council of Europe Guidelines on child-friendly justice.

Existing problems have been documented at length.[37] Even though they differ from country to country, the most common problems include: the lack of legal aid and legal advice; the lack of specialization and training of staff, including judges, prosecutors, lawyers and the police; and increasingly, the lack of

---

34   Including in the landmark decision on corporal punishment *A. v the United Kingdom* Application No. 100/1997/884/1096, judgment of 23 September 1998.

35   See for instance *Scozzari and Giunta v Italy*, Application No. 39221/98 and 41963/98, judgment of 13 July 2000; see also Berro-Lefèvre, I., *Improving Children's Access to the European Court of Human Rights in International Justice for Children*, Council of Europe, 2008.

36   The office of the Ombudsman for children (*Defensor del menor*) of the Madrid autonomous community was closed down in 2012.

37   See, *inter alia*, European Commission, DG Justice, Summary of contextual overviews, *supra* note 11; see also UNICEF, Child Rights in Central and Eastern Europe and Central Asia, *Issue No. 1/2014 of Insights*: Promoting equitable access to justice for all children.

means and time available to justice and police professionals to deal adequately with children, due to budgetary restrictions.

Lengthy judicial proceedings are another issue of particular concern when affecting children as undue delays can have irreversible effects on them. Effective and prompt proceedings are important in criminal justice, but also in administrative and civil matters, including in decisions regarding child custody, adoptions and civil/birth registration. For instance, cumbersome and lengthy administrative procedures to obtain birth registration certificates have in some Member States left a number of children at risk of being stateless and deprived of important rights, such as the right to health care or education.

While efforts have been made in some countries to ensure better respect for the rights of children to be heard and to have their views adequately considered, these rights remain non-existent in some countries and are inadequately applied in others. Children are in fact all too often not considered as full bearers of rights. For instance, as part of my country work I have noticed that in asylum proceedings children are not always considered independently from their parents, even though they can face persecution and risks of persecution of a child-specific nature and, therefore, can claim asylum under the 1951 Convention relating to the Status of Refugees on the grounds of belonging to a particular social group of children.[38]

As mentioned above, human-rights compliant access to justice for children encompasses fair outcomes and decisions that have the best interests of the child treated as a primary consideration. However, outcomes and decisions that are at variance with these principles are still all too common in Europe. One example is the widespread practice in parts of Eastern Europe of placing children in institutions because of abuse or neglect in their families or because they have been abandoned, instead of providing them with foster care or other, more children rights-compliant alternatives.[39] It is also not in the best interests of a child to be taken away from his/her family on the grounds of poor

---

38   *Report* by Nils Muižnieks, Council of Europe Commissioner for Human Rights, following
      his visit to Denmark, from 19 to 21 November 2013, CommDH(2014)4, 24 March 2014,
      §40–42. See also UN High Commissioner for Refugees, *Guidelines on International
      Protection: Child Asylum Claims under Articles 1(A)2 and 1(F) of the 1951 Convention and/or
      1967 Protocol Relating to the Status of Refugees*, 22 December 2009.

39   See UNICEF, Regional Office for Central and Eastern Europe and the Commonwealth of
      Independent States (CEE/CIS), *At Home or in a Home? Formal Care and Adoption of
      Children in Eastern Europe and Central Asia*, September 2010, pp. 4–5. See also the CRC
      Committee, *Concluding Observations on the Russian Federation*, *supra* note 7, §38–40; and
      Recommendation (2005)5 of the Council of Europe Committee of Ministers to Member
      States on the rights of children living in residential institutions. See also Commissioner

socio-economic conditions. Such interferences have been found by the Court to be at variance with the right to respect for private and family life protected in Article 8 of the ECHR.[40] Referrals of children from such families to child protection services, and separation from their families, when the latter should have been provided with health and social support, have also been increasingly reported in Western European countries.[41]

III Towards a Better Protection of Children's Rights

1 Economic Crisis as an Opportunity for Reform

There is a tendency to present human rights compliant systems of juvenile justice as costly and, at the same time, to argue that a heavy-handed approach regarding young people is the most effective way of making societies safer. Against this background, working towards better respect for children's rights in the field of justice can be perceived as superfluous, even more so in the current context of economic crisis, in which resources are limited and the risk of anti-social behaviour might increase.

However, 40 years of international scrutiny, which have led to the elaboration of a comprehensive and detailed set of standards, provide ample evidence to challenge these assumptions. In particular, the most recent of these assumptions, whereby budgetary restrictions due to the economic crisis make child-friendly justice unpractical, should be challenged.

While it is true that juvenile justice has a cost because it requires time, adaptations and the involvement of more actors than in the case of justice for adults, it is also clear that some of the current approaches to youth delinquency have a high monetary cost for the State, too. Of all the possible responses to youth crime, detention is probably the most expensive.

Effectiveness, in turn, can be measured only against clear objectives. The two objectives of juvenile justice most commonly referred to include making societies safer by preventing youth crime and ensuring full respect for

---

for Human Rights, *Report* by Thomas Hammarberg following his visit to Slovakia, from 26 to 27 September 2011, doc. CommDH(2011)42, 20 December 2011, §80–84.

40   In *R.M.S. v Spain*, the Court stated that a situation of material deprivation in itself cannot be a sufficient ground for ordering the separation of a child from his/her natural family and that it constitutes a breach of Article 8. Application No. 28775/12, judgment of 18 June 2013. See also *Havelka and Others v the Czech Republic*, Application No. 23499/06, judgment of 21 June 2007; *Wallová and Walla v the Czech Republic*, Application No. 23848/04, judgment of 26 October 2006.

41   Report of the Commissioner for Human Rights on Spain, *supra* note 24, §23.

children's rights, in order to maximize possibilities for children to develop their full potential. Whether we consider one or the other of these objectives, there can be little doubt that a human-rights compliant juvenile justice system is more conducive to the attainment of these aims. Heavy-handed and cuts-driven responses to juvenile justice needs do not appear to make society safer or more respectful of rights and can, on the contrary, have long-term negative consequences for society. Detention, coupled with the absence of prevention and reintegration strategies, triggers offending and re-offending. The lack of measures to ensure access of all children to justice leads to the alienation from society of a considerable number of them. The weakening of alternative remedies, such as Ombudsmen, results in deprivation of or delayed justice. The adoption of patchy measures relating to juvenile justice, without a comprehensive approach and outside of the context of major reforms of the judiciary, often results in inconsistent policies.

Since the beginning of my mandate I have worked towards ensuring a human rights compliant response to the economic crisis. Governments often tend to argue that the economic crisis is a major factor preventing action in favour of human rights protection. However, the very same policies that are left unaddressed because of lack of resources to change them have proven to be costly and, in many cases, also ineffective. Ultimately, governments may be spending huge amounts of money to preserve systems that violate human rights without achieving tangible long-term results.

Against this background, the economic crisis could be used as a catalyst to review policies in place with a view to making them both more cost-effective and more respectful of human rights. Juvenile justice might be one of these areas.[42] Decision-makers should also bear in mind that children and youth are among the groups most hit by the economic crisis and austerity measures, with potentially long-term damaging consequences for European societies.

2   *The Way Forward*

The authorities of the Member States should firmly anchor their juvenile justice policies on evidence-based approaches. Objective evaluation of past policies, both in terms of enjoyment of rights and cost-effectiveness is crucial. Measures that have not brought about the expected results, including as regards crime prevention, should be abandoned. UNICEF, the European Commission and the Fundamental Rights Agency[43] among others have under-

---

42   See European Council for Juvenile Justice, *supra* note 20.

43   See European Commission, DG Justice, Summary of contextual overviews, *supra* note 11. The Fundamental Rights Agency is currently preparing a qualitative study on the

taken valuable data collection and analysis. Nonetheless, States should also take their responsibilities and carry out regular monitoring of policies and projects regarding juvenile justice.

Politicians should refrain from using "punitive rhetoric" regarding youth criminality and from enacting hasty provisions to quickly pander to public demands for security. They should rather co-operate with all those concerned to define long-term solutions that work.

Effective and human rights-compliant policies to improve the relation between children and justice have been identified throughout the Council of Europe Member States.[44] Coupled with the international standards and guidance, they can be a source of inspiration for States who want to establish or improve juvenile justice.

States should conceive or improve their juvenile justice systems as part of overall processes of reform of the judiciary, as has recently been done in a number of countries such as Armenia, Albania, Bosnia and Herzegovina or Montenegro. Reforms should span across all relevant areas from social work, education and prevention policies to courts and the police. Their primary objective should be to translate the state obligation to treat the best interests of the child as primary consideration into practical arrangements within the justice system.

Prevention and reintegration policies, involving a range of relevant actors and covering areas such as social policy, health, education and police work, should form an essential part of juvenile justice policies. Moreover, diversion should be the core element of juvenile justice systems. Diversion, as prescribed by Article 40(3) of the CRC, involves measures aimed at avoiding resorting to judicial proceedings to deal with children alleged to, accused of or having infringed the law. A number of Member States have diversion strategies in place.[45] They involve, among other options, diversion to health or social services, diversion administered by probation services or implemented by the police and placement in foster care. Diversion can apply both to first-time and

---

participation of children in criminal and civil judicial proceedings in 10 Member States of the European Union.

44   See, *inter alia*, UNICEF, *Good Practices and Promising Initiatives in Juvenile Justice in the CEE/CIS Region*, 2010. See also *Report* by Thomas Hammarberg, Commissioner for Human Rights of the Council of Europe, following his visit to Ireland from 1 to 2 June 2011, doc. CommDH(2011)27, 15 September 2011, §35–36 and Issue Paper on Juvenile Justice, *supra* note 5.

45   For instance the Children's Hearings system set up in Scotland, see: http://www .scotland.gov.uk/Topics/People/Young-People/protecting/childrens-hearings. See also Commissioner for Human Rights, *Report* by Thomas Hammarberg following his visit to Ireland, *ibid.*, §35.

repeat offenders. While diversion is an important tool to promote reoffending and is, therefore, a critical aspect of effective prevention and reintegration policies, it requires due respect for a number of legal safeguards.[46]

When diversion from criminal justice is not possible, detention should be the last resort option, and other non-custodial alternatives should be favoured, such as probation, foster care, educational measures, guidance and supervision orders, community sentences and restorative justice.

Furthermore, the authorities should empower national human rights structures by strengthening their effectiveness and independence as they constitute an important and accessible remedy for violations of children's rights, including for the most vulnerable and marginalized children who would otherwise not approach the justice system.[47] They can provide regular monitoring and early-warning on the human rights situation of children. Some of these institutions indeed have a mandate as a National Preventive Mechanism under the Optional Protocol to the Convention for the Prevention of Torture and can monitor the situation in institutions in which children are deprived of their liberty. In several countries, ombudsmen have also proactively alerted the authorities about the particular impact of austerity measures on the rights of children.[48]

Conclusion

A well-functioning juvenile justice system, compliant with international standards, should contribute to making societies safer for all, by preventing juveniles from offending and re-offending. It should also contribute to making societies safer for children, by ensuring that violations of their rights are adequately remedied.

Numerous international texts dealing with juvenile justice have been issued over the last four decades. However, implementation remains uneven. Firstly, there appears to be a lack of awareness of children's rights and of the relevant standards. Additionally, the two main goals of juvenile justice—prevention and reintegration—remain all too often ignored or neglected by policy-makers, who tend to favour punitive approaches, or still miss the key point that children have a right to be treated differently from adults.

---

46   See Commissioner for Human Rights, Issue Paper, *supra* note 5, pp. 16–19.

47   See Commissioner for Human Rights, Issue paper on safeguarding human rights in times of economic crisis, Strasbourg, November 2013, pp. 51–56.

48   *Report* by Nils Muižnieks, Council of Europe Commissioner for Human Rights, following his visit to Spain, *supra* note 24.

There is a long way to go until all children have effective access to justice and to proceedings that are respectful of their best interests and result in fair outcomes. Despite undeniable progress, children continue all too often not to be considered as full bearers of rights. The need to reduce public expenses has led to important restrictions of the capacity of the judiciary to deal in an appropriate and human rights-compliant manner with children. Nonetheless, austerity budgets could also be considered as an incentive to improve the efficiency of juvenile justice systems along the lines drawn by international human rights bodies over the last decades.

European Court of Human Rights

Elisabet Fura

Introduction

This is not a scientific report, rather I have chosen a case that I find particularly interesting, bearing in mind the topic of this conference namely how to realize child-friendly justice. I offer no exhaustive list of the case law related to the rights of the child of the European Court of Human Rights (hereafter the Court) where I had the privilege to serve during nine years from 2003 to 2012.

The judgment I have chosen to illustrate how child-friendly justice might be realized is a case in which I was the judge rapporteur. Here I had the possibility to influence the outcome in a more direct way than what is normally the case. However, the bench was made up of seven judges and in all the aspects I am concentrating on here, the Court was unanimous. The case is also pertinent since it deals with immigration issues and asylum seekers, an area that is becoming more and more relevant in Europe and elsewhere.

The choices made in this paper are my own and any views expressed are also personal, not necessarily reflecting the views of the Court or of my current position as Chief Parliamentary Ombudsman in Sweden.

Some Basic Facts about the European Court of Human Rights

The role of the Court is a subsidiary one, meaning that it is the obligation of the High Contracting Parties to the European Convention for the Protection of Human Rights and Fundamental Freedoms (hereafter the Convention) to apply the rights and freedoms as interpreted by the Court at home. This is expressed in the first article of the Convention, which reads: "The High Contracting Parties shall secure to everyone within their jurisdiction the rights and freedoms defined in Section 1 of this Convention."

This is a basic principle underpinning the entire case law of the Court. The principle of subsidiarity has been expressed repeatedly in case law and recently it was also added to the preamble of the Convention through the Additional Protocol no 15.

The most important precondition for anyone wishing the Court to consider a complaint is to exhaust all effective domestic remedies. Still the Court struggles with a significant backlog of some 100,000 cases which makes it even more important that rights are respected domestically; the Court's role has never been to act as an appeal court. Note also that the Court cannot deal with *substance* or, differently put, change the outcome of a judgment rendered by a national court – but rather with the *form*. The question the judges ask in every case is whether the responding State Party, in the particular case put to the Court, respected the rights guaranteed by the Convention.

The Court is composed of 47 judges, one elected in respect of each contracting party, by the parliamentary assembly of the Council of Europe in their personal capacity, for a non-renewable period of nine years. They do not represent the party that nominated them but they sit in all cases where this State is the responding party. To have the national judge as a part of the composition is intended to secure the knowledge of the domestic law and other issues related to that State.

The Court most frequently decides cases on the merits in a chamber of seven, including the national judge. One judge, the judge rapporteur, has the specific task to prepare the case and propose solutions as to procedure in general and the drafting of the judgment in particular. The case discussed here is that of *Popov v France* (judgment 19 January 2012, only in French) a landmark case concerning children's rights.[1]

Factual Background

The applicants were Vladimir and Yekaterina Popov, Kasakhstani nationals, accompanied by their two children who were born in France in 2004 and 2007 respectively. Fleeing recurrent persecution in their country because of their Russian origin and Orthodox faith, Mrs. Popov arrived in France on 15 December 2002, with a two-week visa. Her husband joined her in France on 19 June 2003.

The applicants' application for asylum was rejected, as were their applications for residence permits. On 27 August 2007 the applicants and their children, then aged five months and three years, were arrested in their home and taken into police custody. Their administrative detention in a hotel in Angers was ordered the same day. The following day they were transferred to Charles-de-Gaulle Airport to be flown back to Kazakhstan. The flight was cancelled however, and they never boarded the plane. The applicants and their children were then taken to the Rouen-Oissel administrative detention centre, which was authorized to accommodate families. On 29 August 2007, a judge decided a two-week extension to their detention. The applicants were taken back to

---

1 *Affaire POPOV c. France*, requêtes 39472/07 et 39474/07 arrêt 19 janvier 2012.

Charles-de-Gaulle Airport on 11 September 2007, but this second attempt to deport them also failed. Noting that that failure was not the applicants' fault, the judge ordered their release.

On 16 July 2009, the refugee status the applicants had applied for prior to their arrest was granted, on the grounds that the enquiries the Ardennes Prefecture had made to the authorities in Kazakhstan, disregarding the confidentiality of asylum applications, had made it dangerous for them to return there.

Relying on Articles 3 (prohibition of inhuman or degrading treatment), 5 (right to liberty and security) and 8 (right to respect for private and family life) of the Convention, the applicants complained about their two-week administrative detention at the Rouen-Oissel centre pending their removal to Kazakhstan.

The application was lodged with the Court on 10 September 2007 and the Court notified the government of France of the complaints under Articles 3 and 8 on 19 October 2009 and of the Article 5 complaint on 12 May 2011.

Decision of the Court

Article 3
The Court noted that arrangements at detention centres in France authorized to accommodate families were left to the discretion of the head of the establishment, including the existence of amenities suitable for young children. While families were separated from other detainees at the Rouen-Oissel centre, the only beds available were iron-frame beds for adults, which were dangerous for children. Nor were there any play areas or activities for children, and the automatic doors to the rooms were dangerous for them. The Commissioner for Human Rights and the European Committee for the Prevention of Torture known as the CPT also pointed out that the promiscuity, stress, insecurity and hostile atmosphere in these centres were bad for young children, in contradiction with international child protection principles according to which the authorities must do everything in their power to avoid detaining children for lengthy periods. Two weeks' detention, while not in itself excessive, could seem like a very long time for children living in an environment ill-suited to their age. The conditions in which the applicants' children—a three-year-old girl and a baby—were obliged to live with their parents in a situation of particular vulnerability heightened by their detention were bound to cause them distress and have serious psychological repercussions.

The Court found that the authorities had not measured the inevitably harmful effects on the children of being held in a detention centre in conditions that exceeded the minimum level of severity required by Article 3. That provision stipulates: "No one shall be subjected to torture or to inhuman or degrading treatment or punishment."

The Court held that there had been no violation of Article 3 in respect of the parents, who were the actual applicants, but I will not elaborate here on the reasons for this.

Article 5.1.f and Article 5.4

The Court considered that although the children had been placed with their parents in a wing reserved for families, their particular situation had not been taken into account by the authorities, who had not even sought to establish whether any alternative solution could be envisaged. The court accordingly found a violation of Article 5.1.f in respect of the children. That provision reads as follows:

> 1. Everyone has the right to liberty and security of person. No one shall be deprived of his liberty save in the following cases and in accordance with a procedure prescribed by law; ...
> ... (f) the lawful arrest or detention of a person to prevent his effecting an unauthorized entry into the country or of a person against whom action is being taken with a view to deportation or extradition.

While the parents had had the possibility to have the lawfulness of their detention examined by the courts, the Court noted that children accompanying parents found themselves in a legal void, unable to avail themselves of such a remedy. No removal or detention order had been issued against the applicants' children that they might have challenged. The Court accordingly also found a violation of Article 5.4 in respect of the children. That provision reads as follows:

> 4. Everyone who is deprived of his liberty by arrest or detention shall be entitled to take proceedings by which the lawfulness of his detention shall be decided speedily by a court and his release ordered if the detention is not lawful.

Article 8

The interference with the applicants' family life because of their two-week detention at the centre had been in accordance with the French Code governing the entry and residence of foreigners and the right of asylum. The interference pursued the legitimate aim of combating illegal immigration and preventing crime.

Referring to the broad consensus, particularly in international law, that the children's interests were paramount in all decisions concerning them, the Court noted that France was one of the only three European countries that had systematically placed accompanied minors in detention. The Court also noted that the Office of the High Commissioners for Refugees, the French National Security Ethics Commission (CNDS) and the Defender of Children had all spoken out in favour of alternatives to detention. As there had been no particular risk of the applicants' absconding, their detention had not been justified by any pressing social need, especially considering that their placement in a hotel on 27 August 2007 had posed no problem. Yet the authorities did not appear to have sought any solution other than detention, or to have done everything in their power to have the removal order enforced as promptly as possible.

By way of comparison, in the *Muskhadzhiyeva and Others v Belgium* case,[2] the Court had rejected a complaint similar to the applicants'. However, considering the above factors and the recent case-law developments concerning "the child's best interest" in the context of the detention of child migrants (see *Rahimi v Greece*[3]) the Court considered that the child's best interests called not only for families to be kept together but also for the detention of families with young children to be limited. In the applicants' circumstances, two weeks' detention in a closed facility was disproportionate to the aim pursued. The Court accordingly held that there had been a violation of Article 8.

Why This is a Landmark Case

In this case the Court took children's rights seriously for the first time even though the children were neither applicants nor the objects of the detention order, thus lacking a legal remedy to challenge the order. The description of the conditions in the detention facility and how they influenced the children, is heart-breaking. The little girl developed eating disorders along with other stress-related symptoms. According to other reports quoted in the judgment it is not unusual that children "accompanying" their parents in detention not only suffer mentally and physically but also that their image of their parents, including their authority, is damaged.

The importance civil society attached to the case is reflected in the fact that the Court received third-party interventions from the Commissioner for Human Rights as well as from the Committee on the Prevention of Torture, the CPT.

---

2   Application No. 41442/07, judgment of 19 January 2010.
3   Application No. 8687/08, judgment of 5 April 2011.

The judgment is also interesting from an academic point of view: the Court did not confine its examination to relevant national laws and their compatibility with the requirements of the Convention. It applied other relevant international legal documents (UN Convention of the Rights of the Child[4]), EU-law[5] and even "soft law."[6] This is by no means a new feature but it becomes more and more frequent that the Court relies on other sources and "soft law" in addition to the Convention, a practice appreciated by some scholars while criticized by others.The judgment also includes the application of international law (see paragraph 140 of the judgment).

But in view of the focus of this Conference, perhaps the most important aspect of the judgment is that it furthers the protection of children's rights, taking quite a big step forward, distinguishing the case from a fairly recent one against Belgium[7] (see paragraph 147 of the judgment).

The authorities alleged that they were faced with a dilemma; the interest of the child demanded that the children were not separated from their parents, who had to be detained. So the children were detained, too. My understanding is that the dilemma is a false one; the best interest of the child would oblige the authorities to look for alternative solutions like keeping the family confined at their residence or in a hotel.

The Court highlighted that while the French legislation excluded explicitly that a minor is placed in detention a report quoted in the judgment showed that in 2009 as many as 318 children "accompanying their parents" were detained.

The language of the Court is strong, see for example paragraph 124 where the Court holds that there is absolutely no legal basis for keeping the children in detention and that the children lack a legal remedy "les enfants...tombent dans un vide juridique" – "the children fall into a juridical void."

Although the problem of what is termed "accompanying children in detention" had been identified domestically by NGOs, experts and the national courts of lower instance, the practice continued until the Court ruled against France. Sometimes a push from outside is needed to change bad habits!

---

4 Para. 52 of the judgment.
5 Paras. 59–62 of the judgment.
6 For instance the report of Amnesty International dated 18 June 2005 (eur 45/015/2005) enti-tled "United Kingdom – Seeking asylum is not a crime: detention of people who have sought asylum."
7 *Supra* note 2.

SECTION 2

Africa

∵

What's in a Name? "Child-friendly" Justice in Africa

Julia Sloth-Nielsen

Introduction

This chapter seeks to pave the way for the discussion of the notion of "child friendly justice" in African context. First, it describes the various manifestations of children's contact with justice systems on the continent. Second, it will examine some strengths, weaknesses, gaps and potentials that exist. In this section, the policy orientation understood as Justice for Children (or J4C) will be described. The third section provides the current international legal and policy framework which is uniquely applicable to African States, either via regional treaties, soft law or guidelines. The paper will then provide an assessment of the usefulness of the concept of "systems strengthening" in developing and maintaining "child-friendly justice" for children in Africa. Some conclusions for the ongoing development of justice for children in Africa form the final part of the chapter.

1   Children in Justice Systems in Africa: Setting the Context[1]

For the purposes of this chapter, "justice for children" refers to all situations where children are involved in both criminal and civil justice systems, including administrative or informal (or traditional or customary) justice mechanisms. "Child-friendly justice" describes justice systems that are designed or adjusted to be sensitive to the particular issues that children face when they come into contact with the law and courts (or legal proceedings) for any reason.[2] In relation to the criminal justice system, children may be in contact with the justice system through their having been alleged to be in conflict with the law, or as victims or as witnesses. In civil law proceedings, they may come into contact with the justice system in care and protection proceedings, in disputes involving care, contact, guardianship and even in relation to claims for child support (or maintenance). Either court-based (judicial) or administrative systems may come into play where children are refugees, asylum seekers or are otherwise brought before judicial or quasi-judicial procedures as foreign

---

1   African Child Policy Forum and DCI (2012). Achieving Child-Friendly Justice in Africa (available at www.africanchildforum.org).
2   *Ibid.*, p. iv.

separated or unaccompanied children. Administrative systems are also implicated sometimes through schools (including school disciplinary procedures)
and administrative aspects of the care and protection system.

In most parts of Africa, customary and informal systems of administration
of justice prevail, and these can implicate children as recipients of justice processes in a large number of instances. In a range of places in Africa, religious
(sharia) law is implemented especially for family disputes and these may affect
children.[3] Children may be involved in transitional justice processes in the
aftermath of armed or other conflict, and they may be involved in restorative
justice processes of one or another kind.

The publication "Achieving Child-friendly justice in Africa," prepared for the
Kampala Conference on Child Friendly Justice held in November 2011, is one of
the first synthesis efforts at assessment of progress made, and shortcomings
which still exist. The publication follows the format of the Council of Europe
Guidelines[4] to a significant extent insofar as it focusses on justice before, during and after contact with a justice system is encountered. It further details
elements of justice systems in Africa, such as provision of information to children during justice processes, privacy, safety and special measures of protection, the training of professionals, multidisciplinary approaches to justice for
children, deprivation of liberty of children and the minimum age of criminal
responsibility, diversion of children in conflict with the law away from formal
justice processes, and a special section is devoted to the role of police authorities in relation to justice processes. Overall, the publication is commendable
insofar as a wide range of countries in Africa are included for consideration on
various points, although the weighting is towards Anglophone jurisdictions,
and West and North African jurisdictions are less extensively represented.[5]

The compendium reveals that significant progress has been made in the
arena of legislative reform, with any number of jurisdictions having adopted
child protection and juvenile justice codes since the ratification of the CRC,
notably towards the latter half of the first decade of the millennium. Countries
that have followed through on law reform in this period include Somaliland

---

3 The Khadis court system in Zanzibar is an example. See Sloth-Nielsen, J., "The Children's Act
   of Zanzibar," in Maina Peter, C. (ed.), *The Laws of Zanzibar* (2015), where it is explained that
   the provisions of the Children's Act are subject to the primacy of Khadis courts in family law
   matters (excluding child care and protection).
4 The Guidelines of the Committee of Ministers of the Council of Europe on Child-Friendly
   Justice, adopted by the Committee of Ministers on 17 November 2010 at the 1098th meeting
   of the Minister's Deputies.
5 This is understandable as the work was a desk top study which had to rely on available published material.

(concerning juvenile justice), South Sudan (2008), Sierra Leone (2007), Botswana (2009), South Africa (2005 and 2008), Tanzania (2009), Malawi (2010), Lesotho (2011), Zanzibar (2011) and post the publication of the 2011 book, Swaziland (2012), Angola (2012), Rwanda (Law 54 of 2011), and Burundi.[6] Sudan enacted a child law in 2010, although this is not referred to in the Kampala publication. Namibia's Child Care and Protection Bill, based on an extensive consultation process, has received parliamentary approval, and a draft Children's Act in Zambia is being finalized.

Several salient points can be made about law reform in the sphere of justice for children, and "child friendly justice" in particular, in the African context. First, it is evident that serious endeavours were made to ensure that the legislation in almost all respects complied with essential international treaty law and other guiding standards of international significance. There are exceptions to this general proposition, however, which can be mentioned for the sake of completeness: Botswana has expressly retained corporal punishment— whipping—as a judicial sentence for convicted juveniles, and in many countries the minimum age of criminal responsibility has not been sufficiently raised nor the unworkable rebuttable presumption of criminal incapacity (inherited from Roman Dutch law in many SADC countries which share a similar legal history), which results in a "split" minimum age of criminal capacity, decisively abolished.[7] Also, there are gaps where international standards were significantly enhanced only after the completion of the respective law reform processes, which was often quite a lengthy period before finalisation of the Bill in Parliament: a clear example are the (November) 2009 UN Guidelines on Alternative Care, which provided much more detailed guidance on the functioning of alternative care systems and their constituent principles, elements and institutions than is presently evident in the text of the Acts themselves.

Intercountry adoption, which came to the fore as an African area of major socio-political and practical significance really only arose as an issue in the latter part of this decade too (the first Madonna adoption in Malawi was in 2005). Since African countries are only now ratifying the 1993 Hague Convention on Protection of Children and Co-operation in Respect of Intercountry Adoption in significant numbers (Kenya 2010, Lesotho 2012, Swaziland 2012, Zambia 2013), most have not adopted sufficiently detailed domesticating

---

6 Nigeria's Law of the Child is dated 2003, and Kenya adopted the Children's Act (currently under revision) in 2001. Ghana enacted two separate laws, one on child protection in 1998 and a juvenile justice statute in 2001.

7 See CRC Committee General Comment No. 10 (Child Rights in Juvenile Justice) (2007).

provisions in relation to intercountry adoption in their children's statutes.[8] This is another area of future improvement.

Third, little detail is provided in most child care and protection laws on children in contact with the law as witnesses. Although many legal systems appear to have *ad hoc* provisions concerning issues such as providing evidence in camera where the witness is a child, and from time to time evidentiary provisions have been grafted onto existing law concerning procedure and evidence (*e.g.* rules on the use of intermediaries and provision of testimony through one way mirrors, *etc.*), the search for comprehensive child witness protection must be conducted outside of dedicated child protection laws, and where it is exists, it tends to be limited in scope.[9]

Fourth, it appears that substantive law on sexual offences is usually contained in separate criminal codes on sexual offences, or in the penal code. Thus to the extent that children, especially girls, are victims of sexual offences, there is little in these statutes (sometimes they are not modern) to provide separately for the justice process regarding child victims of sexual offences, *e.g.* in relation to medical examination procedures, interviewing standards and reduction of secondary victimisation in justice processes. This fact has a bearing on some observations later in this paper.

Another observation about law reform relates to the extent to which there was information sharing and intercountry collaboration between various States during drafting and formulation processes. Sometimes this extended to direct involvement of consultants from other African countries in the drafting processes (Zanzibar, Namibia, Mozambique) and sometimes the comparative work was undertaken in the usual course of events by Law Reform Commissions or government legal drafters (South Sudan, Lesotho, Malawi, Tanzania). There is thus obvious similarity discernible in specific provisions of some statutes. An example is the preliminary enquiry procedure devised to serve the central "gatekeeping" function to keep children out of facilities in which they would be deprived of their liberty and to further the (obligatory) consideration of diversion. First mooted in the South African law reform process which lead to the

---

8 South Africa is the exception as the Children's Act contains a dedicated chapter on intercountry adoption, as the Hague Convention was ratified by South Africa in 2003 consequent upon a successful constitutional challenge to statutory provisions requiring adoptive parents to be nationals, ruled overbroad and in violation of the best interests of the child. This in turn left the door wide open to foreign would-be adoptive parents to seek out local children.

9 In Zanzibar and Tanzania, this lacuna has been filled via detailed children's court regulations (or rules), which flesh out the manner in which children's evidence may be presented, the evidentiary weight to be accorded their evidence and so forth.

adoption of the Child Justice Act 75 of 2008, this procedure is now echoed in
the Child Care and Welfare Law of Lesotho, in the Children's Law of Zanzibar,
and in the draft Child Justice Bill of Namibia (in the last version on file, dated
2010), for instance. Elaboration of the contents (normative guidelines) of the
best interests of the child provides another example of where countries have
followed the lead of South Africa (whose draft Children's Act dealing with protection and welfare issues was publically available already in 2002).[10] Angola's
Holistic Law of the Child borrowed in many places from the Lusophone statute
of Mozambique,[11] and the "village child protection committee" concept is
common to both the Lesotho and the Botswanian legislation.[12] Many further
examples of these synergies can be cited, despite the obvious differences in
domestication: differences are notably evident in the fact that some countries
have combined child protection and provisions for children in conflict with
the law in one statute (*e.g.* Malawi, Lesotho) whilst others have drafted separate legislation for procedures governing children brought into contact with
justice systems as alleged offenders. Examples are the juvenile justice law of
Somaliland, the South African Child Justice Act 75 of 2008 and the draft Child
Justice Bill in Namibia.

The next, and final, observation about the legal reform processes alluded
to above concern what I have called "allied processes" which have either
taken place or have been set in motion. Amongst these, the following are
highlighted:

A.   Budgeting or costing of enacted legislation, and their processes was ini-
     tiated already as a pioneering aspect of the development of child justice
     legislation in South Africa in its very initial draft in 1998.[13] The exercise
     continued when the omnibus Children's Act 38 of 2005 was formulated,

---

10   South African Law Reform Commission, "Report on the Review of the Child Care Act"
      (2002), as this Report contained a draft Bill which was subsequently tabled in Parliament.
11   Sloth-Nielsen, J. and Mandlate, A., "The Angolan Holistic Law of the Child: A Preliminary
      Assessment," in Atkin, B. (ed.), *International Survey of Family Law*, Jordan Publishing,
      United Kingdom, 2013.
12   See Sloth-Nielsen, J., "The Family Law Aspects of the Law of the Child of Botswana," in
      Atkin, B. (ed.), *International Survey of Family Law*, Jordan Publishing, United Kingdom,
      2012.
13   Barberton, C. and Stuart, J., *Costing the Implementation of the Child Justice Bill: A Scenario
      Analysis*, Research Monograph Series, Applied Fiscal Research Centre, University of Cape
      Town, 1999. This was when the "design" and content of the proposed system were first
      released for comment in the South African Law Reform Commission Discussion Paper on
      Juvenile Justice (1998).

with some dramatic results.[14] These are explained in the next section. In the meantime, costing of the Lesotho legislation is presently underway and a process of draft budgets and implementation plans for Botswana and Malawi is under discussion. Skills to undertake this specialized type of financial/economic analyses appear however to be in short supply, with the same person anchoring the various costing processes mentioned here.

B.   Some level of training and awareness raising – to varying extents, and at varying times during the reform processes – took place and laid something of the groundwork for the reception of new legislation. As regards my home country, South Africa, this was paradoxically most intense before the finalization of the legislation in Parliament, especially with respect to judicial officers,[15] and to probation officers working in the juvenile justice system. Notable gains were made in getting widespread support for diversion and alternative sentencing, and pre-trial individualized assessment of young offenders took off and became fairly routine. A similar trend is notable in relation to Lesotho (probation officers were appointed and trained in restorative justice practice from 2005/6 already); in Namibia (some level of judicial engagement at a national conference of magistrates during the lead up to the finalization of the Bill, which was recently enacted, took place); and in Malawi (training on diversion and police procedures for government in respect of children was institutionalized at police training college before and during the period when the Bill became law, and non-governmental entities trained to provide diversion programmes).

C.   The necessary development of subsidiary legislation – regulations or rules or national directives – to provide more detail on the "how to," as

---

14   Barberton, C., *The Cost of the Children's Bill – Estimates of the Cost to Government of the Services Envisaged by the Comprehensive Children's Bill for the Period 2005–2010*, Report for the National Department of Social Development, July 2006. The costing is further described in Davel, C.J., and Skelton, A., *Commentary on the Children's Act*, Juta and Co, Cape Town, 2007 (with loose-leaf updates) and UNICEF-IRC, *Reforming Child Law in South Africa: Budgeting and Implementation Planning*, 2009.

15   This was through the efforts of staff at the National Justice Training College to mainstream children's rights courses in the overall curriculum for aspirant judicial officers. Justice Training College has been replaced by a Judicial Training Institute falling under the Office of the Chief Justice, and in the interregnum, the attention to child law and children's rights has dissipated and disappeared.

opposed to more general statements of principle and "hard" law found in primary legislation, has taken place in many countries.[16]

D.   Modern and child rights compliant police training materials have been developed in some places (Zambia, Namibia, Tanzania, Sierra Leone), and implemented in national police training curricula. Training materials for other sectors such a social workers (Lesotho, South Africa) have also been developed, albeit with sporadic implementation.

2   Strengths, Gaps, Weaknesses and Potential

This section is, it must be admitted, based largely on personal experience garnered during technical support activities, training workshops, materials design and participation in law reform at country level in quite a large number of (especially Anglophone) African jurisdictions. The countries on which the assessment provided in this section is based include Mozambique, South Africa, Kenya, Malawi, South Sudan, Somaliland, Lesotho, Botswana, Ethiopia, Tanzania and Zanzibar and Namibia.

Four points arise for consideration. First, the overarching legal systems into which the new child rights-oriented legislation must fit can only be considered as fledgling at best. Legal Aid systems, essential in order for children to have representation in justice systems, are sorely lacking, and although in some places, legal representation is provided by NGO s (such as in Ethiopia, Kenya and Tanzania), this is on an *ad hoc* and sporadic basis. South Africa remains an exception, with the para-statal Legal Aid Board having since 2006 proactively taken steps to develop Children's Units, dedicated to providing legal representation for children in conflict with the law.[17] There is now nearly universal access to legal representation for accused children, which is unique on the continent.

Another example relates to specialized children's or juvenile courts. Whilst these have been developing since around 2000, progress is generally quite slow and often they exist only in the capital city or main centres. Malawi now has 28 children's courts, spread amongst the four regions, and stands out; Kenya has made similar advances.

---

16   For example, detailed regulations have been developed to accompany the Law of the Child of Tanzania (2009), which (to the extent that the principal Act is lacking or deficient) provide a great deal more "meat" relevant to child friendly justice and procedures.

17   Sloth-Nielsen, J., "Seen and Heard: New Frontiers in Child Participation in Family Law Proceedings in South Africa," 23 *Speculum Juris*, 2009, pp. 1–19.

South Africa's experiment with multi-sectoral One Stop Child Justice Centres[18] designed to provide child friendly processes to child offenders, despite initial indications that they were extremely successful in their outcomes, stalled almost immediately after the first two had been commissioned at the turn of the millennium, and it is possible that government is now retreating from continuing with this innovation.[19]

Furthermore, many African justice systems are characterized by long, long delays. In particular, cases involving children in conflict with the law may take not months but *years* to conclude, with concomitant lengthy stays in detention facilities and little progress in finalizing an outcome. It seems too that this ill bedevils child protection cases and instances regularly surface where children in need of care and protection spend long periods deprived of their liberty in "prison like" facilities. A promising project has been noted in relation to active case management in Botswana,[20] to enhance early settlement of civil disputes and "fast tracking" of trials. Case management has been written into the Rules of the Law of the Child of Tanzania as well as Zanzibar's Rules pertaining to the Children's Act. The preliminary inquiry procedure in the South African Child Justice Act attempts a similar process of fast tracking cases. But these are fledgling endeavours and overall, justice is sorely delayed. This problem is as acute, if not more so, for cases involving child witnesses and victims.

Second, it was noted above that the costing of the Children's Act in South Africa had dramatic results: the costing revealed how large the gap was between the availability of social services expected in order to implement the act, and the number of qualified social workers. The scale of divergence was so serious that the South African Government was persuaded to institute a new bursary scheme to attract students to study social work, so as to increase the pool in the medium to long term. Social work was declared a "scarce skill," allowing for salary enhancements.[21] Other initiatives elsewhere on the continent have examined the scarcity of a social workforce, without which "child friendly" justice is difficult—if not impossible—to achieve.[22] The use of volunteers and

---

18   The Centres, concretized in enabling provisions of the Child Justice Act 75 of 2008, were to be dedicated to children in conflict with the law, and would include facilities for police, detention facilities for temporary pre-trial detention, court facilities and offices for diversion service providers and prosecutors.

19   See African Child Policy Forum and DCI, *supra* note 1, pp. 47–48.

20   Presentation by attorneys from Botswana at the Miller du Toit/University of the Western Cape Child and Family Law Conference, March 3, 2014.

21   UNICEF-IRC, *supra* note 14, p. 38.

22   A conference on growing the social workforce was held in Cape Town in November 2011, and drew a large number of delegates from UNICEF offices together. Follow up has ensued

community workers with much more limited training has proved to have its own challenge, as volunteer fatigue sets in after a while and community workers often time demand allowances in order to fulfil their own family responsibilities in resource poor countries.

Third, even where progress has been made, gains can easily be reversed or progress halted. Many building blocks of systems of child friendly justice are to a greater or lesser extent donor dependent: NGO s delivering diversion services, or providing facilities for the alternative care for abused or abandoned children (both victims and children in conflict with the law) often rely on external funding, which can stop or shift; some services governments cannot routinely fund, *e.g.* petrol costs for home visits and community work, funding for supplies, and for equipment maintenance. Child friendly interview and testimony equipment is from time to time installed, and then not maintained, or not properly linked up, or it falls into disuse (the author has personally observed this in Malawi and Lesotho). Thus promising projects and initiatives appear difficult to sustain over time.

Fourth, and I say this with some hesitation insofar as it may challenge current orthodoxy, the clear thrust of juvenile justice reform that was evident around 2000 and shortly thereafter has in my view been diluted by changing programme names, focus and content. Thus around 2006 the Justice for Children (J4C) concept (or appellation) began to take root, drawing together programmes dealing with children in conflict with the law as well as other children in contact with civil law processes, *i.e.* child witnesses and child victims of (especially) sexual assault.[23] In Eastern and Southern Africa, a conference on Justice for Children resulted in the Lilongwe Commitment on Justice for Children of 2009.[24] J4C undoubtedly had laudable intentions, *inter alia* to reduce the stigmatisation of child offenders, to increase the pool of potential donors and supporters by including child victims in the overall conceptual framework, and going as broad as possible to include children in any manner in contact with justice systems (*e.g.* affected by custody and maintenance disputes of their parents, in adoption applications and so forth). "Child protection" became the dominant terminological starting point, and even though it is not disputed that children in conflict with the law are often also in need of protection, the change in emphasis in my view diminished and weakened the once coherent juvenile justice reform agenda which had seen

---

in various guises, including engaging with training institutions and cross border access to training.

23   Resulting in the UN Secretary General's Guidance Note on the UN Approach to Justice for Children (2008).

24   For the detailed contents of this declaration, see ACPF and DCI, *supra* note 1, p. 14.

diversion and alternative sentencing sanctions mushroom and a concentration of training on core international human rights standards relevant to deprivation of liberty.

J4C also drew on different stakeholders to those usually concerned with juvenile justice reform: prisons and detention facilities are a prime site for initial interventions to spearhead reforms and implement the principle of detention as a last resort and for the shortest period of time; however, prison personnel are normally involved in child protection only to the extent that infants are incarcerated with their mothers. They have nothing to do with child victims and other welfare matters.

Seen from another angle, child protection calls upon the alternative care system including kinship and foster care placements, which are seldom if ever concerned with children in conflict with the law as a core issue. Reforming alternative care institutions and the whole thrust towards deinstitutionalization affects (in the main) orphanages, not detention facilities for juvenile justice inmates. Not even the same NGO s are involved: PRI who have played an important role in juvenile justice reform in several African countries do not include child welfare systems in their scope.[25] In sum, by broadening the scope of child friendly justice, momentum for systems reform for children in conflict with the law waned; at the same time, justice systems for abused, neglected and abandoned children were so underdeveloped that little observable progress could be recorded in the period 2006 until now.[26] This point is substantiated further below.

On a positive note, it is apparent that the actual numbers of children in conflict with the law and hence in contact with justice systems are, with respect, extraordinarily low. For instance, it has been recorded that the total number of children in detention in Guinea in 2007 was 1200.[27] In Malawi, where good statistics have been kept by the National Child Justice Forum, "[T]he overall number of children deprived of their liberty in Malawi is arguably low – various figures were supplied by stakeholders, and these do not always synchronize. However, it appears that there are around 100 children in each of the 4 juvenile detention centres. The total number of children arrested each year appears to be around 2200 (for the whole country), indicating considerable success in advancing diversion and non-custodial sentencing."[28] In Lesotho, it was

---

25 The Open Society Foundation is another example here.

26 Anecdotally it has been pointed out to the author that the preponderance of civil children's court matters in (*e.g.*) Kenya and Malawi concern private disputes about paternity and maintenance.

27 Complementary report on the African Charter on the Rights and Welfare of the Child, 2014.

28 Sloth-Nielsen, J. and Mwambene, L., *Malawi Justice for Children 2013*, unpublished report of a field mission to Malawi, commissioned by UNICEF.

indicated that the total number of arrested children is around 600 annually.[29] This surely implies that it is possible to make an impact.

I turn now to the international norms and standards applicable in Africa, the backdrop against which the 2011 Kampala Guidelines on Action on Children in Justice Systems in Africa, discussed below, are premised.

3   Relevant Standards Unique to Africa

The African Charter on Human and People's Rights (in force from 1987), and its monitoring body, the African Commission on Human and Peoples' Rights are a starting point for this discussion. This is not so much because of the contents of the Charter, but because of the focus that the Commission has had on prison conditions, civil liberties, torture and detention over the years. Notable standards include the Robben Island Guidelines[30] and the Principles and Guidelines on the Rights to a Fair Trial and Legal Assistance in Africa, first formulated by the Commission in 1999 and updated at the end of 2011.[31] These Guidelines constitute soft law, but provide considerable detail on criminal justice standards in particular, including the elements of a fair hearing, *locus standi*, the role of prosecutors, access to lawyers, legal aid, the independence of lawyers, access to judicial services, provisions applicable to arrest and detention, principles applicable to criminal proceedings, victims of crime and traditional courts. These are generally applicable to adults, but also to children. Additionally, a lengthy section is devoted specifically to children and their rights to a fair trial.

It must be recorded that these standards relating to children significantly upgrade the norms applicable to children in contact with justice systems contained in the African Charter on the Rights and Welfare of the Child itself.[32]

---

29 Information provided by the police at a training workshop in Lesotho in January 2014.

30 Resolution on Guidelines and Measures for the Prohibition and Prevention of Torture, Cruel, Inhuman or Degrading Treatment or Punishment in Africa (Robben Island Guidelines), 2008. This followed the Ouagadougou Declaration and Plan of Action on Accelerating Prison and Penal Reforms in Africa (2002) and Kampala Declaration on Prison Conditions (1996).

31 The African Women's Protocol (2005) to the African Charter on Human and Peoples' Rights contains some relevant provisions, *e.g.* Article 4 (right to life, integrity and security of the person) and Article 25 (remedies for rights violations). See www.achpr.org for all the documents referred to in this paper.

32 A notable gap in the Charter is the absence of a provision that restricts the use of detention to the minimum period and only as a last resort, as is contained in Article 37(b) of the CRC.

A brief summary of some salient provisions will have to suffice. Training of enforcement officials and judicial officers in dealing with children sensitively and professionally is advocated.[33] Law enforcement officials must ensure that all contact with children respects their legal status, avoids harm, and promotes the wellbeing of children. Children's right to privacy shall be respected at all times, and several provisions enjoin increased access to diversion and community-based sentencing. Detained children are supposed to be provided by the State with legal assistance from the moment of arrest, as well as parental assistance. Appropriate limitations on sentences are set.

Child witnesses are supposed to give evidence with the minimum of distress, and several norms pertain to the collection of evidence/interviewing of child victims, as well as the need to ensure that victims of sexual abuse do not come into contact with alleged perpetrators during justice procedures. The use of intermediaries at interview and evidence stage is encouraged, as well as pre-recorded videos and screens to be used at trials. The wearing of ordinary clothes by office bearers during children's testimony is proposed as well as restrictions on defendants' personally cross-examining child witnesses; finally, restrictions must be placed on the circumstances in which sexual history evidence of alleged child victims may be sought or presented.

Hence, a detailed framework for the elaboration of child friendly justice guidelines (but relating only to criminal procedures involving children) already existed[34] at the time of the drafting of the African Guidelines on Child Friendly Justice, which were adopted at the Kampala Conference on Deprivation of Liberty in November 2011. The Guidelines were endorsed by the African Committee of Experts on the Rights and Welfare of the Child in 2012.

Commencing with a preamble, the Guidelines note that most children in Africa do not enjoy their rights under the African Charter on the Rights and Welfare of the Child,[35] and many do not have access to legal protection or remedial measures. It is recorded that children face persistent barriers to the fulfilment of their rights in the justice system, such as non-existing or partial access to justice, diversity in and complexity of services, discrimination on various grounds, and lack of access to services. The need for more sustained progress towards implementation of child rights in justice systems is emphasized. Participation,

---

33   Rule N(b).

34   At the time of drafting of the African Guidelines on Child Friendly Justice, the fair trial rights norms were those of 1999; however, as the Guidelines were being finalized, these were updated to the 2011 version discussed here.

35   The Charter now has 47 States Parties, and universal ratification is aimed for by 2015. See for the campaign for universal ratification www.acerwc.org.

the principle of a child's best interests, non-discrimination, dignity and the right to survival and development constitute overarching principles. The necessity of information and management systems to underscore national policy is stressed, as is the need for adequate birth registration systems and sufficient resources. Mediation, conflict resolution and restorative justice are regarded as being locally embedded options to formal justice, provided that human rights safeguards are respected. The need for speedy justice is emphasised, and the overall role of social protection systems in reducing children's vulnerability and as a prevention mechanism is highlighted with a view to strengthening social protection programmes. The concrete guidance is found from para. 33 onwards, the text of which draws substantially from the African Commission's Principles and Guidelines on the Rights to a Fair Trial and Legal Assistance in Africa, referred to above. Specific mention is made of migrant children who find themselves outside their country of origin, and it is stated that children shall not be subjects of trials in military courts. Children accused of crimes committed whilst they were members of armed forces or armed groups – child soldiers – shall be treated primarily as victims and not as perpetrators. Traditional courts, religious courts or other similar structures are required to respect international standards on the right to a fair trial and children's rights. Notable here is the attention paid to gender equality, as traditional and religious courts are frequently patriarchal and gender insensitive. Traditional courts are also expected to act impartially, without improper influence, pressure threats or interference.

Paras. 44–62 of the Guidelines deal with fair trial rights for children accused of offences. States Parties are reminded that these fair trial rights apply regardless of the charges, including charges related to terrorism, brought against the child, and are reminded that derogation from the rights enshrined in the African Charter on the Rights and Welfare of the Child is not permitted even during states of emergency.

Paras. 63–71 deal with child victims and witnesses and fair trial rights. States Parties are required to enact legislation to enshrine these rights, a gap that was alluded to earlier in this chapter. This section also contains the guidance that extra judicial settlements, including those negotiated between families, pose particular risks to child victims (and to rights of the girl child in particular where marriage is proposed as the settlement), and actors in affected justice systems should refuse to countenance private arrangements insofar as these do not promote the rights of the child victim.

Paras. 72–85 deal with children as subjects of civil, judicial or administrative proceedings, including alternative care proceedings and family law disputes. Amongst other guidance in family disputes, the choice of measures which diminish or avoid the intensification of conflict (except where these are not conducive to the best interests of the child), the selection of measures which would avoid or minimize further legal or administrative proceedings, the choice of measures which do not result in the separation of siblings, and those which promote the right to the child to be brought up in a stable family environment, and where this is not possible, an environment closely resembling a family environment, are all deemed to be in the best interests of the child. States are required to include legal provisions to this effect in national laws. Specific mention is made in this part of the need for national systems for the regulation of alternative care for children deprived of parental care. All placements of children in alternative care must be subject to periodic review, and institutions for the alternative care of children subject to registration, regular inspection and quality assurance processes. These requirements must be enshrined in national legislation.

States must ensure that orphaned children are assured of the appointment of legal guardians, either by operation of a will, by appointment by a court or other similar structure, or by operation of laws specifying which care-giver, member of the kinship group or other person will hold guardianship. Adequate legislative and enforcement mechanisms in justice systems must exist to ensure that children are not wilfully or otherwise deprived of inheritance rights, and due attention must be paid to the right of the girl child to equality in the distribution or allocation of any estate property, since customary law frequently devolves property to the eldest male heir only.

The final section of the Guidelines, covering paras. 86–93, deals with various dimensions of monitoring of the implementation of the Guidelines. This includes advice to States to consider positively requests for access to institutions and to child friendly justice courts from African Union structures, including the African Committee of Experts on the Rights and Welfare of the Child and Special Rapporteurs of the African Commission on Human and Peoples' Rights; and requesting States to include information on progress towards implementation of the Guidelines in State Party reports to the African Commission and to the African Committee of Experts.

4   "Systems Strengthening" Post J4C

The current orthodoxy being advocated is a "systems strengthening'" approach.[36] This approach is premised on the thesis that children face complex

---

36   See various Save the Child publications, the latest of which is Interagency group on child protection systems in sub-Saharan Africa "Strengthening Child Protection Systems in Sub-Saharan Africa: A Working Paper," 2012.

problems that require a multi-disciplinary response. Dividing children up into subsets for the purposes of programming (children on the street, children in conflict with the law, children without parental care and so forth) splits available resources into tiny sectors, does not permit overarching co-ordination and effective collection of data, and impedes preventive child protection efforts (*e.g.* those aimed at combatting violence in all settings, including in the home and at school). Theoretically, insofar as the "systems strengthening" approach advocates a "holistic" response to the protection of children and implementation of rights, one can have no immediate objection. But the question arises as to whether the current "systems strengthening" approach being advocated by a range of INGO s will enhance the implementation of the required standards for child-friendly justice—or not.

It is proposed that the answer to this is both yes and no. Early intervention and prevention of (for instance) juvenile offending is an unqualified plus that no one in their right mind would argue against, if it is to bring about a long term reduction of children's contact with justice systems. Whether this is achieved through social protection programmes to alleviate poverty and keep children in their families, through community violence prevention, through alternative care systems for orphans or whatever general protection initiatives are appropriate to curb juvenile delinquency, is not material.

Similarly, the "systems strengthening" approach to focussing on areas beyond the capital city of a country to rural and other areas, and its stated intention to develop and extend social welfare services—as mentioned, these are crucial to child-friendly justice systems in any event—can be regarded as essential: since no child-friendly justice system can operate without the minimum level of human resources for assessment, counselling, programme implementation and so forth.[37]

However, "systems strengthening" could at the same time herald a real dilution of what are actually quite clear deliverables for juvenile justice reforms: it diverts attention away from justice processes to a potentially vast array of other interventions concerning vulnerable children. By way of example, in explaining systems strengthening case studies to members of the African Committee of Experts on the Rights and Welfare of the Child in March 2014, the four pilot studies adduced were: the establishment of district child protection committees in Tanzania, the establishment of a police child protection unit and one stop centre for survivors of sexual violence at a hospital (services for women

---

37   *E.g.* probation officers to interview children in conflict with the law, counsellors to prepare children to give testimony in court, intermediaries o assist with the giving of evidence, diversion service provides, *etc.*

and children) in Zanzibar, a broad array of ongoing developments in South African (some of which had commenced in the 1990s, and including a cash transfer scheme which started in 1998), the development of a new Child Protection Policy Framework[38] in Ghana (not yet operationalized), and deinstitutionalization of children in the care system in Rwanda. Notably, none dealt remotely with children in formal contact with justice systems, such as is envisaged in the Council of Europe child-friendly guidelines.

A related concern is that the premises or starting points of the "systems strengthening" approach on the one hand, and child-friendly justice (before, during and after formal contact with the justice system) on the other, differ wholly. "Systems strengthening" ultimately proceeds from a bottom up approach, investing heavily in identifying and capitalizing on community child protection strategies, and support at community and district level, whilst it is axiomatic that child-friendly justice guidelines focus on how a child is treated once contact with the State authorities (police, prosecutors, courts) is already underway. Community referrals (*e.g.* to family group conferences or other restorative justice processes) is a by-product or outcome of (diversion away from) any initial formal contact.

For these reasons, it is proposed that "systems strengthening" offers little to child friendly justice role players over the longer term, and may even drain fiscal and (especially) political support from existing reforms that have taken place to make child justice more child rights compliant.[39]

5   Conclusions

As is evident from the above discussion, the legal framework for driving through reforms which underpin a more child-friendly system of justice for children is in place, both at the continental and by and large at country level too. So where do the systemic difficulties lie?

---

38 Addressing *inter alia*, sexual violence against girls, child labour, lack of access to justice, unnecessary institutionalisation of children, teenage pregnancy and host of social and other ills.

39 Further as noted, the numbers of children in conflict with the law appear to be low enough to achieve quite significant gains with not too much investment: at minimum, this comprises police training in procedures, avoidance of delays in finalizing criminal cases, in fact expediting them through proven case management interventions, and providing organized legal representation for the rather small and easily identifiable number of children who are arrested.

A few observations will conclude. First, as alluded to above, the changing terminology and focus in the children's sector has not had good outcomes for child friendly justice. Donor interest has not been sustained, and juvenile justice (in particular) has been pushed to the back seat. NGO s interested in juvenile justice specifically may ultimately move on.

Second, experiences in the region indicate that the delivery of services for justice for children is multi-sectoral and involve to a significant degree civil society and international organizations. The consequences of this are multifarious, including precarious funding streams, difficulties in coordination across a wide range of government departments and sectors, and different role players being involved in juvenile justice (on the one hand) and child protection and services to victims on the other (*e.g.* health services, one stop centres for survivors of gender based violence, specialized police units geared principally to respond to domestic violence). Wavering commitment to sustained interventions in juvenile justice has shown that skills built up become lost, and that skilled staff move on. In South Africa, it has become clear over the last two decades that constant and ongoing training and sensitization is required far beyond the initial adoption of laws and institutional reform. An assessment of a decade of justice for children reform in Malawi appears to show that strong and credible leadership over a long period of time is a precursor to reforms which are not mere pilot projects and which show gains that have lasting effect. And, since justice sector role-players are at the core of child friendly justice, working in close proximity to the formal trappings of criminal justice architecture (*i.e.* courts, police detention facilities, prisons), it is here that the focus must lie. Generalized training of a social workforce for systems strengthening will not have the desired impact.

Third, the need for the reform (or rethink) of institutions (reformatories, places of safety, re-education centres) linked to children's contact with justice systems remains a serious concern. On the one hand, existing institutions (whatever they are named) are almost uniformly inappropriate and un-child friendly. In 2007, I raised the question as to what appropriate institutions in Africa should look like, and what skills development they should provide that are appropriate to the local context, whilst at the same time not serving to incentivize institutional care as preferable to grinding poverty and lack of access to skills outside?[40] At the same time, the complaint is often heard at the coal face that there are no available institutions at all, hence the overuse of

---

40   Sloth-Nielsen, J. and Mezmur, B.D., "Surveying the Research Landscape to Promote Children's Legal Rights in an African Context," 7 *African Human Rights Law Journal*, 2007, pp. 330–353.

detention in prisons (sometimes even for children in need of care and protection).

Some years ago, in response to the constantly shifting policies and impetuses of the Department of Correctional Services of South Africa (tough on crime sentencing, then restorative justice, demilitarisation and then reintroduction of uniforms, privatisation of prisons which was then abandoned as a long term option, numerous reports of torture perpetrated on prisoners, *etc.*), the then most eminent authority on South Africa prisons said: "Why can't they just implement their (Prisons) Act – all they are required to do is to detain prisoners in conditions of safe custody and humane treatment!"

My final thought then, is that simply implementing the basics of due process and fair trial rights alone – as already provided for in regional and domestic laws – will significantly enhance children's real experience of child-friendly justice in the African context.

SECTION 3

Americas

∴

Access to Justice in the Inter-American System: Standards and Challenges

Rosa Maria Ortiz

I would like to share with you the most important regional challenges that girls, boys and adolescents face in access to justice in the Americas, as well as standards that we have developed on this issue through cases, precautionary measures and thematic reports.

The Commission has stated that any intent to guarantee an adequate respect and protection of the rights of children is reinforced when the access to justice is guaranteed. In this regard, the Inter-American Commission on Human Rights (IACHR) has established that the right to access to justice is a key pillar upon which democracy stands. This same right is applicable to girls and boys with special and reinforced guarantees.

The IACHR has different mandates and functions that include the preparation of thematic reports or studies that it deems pertinent, the request for concrete measures to States for the protection of human rights, and the reception, processing and decision of individual petitions once the internal remedies have been exhausted, of human-rights violations recognized by inter-American human rights instruments.

In relation to children's rights, the protection of their human rights includes a *corpus iuris* that includes several international instruments linked with the purpose of guaranteeing children's human rights, recognizing that human rights treaties are live instruments.[1]

Petitions related to children before the IACHR represent 10% of the total number presented before the Commission (2,000 per year). Of those, a high percentage represent a lack of access to justice. After an initial review, the

---

1　I/A Court H.R., *Case of Gelman v Uruguay*, Judgment of February 24, 2011, Series C No. 221, para. 121; I/A Court H.R., Case of *Chitay Nech et al. v Guatemala*. Preliminary Objections, Merits, Reparations, and Costs. Judgment of May 25, 2010. Series C No. 212, para. 165, 166, 167 and 168; I/A Court H.R., *Case of Contreras et al. v El Salvador*. Merits, Reparations, and Costs. Judgment of August 31, 2011. Series C No. 232, paras. 107 and 112; I/A Court H.R., *Case of the Gómez Paquiyauri Brothers v Peru*, Merits, Reparations and Costs. Judgment of 8 July 2004. Series C No. 110, paras. 166–168. See also I/A Court H.R., Case of the *"Street Children" (Villagrán Morales et al.) v Guatemala*. Merits. Judgment of November 19, 1999. Series C No. 63, para. 193; and I/A Court H.R., *The Right to Information on Consular Assistance in the Framework of the Guarantees of the Due Process of Law*. Advisory Opinion OC-16/99, October 1, 1999. Series A, No. 16, para. 114.

Commission transmits the petitions to the Member State. Of those, we have 121 in the admissibility stage, and 55 at the merits stage. Addressing the relevance that the passage of time has on children, the Commission has decided to give priority to the analysis of those petitions related to children. The Commission created a special rapporteurship for the rights of girls, boys and adolescents in 1989 to promote and protect their rights.

The Commission has established that States have the duty to investigate, prosecute, punish and provide reparations in every human-rights violation case. During its early years, during internal armed conflicts and dictatorships, the IACHR referred basically to disappearances, torture, extrajudicial killings and massacres. In these contexts, the IACHR reminded States of their duty to take all necessary measures (judicial, administrative and/or others) to establish the truth, to prosecute and punish those responsible and to provide adequate reparations for victims. The Commission has established specific obligations of States in cases involving girls and boys, among them specific reparations and the duty to have special diligence in processing their cases.

In more recent years, while most of our region enjoys democracy, and in the light of the incorporation of the Convention on the Rights of the Child to the *corpus iuris*, the Inter-American system has developed more specific parameters that provide content to the effective access to justice of children. The system has established that for this access to be effective and respectful of children's human rights, it must be resolved with exceptional diligence.[2] Girls and boys must also have free and adequate legal counsel to represent their rights and interests in all proceedings that could affect them. Their right to be heard must be guaranteed in accordance with their age and maturity.[3]

Human-rights guarantees include the existence of legal mechanisms to define and protect these rights, with the intervention of a competent, independent and impartial tribunal whose actions are strictly respectful of the law. All judgments must be founded so that the higher protection is detailed as the

---

2   Inter-American Court of Human Rights, *Case of Fornerón and Daughter v Argentina*. Merits, Reparations, and Costs. Judgment of April 27, 2012, Series C, No. 242, para. 51; Inter-American Court of Human Rights Order of July 1, 2011, *Provisional Measures with Respect to Paraguay, Matter of L.M.*, "Considering" part, para. 16.

3   I/A Court H.R., *Case of Furlan and Family v Argentina*. Preliminary objections, Merits, Reparations, and Costs. Judgment of August 31, 2012 Series C No. 246. para. 242, and, *mutatis mutandi*, I/A Court H.R., *Case of Atala Riffo and Daughters v Chile*. Merits, Reparations, and Costs. Judgment of February 24, 2012. Series C No. 239. para. 199. See also the "Brasilia Regulations Regarding Access to Justice for Vulnerable People," which expand on the principles included in the "Charter of Rights of the People before the Judiciary in the Ibero-American Judicial Space" (Cancun, 2002).

base of all decisions. In criminal procedures, the latter is reinforced by the right to recourse.

The Commission can, in urgent matters and when there is a risk of irreparable harm, ask the State to grant precautionary measures to protect those in danger. In relation to childhood, In the case of LM in Paraguay,[4] the Commission and the Court asked for urgent measures to be adopted to avoid irreparable harm to the rights to a family, to identity, and to the physical and psychological integrity of a child without the possibility of relating to its biological family due to the delay in resolving his situation.

Latin America and the Caribbean have seen important developments in the past few decades with the adoption of the Convention on the Rights of the Child and the creation of the National Systems of Promotion and Protection of the Rights of Girls, Boys and Adolescents. The latter has helped to keep social problems away from courts. The region has also advanced in creating specialized judicial assistance and the defence of the rights of girls, boys and adolescents, as well as their participation in their judicial processes. Nonetheless, there are still many important challenges in the implementation of these new policies, institutions and practices. Among the most important ones:

· The specialized training of professionals that work directly with boys and girls and the obligation to denounce before the competent authorities those situations which could amount to a violation of their rights (for example, health professionals from the care facilities or detention centres).
· The existence of offices or services at the local levels that can advise or receive children, that are accessible and friendly and have specialized personnel, within the National Promotions and Protection System, in which children can come with queries, doubts or problems, or to denounce a situation that could threaten their rights. These services and offices must have the legal obligation to inform the competent authorities about possible rights violations.
· Children that live under conditions that could especially endanger the exercise of their rights or being exposed to violence, such as imprisoned children or those living in care facilities, require specially adapted mechanisms to facilitate the denunciation of violations of their rights before the competent authorities and access to justice. A special mechanism for this is an independent monitoring mechanism of these facilities that would allow children to present petitions, or denounce certain situations.

---

4 *Supra* note 2.

In addition to individual petitions and precautionary measures, the Commission produces thematic reports and requests advisory opinions from the Court. The Rapporteurship on the Rights of the Child has published several such thematic reports, among them "Report on Corporal Punishment and Human Rights of Children and Adolescents"; "Juvenile Justice and Human Rights in the Americas"; and the most recent, "Report on the Rights of Girls and Boys to a Family. Alternative Care. Ending Institutionalization in the Americas." These three reports reinforce the Universal System's efforts, particularly those of the Special Representative of the Secretary General on Violence Against Children and of the Committee on the Rights of the Child.

The latest report emphasizes that States have a legal obligation under international law to strengthen the development and capabilities of the family and the community surrounding the child to guarantee in the most effective manner the protection of his/her rights.

Children must feel empowered, as must their families and communities, and they must know their rights and the necessary means to achieve them or denounce situations that endanger them. The IACHR is convinced that inclusive communities and families, strengthened by the State to take care of their children and adolescents, will, along with the children's own protagonism, be the necessary counterpart so that specialized justice can bear its best fruits.

Index